NOT ACCORDING TO PLAN

NOT ACCORDING TO PLAN

Filmmaking under Stalin

Maria Belodubrovskaya

CORNELL UNIVERSITY PRESS   ITHACA AND LONDON

First published 2017 by Cornell University Press

Printed in the United States of America

Library of Congress Cataloging-in-Publication Data

Names: Belodubrovskaya, Maria, author.
Title: Not according to plan : filmmaking under Stalin / Maria Belodubrovskaya.
Description: Ithaca : Cornell University Press, 2017. | Includes bibliographical
    references and index.
Identifiers: LCCN 2017014439 (print) | LCCN 2017015516 (ebook) |
    ISBN 9781501713811 (epub/mobi) | ISBN 9781501713804 (pdf) |
    ISBN 9781501709944 | ISBN 9781501709944 (cloth : alk. paper)
Subjects: LCSH: Motion picture industry—Soviet Union—History. | Motion
    pictures—Soviet Union—History. | Stalin, Joseph, 1878–1953—Influence.
Classification: LCC PN1993.5.R9 (ebook) | LCC PN1993.5.R9 B385 2017 (print) |
    DDC 384/.80947—dc23
LC record available at https://lccn.loc.gov/2017014439

Cornell University Press strives to use environmentally responsible suppliers and materials to the fullest extent possible in the publishing of its books. Such materials include vegetable-based, low-VOC inks and acid-free papers that are recycled, totally chlorine-free, or partly composed of nonwood fibers. For further information, visit our website at cornellpress.cornell.edu.

To Scott

Contents

Terms and Abbreviations   ix
Note on Transliteration   xi

Introduction   1

1. Quantity vs. Quality: Soviet Film Policy and the
   Intolerance of Imperfection   12
2. *Templan*: "Bastard" Plans and Creative Counterplanning   52
3. The Masters: The Director-Centered Mode of Production
   and the Tradition of Quality   90
4. Screenwriting: Lack of Professionalization and the
   Literary Scenario   130
5. Censorship: Industry Self-Censorship and
   Extreme Uncertainty   165

Conclusion: The Failure of Mass Cinema under Stalin
   and the Institutional Study of Ideology   213

Acknowledgments   223
Appendixes   227
   1. Soviet Feature-Film Production
   2. Soviet Cinema Administrations (1930–1953)
   3. The Institutions of Soviet Film Censorship
Bibliography   231
Index   243

Terms and Abbreviations

ARRK	Association of Workers of Revolutionary Cinema (1924–1935)
Central Committee	Chief administrative body of the Communist Party of the Soviet Union
Glavkinoprokat	Main Film Distribution Administration (1938–1953)
Glavrepertkom	Main Repertory Control Committee (1923–1933)
Gosfilmofond	State Film Foundation
Gosplan	State Planning Agency
GUK	Main Cinema Administration (1936–1938)
GUKF	Main Administration for Cinema and Photo Industry (1933–1936)
GURK	Main Administration for Repertory Control (1934–1936)
KhPO	Artistic-production unit
Komsomol	Young Communist League
Narkompros	People's Commissariat of Education
NKVD	People's Commissariat of Internal Affairs, successor to OGPU (Joint Chief Political Directorate) and precursor to KGB (Committee for State Security)
ODSK	Society of Friends of Soviet Cinema (1925–1934)
politprosvetfilm	Lit., political and enlightenment film
RGALI	Russian State Archive for Literature and Art
RGASPI	Russian State Archive for Social and Political History
RSFSR	Russian Soviet Federative Socialist Republic
Soiuzkino	All-Union Combine for the Cinema and Photo Industry (1930–1933)
Sovnarkom	Council of People's Commissars, chief executive body of the Soviet government, succeeded by the Council of Ministers in 1946
templan	thematic plan
TsGALI	Central State Archive for Literature and Art in St. Petersburg
TsOKS	Central United Film Studio for Feature Films

URK	Administration for Cinema Repertory Control (1938–1946)
VGIK	State Cinema Institute in Moscow
VSNKh	Supreme Council for National Economy

Archival designations f., op., d., l., and ob. stand for fond (depository), opis' (register), delo (file), list (page), oborot (reverse).

Note on Transliteration

I transliterate Russian-language material using the Library of Congress system, with a few exceptions for well-known figures (e.g., Sergei Eisenstein, Viktor Shklovsky, Yakov Protazanov, and Lazar Kaganovich). I also drop the apostrophe (') for the Russian soft sign in words that appear commonly in English-language literature on Russian cinema (e.g., Mosfilm and *kulturfilm*). I spell the names of Russian authors writing in English as published.

NOT ACCORDING
TO PLAN

INTRODUCTION

No statement in the history of Soviet cinema is more famous than Vladimir Lenin's "of all the arts, for us the most important is cinema."[1] Lenin's successor, Joseph Stalin, also recognized cinema as a "mighty instrument of mass agitation and propaganda" and strove to harness the Soviet film industry to serve the Communist state.[2] The conventional wisdom is that he succeeded: under Stalin the Soviets built a propaganda state and the regime had control over the arts and media, including cinema.[3] Scholars have also called Stalin-era cinema a "dream factory," a communist equivalent to Hollywood.[4] Yet even a cursory look at the performance of Soviet cinema under Stalin reveals that it was never a mighty propaganda machine. In the 1930s the American film industry released more

1. For the context of Lenin's quote, see Richard Taylor and Ian Christie, eds., *The Film Factory: Russian and Soviet Cinema in Documents, 1896–1939* (London: Routledge, 1994), 56–57. It needs to be noted that the quote comes to us only as a recollection (Anatoly Lunacharsky spoke with Lenin and reported his conversation three years later to Grigorii Boltianskii). Also, if Lenin indeed uttered these words, he was referring to cinema as a whole (including newsreels and educational films) and taking it as a medium that could communicate without requiring literacy.

2. "Ukrepit' kadry rabotnikov kino," *Pravda*, February 3, 1929, 4, translated in Taylor and Christie, *Film Factory*, 100.

3. Peter Kenez, *The Birth of the Propaganda State: Soviet Methods of Mass Mobilization, 1917–1929* (Cambridge, UK: Cambridge University Press, 1985).

4. Boris Groys and Max Hollein, eds., *Dream Factory Communism: The Visual Culture of the Stalin Era* (Frankfurt: Schirn Kunsthalle, 2003).

than five hundred films per year, Japan up to five hundred films, Britain two hundred films, and France, Italy, and Nazi Germany each about one hundred features. In contrast, Soviet feature-film output plummeted from more than a hundred annual titles in the late 1920s, to an average of fifty in the 1930s, twenty in the 1940s, and the low of only seven features in 1951. In terms of film releases, Soviet Russia under Stalin looked more like China or Czechoslovakia than its authoritarian counterparts (Germany, Italy, and Japan), and it certainly never became an alternative to Hollywood.

This book is a history of Soviet filmmaking under Stalin (1930–1953). It examines what happened to "the most important of the arts" and why the Stalin regime, despite explicit intent, failed to construct a controlled mass propaganda cinema. In telling this story the book pursues three goals. First, to revise some of the persistent myths about this period, such as that Stalin was the chief censor, that thematic planning was an effective censorship tool, or that film directors had no autonomy. Stalin was only one, albeit a crucial, authority in a larger system of Soviet filmmaking, and filmmakers and executives had substantial agency in developing and determining content. Second, it is time to shake the label "Stalinist" from this cinema. As isolated as Russia might have been under Stalin, film practitioners saw themselves as contributors not only to Stalin-era culture but also to the global cinema process. Soviet films circulated abroad, and Soviet filmmakers never lost sight of Hollywood as a competitor and counterpart. Nor should we view the Stalin period as a break from the pre- and post-Stalin eras. Stalin-era cinema was built on the film industry of the 1920s and prepared the cinema of the 1960s, and it was only a particularly constrained episode in the rich Russian filmmaking tradition. Finally, and most broadly, this history suggests that there are limits to totalitarianism. The Stalinists did not succeed in establishing a communist culture industry because, even in a highly politicized and repressive environment, industry-specific institutions and incentives counteracted top-down control.

The Bolsheviks expected the Soviet film industry to mount a mass communist cinema, a "cinema for the millions."[5] Before the 1917 revolution, Russia had a robust and well-respected movie-making tradition. After the revolution, in 1919, the Bolsheviks nationalized film production and put effort into developing filmmaking that would support the state's political needs. State-owned

---

5. The phrase comes from the title of Boris Shumiatskii's *Kinematografiia millionov: Opyt analiza* (Moscow: Kinofotoizdat, 1935). It goes back to the slogan "intelligible to the millions," propagated at the 1928 Party Conference on Cinema. B.S. Ol'khovyi, ed., *Puti kino: 1-oe vsesoiuznoe partiinoe soveshchanie po kinematografii* (Moscow: Tea-kino pechat', 1929), 17, 429–444.

but diversified Russian cinema of the 1920s achieved global renown and showed promise of becoming a communist Hollywood. In the early 1930s, however, the Stalin regime centralized all film production in the country under one Moscow-based cinema administration, and then put pressure on the industry to produce high-quality popular hits. The ambitious goal of high quality and the intolerance of anything less interrupted the project of mass communist cinema: risk aversion set in, studios began to operate under capacity, production schedules lengthened, and fewer new releases made their way to audiences.

Actual production of feature-length films fell even further when compared to what was considered ideal. In 1935–1936 Boris Shumiatskii, the head of the cinema administration, projected an annual output of three hundred to eight hundred features. This quantity was required for the Soviet Union to "catch up and overtake" the United States in film production. By the late 1930s, it became clear that this target was unattainable. Production potential was reset to a modest eighty films per year, but the film industry failed to deliver this target number as well. Then in 1948, in a major policy retreat, Stalin announced that it was not necessary for the Soviet Union to compete with Hollywood and set the yearly production goal to four or five "masterpieces." Under the expectation that every film would be far above average in artistic achievement and political impact, annual production fell so low in 1948–1952 that contemporaries dubbed the period the "film famine" or "cine-anemia" (*malokartin'e*). To compensate, the film industry released old films, both Soviet and foreign. The release schedule for 1949, for instance, was made up of only thirteen new Soviet films, in addition to sixty-one foreign titles dating primarily from the 1930s.[6] (For a summary of film output, see appendix 1.)

The Soviet film industry underproduced under Stalin not because it lacked resources. Cinema not only paid for itself but was also profitable. A top-grossing film in 1937 could earn fifty times its cost.[7] In 1939 cinemas sold or distributed 950 million tickets, one-third of that in the United States, which is impressive given that the Soviet film industry made only one-tenth as many films.[8] Yet making a profit was never this industry's top priority, and, even if in the later Stalin

---

6. Kirill Anderson et al., eds., *Kremlevskii kinoteatr, 1928–1953: Dokumenty* (Moscow: ROSSPEN, 2005), 836.

7. Thorold Dickinson and Alan Lawson, "The Film in USSR—1937," *The Cine-Technician* (August–September 1937): 105.

8. These data are adjusted to population size. "Kinematografiia v tsifrakh," *Kino*, February 15, 1940, 7; John Sedgwick and Michael Pokorny, eds., *Economic History of Film* (New York: Routledge, 2005), 154.

period many productions ran over budget, there were always finances, equipment, and studio capacity that remained unutilized. Nor was there a shortage in film talent. In 1938 Soviet film studios employed over 160 film directors.[9] This number was only marginally lower than the concurrent estimates for the US film industry.[10] According to the film industry's self-assessment in 1936, it had the capacity to produce at least 120 features per year—almost ten times the number of films it made during the worst years of the Stalin period.[11] In fact, before it was consolidated in 1930, and immediately after Stalin's death in 1953, Soviet feature output gravitated toward what seems to have been its natural level of just over 100 films a year.

The few films the industry did produce were typically skillful works. As opposed to what is often assumed, they appealed to Soviet film viewers not because they did or did not contain propaganda (they always did), but because they were attractive and professionally made. Movies told engaging stories, featured excellent actors, and dealt with compelling characters acting in accordance with their own belief systems, which included but were not limited to a socialist worldview. In the 1930s films spanned a variety of themes and genres. By the 1940s, however, and against the party-state leaders' wishes, the balance shifted toward historical epics and children's films and away from genres dealing with contemporary subjects.[12]

Yet the content and quality of new Soviet releases often failed to meet party-state standards. In 1933 Shumiatskii said that of the films produced in 1932, half were completely unacceptable as Soviet products.[13] Eight years later, there was little progress. Andrei Zhdanov, the chief Communist Party Central Committee member in charge of cultural policy, complained that "at least half" of new films produced in 1940 were politically "unusable."[14] Throughout the period, many "unusable" films were nevertheless released to fill the screens and generate revenue, but a significant number of completed films were banned altogether.

---

9. A. Dubrovskii, "O 'predelakh' i vozmozhnostiakh sovetskoi kinematografii," *Iskusstvo kino* 1 (January 1938): 27. See also RGALI, f. 2456, op. 1, d. 312. All titles for the files from RGALI can be found on the archive's website through the search where you enter f. #, op. #, d. #.

10. In 1936, 244 directors worked in Hollywood. Tino Balio, ed., *Grand Design: Hollywood as a Modern Business Enterprise, 1930–1939*. Berkeley: University of California Press, 1995), 80.

11. Anderson et al., *Kremlevskii kinoteatr*, 306.

12. On the genre dynamic under Stalin, see Maria Belodubrovskaya, "The Jockey and the Horse: Joseph Stalin and the Biopic Genre in Soviet Cinema," *Studies in Russian and Soviet Cinema* 5, no. 1 (2011): 29–53.

13. Boris Shumiatskii, "Kak sostavliat' templan khudozhestvennykh fil'm," *Kino*, August 4, 1933, 2.

14. Anderson et al., *Kremlevskii kinoteatr*, 607.

The existence of film bans under Stalin is particularly surprising. To produce a banned film was to commit a crime against the state and waste millions of rubles on productions considered so harmful they could not be shown to the public. Why did film directors, their studios, and film executives in Moscow repeatedly fail? Couldn't the supposedly formidable Stalinist state prevent the film industry from producing the wrong films? And more generally, why couldn't filmmakers and the state cooperate on improving film output when both had the resources and the will to do so?

The typical explanation for Soviet cinema's poor performance during this period is political repression and resistance under Stalin.[15] This thesis, although compelling in some respects, is not borne out by the history of Soviet cinema. What, for example, accounts for the fact that the filmmakers who made banned films were sometimes allowed to continue to work rather than being replaced by other filmmakers? Similarly, may we speak of resistance when filmmakers wanted to produce on demand but failed unintentionally? As has been shown in other contexts, many among the Soviet elite embraced the state's agenda; this was the case for most filmmakers as well.[16] There is no doubt that fear played a major role in the relationship between Soviet film practitioners and the party-state. To live under Stalin was to live in a police state. Yet to argue that fear was the filmmakers' primary motivation is to present them as largely passive agents who lived solely to survive. In reality, Soviet filmmakers were an active and privileged group who protected their art and felt entitled to their works as much as the films' actual sponsor and owner, the state, did. Such notions as authorship, mastery, peer competition, and international reputation were indispensable to Soviet filmmakers, perhaps more so than in other contemporary nonauthoritarian film contexts such as Hollywood. Moreover, the Stalinist party-state helped to cultivate this stance by delegating content development, production, administration, and even censorship to the filmmakers themselves.

Stalinism was undoubtedly a crucial context for the story of Soviet cinema, but the more pertinent explanation for its performance can be found in the operation of the film industry itself. Although Stalin's hope was to build a mass-producing cinema machine, the regime did very little to equip the Soviet film industry for

---

15. See, e.g., Peter Kenez, *Cinema and Soviet Society from the Revolution to the Death of Stalin* (London: I. B. Tauris, 2001).

16. Igal Halfin writes about this in reference to the communists who perished during the Great Terror. *Terror in My Soul: Communist Autobiographies on Trial* (Cambridge, MA: Harvard University Press, 2003).

controlled mass production. In the Stalin period, Soviet studios operated under an artisanal, underprofessionalized mode of filmmaking, which lacked a division of labor or standardization that could distribute authority over the final product among multiple agents. Film directors were in charge of most aspects of production, there were no producers in the Hollywood sense, and executives and censors never had the clout to completely overwhelm filmmakers. Even though proposals were made in the mid-1930s to industrialize Soviet filmmaking based on the Hollywood model, these were quickly abandoned due to pressure from the more immediate goal: the production of a few major hits.

Soviet leaders were ardent industrializers, but when it came to cultural production, the impulse to increase output clashed with the impulse to control quality.[17] What the Stalin regime wanted most of all was for Soviet cinema to produce politically useful masterpieces. Soviet cinema could produce political blockbusters, and *Battleship Potemkin* (1925) and *Chapaev* (1934) were widely recognized as models. With such films, the masterpiece goal was always within grasp, and no structural change seemed necessary. These and similar film achievements validated existing nonindustrial practices, elevated director-masters, and obviated any need for institutional reform. Meanwhile, *Potemkins* and *Chapaevs* were rare occurrences. Yet instead of being satisfied with half-successes and allowing the industry some breathing room—as Joseph Goebbels, for instance, did under Hitler in Nazi Germany—the party-state refused to tolerate imperfection.[18] Too impatient to wait and see what new formulas of propagandistic expression the filmmakers might develop, Stalin, his associates, and official critics rejected or censured the movies that did not meet their standards. The strategy of pressuring the already poorly developed industry without strengthening it backfired.

The industrial conditions of Soviet cinema explain more about its failures and successes than we have been willing to consider. The "resistance" and entitlement Stalin-era filmmakers as a group appeared to display was not personal but institutional and systemic. Under urgent pressure to produce masterpieces, the industry invested in top directing and screenwriting talent, but failed to cultivate middle management or industrial processes that could have improved censorship and control. No sophisticated mechanisms were developed to absorb inefficiencies, generate "usable" story ideas, rewrite hundreds of screenplay submissions into high-quality propaganda, control directors, and turn censorship into a

17. See David Priestland, *Stalinism and the Politics of Mobilization: Ideas, Power, and Terror in Inter-War Russia* (Oxford: Oxford University Press, 2007).

18. David Welch, *Propaganda and the German Cinema, 1933–1945* (London: I. B. Tauris, 2001).

productive activity. In the absence of sophisticated management and structural change, repression-like measures—film bans, public shaming, and other types of persecution—were the only tools of control available.

Instead of repression and resistance, it is more useful to think about the interaction between Soviet filmmakers and the state as a complex give-and-take within limited industrial conditions that resulted in a compromise detrimental to both parties. In the absence of midlevel managers, writers, or directors who could easily adjust to new requirements, and needing to protect itself in response to the Stalinist intolerance of imperfection, the film industry curtailed its productive activities. Faced with low productivity, the party-state was forced to settle on a minimum program—four to five masterpieces—and compromise on its ultimate ambition of mounting a controlled mass propaganda cinema. After Soviet cinema failed repeatedly to produce "usable" films on urgent and politically mobilizing topics such as collective farms, industrial construction, the new Soviet man, and Soviet superiority, the party-state accepted that, with rare exceptions, the film industry would handle only such familiar propaganda appeals as patriotism, nationalism, and heroism. The later Stalin-era films were more formulaic and less useful politically, but without them there would have been hardly any films at all.

To date the literature on Stalin-era cinema has primarily focused on political history and the films themselves.[19] The Soviet film industry and its institutions have been given only a cursory treatment.[20] Scholars note the dysfunctional nature of Soviet cinema, but do not explain its structural logic: which is that while trying to be a propaganda factory, the Soviet film industry was run as an artisan's workshop. As opposed to Hollywood, which was a model of coordination and efficiency, the Soviet film industry was not vertically integrated: only one of its branches, film production, was centrally controlled, while film distribution and exhibition were administered separately from production.[21] (For a list of Soviet cinema administrations and their jurisdictions over branches of the industry,

19. Jay Leyda, *Kino: A History of the Russian and Soviet Film* (New York: Collier Books, 1973); Denise Youngblood, *Soviet Cinema in the Silent Era, 1918–1935* (Austin: University of Texas Press, 1991); Richard Taylor and Derek Spring, eds., *Stalinism and Soviet Cinema* (London: Routledge, 1993); Kenez, *Cinema and Soviet Society.*

20. Paul Babitsky and John Rimberg, *The Soviet Film Industry* (New York: Praeger, 1955); Jamie Miller, *Soviet Cinema: Politics and Persuasion under Stalin* (London: I. B. Tauris, 2010).

21. Vertical integration is a system in which film production companies control distribution and own theaters, and therefore can fully exploit the profit potential of their products. It was in place in Hollywood in the 1930s and 1940s. See Tino Balio, ed., *The American Film Industry* (Madison: University of Wisconsin Press, 1985).

see appendix 2). Distribution was centralized in 1938, but theaters, state-owned but decentralized, had their own priorities. Because of this dispersed industry structure, the party-state did not have a full grasp of distribution and did not mandate to theaters what to show. Unlike national film industries in Europe and Asia, the Soviet Union had a key fertile condition for Hollywood-type mass cinema: a large domestic market free of competition with new foreign releases. Having refused the Hollywood vertical-integration model, the Soviet party-state also failed to utilize this market advantage.[22] The lack of vertical integration constrained how much centralized control was possible, let alone achieved, and it focused all the political pressure on film production.[23]

To suggest an industrial explanation for Soviet cinema's trajectory under Stalin is not to deny the role of ideology. In fact, the party-state's shortsightedness in handling the film industry is itself explained by its unrealistic ideological ambitions. As much recent literature on Stalinism shows, Stalin had enormous aspirations for building a new communist society, of which mass propaganda cinema was one element, and many of his destructive actions originated in his unwavering desire to realize this program.[24] One reason the outcomes diverged from intentions under Stalin was that the Stalinist vision presupposed that it was possible to build socialism simply by creating a correct, revolutionary proletarian consciousness in the Soviet population. Equipped with this special consciousness, the Soviet people would *automatically* acquire the will and energy to participate

---

22. I am indebted to Ben Brewster for pointing this out to me.

23. The focus of this book is Soviet feature-film production. Film exhibition (and "cinefication," the expansion of the theater network) was also crucially important for the project of building a mass propaganda cinema. So was distribution: as output of new films decreased, the number of distribution prints for each new release grew from 50 prints in the early 1930s to 300 by 1940 and 1,500 at the end of the Stalin period. Jamie Miller has argued that in the 1930s the number of prints for each release did not adequately service the Soviet screens, but more research into distribution and exhibition is needed. Jamie Miller, "Soviet Cinema, 1929–41: The Development of Industry and Infrastructure," *Europe-Asia Studies* 58, no. 1 (2006): 103–124. Nor does this book provide an account of filmmaking in the national republics. Even though the dysfunctional state of the industry extended to the republics, major differences existed among them, and the histories of such important cinemas as those of Ukraine and Georgia under Stalin remain to be written. This history also does not cover Soviet shorts, nonfiction, and animation.

24. See, e.g., Stephen Kotkin, *Magnetic Mountain: Stalinism as a Civilization* (Berkeley: University of California Press, 1995); David L. Hoffmann, *Stalinist Values: The Cultural Norms of Soviet Modernity, 1917–1941* (Ithaca, NY: Cornell University Press, 2003); Francine Hirsch, *Empire of Nations: Ethnographic Knowledge and the Making of the Soviet Union* (Ithaca, NY: Cornell University Press, 2005). As Peter Holquist suggests, the Bolshevik project was never about control; it was about transformation and enlightenment. Peter Holquist, "Information Is the Alpha and Omega of Our Work: Bolshevik Surveillance in Its Pan-European Context," *The Journal of Modern History* 69, no. 3 (1997): 415–450.

in building a communist state. This "revivalist" position, as David Priestland calls it, dictated that revolutionary and inspirational ideas (politics and ideology) rather than rational economic systems, technology, and gradualism were required for the socialist project to succeed.[25]

This stance explicates why the party-state leadership instructed film executives to invest in top talent rather than to mount systematic industrial reform. A greater division of labor, for example, could have stripped Soviet film directors of their overarching authority, but it was not implemented because the institution of the director-master was supposed to secure voluntary ideological commitment and exemplify Soviet superiority over the West.[26] Stalinist ambition also explains why the party-state acted surprised when the filmmakers failed to automatically fall in line, and why it responded with aggressive stopgap measures (bans, personnel restrictions, artistic campaigns, and administrative buildup) to force cinema onto a path of success. Because of this ideological posture, the party-state never had a development strategy for Soviet cinema, while Stalin's intolerance of imperfection proved too disruptive and inflexible to produce satisfying results.[27] Ironically, this meant that free-market, capitalist Hollywood had far more sophisticated censorship and content control than the totalitarian, communist Stalin-era film industry.[28]

This book looks at a crucial period in the history of Soviet cinema when its institutions as a whole were established. It explores how the unhappy compromise

---

25. Priestland, *Stalinism and the Politics of Mobilization*, esp. 35–49. On the Stalin era's failures at mobilization, see David Brandenberger, *Propaganda State in Crisis: Soviet Ideology, Indoctrination, and Terror under Stalin, 1927–1941* (New Haven, CT: Yale University Press, 2012).

26. On Soviet superiority, see Michael David-Fox, *Showcasing the Great Experiment: Cultural Diplomacy and Western Visitors to the Soviet Union, 1921–1941* (Oxford: Oxford University Press, 2011), 285–311.

27. In his book *Soviet Cinema: Politics and Persuasion under Stalin*, Jamie Miller offers a contrasting explanation, arguing that party-state actions can be explained by its defensive stance. Always afraid of losing power, the party-state had little flexibility and failed to adjust to the inefficiencies of the film industry. I suggest that inflexibility, which is a keen characterization of this system, was a product of a lack of industrial development and an absence of sophistication. That in turn was caused by the Stalinist offensive stance and Stalin's intolerance of imperfection. *Soviet Cinema* also does not distinguish between the party-state and the cinema administration. According to Miller's account, the head of the film industry represented the interests of the party-state, a position with which I disagree. As I hope this book shows, the cinema chiefs Boris Shumiatskii and Ivan Bol'shakov represented the industry first and the party-state second.

28. On Hollywood censorship, see, e.g., Lea Jacobs, *The Wages of Sin: Censorship and the Fallen Woman Film, 1928–1942* (Madison: University of Wisconsin Press, 1991); Thomas Doherty, *Hollywood's Censor: Joseph I. Breen and the Production Code Administration* (New York: Columbia University Press, 2007).

of Stalin-era cinema emerged and what role ideology played in it. Much of this account is based on published and unpublished archival sources. The author approached the project with largely the same preconceived notions about Stalinist totalitarian control as everyone else, but the documents told a different story. That story was that in many ways Soviet film practitioners operated as international professionals using largely the same standards of entertainment, artistry, and craftsmanship as elsewhere. Documents suggested that Soviet filmmaking functioned poorly and inefficiently, but that the inefficiency and lack of standardization made Soviet cinema far less susceptible to pressures from the Stalinist leadership than previously understood. Because no substantial institutional reform was implemented under Stalin, Stalinism restricted how Soviet cinema operated but did not fundamentally alter its mode, and the filmmakers themselves—the men and women who cared about the art and craft of film far more than they did about ideology and politics—were this system's major players.

The chapters that follow focus on the thick layer of agents whom ideology targeted and who produced the film artifacts: filmmakers (directors and screenwriters) and administrators (executives and censors). Chapter 1 discusses Soviet film policy. Until 1948, the Stalin government pursued two goals: a short-term objective to make masterpieces (quality) and a longer-term project of building a mass cinema (quantity). It shows how, against intent, the masterpiece policy and its correlate, the intolerance of imperfection, set Soviet cinema under Stalin on a path of contraction. Chapter 2 addresses thematic planning, which is often seen as the party-state's primary tool of content control. I show that thematic plans were compiled out of studio proposals and never satisfied their top-down function.

The reason thematic planning did not work was because studios operated under what I call the director-centered mode of production and had to accommodate the interests of their directors. Chapter 3 discusses the implications of this mode and suggests why entrusting self-governance and self-censorship to a select group of director-masters, whose artistic commitments diverged from party-state goals, was counterproductive. Another bottleneck was screenwriting, which is addressed in chapter 4. Lacking a large contingent of professional screenwriters who could write on order, the industry focused on mobilizing established writers to produce high-quality screenplays. Writers did not deliver masterpieces and weakened censorship, making it only more difficult to produce ideologically correct films on a large scale.

Censors, the subject of chapter 5, were also poorly equipped to guide filmmakers. Censorship was primarily carried out by the industry, which created conflicts of interest and contributed to risk aversion. Failures of self-censorship forced Stalin and his associates to review films themselves. Stalin's involvement, which was unpredictable, produced extreme uncertainty and lack of responsibility among the censors. While industry censors multiplied, film production slowed. In addition to this account, chapter 5 contains censorship case studies of three important films: Aleksandr Medvedkin's *The Miracle Worker* (1936), Leonid Lukov's *A Great Life*, part 2 (1946), and Konstantin Iudin's *Brave Men* (1950).

I conclude by proposing that an institutional approach to cinema history can give us specific answers about how ideology operates in cinema. Films are produced not by ideologies but by filmmakers and film executives working within a certain institutional environment. What ideology determines are the institutions. And the institutional structure can work both ways. It can either support the trickling of ideology all the way down to films or it can block such a transfer. Against expectation, Stalin-era cinema manifested the latter alternative. The institutions of Soviet cinema were ill-equipped to mass-produce propaganda films because the Stalinist ideological ambition to make "superior" films precluded industrial development. The combination of strong political ambition and weak institutional policy was detrimental to the success of the Soviet mass-cinema project. The low yield of the "most important of the arts" was an accident of ideology.

QUANTITY VS. QUALITY

Soviet Film Policy and the Intolerance of
Imperfection

In 1952, Harry Schwartz, *The New York Times* editorial writer and an expert on
the Soviet Union, reported on the "sagging Soviet screen scene": "Here is surely
a phenomenon to cause a mass lifting of the eyebrows. Even Stalin's most skilled
dialectician can hardly be making a Communist propagandist out of Tarzan as
played by Johnny Weissmuller and produced in Hollywood. Edgar Rice Bur-
roughs' original version of nature boy has always been strong on thrills and
action, and way low on social significance of the kind the Kremlin prizes so
highly. Yet facts are facts. Moscow has resurrected the old Tarzan films, showing
them in its theaters, and finding the customers love them. All this after years of
raging about Hollywood's 'bourgeois decadence.'" The reason for Moscow's radical turnabout in screen policy, Schwartz suggested, was desperation. The Stalin
government had too few Soviet movies to screen.[1]

Indeed, perhaps the most striking feature of the Soviet film industry under
Stalin was its decline in film output (figure 1.1). The purpose of this book is to
explain this decline. To start, it might be useful to establish the tenets of Soviet
cinema policy. Was the low output that caused the release of old American films
in the late Stalin period part of the party-state's deliberate policy or an outcome
of an unintended policy failure? We now have access not only to Stalin's public

---

1. Harry Schwartz, "Scanning the Sagging Soviet Screen Scene," *The New York Times*, March 9,
1952, x5.

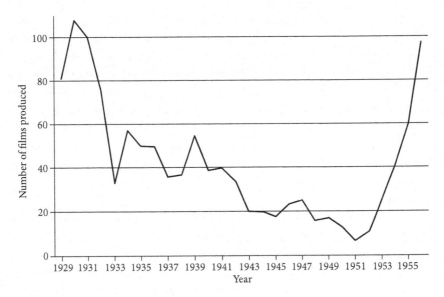

FIGURE 1.1 Soviet film production, 1929–1956

pronouncements but also to the Communist Party Central Committee's internal deliberations. If we investigate the party-state's decisions on cinema, as well as the industry's attempts to implement them, we shall discover that neither low output nor Tarzan were ever part of the plan.

The goal was a "cinema for the millions," an objective that had both a quantitative and a qualitative dimension. Ideally, the Stalin government, just like Soviet governments before and after Stalin, wanted a mass quantity of successful propaganda films. Both quantity and quality were required to convince naysayers at home and abroad of the superiority of the Soviet regime. Accordingly, Stalin's Central Committee pursued two policies. The maximum program, as I shall call it, dictated that the film industry make hundreds of mass films and compete with Hollywood. The minimum program prescribed the release of at least a few political and artistic "masterpieces" each year. The implementation of this bifurcated agenda proceeded in spurts that depended on current output. When the number of films made was on the rise, the party-state demanded higher quality and greater selectivity. When quality improved, the industry was instructed to produce more films.

The Soviet mode of film production, however, constrained the implementation of both programs. At the start of the Stalin period, Soviet filmmaking operated under a largely "artisanal" (*kustarnyi*), or nonindustrial, director-centered mode established in the 1920s. Between 1930 and 1937, the new head of the Soviet cinema administration, Boris Shumiatskii, an ambitious man and a great proponent of genre cinema, tried and failed to reform this mode.[2] In 1935 he proposed a project to modernize the industry based on the Hollywood model and to build a cinema city, a "Soviet Hollywood," in the south of Russia. This proposal, which Stalin initially supported, was part of a policy swing toward the maximum program and had the potential of boosting both quantity and quality. In 1936, however, the policy pendulum swung back to masterpieces and Stalin abandoned the project. The failure of the Soviet Hollywood initiative, with its promise of mass production and comprehensive controls, determined the course of Soviet cinema once and for all. The existing mode of production could not support expansion, precluding the success of the maximum program.

The implementation of the minimum program also backfired, and the Stalin period ended with "the film famine," a desperate dearth of new releases. This was because every swing toward selectivity was accompanied by sharp criticisms of "average" and "poor" films, which comprised most of the output, as well as by emphatic film bans. Quality was always the priority under Stalin, but his intolerance of imperfection grew over time. Each attack on the industry undermined its productivity, eventually collapsing filmmaking to only a handful of features. In 1948, having realized that the industry was incapable of producing "good" films on a large scale, Stalin had to accept the reality of the vastly reduced minimum program.

From Quantity to Quality, 1930–1933

One of the first major pronouncements by a Bolshevik leader on the role of mass cinema was Leon Trotsky's article "Vodka, Church, and the Cinema" published in *Pravda* in July 1923. Not unlike Lenin, who in 1922 reportedly declared cinema a crucial educational medium, "the most important of the arts," Trotsky argued that cinema was the most critical tool of the party-state for providing the working class with enlightening entertainment during nonwork hours. Trotsky, however, went further than Lenin to suggest that cinema could compete with drinking establishments as both leisure and a revenue source for the state. This fiscal proposition was particularly ambitious given that in 1927–1928 state receipts from vodka sales were projected to reach more than 600,000,000 rubles, whereas

---

2. Shumiatskii was a seasoned Communist who had worked for the Communist Party underground before 1917 and later, among other party appointments, served as Soviet Ambassador to Persia.

receipts from movie theaters in 1926–1927 amounted to less than 20,000,000 rubles.[3] Trotsky further proposed that cinema could replace the church. Unlike religion, he said, cinema could tell a different story every hour.[4] To displace religion and alcohol, cinema would have to provide not only enlightenment and entertainment but also many new stories in a large number of venues. It had to become a mass phenomenon.

In the 1920s, Soviet cinema showed the potential of meeting this goal. Under the quasi-free-market conditions of the New Economic Policy (1921–1928), studios were mostly self-financed entities selling their products to large regional distributors on a contractual basis. The distributors, in turn, rented films to a dispersed network of exhibitors. Soviet films competed for audiences not only among themselves but also with foreign pictures, and some of them were quite successful at this. The single greatest change that happened under the First Five-Year Plan (1928–1932), which replaced the New Economic Policy when Stalin solidified his power, was that imports of foreign films were curbed in 1930.[5] The measure targeted economic frugality—foreign currency was in limited supply, and far more important commodities could be purchased with it than motion pictures—but it also pursued ideological goals: it helped the Stalin regime to monopolize cultural and political communication.[6]

Despite this change, the party-state's conception of cinema as a potential revenue maker persisted to the end of the Stalin period and beyond. In combination with the Bolsheviks' ambitious ideological agenda, which included transforming everything from the economy to the human psyche, the conception of cinema as a revenue source produced the program maximum for Soviet cinema: "One hundred percent ideology, one hundred percent entertainment, one hundred percent commerce."[7] In a policy speech in 1927, Stalin echoed Trotsky's idea of replacing

3. Ol'khovyi, *Puti kino*, 42. Vodka production and sales were banned by the tsarist government prior to 1917, a policy that continued for a few years until the Bolsheviks reinstituted vodka trade as a state monopoly in the mid-1920s. Julie Hessler, *A Social History of Soviet Trade: Trade Policy, Retail Practices, and Consumption, 1917–1953* (Princeton, NJ: Princeton University Press, 2004), 164.

4. L. Trotskii, "Vodka, tserkov' i kinematograf," *Pravda*, July 12, 1923, 2, reprinted with commentary by Vladimir Zabrodin in *Kinovedcheskie zapiski* 45 (2000): 184–188.

5. For import statistics and domestic production in the 1920s, see Denise Youngblood, *Movies for the Masses: Popular Cinema and Soviet Society in the 1920s* (Cambridge, UK: Cambridge University Press, 1992), 20. See also, Vance Kepley, Jr. and Betty Kepley, "Foreign Films on Soviet Screens, 1921–1931," *Quarterly Review of Film Studies* 4, no. 4 (1979): 429–442; Vance Kepley, Jr., "The Origins of Soviet Cinema: A Study in Industry Development," *Quarterly Review of Film Studies* 10, no. 1 (1985): 22–38.

6. Vance Kepley, Jr., "The First 'Perestroika': Soviet Cinema under the First Five-Year Plan," *Cinema Journal* 35, no. 4 (1996): 31–53.

7. Youngblood, *Movies for the Masses*, 46. See also, Ol'khovyi, *Puti kino*, 431–432.

vodka sales with "such revenue sources as radio and cinema."[8] In November 1934, when cinema revenues stood at about 200,000,000 rubles, Stalin told Shumiatskii that this was not enough. He added, "You need to seriously prepare yourself to replacing vodka receipts with cinema revenues."[9] Earlier that year Shumiatskii submitted to the Central Committee a proposal that promised to start achieving this goal by the Third Five-Year Plan (1938–1942), when cinema receipts would reach 1 billion rubles.[10]

It was under the assumption that cinema was a powerful cultural force that in 1930 the Central Committee made all but one of the Soviet Union's fourteen feature-film studios answerable to one administration, the All-Union Combine for the Cinema and Photo Industry (Soiuzkino), and appointed Shumiatskii at its helm. Soiuzkino's predecessor, Sovkino (1924–1930), controlled production and distribution in the Russian Republic (RSFSR) alone. Although the names of these studios changed over time, Soiuzkino incorporated the RSFSR studios Mosfilm (Moscow), Lenfilm (Leningrad), and Vostokfilm (which in 1930–1936 also operated the Yalta Studio), as well as studios in the national republics: the Odessa Studio and the Kiev Studio (Ukraine), Belgosfilm (located in Leningrad but producing in the name of Belarus), Gruziiafilm (Tbilisi), Azerfilm (Baku), Armenfilm (Erevan), Turkmenfilm (Ashgabat), Tadjikfilm (Dushanbe/Stalinabad), and Uzbekfilm (Tashkent). The only studio outside of Soiuzkino's jurisdiction was Mezhrabpomfilm (Moscow). Funded by the Workers International Relief (Mezhrabpom in the Russian abbreviation), a German-Soviet communist organization affiliated with Comintern and headquartered in Berlin, the studio was formed in 1922 as Mezhrabpom-Rus' and renamed Mezhrabpomfilm in 1928. By the 1930s, it was a flagship studio known for its high ticket sales and international filmmaking practices. It employed the A-list directors Vsevolod Pudovkin, Lev Kuleshov, and Yakov Protazanov, as well as immigrant directors, such as Erwin Piscator, who fled the Nazi regime. It was one of the bastions of Soviet internationalism. Mezhrabpomfilm and Vostokfilm were closed in 1936. Soiuzdetfilm, formed out of Mezhrabpomfilm in 1936, inherited the Yalta Studio from Vostokfilm.[11] In the 1930s, Mosfilm, Lenfilm, Kiev/Odessa, and Mezhrabpomfilm/Soiuzdetfilm produced the vast majority of all Soviet films.

---

8. I.V. Stalin, "XV s"ezd VKP(b)," in *Sochineniia*, vol. 10 (Moscow: Gosudarstvennoe izdatel'stvo politicheskoi literatury, 1949), 312.

9. Anderson et al., *Kremlevskii kinoteatr*, 960.

10. Anderson et al., *Kremlevskii kinoteatr*, 240–242; Valerii Fomin, ed., *Letopis' rossiiskogo kino, 1930–1945* (Moscow: Materik, 2007), 282.

11. Vostokfilm represented the Crimea, North Caucuses, Volga, and Siberian regions, along with Kazakhstan. Kazakhfilm (Alma-Ata) was formed in 1934.

As head of Soiuzkino, Shumiatskii's task, along with centralized coordination of production, was to expand output, grow the theater network, and develop domestic manufacturing of film equipment. Soiuzkino and its studios were not vertically integrated, however. In the republics, distribution and exhibition were run by disintegrated administrative units within the national republic governments. Soiuzkino nominally incorporated the republic cinema administrations, but had operational control over distribution and exhibition only in RSFSR. Moreover, the republics, and Ukraine in particular, never accepted Soiuzkino's monopoly over production. Under their pressure, by the end of 1931 production was again decentralized such that the studios located in the republics were transferred to the republic cinema authorities. This, however, did not establish vertical integration in the republics either, as studios were run separately from distribution and from exhibition. In 1933, Soiuzkino was further decentralized as the Main Administration for Cinema and Photo Industry (GUKF). GUKF no longer incorporated the republic cinema administrations and had veto power only over the production programs of the national studios, such as Mosfilm and Lenfilm. It also lost its control over distribution and exhibition in RSFSR. In parallel with the other republics, these branches were now run by the RSFSR government.[12]

During Shumiatskii's tenure the Soviet Union started to manufacture its own film stock, cameras, and projectors, even if of vastly inferior quality compared with imports. A major "cinefication" effort—the expansion of the theater network—also continued, and the number of establishments equipped, nominally at least, to screen silent films grew from seven thousand in 1928 to twenty-eight thousand in 1940.[13] Film production, arguably the core factor in the mass-cinema project, however, started to decline in 1931. One hundred and eight films were made in 1930 and one hundred in 1931, but only seventy-five in 1932 and thirty-three in 1933. This drop in output defied the leadership's explicit wishes. In the summer of 1931, at a conference with screenwriters, Central Committee Propaganda Department Chairman Aleksei Stetskii stated in his opening remarks: "It is absolutely clear that we need to do something to increase output and bring the matter of agitprop and sound cinema up to the mark." He added that one year after the formation of Soiuzkino, Shumiatskii had failed to deliver

---

12. For more on the restructuring of the Soviet film industry, see Babitsky and Rimberg, *Soviet Film Industry*, 1–65. See also appendix 2.

13. It needs to be noted that the target number of screens at the start of the 1930s was seventy thousand by the end of the decade. On cinefication problems and the shortage of prints in the 1930s, see Miller, *Soviet Cinema*, 23–33.

on this task.[14] The December 1931 Central Committee resolution on cinema also stated: "the Central Committee believes that Soviet cinema should undergo both quantitative and qualitative expansion to a degree that would correspond to the overall level and pace of both socialist construction and the growing cultural demands of the masses."[15]

One reason for contraction was economic. In parallel with imports of films, the importation of film stock was drastically reduced by 1931. Since the manufacture of domestic stock had hardly begun, 1931 and 1932 saw a major drop in supplies, affecting the output of 1933. The shortage of stock proved quite consequential indeed. Early in 1931 Soiuzkino was forced to cut production by 50 percent, and some studios were on the verge of closure.[16] The leadership of Soiuzkino told the Council of People's Commissars that the only solution to maintaining film industry momentum was to expand film stock importation once more.[17] Apparently this was not done.[18] By January 1933, Soiuzkino's Feature Production Department fired four hundred employees, its studios planned layoffs of five hundred workers, and even Mezhrabpomfilm fired nine directors.[19]

Yet, as Maya Turovskaya puts it, "party criticisms" of the majority of Soviet films were clearly instrumental in the output decline as well.[20] According to the Central Committee member Lazar Kaganovich, in 1931 the situation with cinema was "dreadful": "not a single serious picture" had been made in the preceding few years. In Europe, Kaganovich said, cinema was developing in leaps and bounds, but Soviet talent was underproducing. Kaganovich commented that there was little point in writing resolutions or setting quantitative targets, since the situation was so bad that "just a couple of [good] films" would have been a vast improvement.[21] Picking up on this assessment, Shumiatskii thus characterized the 1932 film output, which, by Shumiatskii's count, consisted of seventy-nine titles: Five films were "good" (*Counterplan*, *Men and Jobs*, *26 Commissars*, *Three Soldiers*, and *Ivan*). Thirty-six films were "mediocre" and could be released only

---

14. RGALI, f. 2497, op. 1, d. 37, l. 1.

15. Anderson et al., *Kremlevskii kinoteatr*, 155.

16. RGALI, f. 2497, op. 1, d. 18, esp. ll. 269–271.

17. Anderson et al., *Kremlevskii kinoteatr*, 128.

18. Jamie Miller reports that in 1930 46 million meters of film stock were imported and in 1933 only 1 million (Miller, *Soviet Cinema*, 30).

19. RGALI, f. 2497, op. 1, d. 69, ll. 13, 31.

20. Maya Turovskaya, "The 1930s and 1940s: Cinema in Context," in Taylor and Spring, *Stalinism and Soviet Cinema*, 44 n.18.

21. Anderson et al., *Kremlevskii kinoteatr*, 160.

because there was nothing better. Thirty-eight films were "unquestionably bad" or unsuitable for release.[22] Of almost eighty titles, only five were good enough to carry the party-state trademark. In fact, at least fifteen films completed in 1932, as many as in 1931, never saw the screen. The push to improve film quality was an important contributor to the output decline, along with technological issues such as stock shortage and the transition to sound.[23]

Already on the brink of the 1930s, there was an ongoing debate over whether the average quality of Soviet film product ought to be higher than it was in the West. At the 1928 Party Conference on Cinema, a major cinema event of the period, two opposing positions on this question were voiced. According to Il'ia Trainin, an executive at Sovkino who was known for his practical and commercial inclinations, it was unrealistic to expect every film to be above average. In the Western film industries, Trainin reasoned, the majority of pictures were of average quality; there were many failures and very few hits.[24] In contrast, the Central Committee Propaganda Department official Platon Kerzhentsev insisted that Soviet cinema should not submit to the Western model advocated by Trainin as natural. Instead, Kerzhentsev suggested Soviet cinema should follow the theater model. In theater, Kerzhentsev said, a play might have a run of twenty to thirty years. Soviet cinema too ought to make films that would screen for one to two decades. Moreover, he noted, this was quite possible: Sergei Eisenstein's *Battleship Potemkin* was a film for the ages.[25]

Trainin's position was realistic; Kerzhentsev's was idealistic and entirely far-fetched. Masterworks of *Potemkin*'s scale were unusual. Moreover, while *Potemkin* may have been a masterpiece, it was largely unpopular with Soviet audiences. It played in two Moscow theaters for only four weeks, whereas a popular American film, such as Douglas Fairbanks's *Robin Hood* (1922), stayed at eleven Moscow theaters for months.[26] Even if it were possible to make a hundred *Potemkin*s a year, Soviet exhibitors would not screen them. Between 1931 and 1938 film

22. Glavnoe upravlenie kino-foto-promyshlennosti, *Korennye voprosy sovetskoi kinematografii* (Moscow: GUKF, 1933), 51.

23. The transition from silent to sound cinema—both the production of sound films and equipping theaters to screen them—which started internationally in 1927, took far longer in Soviet cinema than it did in the West. See, e.g., Vincent Bohlinger, "The Development of Sound Technology in the Soviet Union during the First Five-Year Plan," *Studies in Russian and Soviet Cinema* 7, no. 2 (2013): 189–205.

24. Ol'khovyi, *Puti kino*, 136.

25. Ol'khovyi, *Puti kino*, 191.

26. Richard Taylor, *Battleship Potemkin: The Film Companion* (London: I. B. Tauris, 2001), 65. Although *Potemkin* was available and even recommended for distribution in the 1930s (see, e.g., TsGALI, f. 257, op. 12, d. 32, l. 9), it is unlikely that it garnered bigger audiences then.

distribution was decentralized, and theaters, controlled by local authorities (regions, municipalities, and enterprises) and interested in making money, tended to screen commercially viable films, including older foreign titles. As Jamie Miller writes about the 1930s, "it was clear by the way that films were being advertised that urban film exhibition still had an essentially commercial face."[27] Yet, however extreme and unrealistic, Kerzhentsev's masterpiece-only model accorded with the Soviet superiority thesis: if Soviet society was to be superior to the capitalist West, all of its films must be superior as well. As we shall see, having attempted and discarded alternative possibilities under Shumiatskii, this masterpiece-only extreme became the model Soviet cinema adopted after 1936.

Kerzhentsev's comments also fit the extreme rhetoric of the First Five-Year Plan. This was the period of "socialism in one state" when the Stalin regime instituted economic self-reliance, forced industrial growth, brutal collectivization, and central planning. It was also a period of the cultural revolution when an attempt was made to create new socialist art, art designed to provide activist enlightenment and political education in rejection of the traditional and passive "bourgeois" entertainment.[28] In cinema, formal avant-gardism in fiction, exemplified by Eisenstein, was one version of such art, and nonfiction reportage, represented by Dziga Vertov, was another. Yet this period also saw the development of a lesser-known but historically important genre of agitprop cinema (*politprosvetfilm* or *agitpropfilm*, a successor to the 1920s' *kulturfilm*). Rather than focusing on storytelling, agitprop films informed, educated, or made persuasive arguments. On average, they were shorter, combined documentary and fiction, had lower budgets, and were made by less-experienced filmmakers.[29] *Potemkin*, in fact, was considered an agitprop film about the 1905 revolution, and many agitprop films were also experimental. Although to us in retrospect the boundary between agitprop and avant-garde feature seems blurry, in the industry discourse agitprop was a separate and sizable category. During the 1929–1930 season,

---

27. Miller, *Soviet Cinema*, 26.

28. On the cultural revolution, see, e.g., Sheila Fitzpatrick, ed., *Cultural Revolution in Russia, 1928–1931* (Bloomington: Indiana University Press, 1977). On the entertainment versus enlightenment debate, see Denise Youngblood, "Entertainment or Enlightenment? Popular Cinema in Soviet Society, 1921–1931," in *New Directions in Soviet History*, ed. Stephen White (Cambridge, UK: Cambridge University Press, 1992), 41–61.

29. A January 1931 Soiuzkino report said that the percentage of agitprop films in production in 1930 was "under 55 percent," while their budgets amounted to 29 percent of total production budget (Anderson et al., *Kremlevskii kinoteatr*, 120). By a Council of People's Commissars decree "On Strengthening the Production and Exhibition of Political-Enlightenment Films" (December 7, 1929), studios were obligated to allocate 30 percent of their budgets to the production of agitprop films (Babitsky and Rimberg, *The Soviet Film Industry*, 27).

about half of all Soviet full-length films reviewed by the state censorship office, Glavrepertkom, were categorized as agitprop films. A ratio of ninety agitprop films to ten fiction features was suggested as desirable for 1932, a position that Shumiatskii, a huge proponent of narrative fiction, never tired of ridiculing.[30]

Agitprop cinema answered the goals of the cultural revolution, but, not unlike *Potemkin*, it failed to become a staple of the exhibition market. Agitprop films were not entertaining enough, and theater managers were reluctant to include them in their programs. Of the ninety-five agitprop films Glavrepertkom approved in 1929–1930, only thirty-six were screened.[31] It was also the case that many were of inferior quality, and a substantial number of titles banned in 1931 and 1932 were agitprop films.[32] When the December 1931 Central Committee resolution mandated that the film industry "decisively combat the wide-spread practice of pursuing quantity at the expense of quality, which results in enormous harm from the point of view of finances, resources, and ideology," it was a statement against agitprop cinema.[33]

In response to the commercial unviability and unpopularity of agitprop (and facing the reality of the exhibition network that he had little control over), as well as to respond to the Central Committee's call for better quality, in 1931 Shumiatskii shifted his priorities away from agitprop to the mass feature. Likely at Shumiatskii's suggestion, in December 1931 the Central Committee established within Soiuzkino a unit for the production of "mass fiction films" (*massovye khudozhestvennye kartiny*).[34] As Shumiatskii later explained in his programmatic book *Cinema for the Millions* (1935), a mass film was a film for the masses. More specifically, he wrote, paraphrasing Stalin, it was "a highly ideologically principled fiction film with a thrilling and engaging plot and strong acting performances."[35] It was a compromise between Kerzhentsev's ideological masterpiece and Train-in's commercial narrative cinema. The mass film's first prototype was *Vstrechnyi* (*Counterplan*, Sergei Iutkevich, Fridrikh Ermler, and Leo Arnshtam, 1932), and the archprototype became *Chapaev* (Georgii Vasil'ev and Sergei Vasil'ev, 1934).

The production plan for 1932 estimated that only 22 percent of films would fall into the newsreel and agitprop category, 32 percent would be fiction features,

30. RGALI, f. 2497, op. 1, d. 39, l. 158.

31. RGALI, f. 2497, op. 1, d. 39; RGALI, f. 2497, op. 1, d. 37, l. 104.

32. Evgenii Margolit and Viacheslav Shmyrov, *Iz"iatoe kino, 1924–1953* (Moscow: Dubl'-D, 1995).

33. Anderson et al., *Kremlevskii kinoteatr*, 157.

34. Anderson et al., *Kremlevskii kinoteatr*, 155–160. It is very likely that Shumiatskii wrote this resolution. It was customary for the Central Committee to edit and approve as official decisions documents prepared by the relevant agencies themselves.

35. Shumiatskii, *Kinematografiia millionov*, 122.

and 46 percent would be technical (*tekhnicheskii*) and instructional (*uchebnyi*) films.[36] In other words, the majority of all films meant for general distribution (technical and instructional films were made largely for specialized audiences) were now to be nonagitprop features. Compared with 1930–1932, when the percentage of agitprop films in each year's production schedule was at least 50 percent, 22 percent of *both* agitprop and newsreels was a radical reduction. By 1933 the agitprop film as a category became a thing of the past, as were overt avant-garde films.[37]

The elimination of agitprop cinema and the transition to the mass feature probably provide the best explanation as to why film output had dropped by more than half between 1932 and 1933. It is especially so given that this transition was part of a general policy shift that started in 1932 in anticipation of the Second Five-Year Plan (1933–1937). Forced collectivization and industrialization of the First Five-Year Plan did not produce economic prosperity, and in 1932 and 1933 the Soviet Union suffered the worst famine in its history. The Stalin government felt the need to scale back, and the policy pendulum moved from quantity and forced growth to quality, technological advancement, and relative consumerism.[38] The year 1932 marked the end of the cultural revolution. In April 1932 the Central Committee issued a resolution that abolished all artistic literary organizations and united all writers who wanted to work for the regime under the Soviet Writers' Union. The stated goal of the resolution was to interrupt the bitter bickering among artistic factions. The actual goal was to transition Soviet culture toward one party-sponsored and consumer-friendly approach: socialist realism. Stalin recognized that both the so-called authentic proletarian art and avant-garde experimentation, encouraged during the cultural revolution, failed to captivate the Soviet masses.[39] As for cinema, also in April 1932, the Central Committee appointed a special commission to oversee the production of mass fiction films in 1932, including ten "most significant" titles to be produced under

---

36. Fomin, *Letopis' rossiiskogo kino, 1930–1945*, 126. Percentage is a better estimation here than number. Similarly to newsreels, many agitprop films were shorts and numerically overwhelmed the production program in 1930–1932. For example, according to one report, Soiuzkino planned to produce 112 fiction films, 320 agitation films, and 527 newsreels in 1931 (RGALI, f. 2497, op. 1, d. 2, l. 9).

37. The production of shorts was curtailed as well. In 1936, for example, only seventeen short-length films were planned and twenty produced ("Doklad nachal'nika GUK tov. B. Z. Shumiatskogo," *Kino*, January 21, 1937, 2). Documentary film production was also down during the 1930s.

38. Priestland, *Stalinism and the Politics of Mobilization*, chap. 4.

39. See Evgenii Margolit, "Fenomen agitpropfil'ma i prikhod zvuka v sovetskoe kino," *Kinovedcheskie zapiski* 48 (2007): 255–266.

the commission's direct guidance.[40] This decision solidified Shumiatskii's focus on the mass film and put a specific low target—ten—on the number of hits he was expected to make in the near future.

The transition to the quality mass film was the first bout of the minimum "masterpiece" policy. On the surface, the ten quality hits were to temporarily fill the gap between the reality of many "bad" films and the ideal of many "good" features. And by instructing Shumiatskii to focus of these masterpieces and produce quality mass films in general, the authorities never intended to permanently cut film production in half or stop the production of films in popular genres. Yet the implication of this policy was that films in the "mediocre" and "bad" categories— seen as politically useless, insubstantial, or lacking in mass appeal—would no longer be supported. In one blow, all the so-called inferior films, including not only agitprop titles but conventional genre pictures such as everyday dramas and comedies, as well as short, experimental, and nonfiction films, were swept under the rug of perfection.[41] Despite its intent, the selectivity policy became a policy of restriction.

The Second Five-Year Plan emphasized not only technology and selectivity but also expertise. In July 1931, at a meeting of economic managers, Stalin made a speech entitled "New Situation—New Tasks in Economic Construction," in which he listed what became known as "Stalin's six conditions." This speech reshuffled the Soviet attitude to labor relations. One of Stalin's conditions called for ending equal pay (*uravnilovka*) and introduced preferential compensation for more qualified workers. Another condition reversed the policy of suspicion toward "old specialists," or experts who had been professionally active under the previous regime. The April 1932 decree and the new policy of engagement with talent and specialists, including artists and filmmakers, regardless of their class origin and ideological commitments, were part of this trend toward expertise. Yet another condition mandated dividing large enterprises into smaller units headed by one manager (*edinonachal'nik*), who would be directly responsible for a limited scope of operations.[42] In 1934, speaking at the agenda-setting Soviet Writers'

---

40. Anderson et al., *Kremlevskii kinoteatr*, 168. The idea was abandoned months later. Of the films the Commission reviewed, none were good enough to be explicitly sponsored by the Central Committee (Anderson et al., *Kremlevskii kinoteatr*, 185–186).

41. Turovskaya has written about this process in "1930s and 1940s," 44. Leonid Heller writes about this same slashing of everything but the "best" books in literature. Leonid Geller [Heller], "Printsip neopredelennosti i struktura gazetnoi informatsii stalinskoi epokhi," in *Slovo mera mira: Stat'i o russkoi literatrue XX veka* (Moscow: MIK, 1994), 159–160.

42. Joseph Stalin, "Novaia obstanovka—novye zadachi khoziaistvennogo stroitel'stva," *Pravda*, July 5, 1931, 1.

Congress, the Central Committee member Nikolai Bukharin explicitly linked expertise and craftsmanship with quality and Soviet superiority over the West.[43]

These new priorities directly affected the film industry's approach to its creative personnel. Whereas in 1928–1931 the strategy was to attract a new crop of young directors, preferably of proletarian origin, by 1933 it shifted toward "educating" (*vospitanie*) or incentivizing the existing pool of talent.[44] In parallel with discrimination in film types, Soiuzkino began distinguishing between experienced and inexperienced directors and became reluctant to employ talent in the latter category. It also started to pay less attention to the fact that by 1933 the majority of experienced filmmakers, such as Eisenstein, Pudovkin, or Aleksandr Dovzhenko, were political sympathizers with bourgeois backgrounds rather than proletarian activists and party members. Shumiatskii needed the masters to make mass quality films even if these masters, in the words of a contemporary observer, did not "care a rap about ideology."[45]

In 1933 Shumiatskii made a specific decision to entrust film production to only those directors who had proven successful in the past. This decision can be traced back to one specific conversation Shumiatskii reportedly had at the Central Committee. When Shumiatskii proposed to the Central Committee film commission his production plan for eighty titles for 1934, the commission asked him whether he had at his disposal eighty trustworthy directors to deliver this program. Shumiatskii's answer was no. "How many reliable directors do you have?" the Central Committee asked. Shumiatskii's answer was forty to fifty. "Who gave you the right to risk?" they wanted to know. "Structure your plans around the 'masters.'"[46] This exchange compelled Shumiatskii to assign films to a select group of experienced directors.

To implement the policy of "selection" (*otbor*) for 1933, Shumiatskii's office issued an order that prohibited studios from "assigning sound films to directors who have not worked as assistants or codirectors on at least one full-length sound film." The order required that studios reassign directors for all films under development that violated this rule.[47] Then the summer 1933 film planning

43. *Problems of Soviet Literature: Reports and Speeches at the First Soviet Writers' Congress* (New York: International Publishers, 1935), 185–186, cited in Priestland, *Stalinism and the Politics of Mobilization*, 269.

44. See, e.g., Anderson et al., *Kremlevskii kinoteatr*, 97–99; Shumiatskii, *Kinematografiia millionov*, 110–112.

45. TsGALI, f. 257, op. 6, d. 19, l. 22.

46. Boris Shumiatskii, "Kak sostavliat' templan khudozhestvennykh fil'm," *Kino*, August 4, 1933, 2.

47. "Tol'ko opytnym rezhisseram," *Kino*, July 4, 1933, 1. In 1933, only 48.3 percent of all films produced were sound films (Taylor and Christie, *Film Factory*, 424).

conference established "a commission to select directors who had the right to work on their own feature films" in 1934. This commission, which included the directors Dovzhenko, Pudovkin, Eisenstein, and Nikolai Shengelaia, among other members, selected seventy-seven directors and director teams (eighty-five individuals) working at all studios, including Mezhrabpomfilm, and the list of directors planned for 1934 was published in the newspaper *Kino*. On the list were most of the "old masters," the directors who made major films in the 1920s: Eisenstein, Pudovkin, Dovzhenko, Vertov, Kuleshov, Protazanov, Barnet, Room, Iutkevich, Pyr'ev, Medvedkin, and so forth. Only a handful of less-established filmmakers, such as Mikhail Romm and Mikhail Korostin, were included. Among the selected were nonfeature directors, such as the animator Nikolai Khodataev, further reducing the list of those with credentials to make features.[48] Although the 1934 production plan still included seventy-two titles, precedent was established that only seasoned directors received film assignments.[49]

Seasoned filmmakers supported the purge of the director ranks, for it only increased their status and likelihood of getting work.[50] In the eyes of the Central Committee and perhaps Shumiatskii himself, the selectivity policy sent a very strong signal to directors: deliver or be out of work. However, similarly to selectivity in film projects, the talent selection policy proved disastrous for the industry. In 1933, 180 directors worked at Soviet studios, and when their ranks were cut, production capacity suddenly became underutilized.[51] Many potentially politically loyal filmmakers found themselves cut off from professional employment.

Once again, elimination as such was not the thrust of this decision. If Shumiatskii had told the Central Committee that he had an army of reliable directors but few good screenplays, they would have probably instructed him to get more screenplays. The strategy was only to invest in that resource that guaranteed quality: the director. In 1933 both the Central Committee and Shumiatskii thought of quality and production mostly in terms of directors, as opposed to studios, stories, actors, or screenplays. As I will detail in the chapters that follow, this thinking reflected not only the Second Five-Year Plan's focus on expertise but also the director-centered mode of Soviet filmmaking, as well as Stalin's general attitude to creative talent. The problem with this conception of talent was that

48. "Doloi ravnenie na 'seredniachok,'" *Kino*, August 16, 1933, 1.

49. Konstantin Iukov, "Pervye rezul'taty bol'shoi raboty," *Kino*, December 19, 1933, 2.

50. See., e.g., S. Eisenstein, "Razumnoe predpriiatie," *Kino*, November 17, 1935, 4, and other articles in this issue.

51. RGALI, f. 2456, op. 1, d. 132, ll. 265–276, cited in Fomin, *Letopis' rossiiskogo kino, 1930–1945*, 271, 279–280.

as long as directors were considered *the* experts responsible for film output, the number of directors translated into the number of films, thus limiting the number of titles the Soviet film industry could produce in the long run. In addition, since the quality requirement was never subsequently lifted during the Stalin era, film executives always hesitated to entrust productions to new and inexperienced directors, making it difficult to foster new talent and make more films. When in 1935 Stalin encouraged Shumiatskii to expand film output, Shumiatskii had already been working with a constrained industry capacity. Shumiatskii needed a major reform if he wanted to jump-start Soviet cinema.

From Quality to Quantity, 1934–1935

The first masterpiece period was widely considered successful at the time. In November 1934 Shumiatskii showed Stalin a new film, *Chapaev*, a flamboyant Civil War biopic made at Lenfilm by Georgii Vasil'ev and Sergei Vasil'ev. Stalin loved the film, and *Chapaev* was immediately proclaimed the new socialist-realist *Potemkin*. The newspaper *Pravda* wrote, "The Whole Country Will See *Chapaev*."[52] *Chapaev* began a new quantity period, which lasted through the end of 1935. In his address to the film community following the success of *Chapaev* and several other mass hits, Stalin urged: "Soviet power expects new successes from you, new films that, like *Chapaev*, glorify the greatness of the historic deeds in the struggle for workers and peasants' power in the Soviet Union, mobilize us to fulfill our new tasks, and remind us of both the achievements and the difficulties of socialist construction."[53]

If Stalin had been speaking a few months later, he might have said, "*many* new films." At the end of 1935, the Central Committee member Andrei Andreev, addressing filmmakers on behalf of the Central Committee, stated: "We will expand [cinema's] production base in every way conceivable, but for the moment we need to use all extant technology to produce as many films as possible."[54] In his 1936 report to Stalin, Chairman of the Central Committee Propaganda

---

52. "*Chapaeva* posmotrit vsia strana," *Pravda*, November 21, 1934, 1, translated in Taylor and Christie, *Film Factory*, 334–335. Reportedly during the first year of its release *Chapaev* was seen by thirty million viewers and by 1939 by an additional twenty million. Julian Graffy, *Chapaev* (London: I. B. Tauris, 2010), 81.

53. Joseph Stalin, "Congratulations to Soviet Cinema on Its Fifteenth Anniversary" (from *Pravda*, January 11, 1935), in Taylor and Christie, *Film Factory*, 348.

54. "Rech' A.A. Andreeva na VII vsesoiuznom kinosoveshchanii," *Kino*, January 6, 1936, 1.

Department Aleksandr Shcherbakov quoted Andreev as saying in that same speech, "Still we have too few films. You produce dozens, whereas you should make at least hundreds."[55]

In March–May 1935, on the wave of what he took to be his industry's success, Shumiatskii wrote *Cinema for the Millions*, defining Soviet mass cinema. In November 1935 he added a preface to the book, in which he coupled mass film with a plan for "the major reconstruction of Soviet cinema."[56] From Shumiatskii's perspective, with *Chapaev*, his industry had accomplished the objective of creating a mass masterpiece. The next step was to build an industry that would produce masterpieces on a large scale.

In the summer of 1935 Stalin sponsored a trip by Shumiatskii and a group of film professionals to Europe and America to study the developed film industries. A major part of this trip was a visit to Hollywood. The tour resulted in a project to industrialize the Soviet film industry in accordance with the Hollywood model and to construct in the south of Russia a state-of-the-art cine-city, "Soviet Hollywood." Having personally evaluated how the film industries functioned in Europe and America, Shumiatskii apparently realized the problems of the Soviet film industry were systemic and could not be addressed piecemeal. Soviet Hollywood, he wrote, could "with a single blow split the many knots that were impossible to untie in a regular way."[57] Shumiatskii's plan was to introduce a division of labor at film studios and to adopt Hollywood production methods, such as strict specialization and standardization, as well as producers, editors, dialogue and storywriters, mechanized film-development laboratories, and large reusable film sets.[58]

Stalin initially supported the project. Between May 1934 and March 1936, Stalin and Shumiatskii met regularly at Stalin's Kremlin screenings, and Shumiatskii had Stalin's ear.[59] According to Shumiatskii, in December 1935 Stalin agreed with him that the production of films, as opposed to theater construction or equipment manufacturing, had to be the industry's primary growth area. Stalin said,

---

55. Anderson et al., *Kremlevskii kinoteatr*, 307.

56. Shumiatskii, *Kinematografiia millionov*, 9.

57. Fomin, *Letopis' rossiiskogo kino, 1930–1945*, 353.

58. For more on Soviet Hollywood, see Maria Belodubrovskaya, "Soviet Hollywood: The Culture Industry That Wasn't," *Cinema Journal* 53, no. 3 (2014): 100–122.

59. The notes effectively stop on March 9, 1936, as there are no notes between March 9, 1936 and January 26, 1937. Boris Shumiatskii, "Zapisi besed B. Z. Shumiatskogo s I. V. Stalinym pri prosmotre kinofil'mov, 7 maia 1934 g.–26 ianvaria 1937 g.," in Anderson et al., *Kremlevskii kinoteatr*, 919–1053. For a translation, see Richard Taylor, "On Stalin's Watch: The Late-Night Kremlin Screenings: May to October 1934," *Studies in Russian and Soviet Cinema* 7, no. 2 (2013): 243–258; and "On Stalin's Watch: The Late-Night Kremlin Screenings: October 1934 to January 1937," *Studies in Russian and Soviet Cinema* 8, no. 1 (2014): 138–163.

"We need not only good films, but way more of them in terms of both quantity and prints. It is sickening that all theaters are showing the same picture for months in a row." Responding to Shumiatskii's complaints that Gosplan, the state planning agency, preferred to build new film theaters, Stalin added, "Who needs theaters, when there is nothing to show?"[60] Encouraged by these comments, which he himself helped articulate, Shumiatskii set out to develop his vision for an industrialized mass-producing cinema that could compete with Hollywood. In mid-December 1935 he presented this vision to filmmakers in a nine-hour address, subsequently published as *Sovetskaia kinematografiia segodnia i zavtra* (Soviet Cinema Today and Tomorrow).[61]

The initial phase of Soviet Hollywood the city, Shumiatskii proposed, was to cost 305,000,000 rubles (USD 61,000,000 or about 1 billion in today's dollars).[62] It was to comprise 4 studios with 40 sound stages on a territory of about 2 square miles. Some 240 standing sets were to span an additional 1.5 square miles. The staff of the 4 studios was to include 40 producers, 100 directors, 110 assistant directors, 72 chief cameramen, 55 "montage directors" (film editors), 80 screenwriters, 32 dialogue writers, and at least 500 actors. By December 1940 Soviet Hollywood was to employ 9,000 workers, and the cine-city was to have a population of over 20,000.[63]

As for the scope of output, Shumiatskii estimated that the number of films needed each year was 300 at the minimum and 1,000 at the maximum. At least 300 films were required, he argued, because in small towns and on collective farms a film should not stay in the theater for more than one day. Given that old films should be shown no more than once a week, six new features each week were required.[64] Shumiatskii's vision was thus one of saturating the market with new releases, in accordance with the cinema-replaces-vodka model. He wanted to make it possible for a rural consumer to feel compelled to go to the cinema every single evening of the week. The maximum number, 1,000 films, was the number needed to outstrip America, which according to Shumiatskii was producing 800 films a year.[65] How would Shumiatskii get to the maximum? In 1935

---

60. Anderson et al., *Kremlevskii kinoteatr*, 1032–1033.

61. Boris Shumiatskii, *Sovetskaia kinematografiia segodnia i zavtra* (Moscow: Kinofotoizdat, 1936).

62. "Kinogorod," *Pravda*, December 22, 1935, 6; also cited in Anderson et al., *Kremlevskii kinoteatr*, 1033; and Valerii Fomin, "Sovetskii Gollivud: Razbitye mechty," *Rodina* 5 (2006): 100.

63. See, e.g., Glavnoe upravlenie kinematografii, *Osnovnye polozheniia planovogo zadaniia po iuzhnoi baze sovetskoi kinematografii (kinogorod)* (Moscow: Iskra revoliutsii, 1936).

64. *Doklad komissii B. Z. Shumiatskogo po izucheniiu tekhniki i organizatsii amerikanskoi i evropeiskoi kinematografii* (Moscow: Kinofotoizdat, 1935), 147.

65. Vs. Vishnevskii et al., "Boevye zadachi sovetskogo kino," *Izvestiia*, December 6, 1935, 4. In reality, the Hollywood feature output in the mid-1930s was between five hundred and six hundred titles.

the production capacity of the Soviet film industry—based on the number of available directors—was estimated at 120 features.[66] With some reform and personnel reshuffling (principally, promoting assistant directors to directors), that capacity would quickly increase to 200 features. The first phase of Soviet Hollywood, to be commissioned in 1939, was to have an annual capacity of another 200 features. The second and the third phases, to be launched by 1942 and 1945, respectively, were to support 200 features each.[67] This would total 800, and boosting output to 1,000 titles would not be difficult. "Acceleration would expand all opportunities," wrote the filmmakers, many of whom wholeheartedly supported Soviet Hollywood.[68]

Soviet Hollywood went as far as selecting in July 1936, with Stalin's blessing, the site for the city—the Laspi area near Foros on the southwestern tip of the Crimean Peninsula. First foundations were laid in November 1936. Soon, however, the project was closed. It appears that Shumiatskii lost Stalin's support in the course of 1936 when Stalin started to receive signals that conflicted with Shumiatskii's rosy picture of Soviet cinema. Stalin learned, for instance, that the film industry was operating at half capacity. Yet instead of focusing on the tasks at hand, Shumiatskii, as the Propaganda Department's Shcherbakov put it, was preoccupied with "sunny cine-cities."[69] It did not help that in October 1936 Shumiatskii's administration underwent an investigation and subsequent closure of one of its subsidiaries, Vostokfilm, whose leadership was accused of squandering state funds. Tellingly, the US press described the Vostokfilm chiefs as executives who "went Hollywood."[70]

It is possible that after all this negative feedback, Stalin decided that the Soviet Hollywood project, as well as the Hollywood-type industrialization implemented by Shumiatskii, might produce poor results and withdrew his support. Yet why did Stalin abandon the project itself? After all, no Soviet Hollywood meant no mass production and no competition with Hollywood. The answer is that Stalin's change of heart was part of a new shift in his thinking, which occurred in 1936 and which set the Soviet Union, once again, on a course toward isolationism, Soviet superiority, and internal security. This course was incompatible with Soviet Hollywood.

---

66. Anderson et al., *Kremlevskii kinoteatr*, 306.
67. "Kinogorod," *Pravda*, December 22, 1935, 6; also cited in Anderson et al., *Kremlevskii kinoteatr*, 1033; Fomin, "Sovetskii Gollivud," 100; "Gde budet postroen Kinogorod?" *Izvestiia*, December 24, 1935, 4; Dubrovskii-Eshke, "Tri ocheredi," *Kino*, January 11, 1936, 3.
68. Vs. Vishnevskii et al., "Boevye zadachi."
69. Anderson et al., *Kremlevskii kinoteatr*, 306–311.
70. "Bad Scenario Helps Send Soviet Film Men to Jail," *New York Times*, October 29, 1936, 1.

In August 1936 two prominent party leaders, Lev Kamenev and Grigory Zinoviev, as well as several others, were accused of anti-Soviet activity, including a plot against Stalin. Their show trial unleashed what became known as Stalin's Great Terror, a witch-hunt for "enemies" among Soviet elites. Shumiatskii experienced the effects of this hunt simultaneously with the Kamenev–Zinoviev trial. Some of his associates and subordinates were purged in 1936, and he fell under suspicion for harboring "enemies of the people" in his administration.[71] Because of spy mania, foreign sympathies and ties were no longer considered welcome. Suddenly, Shumiatskii, before then a Stalin insider and a powerful executive, became the target of ruthless public criticism.[72]

The Soviet Hollywood project was closed sometime in 1937, likely following the arrests of executives associated with it.[73] When Frank Capra and Robert Riskin visited Moscow in May 1937, they discussed the matter with its key proponents, the director Grigorii Aleksandrov and the cinematographer Vladimir Nil'sen.[74] Yet days later *Pravda* wrote that the idea of Soviet Hollywood was "foreign to the spirit of Soviet culture." *Pravda*'s particular contention was that two-thirds of Soviet screens continued to be silent, making Shumiatskii's project—to produce sound films exclusively—utterly divorced from reality.[75] The "foreignness" of Soviet Hollywood was voiced again in August 1937, at which time the newspaper *Izvestiia* referred to Soviet Hollywood in the past tense.[76] Nil'sen, Eisenstein's student and an accomplished cinematographer, who accompanied Shumiatskii to Hollywood and was his collaborator on the industry Americanization project,

---

71. There is no doubt that the purge of such effective executives as the head of Mosfilm Boris Babitskii and his deputy Elena Sokolovskaia, the cinematographer Vladimir Nil'sen, and many others gravely hurt the Soviet film industry. For more on the personalities purged, see Jamie Miller, "The Purges of Soviet Cinema, 1929–1938," *Studies in Russian and Soviet Cinema* 1, no. 1 (2007): 5–26.

72. See, e.g., Al. Morov, "Pochemu zaderzhivaetsia vypusk kartin," *Pravda*, October 7, 1936, 3; Fomin, "Sovetskii Gollivud," 103–104; Richard Taylor, "Ideology as Mass Entertainment: Boris Shumyatsky and Soviet Cinema in the 1930s," in *Inside the Film Factory: New Approaches to Russian and Soviet Cinema*, ed. Richard Taylor and Ian Christie (London: Routledge, 1991). 215.

73. Evgenii Sattel', the man in charge of construction within the cinema administration and the principal executive behind the cine-city project, was arrested in September 1937, charged with antigovernment terrorism, and executed in January 1938. The deputy head for cine-city construction, Iulii Piatigorskii, was arrested in March 1937, charged with terrorism and spying, and executed in September 1937 (Fomin, *Letopis' rossiiskogo kino, 1930–1945*, 472, 503).

74. G. Aleksandrov and V. Nil'sen, "Kak delaiutsia amerikanskie fil'my," *Izvestiia*, May 16, 1937, 4; Maiia Turovskaia, "Gollivud v Moskve, ili sovetskoe i amerikanskoe kino 30-kh–40-kh godov," *Kinovedcheskie zapiski* 97 (2010): 57. For a transcript of Nil'sen and Aleksandrov's conversation with Capra and Riskin, see RGALI, f. 2753, op. 1, d. 29.

75. K. Shutko, "Spornye voprosy kinematografii," *Pravda*, May 19, 1937, 3.

76. Kinorabotnik, "Tak nazyvaemaia rekonstruktsiia," *Izvestiia*, August 22, 1937, 3.

was arrested in October 1937 and executed in January 1938.[77] Shumiatskii, who had lived under a constant threat of arrest for many months, was apprehended in January 1938. After repeated brutal interrogations, where he refused to name his "associates" in an alleged plot to assassinate Stalin at a Kremlin screening, Shumiatskii was executed in July 1938.[78]

The Year 1936 and the Campaign against Formalism and Naturalism in the Arts

The new Soviet constitution released in December 1936 announced that socialism had been achieved. To match that declaration with reality, the party-state leadership again intensified its policies toward accelerated industrial growth, social conformity, and ideological purity and vigilance. By 1936 Stalin was convinced that in the impending war in Europe, Great Britain, Italy, France, and Japan would ally themselves against the Soviet Union. To him, it was time to protect "socialism in one state," which required a unified front in all areas of Soviet life.

On December 16, 1935, the Central Committee created the All-Union Committee for Arts Affairs. To head this agency it appointed Kerzhentsev, who in 1933–1936 was in charge of the Soviet radio authority. Shumiatskii's administration, renamed the Main Cinema Administration (GUK), was demoted to become part of the Arts Committee. The Arts Committee incorporated all the republic film administrations (their units for production, distribution, and exhibition) as well as the RSFSR offices for distribution and exhibition. More important, with Stalin's approval, Kerzhentsev instigated what became known as the campaign against formalism and naturalism in the arts (January–March 1936), which attacked Soviet artists for not adhering to the party-state cultural policy.[79] Stalin could no longer tolerate insubordination. Shumiatskii's fall from favor was directly tied to these developments. The antiformalism campaign "revealed" that in addition to underproducing, Shumiatskii continued to make ideologically flawed films, some of which were later banned following Propaganda Department review.

77. On Nil'sen, see Arkadii Bernshtein, "Gollivud bez kheppi-enda: Sud'ba i tvorchestvo Vladimira Nil'sena," *Kinovedcheskie zapiski* 60 (2002): 251–257.

78. Tat'iana Simacheva, ed., "Boris Shumiatskii," *Kinograf* 18 (2007): 131–133; B.L. Shumiatskii, *Biografiia moei sem'i* (Moscow: Mai print, 2007). I am grateful to both Boris Lazarevich Shumiatskii and Tat'iana Simacheva for information beyond these publications.

79. For the course of the antiformalism campaign, see Leonid Maksimenkov, *Sumbur vmesto muzyki: Stalinskaia kul'turnaia revoliutsiia 1936–1938* (Moscow: Iuridicheskaia kniga, 1997).

The antiformalism campaign started on January 28, 1936 with a *Pravda* article, "Muddle Instead of Music," which attacked Dmitri Shostakovich's opera *Lady Macbeth of the Mtsensk District*, staged by the Bolshoi Theater in Moscow. Stalin saw the opera on January 26 and disliked it, which resulted in the article. Shostakovich was accused of composing a "muddled stream of sounds," "shouts," and "scrapes" in a conscious and leftist attempt to part with everything "classical," "simple," "accessible," "realistic," "human," and "natural." According to the article, *Lady Macbeth* pandered to foreign bourgeois tastes and was "apolitical."[80]

The article and its crude insults were a surprise to many, not least because Shostakovich's opera, written in 1932, had previously been staged by two other theaters without a problem.[81] When similar articles addressing works in other arts—ballet, painting, film, architecture, and sculpture—followed, the Soviet artistic community realized the party leadership was sending a message. Indeed, the campaign was yet another cultural revolution, and its arguments for Soviet uniqueness and superiority were similar to those made during the First Five-Year Plan. The Central Committee's quarrel with cinema was also the same as in the late 1920s, and the same derogative terms returned. Specifically, most Soviet films, now in their reduced quantity, continued to be unsatisfactory. "Good" films were few, and "average" (*seredniaki*) were many. Some films were also "formalist," or only superficially dedicated to the party-state purpose.

The antiformalism campaign has traditionally been interpreted as an antimodernist, taste-based move, a part of the Great Retreat, when Stalinist culture reverted to traditionalism.[82] A more recent account of Stalinism, however, allows suggesting that the campaign and other conservative cultural reforms of the 1930s were an attempt to jump forward rather than to retreat.[83] The ambitious social agenda of the Stalinists remained, but in order to achieve it they needed the across-the-board, active participation of the Soviet masses.[84] In 1936 Stalin

---

80. "Sumbur vmesto muzyki," *Pravda*, January 28, 1936, 3.

81. On this, see Sheila Fitzpatrick, "The *Lady Macbeth* Affair: Shostakovich and the Soviet Puritans," in *The Cultural Front: Power and Culture in Revolutionary Russia* (Ithaca, NY: Cornell University Press, 1992), 183–215. Whether the article was ordered to Kerzhentsev by Stalin or was Kerzhentsev's own initiative remains unclear, but the link to Stalin's visit to the theater is uncontroversial. The article, which appeared unsigned, had been attributed to Stalin, Zhdanov, and Kerzhentsev. However, it has definitively been established that the author was *Pravda*'s staff critic, David Zaslavskii. See Evgenii Efimov, *Sumbur vokrug "Sumbura" i odnogo "malen'kogo zhurnalista": Stat'ia i materialy* (Moscow: Flinta, 2006).

82. Nicholas S. Timasheff, *The Great Retreat: The Growth and Decline of Communism in Russia* (New York: E. P. Dutton, 1946).

83. Kotkin, *Magnetic Mountain*; Hirsch, *Empire of Nations*.

84. Hoffman, *Stalinist Values*. See also David L. Hoffmann and Yanni Kotsonis, eds., *Russian Modernity: Politics, Knowledge, Practices* (Houndsmills, UK: Macmillan Press, 2000); Jochen Hellbeck, *Revolution on My Mind: Writing a Diary under Stalin* (Cambridge, MA: Harvard University Press, 2006).

wanted art and culture to embrace his project, which the adoption of socialist realism in 1932–1934 had failed to achieve. The antiformalism campaign became the next forceful, stopgap attempt to communicate to Soviet artists that it was no longer acceptable to place anything ahead of ideological commitment and national purpose.

When Stalin came out of the Bolshoi having seen *Lady Macbeth*, he certainly realized that the opera—flamboyantly avant-garde as it reportedly was—was not going to be accessible to the majority of Soviet citizens. He must have also been "disappointed" that Shostakovich's work was not teaching the Soviet population any useful ideas, politically or otherwise. The opera's lack of appropriate ideas was a much greater sin than its formal difficulty. "Formalism" (and "naturalism," for these were considered together) was not about focusing on form, but about focusing on form at the expense of content. From Stalin's perspective, Soviet art had to express substantial, socialism-inspired ideas, and the campaign helped to explicate this notion. It did not hurt if Soviet artworks were also conventional and accessible in form, but accessibility did not reject formal mastery, complexity, and quality.[85]

We often think that content censorship was the main reason film production shrank under Stalin. The antiformalist campaign suggests that the situation was more complicated. The agenda Stalin had for Soviet art went far beyond the censored message and incorporated the notion of quality artistic expression. As Stephen Kotkin has argued about the construction of Magnitogorsk (*Magnitostroi*), the new industrial city mounted in the Ural Mountains under Stalin, the exemplars of Soviet achievement had to embody the new "socialist civilization." This, for example, meant that the authorities wanted the housing in Magnitogorsk to be not only functional but also attractive—to show that the proletariat too had its aesthetics.[86] Similarly, when contemporaries said Soviet literature and cinema ought to have their "*magnitostrois*," they meant not only artworks filled with socialist pride, dignity, and monumentality but also aesthetically refined works.[87] In other words, even as the antiformalism campaign emphasized political utility, Soviet art had to maintain its artistic superiority. This is why in contemporary parlance, ideological tendency, substantial theme, and high art were often

85. On my account of the significance of the antiformalism campaign for Soviet cinema, see Maria Belodubrovskaya, "Abram Room, *A Strict Young Man*, and the 1936 Campaign against Formalism in Soviet Cinema," *Slavic Review* 74, no. 2 (2015): 311–333. See also chap. 3.

86. Kotkin, *Magnetic Mountain*, 119.

87. E. Zil'ver, ed., *Za bol'shoe kinoiskusstvo* (Moscow: Kinofotoizdat, 1935), 148.

amalgamated, as in the frequently used modifiers *ideino-khudozhestvennyi* (ideological-and-artistic) or *khudozhestvenno-ideologicheskii* (artistic-and-ideological). It was not censorship that defined Soviet culture past 1936, but a broader and far more fanciful notion of a socialist masterpiece.

The campaign against formalism ended the relative relaxation of the years 1934–1935 and destroyed Shumiatskii's vision of Soviet cinema as a modern enterprise based on international standards. The term "mass film" disappeared, to be replaced by "socialist realism," although the latter absorbed the mass feature's promise of accessible, popular, and mobilizing entertainment. Once again the call was made for selectivity in both screenplays and directors. Shumiatskii reportedly told his subordinates in 1936 that "leader comrades" (*rukovodiashchie tovarishchi*), his euphemism for Stalin and other members of the Central Committee, had instructed him "not to chase after plan fulfillment but supply very big films instead." He added, let the press castigate us for plan nonfulfillment, what matters is "that we are honest before the party, that we don't release drab films (*seriachok*)."[88]

The transition from the mass feature to the "big film" was the second installment of the masterpiece policy. Notably, Shumiatskii's statements come from a denunciation filed by Shumiatskii's associate, the GUK editor-censor Grigorii Zel'dovich, after Shumiatskii's arrest. Zel'dovich ends his discussion of Shumiatskii's statements with an assertion that Shumiatskii, of course, was lying. Since Shumiatskii had been arrested, Zel'dovich assumed the leadership's wishes were the opposite of what Shumiatskii propagated, that is, to make lots of films and fulfill the plan, and that Shumiatskii deliberately sabotaged this policy.[89] In reality, of course, Shumiatskii knew exactly what the policy was: a few big hits at the minimum and as many as possible at the maximum. By 1936, however, Stalin had lost confidence that Shumiatskii was the right person to realize this program and to realize it without humiliating Stalin by resorting to the American model.

The campaign's emphasis on quality and perfection delivered a new blow to the prospect of Stalin-era mass cinema. Filmmaking is a risky endeavor: it is hard to predict whether a film will be successful commercially or ideologically. Every film industry has to find ways to control this risk. One approach, which has proven successful in Hollywood, is mass production. When the volume of production is high, filmmakers capitalize on one another's successes and perfect their skills at a fast rate. This model is: the more, the better. Under

---

88. Anderson et al., *Kremlevskii kinoteatr*, 462–463.

89. Anderson et al., *Kremlevskii kinoteatr*, 463. Zel'dovich was not the only one. See, e.g., Dubrovskii, "O 'predelakh' i vozmozhnostiakh sovetskoi kinematografii," 23–27.

such conditions, hits are more likely, but the majority of films remain "average." The fundamental incompatibility between the Hollywood model and Stalin's ideological agenda was that the party-state was never willing to accept "average." Consequently, after 1936 the Soviet film industry followed the opposite, oxymoronic trajectory: the fewer, the better. As the critic and screenwriter Viktor Shklovsky wrote in 1936, "The primary mistake of cinema leadership is that it wants to film brilliant pictures in small numbers." It was harder, he wrote, to make few films than it was to make many: "To film well one has to film a lot." Comparing making movies to riding a bicycle, Shklovsky reasoned that the more frequently you pedaled, the farther you went, and if you pedaled too slowly, you would be unable to maintain momentum and topple.[90] Momentum was precisely what the intolerance of imperfection interrupted in the Soviet film industry.

After the campaign the film industry switched its strategy from selectivity to risk aversion. A wave of film bans in 1936 prompted studios to discontinue many titles in their production programs out of fear they might be deemed "formalist" or "average." Output shrank from fifty features in 1935 and 1936 to thirty-six in 1937. Another consequence of 1936, although less related to the antiformalism campaign than to the growing suspicion toward foreign influences, was the closure of the Mezhrabpomfilm Studio that June. Due to new tensions in German-Russian relations, the Workers International Relief was abolished in October 1935. The studio too was closed and transformed into a new, Soviet-owned studio for children's film, Soiuzdetfilm. Top Mezhrabpomfilm executives Iakov Zaitsev and Boris Babitskii were executed in 1938.[91]

Plan Fulfillment, Risk Aversion, and the Intolerance of Imperfection, 1936–1953

The closure of Mezhrabpomfilm, a prolific producer—it made 9 features in 1934 and in 1935 each—highlights just how destructive the year 1936 was to the prospect of Soviet cinema's expansion or profitability. The initial plans for 1936

90. Viktor Shklovsky, "Kachestvo i kolichestvo," *Kino*, December 22, 1936, 3.

91. Jamie Miller, "Soviet Politics and the Mezhrabpom Studio in the Soviet Union during the 1920s and 1930s," *Historical Journal of Film, Radio and Television* 32, no. 4 (2012): 521–535; Vance Kepley, Jr., "The Workers' International Relief and the Cinema of the Left, 1921–35," *Cinema Journal* 23, no. 1 (1983): 7–23.

projected 127 features. Then the list was trimmed to 95 titles and revised again in the middle of the year to include only 63 features. Yet Shumiatskii had as few as 40 screenplays in the works at the start of the year, and only 20 of these were ready for production.[92] At the end of 1936, Shumiatskii was even further behind schedule. GUK planned to release 53 films in the last half of the year. As of October 1, only 6 were completed, and GUK's censors shelved 2 of these.[93] Of the 50 films eventually made in 1936, 7 ended up banned.

Nevertheless, since the maximum policy was in place, the press wondered why Shumiatskii could not deliver the films he had promised and more. In 1937 the satirical magazine *Krokodil* published a caricature lampooning Shumiatskii's erratic efforts to adjust the plan. The caption read: "Soviet Viewer: 'Shame on you, Shumiatskii Boris, once again you don't know your subject!'" (figure 1.2). Little did the satirists know how hard it was to fulfill the plan.

When Shumiatskii was arrested in 1938, his successor Semen Dukel'skii was urged to increase production. An *Izvestiia* editorial accompanying the publication of Dukel'skii's new plan for 1938 emphasized that spectator demand for films consistently exceeded supply.[94] However, it proved impossible for Dukel'skii to noticeably expand output. The production plan for 1938 was forty-eight features, but only thirty-seven were made. Even though in 1939 when Ivan Bol'shakov replaced Dukel'skii the cinema administration overfulfilled the plan by 9 percent, this remained the one and only time production exceeded the plan under Stalin.[95]

Failure to meet its own production targets was a perpetual industry problem under Stalin. Each year the cinema administration signed a plan of production—a numbered list of titles—that studios struggled to meet for the remainder of the year. As we shall see in chapter 2, the early 1930s plans were intentionally inflated to give studios and filmmakers choices. After 1931 the plans started to shrink, but the film industry still did not fulfill them (see appendix 1). One reason was

---

92. Anderson et al., *Kremlevskii kinoteatr*, 307–311, 319–321; Glavnoe upravlenie kino-foto-promyshlennosti, *Proizvodstvennyi plan Glavnogo upravleniia sovetskoi kinematografii na 1936 god po proizvodstvu khudozhestvennykh fil'mov* (Moscow: Kinofotoizdat, 1936), 6.

93. Anderson et al., *Kremlevskii kinoteatr*, 352.

94. "Tvorcheskaia programma sovetskogo kinoiskusstva," *Izvestiia*, April 3, 1938, 1.

95. Semen Semenovich Dukel'skii (1892–1960) came from a middle-class family and was a career secret-service functionary. Ivan Grigor'evich Bol'shakov (1902–1980) came from a worker background, and, prior to his appointment as the chief cinema executive, he worked in the leadership of Sovnarkom, the Soviet government, as executive manager. For an excellent assessment of Bol'shakov's activities as the cinema chief, see Valerii Fomin, *Kino na voine: Dokumenty i fakty* (Moscow: Materik, 2005), 408–416.

FIGURE 1.2   Boris Efimov, "I promise to produce [173, etc.] films a year!" *Krokodil* 23 (1937): 16.

simply statistical. Plans covered calendar years, while production schedules were often longer. Titles traveled from plan to plan, as crossover (*perekhodiashchie*) units, and counted toward the projected total more than once. For example, Eisenstein's banned *Bezhin Meadow* was in the industry plan (and counted toward the projected output) in 1935, 1936, and 1937.[96] Another reason was that under Shumiatskii plan fulfillment was never actually required. As we have seen, Shumiatskii's task was to deliver masterpieces, and this goal conflicted with efficient planning. Instead of working to fulfill the plan, Shumiatskii cultivated the directors and studios that could produce high-quality hits. His director-centered strategy was successful as far as it went, but he let several aspects of the industry—nonfiction and short film, as well as studios in the national republics—slide. In the atmosphere of 1936–1938, his skewed strategy was interpreted as a deliberate sabotage of industry development.[97]

Yet plan fulfillment and quantity mattered because theaters had to have content to screen. Even if the importation of new foreign films was stopped in 1930, the pressure of competition from old films remained. The depository of films available for distribution was repeatedly purged of older Soviet and foreign titles deemed no longer appropriate.[98] Nonetheless, in the absence of new releases available from Soviet studios, old titles were still widely distributed. This competitive exhibition reality occasionally forced even the Central Committee Propaganda Department to insist the cinema administration proceed with poor screenplays just to supply new releases. In 1938, for instance, a Propaganda Department official in charge of cinema, Georgii Stukov, sent a note to the Central Committee to overrule a decision by Dukel'skii, who stopped the production of twenty films because they did not satisfy quality requirements. Stukov pleaded with the Central Committee that this decision be reconsidered "taking into account the general shortage of films in the country." Since the Central Committee prioritized purity of content and perfection over quantity, it refused Stukov's request.[99] Dukel'skii put an end to the liberal policy of distributing old films in 1938 in part

96. For a discussion of delays that slowed production schedules, see Miller, *Soviet Cinema*, chap. 4. On *Bezhin Meadow*, see, e.g., Peter Kenez, "A History of *Bezhin Meadow*," in *Eisenstein at 100: A Reconsideration*, edited by Al LaValley and Barry P. Scherr (New Brunswick, NJ: Rutgers University Press, 2001), 193–206; Peter Kenez, "*Bezhin lug* (*Bezhin Meadow*)," in *Enemies of the People: The Destruction of Soviet Literary, Theater, and Film Arts in the 1930s*, edited by Katherine Bliss Eaton (Chicago: Northwestern University Press, 2002), 113–126.

97. See, e.g., G. Ermolaev, "Chto tormozit razvitie sovetskogo kino," *Pravda*, January 9, 1938, 4; A. Zelenov, "Plody gnilogo rukovodstva," *Kino*, January 11, 1938, 2; Dubrovskii, "O 'predelakh' i vozmozhnostiakh sovetskoi kinematografii," 23–27.

98. Directories of permitted and banned titles were published in 1931, 1934, 1936, 1940, and 1943. Narkompros RSFSR, *Repertuarnyi ukazatel', tom 3, Kino-repertuar* (Moscow–Leningrad: GIKhL, 1931); P. Bliakhin ed., *Repertuarnyi ukazatel': Kinorepertuar* (Moscow: OGIZ-GIKhL, 1934); A. Katsigras, *Repertuarnyi ukazatel': Kinorepertuar* (Moscow: Kinofotoizdat, 1936); N.I. Ivlieva ed., *Repertuarnyi ukazatel' deistvuiushchego fonda kinokartin* (Moscow: Goskinoizdat, 1940); N. Ivlieva ed., *Repertuarnyi ukazatel' deistvuiushchego fonda kinokartin* (Moscow: Goskinoizdat, 1943).

99. Anderson et al., *Kremlevskii kinoteatr*, 495–496.

because it hurt plan fulfillment: it allowed studios to survive financially by drawing income from old titles without releasing many new ones.

Vertical integration of production, distribution, and exhibition, which thrived in Hollywood in the 1930s and 1940s and was a part of Shumiatskii's Soviet Hollywood proposal, was never implemented.[100] In 1938 GUK became independent of the Committee for Arts Affairs. It was restructured as the Committee for Cinema Affairs. All the republic film administrations, including the RSFSR units for distribution and exhibition, were subordinated to the Cinema Committee. The Cinema Committee formed a unified distribution office, Glavkinoprokat (Soiuzkinoprokat in 1938), establishing centralized monopoly over distribution. As before, however, within the Cinema Committee, distribution was financially and strategically segregated from production and from exhibition. In addition, the party-state clearly wanted to maintain what Vance Kepley has called the "federal" principle in film exhibition, for exhibition continued to be decentralized.[101] The regional exhibition administrations, still subordinated to the republic governments (in the RSFSR, to territorial units) even if also under Cinema Committee's jurisdiction, continued to be controlled by local, often commercial, interests. The Cinema Committee was again decentralized in 1946 when it became the Ministry of Cinema. Under this fourth and final administrative restructuring of the period, the national republics, including RSFSR, formed their own ministries of cinema, and production and exhibition in the republics were again subordinated to the republic authorities alone. The All-Union Ministry of Cinema maintained direct control over distribution and over feature-film production at Mosfilm, Lenfilm, Soiuzdetfilm, and the Sverdlovsk Studio, which opened 1943.[102]

In the absence of sophisticated distribution and exhibition pathways and similarly to his predecessors, Bol'shakov had enormous difficulty balancing out quality and quantity. Even though it was obvious that quality mattered more, in 1941 Bol'shakov maintained that the plan signed by the government had the status of a law and therefore demanded implementation. He lamented, self-critically of course, "In our [film industry] the fulfillment of the plan plays the main role, whereas the quality of films remains a secondary priority."[103] The bias in favor of plan fulfillment over what Donald Filtzer calls "use value" (or quality), which

100. *Doklad komissii B. Z. Shumiatskogo*, 178–179.

101. The 1946 Russian term was "union-republic" (*soiuzno-respublikanskii*). Vance Kepley, Jr., "Federal Cinema: The Soviet Film Industry, 1924–32," *Film History* 8, no. 3 (1996): 344–356.

102. The Odessa Studio also remained under USSR jurisdiction at least through 1947. See Valerii Fomin, ed., *Letopis' rossiiskogo kino, 1946–1965* (Moscow: Kanon+, 2010), 51–52. In 1948, Soiuzdetfilm was renamed the Gorky Studio.

103. Fomin, *Kino na voine*, 46.

is much harder to measure, was an unintended outcome of the structure of incentives in the centrally planned Soviet economy in general.[104] The pressure of planning accountability compelled Bol'shakov's administration to authorize for production more screenplays than it had time to doctor in accordance with censorship reviews. As a result, many films produced were not up to political and artistic standards, and this made the industry in turn vulnerable to accusations of low quality.[105]

Under Bol'shakov, the plan for each year became a numerical compromise between the external imperative to fulfill the plan and internal pressure to reduce the risks of imperfection. The pressure to control risks was ultimately stronger, thus the plans shrank from year to year. Yet plans continued to be overly optimistic numerically. In the 1940s the industry executives' inclination was to list in the plan as few projects as possible, namely, the projects they were certain directors could deliver. According to Romm, the film director who between 1940 and 1943 was the top executive responsible for feature film production at the cinema administration, out of the forty-five films planned for 1941, ten "do not let me sleep at night because I am afraid that these will be bad films, and no one can guarantee that they will be good."[106] That is, Romm's own preference was to plan only thirty-five films. But executives could not reduce the plan substantially from year to year because they had to appear to be trying to increase output. Moreover, studios had to produce films to justify their large staffs. In 1940 Mosfilm had thirty-two directors on staff, but only twenty-one were "in the plan" for 1941. Out of forty-one cinematographers available, only seventeen were scheduled to work on planned pictures.[107] The plan for forty-five features in 1941 was a compromise based on 1940 when fifty-eight films were planned and thirty-nine produced.

Bol'shakov's appointment to replace Dukel'skii in 1939 was a sign of a relative relaxation after the Great Terror (1936–1938). The years 1938 and 1939 were relatively successful for Soviet cinema in the sense that very few films were

104. Donald Filtzer, *Soviet Workers and Stalinist Industrialization: The Formation of Modern Soviet Production Relations, 1928–1941* (Armonk, NY: M. E. Sharpe, 1986), 266.

105. On this, see "Protokol zasedaniia khudozhestvennogo soveta pri direktsii Leningradskoi kinofabriki po obsuzhdeniiu stsenarnogo polozheniia," in *Iz istorii Lenfil'ma*, vol. 3, ed. N.S. Gornitskaia (Leningrad: Iskusstvo, 1973), 135; Lev Parfenov, ed., *Zhivye golosa kino* (Moscow: Belyi bereg, 1999), 378. Natacha Laurent calls this a conflict between industry and ideology or between economics and censorship. Natacha Laurent, *L'œil du Kremlin: Cinéma et censure en URSS sous Staline, 1928–1953* (Toulouse: Privat, 2000), 251. See also Fomin, *Kino na voine*, 453.

106. RGALI, f. 2456, op. 1, d. 710, l. 143.

107. RGALI, f. 2453, op. 2, d. 336, l. 2.

banned. Since quality was up, Bol'shakov was instructed to expand production. In parallel to 1935 when the industry celebrated its fifteenth anniversary after the release of *Chapaev*, February 1940 saw the official celebration of its twentieth birthday.[108] In its "Greeting to Soviet Cinema Workers" issued for the occasion, the Central Committee asked film practitioners again "to develop and advance the most important and mass art: give the country more high-quality films and other films that contribute to the comprehensive cultural uplifting of the working people."[109] In May 1941, at a meeting between the Central Committee member Andrei Zhdanov and filmmakers, Bol'shakov confirmed he was working on increasing screenwriter and director ranks. Once that increase was underway, he said, the number of films would grow as well.[110] He estimated that eighty features would be possible by 1943, but only thirty-nine were made in 1940 and forty in 1941.[111]

This was partly because the "quality" field was narrowed again in August 1940 by the sudden banning of Mosfilm's *Zakon zhizni* (*The Law of Life*, Aleksandr Stolper and Boris Ivanov, 1940). A week after the film's release, *Pravda* published an anonymous review, "False Film," edited by Zhdanov, which attacked the film for its message. *The Law of Life* told the story of Evgenii Ognerubov, a morally corrupt head of a regional branch of the Komsomol (Young Communist League) exposed by his subordinates. *Pravda* objected that to devote a film to a richly drawn and highly negative Komsomol leader and party member was to falsify Soviet reality, where such individuals may have been possible but were not typical. *Pravda* found it particularly objectionable that the film depicted rank-and-file Komsomol members repeatedly falling under the influence of the corrupt Ognerubov. This taught the audience the wrong message, *Pravda* suggested, for the vigilant Komsomols should have had unmasked Ognerubov early in the film, as would have been the case in real life.[112]

108. On the 1919 decree and its status as the birth of Soviet cinema, see Natalie Ryabchikova, "When Was Soviet Cinema Born? The Institutionalization of Soviet Film Studies and the Problems of Periodization," in *The Emergence of Film Culture: Knowledge Production, Institution Building and the Fate of the Avant-Garde in Europe, 1919–1945*, ed. Malte Hagener (New York: Berghahn, 2014), 118–139.

109. "Privetstvie TsK VKP(b) i SNK SSSR rabotnikam sovetskoi kinematografii," *Kino*, February 15, 1940, 1.

110. Fomin, *Kino na voine*, 45.

111. A. Kur'ianov, "Chto dast khudozhestvennaia kinematografiia v 1939 godu," *Kino*, February 17, 1939, 2.

112. "Fal'shivyi fil'm," *Pravda*, August 15, 1940; Anderson et al., *Kremlevskii kinoteatr*, 601; Vladimir Nevezhin, "Fil'm *Zakon zhizni* i otluchenie Avdeenko: Versiia istorika," *Kinovedcheskie zapiski* 20 (1993/94), 96–97.

The ban on *The Law of Life* was another campaign against cinema's imperfection, and, in parallel with 1932 and 1936, cinema leadership instructed all studios to reconsider all films currently in production in connection with the ban. As a result, production on seven films was shut down and sixteen more were suspended for reworking.[113] Even so, Bol'shakov told Zhdanov that he could not guarantee that all films would be "good" in 1941. He estimated that fifteen would be "good," twenty to twenty-five would be "average," and seven to eight would be "mediocre."[114] Bol'shakov also pointed out that some percentage of failure was inevitable and therefore should be accounted for in the plan. In response, Zhdanov rejected that the industry had "the right to fail" (*pravo na brak*). If you plan for failure, Zhdanov said, you get failure. "Risks" can be taken, he added, but "not at the expense of the population and the state."[115] In other words, for all practical purposes, Bol'shakov was not allowed to take risks and had no way of accounting for error.

Months later, the Central Committee Film Commission, established in the aftermath of *The Law of Life*'s ban and comprising the Central Committee members Zhdanov, Andrei Andreev, and Georgii Malenkov, as well as the former Chief Prosecutor Andrei Vyshinskii, banned several more films, including two Mosfilm comedies, *Serdtsa chetyrekh* (*Four Hearts*, Konstantin Iudin, 1941) and *Staryi naezdnik* (*The Old Jockey*, Boris Barnet, 1940). In March 1941 Zhdanov told filmmakers: Let there be fewer pictures but no failures. As long as successful films are few, the industry should stop thinking about quantity.[116] This was another instance of the masterpiece policy. Two months later Zhdanov explained: "Every film in our country is a social and political event. This is how the Central Committee views the matter."[117] Sergei Eisenstein recorded "a major social and political event" in his notes, adding that the meaning of this phrase immediately put filmmakers, who might have had objections to the bans, in their place. As long as films were few in number, he wrote, every single film had to be treated with "deep responsibility."[118] In 1943, again referring to this meeting in his notes,

113. RGALI, f. 2450, op. 4, d. 35, ll. 32–36. See also Nevezhin, "Fil'm *Zakon zhizni* i otluchenie Avdeenko," 97–98.

114. Anderson et al., *Kremlevskii kinoteatr*, 622; Fomin, *Kino na voine*, 48.

115. Anderson et al., *Kremlevskii kinoteatr*, 626; Fomin, *Kino na voine*, 50.

116. Fomin, *Kino na voine*, 28–30.

117. O.G. Iumasheva and I.A. Lepikhov, "Fenomen 'totalitarnogo liberalizma' (opyt reformy sovetskoi kinematografii)," *Kinovedcheskie zapiski* 20 (1993/94): 126; see also Grigorii Mar'iamov, *Kremlevskii tsenzor: Stalin smotrit kino* (Moscow: Kinotsentr, 1992), 49.

118. Artem Sopin, "'. . . Idem na soveshchanie v TsK,' ili 'Sporit' ne o chem': Tri teksta Sergeia Eizenshteina ob odnom predvoennom soveshchanii," *Kinovedcheskie zapiski* 104/105 (2013): 302, 304.

Eisenstein used Abraham Lincoln's famous words, "by the people, for the people," to explain how Zhdanov and Stalin viewed every Soviet film release.[119]

After 1940 the Stalinist intolerance of imperfection expressed itself not only in bans but also in constant criticism of films deemed average. To Zhdanov and other critics, the vast majority of Soviet films continued to be light, trite, vain, and tedious, and had little to contribute to "the urgent tasks of socialist construction and the communist upbringing of the working people."[120] Out of thirty-nine titles Zhdanov criticized as faulty throughout 1941, seventeen were contemporary dramas, eleven were comedies, five were adventure films, five more were children's films, and one was a historical-revolutionary film. The only Soviet genre of any prominence not included in the problematic list was the historical-biography film.[121] Biographical epics also overwhelmed the list of the films awarded the inaugural Stalin Prize in 1941. The message was clear. Regardless of what the party-state expected in expansion or genre diversity, very few film types satisfied the leaders, and the biopic was the safest genre.

Not surprisingly, many filmmakers wanted to make historical epics. In 1940 the writer and occasional screenwriter Leonid Lench described this situation in a satirical piece, "The Monument." Lench's protagonist was a fictional film director who, instead of working on his next film, celebrated the fifth anniversary of the release of his last film, *The Tatar Yoke*. The director had not made any films since *The Tatar Yoke* because he had been waiting for a chance to direct another "monument." For this director, Lench wrote, every film was like a baby mammoth: it needed a very long gestation period. Lench concluded by reminding his director that the mammoths were extinct, implying that the same fate awaited the director as well.[122] Yet, arguably, the strategy of underproducing and waiting for a chance to make a masterpiece allowed many filmmakers to persevere, while Soviet cinema as a whole come to near extinction.

During the Second World War (1941–1945), film output continued to dwindle. The staff and plant of Mosfilm and Lenfilm were evacuated to Central Asia and joined together to form the Central United Film Studio (TsOKS). Amidst calls on cinema to assist the war effort and expand, another relative relaxation in production followed, and many exceptional war films were made.[123] Again,

---

119. Sopin, "'. . . Idem na soveshchanie v TsK,'" 312–313.
120. Fomin, *Kino na voine*, 38.
121. RGALI, f. 2456, op. 1, d. 709, ll. 9, 18; Andrei Artizov and Oleg Naumov, eds., *Vlast' i khudozhestvennaia intelligentsiia: Dokumenty, 1917–1953* (Moscow: Demokratiia, 2002), 470–472; Fomin, *Kino na voine*, 20–23, 33–35, 37–43, 347–349.
122. Leonid Lench, "Pamiatnik," *Kino*, May 1, 1940, 4.
123. On film production during the war, see Fomin, *Kino na voine*.

however, a larger percentage of films were banned in 1942 and 1943 than in 1940–1941, including several war-themed film almanacs (*Boevye kinosborniki*). A 1943 caricature of Bol'shakov captured that he strived to produce more films during the war but continued to be attacked for their quality (figure 1.3).[124] The accompanying caption, as if spoken by Bol'shakov, read: "Who says that we make few films? Last year we released over twenty and both were good."

At the end of the war, the Soviet Union gained access to a new market in Eastern Europe, and Bol'shakov urged filmmakers to increase film output to up to one hundred films.[125] In April 1946, in yet another effort to inform the film-making community of what was expected of it, Zhdanov met with the leading filmmakers and asked them to improve and expand film output. He told them cinema policy had never changed. Stalin and the Central Committee wanted to see a diversity of genre films, and the best Soviet comedies—Ivan Pyr'ev's *Tractor Drivers*, *The Rich Bride*, and *Swineherd and Shepherd*—in particular continued to "enjoy great trust and respect" of the Central Committee. He said filmmak-ers should stop being shy about propagating their country's ideology in their films, since "any Western film" did that. American hits like *The Charge of the Light Brigade* (Michael Curtiz, 1936) and *San Francisco* (W. S. Van Dyke, 1936), Zhdanov specified, blatantly promoted imperialist colonial policy in India and political corruption, respectively. He could not comprehend why it was so hard for filmmakers to openly and effectively publicize the Soviet way, especially given that the Soviet way had just been vindicated "in the eyes of the entire country, the entire world" by the Soviet victory over Nazi Germany. Sharing his own ideas on what films could be about, he reminded his audience that the Soviet people were eagerly awaiting new films and that cinema was the mightiest propaganda weapon in the hands of the state.[126]

However, once again, in August 1946 a ban by the Central Committee sud-denly undercut these aspirations. The banned film, Soiuzdetfilm's *Bol'shaia zhizn'* (*A Great Life*, part 2, Leonid Lukov, 1946), was the sequel to Lukov's very success-ful part 1 of 1939. It dealt with the postwar reconstruction of a coal mine. Every-one within the film industry loved Lukov's film, and its ban created significant turmoil among the filmmakers.[127] All industry censorship bodies approved the

---

124. See, e.g., Anderson et al., *Kremlevskii kinoteatr*, 676. On Bol'shakov's reaction to this carica-ture, see Fomin, *Kino na voine*, 484–485.

125. I. Bol'shakov, "Nashi blizhaishie zadachi," *Iskusstvo kino* 1 (October 1945): 2–5. See also, Sarah Davies, "Soviet Cinema and the Early Cold War: Pudovkin's *Admiral Nakhimov* in Context," *Cold War History* 4 (2003): 49–70.

126. Anderson et al., *Kremlevskii kinoteatr*, 724–729.

127. See, e.g., RGALI, f. 2372, op. 12, d. 79.

FIGURE 1.3 Konstantin Eliseev, "Segodnia v kino" [Today at the Cinema], *Krokodil* 30–31 (1943): 8.

release, and the Ministry of Cinema planned to send it to the first-ever Cannes Film Festival that year.[128] Once more, however, the characters who represented Soviet youth in the sequel were found objectionable by the Central Committee, and the film's message about the nature of reconstruction was deemed unacceptable.[129] And once more the ban prompted the film industry to abandon a few projects, and, since there was nothing to replace them, shrinkage continued.

The ban of *A Great Life* was yet another campaign signaling that Stalin's patience had again run out. Like the 1936 campaign, this one also stemmed from changes in Stalin's foreign policy in 1946, an upsurge in his suspicion toward the West, and the start of the Cold War.[130] Eisenstein's *Ivan the Terrible*, part 2, had been banned in March 1946, and in May 1946 five other new films were condemned as deficient.[131] Literature also became a target. The Central Committee attacked the Leningrad journals *Zvezda* and *Leningrad* for publishing certain works by Mikhail Zoshchenko and Anna Akhmatova, and both writers were expelled from the Soviet Writers' Union.[132] When someone mentioned at one of the Kremlin meetings that the journal *Znamia* published works similar to those in *Zvezda* and *Leningrad*, Stalin responded, "We will get to *Znamia* as well. We will get to all of you."[133] Soon the Central Committee launched campaigns against the other arts. This was the start of the period of cultural tightening known as *zhdanovshchina*, which was accompanied by a new bout of purges, pronouncements on Soviet superiority, xenophobia, and isolationism.

The notion of "quality" was again reinforced. As Pyr'ev reported after the banning of *A Great Life*, "it turns out that a motion picture has not exactly the significance that we, the workers of cinema and the related arts, have been ascribing it. It turns out that every motion picture has great significance in its country.... Every picture equals fifteen, twenty, thirty thousand agitators." He added that the ban finally made filmmakers realize that every Soviet picture was "an affair of the state" (*gosudarstvenoe delo*).[134] This was exactly the same message that Eisenstein took from a meeting with Zhdanov five years prior. Indeed, this was the

---

128. Fomin, *Letopis' rossiiskogo kino, 1946–1965*, 25.

129. Anderson et al., *Kremlevskii kinoteatr*, 747–767; RGALI, f. 2372, op. 12, d. 79.

130. On this, see Davies, "Soviet Cinema and the Early Cold War," 54–56. Renaming the cinema administration the Ministry of Cinema in March 1946 to emphasize cinema's enormous propaganda potential was part of this shift.

131. Anderson et al., *Kremlevskii kinoteatr*, 732.

132. Artizov and Naumov, *Vlast'*, 559–581.

133. Artizov and Naumov, *Vlast'*, 572. See also 549–550.

134. RGALI, f. 2372, op. 12, d. 79, l. 3.

same message that Kerzhentsev had voiced back in 1928. In February 1947, when Eisenstein met with Stalin to discuss the revisions to his banned *Ivan the Terrible* part 2, Stalin told Eisenstein to take his time with the revisions: "As a rule we cancel films being made in a hurry and they never go out on release. Repin spent eleven years painting *The Zaporozhian Cossacks.*" Stalin added, "The overall task now is to improve the quality. Higher quality, even if it means fewer pictures."[135]

Evidently by then Stalin had given up on the maximum policy, but this was not made official. In 1946–1947 insufficient output and failures of plan fulfillment continued to be part of every discussion of Soviet cinema's problems. At the end of 1946 the newspaper *Kul'tura i zhizn'*, the official Propaganda Department mouthpiece, attacked the Ministry of Cinema by reporting that it planned to release twenty-one films in 1946, but as of December 31 had completed twelve and released five. These statistics were especially problematic, the newspaper lamented, given that the capacity of the Soviet Union's fourteen feature-film studios was two to three times larger than twenty.[136] As late as 1947, citing the urgency to compete with Hollywood in postwar Europe, *Pravda* asked the industry to expand production to fifty films in 1948 and one hundred by 1950.[137] Vasilii Katinov, chief editor at the Ministry of Cinema's Scenario Studio, said the goal of fifty screenplays in 1948 was an "energetic increase."[138] Indeed, output had been averaging twenty films for five years. Yet this increase made sense to the filmmakers. As the screenwriter Vladimir Kreps said, Americans were making cinema a vanguard in the American conquest of Europe. "We need to counter this with an avalanche of our films."[139] In January 1948 even Zhdanov argued that "forty good features" should be made each year.[140]

Finally in mid-1948 the quantity drive was officially abandoned. On June 14, 1948 the Central Committee resolved that it was an error on the part of the film industry to aim for "a large number of films at the expense of their quality," for

135. Sergei Eisenstein, "Stalin, Molotov, and Zhdanov on *Ivan the Terrible, Part Two* (1947)," in *The Eisenstein Reader*, ed. Richard Taylor (London: BFI, 1998), 165.

136. "V kratchaishii srok preodolet' otstavanie sovetskoi kinematografii," *Kul'tura i zhizn'*, December 31, 1946, 2.

137. "Povyshat' uroven' sovetskogo iskusstva!" *Pravda* 247, September 4, 1951, 1; John Rimberg, *The Motion Picture in the Soviet Union, 1918–1952: A Sociological Analysis* (New York: Arno Press, 1973), 38–39; Fomin, *Letopis' rossiiskogo kino, 1946–1965*, 75–76.

138. RGALI, f. 2372, op. 14, d. 59, ll. 7, 71. This document is dated February 1947, but its content, and specifically its multiple references to the year 1947 as the past and 1948 as the present, dates it February 1948.

139. RGALI, f. 2372, op. 14, d. 59, l. 59.

140. Anderson et al., *Kremlevskii kinoteatr*, 798–799.

quality continued to be poor. It requested that the Ministry of Cinema "decisively increase the quality of the films it releases by lowering their quantity" and by attracting to film production the best film talent.[141] This was the first time the Central Committee expressly asked for low quantity in a policy statement. According to the head of the Propaganda Department, Dmitrii Shepilov, who was present when Stalin and the others discussed the matter three days earlier, the decree was instigated by the following comments by Stalin:

> The Ministry of Cinema conducts incorrect policy in film production. It strains to produce more films. The costs are high. Rejects are many. They have no concern for the budget, while we could be getting 2 billion rubles of pure profit from the movies. They want to make sixty films a year. We do not need this. This is incorrect policy. We need four or five features a year, but good ones, outstanding ones, plus several newsreels and popular-science films. We approach cinema extensively, as if it were agriculture. We should make fewer films, but good ones. And then expand the theater network and release more prints. In cinema we should not try to measure up to the United States. They have very different tasks for cinema. They make many films and get colossal profits. We have different tasks. Here, I am looking at the plan of film production. How much rubbish is planned here![142]

Following this decision, the goal of competing with Hollywood in terms of output was finally explicitly abandoned, as was the idea of reaping substantial fiscal benefits from Soviet releases. Stalin was not happy about this loss, but he had no choice. Zhdanov elucidated Stalin's position. Retreating from his 1946 statements about comedy and genre diversity cited above, as well as from the original 1920s Bolshevik goals, he said that in Hollywood profit was the end-all to everything. American studios and exhibitors were interested in screening as many new films as possible. In Soviet Russia, in contrast, films were valued for their propaganda content. Therefore the Soviet regime was not interested in turning films out as fast as possible. Instead, the goal was to make sure the maximum number

---

141. Artizov and Naumov, *Vlast'*, 635–636.

142. D. T. Shepilov, "Vospominaniia," *Voprosy istorii* 5 (1998): 24–26; also cited in Artizov and Naumov, *Vlast'*, 789 n.39. (In these memoirs, Shepilov suggests, like I do, that Stalin's preference for masterpieces destroyed Soviet cinema.) The agricultural analogy invoked here may explain why Stalin thought that it was possible to get results from the formula "the fewer, the better." In the extensive model of agriculture, to get a set amount of product one utilizes a lot of land with lower yield per area. In the intensive model, which is what Stalin proposed for cinema, one concentrates labor, supplies, and machinery to get the maximum yield possible from a small area of land.

of people saw each film, as long as it was a "good" one. Bol'shakov gave this policy a face-saving Soviet-superiority justification. He wrote that although Hollywood produced more films, these films were low in quality. If the Soviets wanted to produce low-quality films, the film industry could release five hundred to six hundred films a year.[143] What would ultimately distinguish Soviet film production was its high quality, and so quality, and not mass output, should be its focus.

As in 1936, Stalin's mistrust of foreign ideas and a desire to chart a unique Soviet path overwhelmed an inclination to emulate the West or to exploit real opportunities offered by the Soviet and European markets. And, as under Shumiatskii, the solution to the quality problem was the director-masters. According to Shepilov, Stalin also said in June 1948, "In general, all important pictures should be assigned to experienced directors. Romm, for instance, is good, Pyr'ev, Aleksandrov, Ermler, Chiaureli. Assign to them. Their kind won't let you down. Assign color pictures to them as well. That is an expensive thing. Kozintsev is good. Lukov should be chased away. Pudovkin is good."[144] Under the existing industry structure, everything depended on the directors.

As soon as Stalin spoke about "four or five good features a year," the rhetoric of quality became, for a time, the only standard. In its July–August 1948 issue, the film journal *Iskusstvo kino*, published an editorial, "To Improve the Quality of Soviet Films," criticizing the Ministry of Cinema for entrusting productions to inexperienced directors, for filming unfinished and poor screenplays, and for producing "empty, artistically unconvincing" films.[145] According to Bol'shakov's article that followed this editorial, filmmakers had "no right to create mediocre, inferior, and weak works. . . . The release of every film is a matter of great state importance."[146] He added that the Ministry of Cinema screenplay portfolio had just been reconsidered in the light of this imperative, and work on no fewer than 143 screenplays was cancelled due to their discrepancy with the new quality requirements.[147]

To substitute for the lack of domestic entertainment, between 1947 and 1952 the Central Committee authorized the release of at least ninety "trophy" films,

143. I. Bol'shakov, "Za vysokoe ideino-khudozhestvennoe kachestvo fil'mov," *Iskusstvo kino* 5 (September–October 1948): 3–5; I. Bol'shakov, "O predstoiashchikh mezhdunarodnykh kinofestivaliakh vo Frantsii i Italii," *Pravda*, June 29, 1949, 3 (also cited in Rimberg, *Motion Picture in the Soviet Union*, 175).

144. Shepilov, "Vospominaniia," 24–25.

145. "Vyshe kachestvo sovetskikh fil'mov," *Iskusstvo kino* 4 (July–August 1948): 1–2.

146. Bol'shakov, "Za vysokoe ideino-khudozhestvennoe kachestvo fil'mov," 3.

147. Bol'shakov, "Za vysokoe ideino-khudozhestvennoe kachestvo fil'mov," 5.

foreign-made films captured in Europe, most of them German and American genre pictures from the 1930s to early 1940s. Among them were four American Tarzan adventures.[148]

Unable to fulfill their maximum policy or reverse the decline in output, the Stalinists went for the minimum program: distribute a handful of masterpieces to a large number of spectators. By the end of the Stalin period each major title was released in up to two thousand prints. This model of countrywide "saturation booking," as Kepley calls it, was first stumbled upon in 1934 when *Pravda* declared "The Whole Country Will See *Chapaev*."[149] This was a distribution-only model of mass cinema. Not realizing that films such as *Chapaev* or *Potemkin* occur only occasionally and under conditions of vibrant innovation, the Stalin leadership refused to accept anything less. The extreme pressure to produce masterpieces in an industry that was never equipped to do so consistently precluded the possibility of a controlled mass cinema. Only after Stalin's death could Soviet cinema grow again, finally approaching the program maximum: an annual output of over a hundred features. In 1954 Georgii Aleksandrov, the Minister of Culture and former head of the Propaganda Department, citing the head of the Soviet government Malenkov, said that one of the goals of his ministry was to crowd out vodka and cultivate cinema.[150] The program maximum never changed, but in the post-Stalin period, the intolerance of imperfection was finally relaxed.

Conclusion

Maya Turovskaya has argued that the story of Stalin-era cinema is where "ideology" won over popular cinema.[151] Yet popular cinema and the Soviet Hollywood project were part of the ideological program to create a *mass* cinema, "a cinema for the millions." From the Stalinist perspective, there was no distinction between

148. Artizov and Naumov, *Vlast'*, 635–637, 639; Anderson et al., *Kremlevskii kinoteatr*, 801–811, 836. For a summary account of trophy films, which includes a list of films, see Claire Knight, "Stalin's Trophy Films, 1947–52: A Resource," *KinoKultura* 48 (April 2015): http://www.kinokultura.com/2015/48-knight.shtml. Knight says eighty-six films are confirmed releases, but Fomin, *Letopis' rossiiskogo kino, 1946–1965*, 66, lists four additional films, and there were probably others.

149. On Soviet distribution prints, see Kepley, "Federal Cinema"; Kepley, "First 'Perestroika,'" 31–53; Babitsky and Rimberg, *Soviet Film Industry*, 243, 281; Denise Youngblood, *Russian War Films: On the Cinema Front, 1914–2005* (Lawrence: University Press of Kansas, 2007), 88.

150. Central Archive for Socio-Political History of Moscow (TsAODM/TsAOPIM), f. 957, op. 1, d. 18, l. 18, cited in M.M. Gol'din, *Opyt gosudarstvennogo upravleniia iskusstvom: Deiatel'nost' pervogo otechestvennogo Ministerstva kul'tury* (2000), http://www.rpri.ru/min-kulture/MinKulture.doc.

151. Turovskaya, "1930s and 1940s," 44.

popular cinema and ideology (quality propaganda). The development of Soviet mass cinema did not go as planned because in 1936, as well as during every other "quality" campaign, short-sighted intolerance of imperfection systematically undermined the long-term project of transforming Soviet cinema into a controlled and industrialized socialist Hollywood. To mass-produce successful propaganda features, the film industry needed not only major facilities but also a massive creative workforce and an efficient production process. Instead of being given these tools, the industry was put under pressure to improve the quality of its product, and in response it eliminated risk.

The reality of Soviet cinema's low output was not just imposed from above but also resulted from an institutional environment structured by the unrealistic ambition of superiority and masterpieces. The Soviet leadership wanted all films, and as many as possible, to match the mobilizing quality of the best 1930s examples. Every film had to be like *Chapaev*. The low volume of production, however, meant that every film was new and unpredictable. As Eisenstein once said, the mistakes Soviet filmmakers made were not out of "negligence or criminal intent," but because of the "complete novelty" of what they were doing.[152] Yet whenever the industry produced failures, it was punished by bans and public humiliation. Being repeatedly castigated this way discouraged filmmakers, industry censors, and film executives from trying anything remotely similar to the banned film again. This hurt the process of incremental improvement, not to mention expansion, and made everyone in the industry more reluctant to produce.

Soviet cinema did not work as the party-state intended because the objective to produce masterpieces precluded industrial reform and development. That alone was sufficient to curtail Soviet film output. Yet the intolerance of imperfection also dictated that every key institution of Soviet filmmaking—planning, production, screenwriting, and censorship, to be discussed in the chapters that follow—functioned to avoid the risk of imperfection. Over time, the nonindustrial mode of production, low volume, and risk aversion led to severe shortages of ideas and talent. The handicaps of Soviet filmmaking as such started with production planning. As the next chapter shows, the quality objective dictated that all production began with serious and politically relevant themes, but no mechanism for efficiently developing such themes ever emerged.

---

152. Sopin, "'. . . Idem na soveshchanie v TsK,'" 306.

TEMPLAN
"Bastard" Plans and Creative Counterplanning

The main planning unit, as is well known, is the director.

—A. Orlovskii, *Kino*, December 22, 1937

As part of the Soviet command economy, film production was supposed to be administered in a centralized manner. The primary instrument through which the cinema administration managed film production was the thematic plan, or *templan*, a list of films to be made each year. It is commonly understood that thematic planning was "the primary instrument for party-state control over cinema" in that it provided filmmakers with content requirements.[1] Yet content was rarely imposed on filmmakers from the top down. Rather, the film industry developed the thematic plans internally based on projects filmmakers themselves proposed. The director, not the theme, was the primary planning unit. The plans reflected the regime's thematic imperatives only in the most general sense.

Early in the 1930s, the Soviet film industry switched from thematic planning to what I shall call creative counterplanning. For the remainder of the Stalin period, thematic plans identified films not by theme but by title and generic category, such as history, industry, collective farms, defense, or everyday life. In these plans, "theme" was synonymous with "project," that is, a screenplay that a

---

1. Leonid Maksimenkov, "Vvedenie," in Anderson et al., *Kremlevskii kinoteatr*, 29. See also, Richard Taylor, "Red Stars, Positive Heroes and Personality Cults," in Taylor and Spring, *Stalinism and Soviet Cinema*, 74, 240 n.19.

director agreed to produce. No effective system to develop screenplays on party-required themes was ever created. Being unable to generate stories themselves, Soviet studios exercised careful selection from among the film projects screen-writers and directors proposed. Selectivity in planning constricted output, and many subjects the party-state desired were not covered. By the end of the period, Soviet cinema was at the mercy of a small group of filmmakers to make any planning and production possible.

Thematic Thinking

Planning by subject matter in Soviet film production dates back to at least 1925. In March of that year, a government commission charged with celebrating the twentieth anniversary of the 1905 revolution mandated that films with a revolution theme be produced. Eisenstein's *Potemkin* was one of these films. In September 1926 the Central Committee Propaganda Department also decided to launch several new films to mark the tenth anniversary of the 1917 revolution. Eisenstein's *October*, Vertov's *Eleventh Year*, and Shengelaia's *26 Commissars* were slotted for this purpose.[2] The first thematic plan was probably the Sovkino production program for 1927–1928. The Propaganda Department considered it in February 1927. This plan contained fifty-eight fiction and twenty-five "scientific" films.[3]

The earliest thematic plan to be published was the Sovkino plan for feature films in the 1928–1929 season.[4] It contained a list of more than 160 potential "themes" (*temy* or subjects) that studios were to work on, with the idea that sixty of them would be selected for eventual production. Each of the themes had a title, a thematic annotation (*tematicheskaia ustanovka*), and a note specifying what kind of material Sovkino had available for it: no material, a theme proposal, a synopsis (*libretto*), a screenplay, or a preexisting literary work. One example of a theme without a proposal was *Miners*: "Life and work of Soviet miners." Another was *Chemicalization of the Country*: "The importance of chemical weapons under the threat of war." A proposal, synopsis, or screenplay meant an author had submitted the subject. Many projects were marked "Screenplay ordered," indicating

---

2. Valerii Fomin, ed., *Letopis' rossiiskogo kino, 1863–1929* (Moscow: Materik, 2004), 479, 543.

3. "Rabota Sovkino v 1927 godu," *Pravda*, February 3, 1927, 5, cited in Fomin, *Letopis' rossiiskogo kino, 1863–1929*, 567.

4. In the 1920s, cinema scheduling was done by season. The season started in the fall and ended in the summer. Planning by calendar year started under Shumiatskii in January 1931.

that a studio had signed an agreement with an author to write on the subject.[5] The eventual features were to fall into the following generic categories:

- Political issues and economic construction in urban areas
- Political issues and economic construction in rural areas
- Cultural revolution and everyday life (*byt*)
- International themes
- Youth themes
- Films for children
- Historical and historical-revolutionary films
- Comedy films[6]

Although the list included some subjects suggested by Narkompros, the People's Commissariat for Education, or by the 1928 Party Conference on Cinema, most themes originated at the studios. As such, the thematic coverage was far from ideal. The Sovkino board criticized the plan for a shortage of comedies in particular, admitting it was reluctant to include comedy themes because it could not guarantee successful films could be made based on them.[7] It was the studios' job to select some of the titles in accordance with the interests of their directors and affiliated screenwriters. This was why almost three times the number of themes was listed for the eventual target of sixty films.

The 1928–1929 plan was not unique. Never in the history of thematic planning under Stalin was a list of film projects or themes imposed from the top. Even the term *theme* referred to both the subject of the film and/or the screenplay proposal, conflating thematic content planning with project-by-project production planning from the start.[8] Moreover, according to the Sovkino executive Vladimir Sutyrin, writing in 1929, *theme* used in the former sense meant different things to different people: the project's story summary, its dominant meaning, or its "philosophical kernel." Sutyrin added that the actual theme of a screenplay was only possible to determine after the screenplay was complete,

---

5. RGALI, f. 2496, op. 1, d. 30.

6. Sovkino, *Tematicheskii plan Sovkino na 1928–29 god* (Moscow: Teakinopechat', 1928), 3; RGALI, f. 2496, op. 1, d. 30, ll. 7–8, 10. This plan is also discussed in Ekaterina Khokhlova, "Neosushchestvlennye zamysly," in *Kino: Politika i liudi. 30-e gody*, ed. Liliia Mamatova (Moscow: Materik, 1995), 124; Miller, *Soviet Cinema*, 99.

7. Sovkino, *Tematicheskii plan Sovkino*, 6.

8. This double meaning was explicitly acknowledged in a contemporary screenplay manual. M. Liadov, *Stsenarii: Osnovy kino-dramaturhiï ta tekhnika stsenariia* (Kiev: Ukrteakinovydav, 1930), 9.

and, since the original theme could change or disappear by the film's completion, planning around themes was largely pointless.[9]

Themes were also too abstract to serve as practical planning units. In 1931 Sutyrin, by then Shumiatskii's deputy at Soiuzkino, wrote that some themes in the plan took the utilitarian function of cinema too literally. His examples were: "The creation of national cadres to help the periphery" and "The system of industrial management and one-man leadership."[10] Similarly, the critic and occasional screenwriter Osip Brik noted that general audiences would not find films with such subject matter compelling. Both Sutyrin and Brik also contended that theme-based thinking forced screenwriters into "formalism" when they tried to artificially incorporate a rigid theme into story action.[11] Even a Central Committee member complained in 1931 that plans that passed his desk were inadequate, for all they contained were vague thematic annotations such as "On the interrelationship between personal and social; the struggle for technology." The screenplay this theme referred to was Vladimir Nedobrovo's *Kachestvo liubvi* (The Quality of Love), whose title must have also rubbed this unnamed commentator the wrong way.[12]

What the early plans show, however, is that cinema executives in Moscow, studio heads, screenwriters, and directors were all thinking in terms of subject matter. Only in this sense was Soviet film planning "thematic." When Eisenstein wrote to Stalin to explain the delays with his *Ivan the Terrible* project, he twice mentioned that he was working on the "theme" of Ivan.[13] What Eisenstein was producing was not just another tsar biopic but a masterpiece on an important subject. Screenplays too were evaluated not just on the author's pedigree but also on the theme. Still, whereas in the 1920s thematic thinking was the overall approach to project selection, by the 1940s, when Eisenstein made *Ivan the Terrible* and the film industry produced very few films, it became only a rhetorical ploy that protected the industry against accusations of working on insubstantial subjects.

Thematic thinking meant that film projects were more likely to be conceived in terms of the subject, the director, the screenwriter, and the film type than in terms of the storyline, and they were never discussed in terms of stars. Here is a description of a 1950 Lenfilm project, *Grazhdanin Sovetskogo Soiuza* (Citizen of

9. V. Sutyrin, "Literatura, teatr, kino," *Na literaturnom postu* 10 (1929): 39–40.

10. V. Sutyrin, "Problemy planirovaniia," *Proletarskoe kino* 8 (August 1931): 7.

11. O.M. Brik, "O zanimatel'nosti," *Kino*, June 4, 1933, 2; Sutyrin, "Problemy planirovaniia," 4–16.

12. Anderson et al., *Kremlevskii kinoteatr*, 167.

13. Fomin, *Kino na voine*, 340–341.

the Soviet Union), which did not have an author attached: "The protagonist of the screenplay is a young man who gets his passport. This is a story of the formation of a young Soviet citizen in front of whom all paths to excellence and growth are open."[14] The emphasis here is not on the storyline but on the contemporary setting, character type, and ideological message. Although authorless theme-only ideas were rare in production planning, the dry language was quite typical. For example, the projected screenplay on a similar subject, *Na poroge budushchego* (At the Brink of the Future), that Iurii German was writing for Grigorii Kozintsev in 1950, was described as: "About the paths of a young Soviet man who is determining his future."[15]

Thematic planning did not go beyond the requirement to articulate a thematic summary for each film story. The rest of Soviet film planning was based on selecting projects (often referred to as "themes") from those proposed by screenwriters and directors based on very broad thematic categories (also "themes") that functioned similarly to genres. Let us first look at where film projects came from and then consider the thematic confines of Soviet production planning.

Bottom-Up Planning or Where Stories Came From

From everyone's perspective, it was always best when subject matter was suggested from above. As is well known, Stalin asked Dovzhenko to make a Ukrainian version of *Chapaev* and suggested the civil war commander Nikolai Shchors, a Ukrainian, as its subject. Zhdanov, communicating Stalin's wishes, asked Eisenstein to make a film about Ivan the Terrible. Many film projects during this period also shared subject matter with other arts when information was disseminated that certain themes would be welcome. This was the case with *Ivan the Terrible* as well.[16] To give another example, at a meeting in 1947 devoted to the Stalin Prizes, Zhdanov said that all arts should work on the theme of patriotism among Soviet scientists, after which Abram Room made *Sud chesti* (*The Court of Honor*, 1948) on this topic.[17] However, such top-down suggestions were rare, and few

14. TsGALI, f. 257, op. 16, d. 1893, l. 15.

15. TsGALI, f. 257, op. 16, d. 1893, l. 21. The writer Iurii German was the father of the film director Aleksei German.

16. On Ivan-related artworks, see Maureen Perrie, *The Cult of Ivan the Terrible in Stalin's Russia* (New York: Palgrave, 2001); Bernd Uhlenbruch, "The Annexation of History: Eisenstein and the Ivan Grozny Cult of the 1940s," in *The Culture of the Stalin Period*, ed. Hans Günther (London: Macmillan, 1990), 266–286.

17. Anderson et al., *Kremlevskii kinoteatr*, 796–797.

subject offers were available. The creative workers were always hungry for ideas. In 1946, after the Soviet government established the Orders of Nakhimov and Ushakov, the first two directors asked by Bol'shakov to make films about these figures immediately agreed.[18]

Some film ideas originated at various government agencies and interest groups. The Ukrainian Central Committee wanted a film about Taras Shevchenko (*Taras Shevchenko*, Igor' Savchenko, 1951). It was at the insistence of the Azerbaijani Central Committee that the 1947 plan included a film about an Azeri ruler, Fatali Khan of Quba (*Fatali Khan*, Efim Dzigan, 1947, subsequently banned). Ideas also came from the cinema administration, and from Shumiatskii and Bol'shakov personally. Mikhail Romm's film *Trinadtsat'* (*The Thirteen*) was suggested to Romm and the screenwriter Iosif Prut by Shumiatskii. According to Romm, Shumiatskii saw John Ford's *The Lost Patrol* (1934) when in Hollywood in 1935, brought a print to Russia, showed it to Stalin, and Stalin asked whether a Russian version could be made.[19] To rework a Leonid Utesov music-hall production into Grigorii Aleksandrov's *Veselye rebiata* (*Jolly Fellows*, 1934) was also Shumiatskii's idea.[20] Such requests continued under Bol'shakov. According to the head of the Lenfilm screenplay department, Leonid Zhezhelenko, German was writing a screenplay about the history of the Russian Navy in 1947 "at the request of" the cinema administration.[21] The head of the Scenario Studio, Ivan Astakhov, commented in 1944 that "a long time ago the [cinema administration] gave us a task to create a screenplay about railway workers."[22]

Although these and other cases qualify as orders from the top, they were never treated as orders. As one official put it, themes were "hinted at" to authors, or authors already interested in a topic were approached to develop it.[23] Most Soviet screenwriters of the later Stalin years were well-established authors, whose creative aspirations were taken into account. In addition, there was constant pressure to give authors some sense of who might adapt their future screenplay, as authors were much more willing to write when they had a specific director or at least a studio for an addressee. To quote the successful writer Konstantin Simonov, "A great number of script writers have refused to write scripts until they are

---

18. RGALI, f. 2372, op. 12, d. 79, l. 24.

19. Mikhail Romm, *Besedy o kino* (Moscow: Iskusstvo, 1964), 15. Shumiatskii remembered the film as *The Last Patrol*.

20. See, e.g., Rimgaila Salys, *The Musical Comedy Films of Grigorii Aleksandrov: Laughing Matters* (Chicago: Intellect, 2009), 24.

21. TsGALI, f. 257, op. 16, d. 1556, l. 14.

22. RGALI, f. 2372, op. 8, d. 75, l. 6 ob.

23. RGALI, f. 2372, op. 8, d. 75, ll. 11.

informed as to the director with whom they will be working. I, for instance, have set the condition that from the day I begin to write the script I know with what director I am going to be working, or else I do not write the script."[24]

Many more stories originated from solicitations of studio screenplay department staffs. Lenfilm, had a history of such collaboration, in particular in 1928–1937, when Adrian Piotrovskii supervised its screenplay department. According to the director Sergei Gerasimov, Piotrovskii "did not wait for screenwriters and directors to come to him with their creative plans." He knew the creative personnel of his studio well and approached each one with ideas for projects tailored to particular individuals.[25] Raisa Messer, a longtime Lenfilm screenplay editor, reported that Piotrovskii expected his staff to familiarize themselves with all the newly published fiction and periodicals in order to find potential stories and authors. She said the idea for a film based on the life of Kliment Timiriazev (*Deputat Baltiki/Baltic Deputy*, 1936) came from Piotrovskii, and that she suggested the screenwriter, Leonid Rakhmanov, based on her familiarity with Rakhmanov's prose. The Lenfilm screenplay department also stayed in regular contact with its freelance authors.[26] Both Messer and Gerasimov credit the studio's leading position in the Soviet film industry in the 1930s to Piotrovskii and the creative atmosphere he fostered at Lenfilm. Piotrovskii was arrested and executed in 1938, and things changed at Lenfilm. In 1946 the director Fridrikh Ermler said that no one stopped by the screenplay department any more. Clearly referring to Piotrovskii's tenure, he added that the department ought to (again) become a "small academy, where anyone can come, smoke a cigarette, and hear one or two jokes." Lamenting the fact that editor-censors, not screenwriters, staffed the Lenfilm screenplay department, he noted that in America screenplays were sent to "gagmen" (*vydumshchiki*), not editors.[27]

Yet this did not mean that Lenfilm's editors stopped proposing ideas. In 1946, when Anna Shishmareva, the head of the Lenfilm screenplay department, reported to the studio Artistic Council on the studio thematic plan for

24. "An Analysis by Konstantin Simonov: The Soviet Film Industry," *The Screen Writer* 11, no. 1 (1946): 17. I am grateful to Robert Appleford for this source.

25. Sergei Gerasimov, *Zhizn'. Fil'my. Spory* (Moscow: Iskusstvo, 1971), 192; see also Grigorii Kozintsev et al., "Chto mozhet redaktor: Kollektivnaia povest' ob Adriane Piotrovskom," *Iskusstvo kino* 12 (1962): 40–63.

26. R. Messer, "A. I. Piotrovskii i stsenarnyi otdel 'Lenfil'ma' (30-e gody)," in Gornitskaia, *Iz istorii Lenfil'ma*, 3: 139–150; RGALI, f. 2450, op. 2, d. 50, l. 54.

27. TsGALI, f. 257, op. 16, d. 1354, l. 136.

1946–1947, she mostly discussed the screenplays already available.[28] However, she also suggested the studio sign an agreement with the writer Vissarion Saianov to write a screenplay about the nineteenth-century critic Vissarion Belinskii in conjunction with the hundredth anniversary of Belinskii's death. This "thematic" suggestion, presumably Shishmareva's own, was put into effect. Lenfilm soon signed a screenplay contract with Elena Serebrovskaia. After a long and tortuous process, Grigorii Kozintsev made *Belinskii* in 1951 based on the screenplay he coauthored with Serebrovskaia and German.[29] And Lenfilm was no different than other studios in this respect. When working on a set of six anniversary pictures for 1942, Nikolai Semenov, the head of Mosfilm's screenplay department, proposed two biopics about the prominent Bolsheviks Feliks Dzerzhinskii and Valerian Kuibyshev, as well as four contemporary themes: the hero of the Soviet Union, the Soviet woman, Moscow, and the manager of a large industrial enterprise. Semenov also proposed names of prominent screenwriters who might work on these subjects.[30] Semenov reported that he had discussed "The Hero of the Soviet Union" with the writer Nikolai Pogodin, who "wanted to work on it." Given that Semenov had considered assigning "The Hero of the Soviet Union" to Valeriia Gerasimova, Pogodin, and Simonov as well, the project must have been Semenov's own brainchild.[31]

In another indication that screenplay departments were continually searching for film ideas, Shishmareva asked Lenfilm Artistic Council members to suggest to her department new themes and authors.[32] This was a routine request, since members of the central Artistic Council, as well as those in the studio Councils, often shared film ideas when they had them.[33] For example, at the meeting of the central Artistic Council in 1944, the director Igor' Savchenko, who was responsible for reviewing the children's-film portion of the plan, suggested one screenplay be created about Soviet schools and one about Komsomol members restoring, "for example," Stalingrad. At the same meeting, the major general and military historian Mikhail Galaktionov suggested bolstering the war-film subsection of the plan with a screenplay about a contemporary battle. Galaktionov

---

28. In the later Stalin period planning was projected two or three years into the future to account for the fact that productions lasted for more than twelve months and that very few projects came to fruition.

29. TsGALI, f. 257, op. 16, d. 1354, ll. 116–125.

30. RGALI, f. 2453, op. 2, d. 509, ll. 1, 2.

31. RGALI, f. 2453, op. 2, d. 506, l. 7; RGALI, f. 2453, op. 2, d. 507, l. 7; RGALI, f. 2453, op. 2, d. 97, l. 20.

32. TsGALI, f. 257, op. 16, d. 1354, ll. 116–125.

33. The two types of Artistic Councils are discussed below and in chap. 3.

proposed that Mikhail Bragin be approached to write this screenplay: Bragin had just published an impressive essay on the topic in *Pravda*, he said. There is no evidence that Bragin ever submitted a screenplay, even though someone in the audience volunteered that Bragin had already been to the cinema administration's screenplay unit, the Scenario Studio.[34]

In the later Stalin period, many films also originated from preexisting literary properties. Again, the idea of adapting a play or novel tended to come from screenplay editors, who then sought collaboration from the works' authors. Studios approached a different author only if the original one refused to work with them.[35] Yet the cases of editor-proposed themes were a minority, and these themes tended to be variations on previously successful models. Screenplay editors did not consider the development of stories their primary job. They called it "bureaucratic planning" (*kantseliarskoe planirovanie*) and instead organized meetings with industrial workers, local party activists, writers, and scientists to generate ideas.[36] Each Friday in the early 1950s a representative of the Lenfilm screenplay department was "on duty" at the Leningrad chapter of the Writers' Union in case the writers had new story ideas to offer the studio.[37]

At one point, studios attempted to develop content by running "screenplay workshops" (*stsenarnye masterskie*) to train new screenwriters. Such workshops operated at Sovkino and at Lenfilm in 1927–1929 and at Mezhrabpomfilm in 1928–1930. However, screenwriting instructors were in short supply, and the shrinking production volume soon made it impossible for studios to employ the trainees. An attempt at creating a screenwriting powerhouse and improving thematic planning was the Scenario Studio (1941–1958), a financially independent screenplay agency of the central cinema administration, located in Moscow.

When created in 1941, the Scenario Studio was to be a collaborative institution that employed writers, developed "themes," advised screenwriters on defective screenplays, and readied screenplays for production.[38] It was organized in part "using the American experience," and at the beginning employed such prominent figures as Viktor Shklovsky, Aleksei Kapler, Mikhail Bleiman, Petr Pavlenko, and Manuel' Bol'shintsov.[39] The Scenario Studio employed a two-step planning process, first submitting to the cinema administration a list of "themes"

---

34. RGALI, f. 2456, op. 1, d. 1080, l. 9.
35. TsGALI, f. 257, op. 17, d. 254; TsGALI, f. 257, op. 16, d. 1893; TsGALI, f. 257, op. 16, d. 1894.
36. TsGALI, f. 257, op. 17, d. 251, l. 9.
37. TsGALI, f. 257, op. 17, d. 250, l. 8.
38. RGALI, f. 2456, op. 1, d. 710, l. 139.
39. RGALI, f. 2456, op. 1, d. 710, l. 46.

that emerged from the proposals of affiliated authors and then signing screen-play agreements.[40] Although this process allowed the Scenario Studio to be more sophisticated about subject matter, and some screenplay subjects originated with its editors, not unlike studio screenplay departments, the Scenario Studio mostly relied on outside authors to generate stories.[41] Moreover, at least some of the stories the Studio offered were instantly tied to specific directors, undermining thematic planning proper. Days after the Studio's formation, Bol'shintsov, its enthusiastic head, reported that the Studio was already working on a project called *Labyrinth* "for Aleksandrov" and a youth screenplay "for Iutkevich."[42] The perception in the industry in fact was that the Scenario Studio was just a branch of Mosfilm: both Aleksandrov and Sergei Iutkevich were Mosfilm directors.

Before and after the formation of the Scenario Studio, studios received pro-posals from amateur and unaffiliated authors (as opposed to "studio" authors, who had previously worked with the studio). The vast majority of these propos-als were rejected, and screenplay editors wrote hundreds of thoughtful rejection letters each year. Screenplays were typically turned down because their topics were inadequate or already covered, and for poor writing or spelling. Neverthe-less, screenplay editors took the inflow of unsolicited submissions as a potential source of stories, and when a submission looked promising they asked the author to send them more.[43]

The final alternative practice of story procurement was the screenplay com-petition. Several competitions, both open and closed (i.e., by invitation only), were held in the 1930s.[44] In the 1940s the Scenario Studio replaced the practice, but the competition strategy was revisited at least once more in 1953.[45] Compe-titions promised substantial rewards to winners (into thousands of rubles) and

---

40. E.g., RGALI, f. 2372, op. 14, d. 61, ll. 1–14.

41. RGALI, f. 2456, op. 1, d. 710, ll. 44–50. Members of the Scenario Studio did engage in some rewriting themselves. See, e.g., Mikhail Zoshchenko's recollections of his experience in Parfenov, *Zhivye golosa kino*, 240–241.

42. RGALI, f. 2456, op. 1, d. 710, l. 51.

43. E.g., TsGALI, f. 257, op. 16, d. 1895.

44. In 1932 Soiuzkino held an open competition for screenplays in any genre that commemo-rated the fifteenth anniversary of the October revolution. In 1933 both the Ukrainian and Georgian cinema administrations held open competitions. In 1936 the Committee for Arts Affairs held a closed competition for anniversary screenplays to mark the twentieth anniversary of the revolution. In 1938 and 1939 the Committee for Cinema Affairs organized two open competitions, one for screenplays on contemporary subjects and another for comedy screenplays, respectively. The former was held concurrently with a closed competition for contemporary themes. To support the latter the newspa-per *Kino* ran a series of articles on comedy and the House of Cinema (*Dom kino*) organized a series of related lectures and screenings. Screenplay competitions were held in the 1920s as well.

45. Anderson et al., *Kremlevskii kinoteatr*, 909–910; Babitsky and Rimberg, *Soviet Film Industry*, 108.

generated a flood of submissions, but hardly any screenplay submissions were ever used. Of the five thousand submissions, fifty-two winners, and a score of special notices in the 1938 open competition, for example, only about a dozen screenplays were accepted for production.[46] None of the screenplays submitted to the 1939 competition met expectations of perfection: no screenplay was good enough to receive first, second, or third place. Fourth-place prizes were awarded to three screenplays, but these never became films.[47]

The practice of running screenplay competitions not only shows how desperate the film industry was for stories and screenwriters, but also that lots of potential stories and would-be screenwriters could be found. However, as chapter 4 explains in greater detail, because studios did not have personnel to turn underdeveloped screenplays around, and the majority of ideas and scripts sent to competitions were not production-ready, they were considered useless. Only if a screenplay appealed to a director did it have a future.

Indeed, the most successful model for generating workable film projects in Stalin-era cinema was the director–screenwriter collaboration. In the 1930s, such collaborations mostly emerged spontaneously. In the later Stalin period, studios or the cinema administration sometimes arranged them. Examples of repeated collaborations in the Stalin period include Dzigan and Vsevolod Vishnevskii, Iutkevich and Pogodin, Iulii Raizman and Evgenii Gabrilovich, and Gabrilovich and Romm. Professional screenwriters typically approached directors and not screenplay departments with their screenplay ideas, and the other way around. Note that this is how A-list directing and screenwriting talent operated in contemporary Hollywood and elsewhere. The problem was that the Soviet model did not accommodate other, less-individualized options well, and this made content planning less attainable.

Directors were always a crucial source of film ideas in Soviet cinema, and this continued to be the case even in the late Stalin period. Lenfilm, for example, had a practice where film directors submitted their plans and wishes (titled "Creative Plans" or "Creative Aspirations") to the screenplay department. In 1950, Ermler, Kozintsev, Aleksandr Faintsimmer, Sergei Vasil'ev, Nikolai Lebedev, Grigorii Roshal', Aleksandr Ivanov, Gerbert Rappaport, Aleksandr Ivanovskii,

---

46. M. Tokareva, "Pervye itogi," *Kino*, February 17, 1939, 3. For the list of winners, see Aleksandr Fadeev et al., "Informatsionnoe soobshchenie zhiuri konkursa na kinostenarii," *Kino*, February 17, 1939, 3. For a report on which screenplays were used, see "Konkursnye stsenarii," *Kino*, May 23, 1939, 4. This article lists ten screenplays; however, it is conceivable that other screenplays/librettos were also used at a later point under different titles.

47. "Itogi vsesoiuznogo konkursa na komediinyi kinostsenarii," *Kino*, September 13, 1940, 3.

Aleksandr Zarkhi, and Iosif Kheifits submitted such "plans," listing one to four projects. Vasil'ev wrote: "My first and main theme, the realization of which I consider a matter of honor, remains the theme of patriotism and the extraordinary heroism of ordinary Soviet people at the time of a great test, the heroic epic of the defense of Leningrad." He added, "the theme 'the people and the party, the leader and the people' is a natural extension of my work from *Chapaev* [1934] to *Front* [1943]." Both patriotism and the theme of the party were central to Vasil'ev's project about the battle for Leningrad, planned several times but never realized. Several directors listed screenwriters they were working with already or had in mind. Vasil'ev listed as his second project "a film about new [Soviet] people, new relations among them," and named several authors that he wanted to contact. Rappaport was interested in "the international theme—the theme of the struggle for peace," and specified that he wished that German or Konstantin Isaev would write for him. He added that Isaev was busy, however, and could start this work only in three months.[48] Thus when negotiating their plans with the studio, directors used thematic language but thought of themes in terms of authors.

The Lenfilm screenwriting department followed the director's wishes very closely. Of the twenty-three proposals contained in the "Creative Plans," all were included in the Lenfilm thematic plan for 1951–1952. Moreover, the screenplay editors copied many of the project descriptions into the plan from the directors' statements. Other than these projects, the thematic plan for 1951–1952 contained four films by minor directors whose creative plans were not included in the archival file (either not solicited, lost, or not submitted), and two screenplays without a director.[49] The screenplay department also signed agreements with screenwriters to deliver many of the director-proposed titles.[50] However, only one was eventually produced: Rappaport's *Svet v Koordi* (*Valgus Koordis*, 1951). The industry-wide plan for 1951–1952 underwent a major revision, and Lenfilm made only two films in 1951 and 1952 each.[51]

That directors learned to formulate their creative aspirations in terms of dry themes does not diminish the fact that they had their own screenplay ideas. Moreover, from everyone's perspective, the director was a tangible production unit, whereas themes and screenplays were more abstract entities. The practice of

48. TsGALI, f. 257, op. 16, d. 1893, ll. 27–35. See also TsGALI, f. 257, op. 16, d. 1894.

49. TsGALI, f. 257, op. 16, d. 1893, ll. 39–44. *Dneproges*, a project Ermler mentioned in his proposal, was not included in this plan but was mentioned in other planning documents.

50. TsGALI, f. 257, op. 17, d. 251, ll. 11, 76–88; TsGALI, f. 257, op. 16, d. 1893, ll. 11, 20 ob.

51. Artizov and Naumov, *Vlast'*, 668–689.

assigning projects to directors only started in the final years of Stalin's life. However, then, as before, directors could refuse assignments, and executives were at the mercy of directors to agree to take on projects. To give just one example, according to Leonid Trauberg, the idea to make a film about Karl Marx was proposed to him and Kozintsev by the Lenfilm screenplay department. The project was planned for production in 1939. The screenplay by the two directors was finished, published, approved by the central film executives, and launched into production in 1940. Later in 1940, however, Zhdanov told Kozintsev and Trauberg that he did not like it that they portrayed Marx as a human being rather than as a great leader.[52] Then in 1941, Zhdanov informed them that the project was "premature" in the present international climate and they should work on something else. Trauberg, who recalled this story years later, said: "They very much wanted us to make a film about Stalin defending Leningrad [in 1919]." Yet Kozintsev proposed they would make a biopic instead—the screenplay by German about the nineteenth-century surgeon Nikolai Pirogov was available at Lenfilm. Trauberg objected that *Pirogov* was not their kind of project, but Kozintsev insisted: it was better to make that than to be without a film. Once they made this decision, *Pirogov* was included in the plan.[53]

Thematic thinking lived on past Stalin's death, and it continued to coexist with planning based on directors, authors, and film types. The first post-Stalin thematic plan, for 1954, contained a list of film projects organized by studio and title. An introduction to the published version of the plan summarized the list thematically and in terms of genre.[54] This became the standard format of Soviet film planning, and the director continued to be the primary planning unit. According to the screenwriter Aleksei Kapler, as quoted in a secret KGB report, in 1969 the Soviet film industry did not have a plan. Rather, it had a list of "themes" directors wished to produce.[55] As we shall see, the director-centered approach to planning, introduced under Shumiatskii, was standardized by Bol'shakov to remain in place for the rest of the Soviet period.

---

52. V.T. Kozintseva and Ia. L. Butovskii, "*Karl Marks*: Istoriia nepostavlennoi postanovki," *Kinovedcheskie zapiski* 18 (1993): 198–205; Anderson et al., *Kremlevskii kinoteatr*, 566.

53. Leonid Trauberg, "O fil'me *Karl Marks*," *Kinovedcheskie zapiski* 18 (1993): 206–209. The involvement of Zhdanov (and Stalin) in this case should not be surprising given the subject. *Pirogov* was made in 1947.

54. *Tematicheskii plan proizvodstva khudozhestvennykh fil'mov na 1954 god* (Moscow: Iskusstvo, 1953).

55. Valerii Fomin, *Kino i vlast': Sovetskoe kino, 1965–1985: Dokumenty, svidetel'stva, razmyshleniia* (Moscow: Materik, 1996), 92.

Planning under Boris Shumiatskii (1931–1937)

Shumiatskii's intervention in Soviet film planning was to stop planning abstract themes and plan only specific individuals—screenwriters and directors—committed to the projects they proposed or agreed to make. In 1932 he replaced the Sovkino "system of orders" (*sistema zakaza*) with the "system of creative counterproposals" (*sistema vstrechnykh tvorcheskikh zaiavok*).[56] Shumiatskii called his approach "counterplanning" because it involved composing the plan out of proposals the creative workers wrote in response to the general thematic needs communicated to them from the top.[57] In effect, to control the unpredictability of theme-based planning, the new system eliminated any "themes" with no screenplay or director attached.

Shumiatskii launched the first version of this system in 1931 to plan production for 1932. First, in May 1931 Soiuzkino distributed to the studios a "framework document" explaining the quantitative, qualitative, creative, and thematic goals of Soviet cinema in 1932.[58] This was "a guide to action" that replaced the bureaucratic "piece of paper," as Shumiatskii derogatively referred to the thematic plans from years prior.[59] Then Soiuzkino officials traveled to the studios to see what proposals were available on the ground. Finally, in November 1931 the Soiuzkino leadership held a conference with studio representatives to draft the actual plan. Shumiatskii insisted that his system allowed studios and creative cadres to become the decisive force in thematic planning.[60] Indeed, the 1932 thematic plan was entirely based on proposals submitted by studios. It listed the title, screenwriter, director, and a brief description of each project.

---

56. G. Kholmskii, "K voprosu o templane," *Proletarskoe kino* 6 (June 1932): 10, also cited in Miller, *Soviet Cinema*, 92. Sutyrin, "Problemy planirovaniia." See also Taylor, "Ideology as Mass Entertainment," 200.

57. "Counterplan" (*vstrechnyi plan*) was an industrial concept from the period, and it referred to a better, more daring target developed through local initiative as a challenge in response to a target request from the top. *Vstrechnyi* (*Counterplan*), which told the story of one such plan, was one of Shumiatskii's favorite films.

58. B.Z. Shumiatskii and Iu. M. Liss, "Vsem trestam, direktoram kinofabrik, direktoram s"emochnykh grupp, rezhisseram, stsenaristam i operatoram," in Soiuzkino, *K templanu Soiuzkino na 1932 god* (Moscow: Soiuzkino, 1932).

59. "O tvorcheskikh zadachakh sovetskoi kinematografii," in Soiuzkino, *K templanu Soiuzkino na 1932 god*, 2.

60. Boris Shumiatskii, "Boevoi templan," *Kino*, October 27, 1931, 4.

The "thematic" aspect of the plan was maintained only in the general film categories, which for the Moscow film studio (future Mosfilm), for example, were as follows:

- Historical-revolutionary films
- Growing revolutionary movement in capitalist countries
- Communism vs. capitalism
- Socialist reconstruction in industry
- Socialist reconstruction in agriculture
- The role of Komsomol in socialist construction
- Growth and evolution of human consciousness
- Intelligentsia joins the proletariat's struggle for socialist society
- Socialist upbringing of the young[61]

When in April 1932 Shumiatskii submitted an adjusted version of this plan to the Central Committee, it included fifty-four mass features organized primarily by title. Eight of these films, he said, marked the fifteenth anniversary of the revolution, while seven other "leading" features (*vedushchie fil'my*) addressed substantial subjects and were attached to leading filmmakers. Most of the rest, Shumiatskii wrote, also had attached to them good-quality screenplays and cadres. In other words, Shumiatskii proposed a program of fifteen prestige pictures and thirty-nine other quality pictures without specifying each picture by theme.[62] The Central Committee pushed back. It rejected Shumiatskii's plan, saying the inclusion of certain directors, such as the "formalist" Mikhail Tsekhanovskii, and certain film titles, such as *The Quality of Love*, indicated that Shumiatskii would fail to meet quality expectations in 1932. Instead the Central Committee instituted fifteen commissions to oversee the production of "significant fiction films" in the following ten thematic categories:

- The Civil War
- The Komsomol
- Sports
- Education

---

61. N. Kiva, "Uslovnyi plan moskovskoi fabriki," *Kino*, October 16, 1931, 4.

62. The term "prestige picture" comes from Hollywood, which divided films not only by genre but also by type. Tino Balio, "Production Trends," in Balio, *Grand Design*, 179–211. In the 1940s, Mikhail Romm called prestige films "showcase" (*pokaznye*) pictures (Fomin, *Kino na voine*, 542). I am grateful to Vincent Bohlinger, who suggested to me that the distinction between ordinary and prestige pictures can be applied to the Soviet context.

- The economy and industrial achievements
- Central Asia
- Transcaucasia
- Pioneers
- International themes
- Party history[63]

The thematic emphasis of the Central Committee's decision is unmistakable. Yet the document also included a roster of potential writers and directors who might work on each subject, indicating that Shumiatskii's filmmaker-based approach was being accepted as well. Shumiatskii welcomed the Central Committee's intervention since, as he suggested elsewhere, the plan "reflected the worldview of the creative personnel and corresponded to [their] political and ideological level," or, in other words, was not pitched at the right ideological level.[64] As for the scope of subjects, love was clearly not on the Central Committee's list, but neither was it on Mosfilm's list. With the exception of sports and region-specific travelogues, the two lists were quite comparable. They were both unspecific and contained subjects that were already on the front pages of Soviet newspapers.

Shumiatskii held the second industry-wide planning conference in December 1932. This time he invited leading film directors, and Eisenstein, Dovzhenko, Pyr'ev, and Room were among the speakers.[65] The conference settled on a program for 1933 containing 126 short and feature-length fiction films, only one-third of which was to start and complete production within that year. Whether already in production or only being developed, all projects were based on filmmakers' proposals.[66] The plan was organized by studio, and the planning unit was the title and the director. Planning materials stated: "As opposed to the thematic plans of the last few years, when only bare themes and sometimes mere clichéd political slogans . . . were included in the plan, the 1933 thematic plan designates each theme to a creative worker, and in particular the director."[67] If a studio had no director for a particular title, that title was moved to the reserve.

63. Anderson et al., *Kremlevskii kinoteatr*, 163–173. The list of films Shumiatskii submitted is absent from the document, but he describes them.

64. RGALI, f. 2497, op. 1, d. 73, l. 20.

65. Fomin, *Letopis' rossiiskogo kino, 1930–1945*, 195.

66. RGALI, f. 2497, op. 1, d. 98, ll. 30–132.

67. RGALI, f. 2497, op. 1, d. 98, l. 24.

Each title had its own specific theme, and in the summary discussion of the plan, five broad thematic categories were specified as primary:

- Socialist construction and contemporary Soviet themes
- International themes
- War and defense
- Historical-revolutionary themes
- Literary classics[68]

The Shumiatskii planning system was not perfect. As before, many films planned were never produced. The difference between the proposal and the screenplay, and the screenplay and the film, remained substantial. And, as critics wrote, many crucial themes—the new Soviet hero, children, collective farms, and so forth—went underrepresented.[69] To improve the plan's realization and thematic coverage, Shumiatskii decided to hold planning conferences semiannually. For the next three years he gathered executives and filmmakers in the summer to draft the plan for the next calendar year and in the winter to finalize it. During the summer meeting he communicated the general thematic needs and models to follow, and the idea was that, between summer and winter, studios would both solicit new proposals and complete the screenplays already approved and contracted.

The first semiannual planning conference was held in July 1933.[70] At this conference Shumiatskii implemented the selective approach to talent discussed in chapter 1, when a list of eighty-five "planned" directors was published in the press. The materials for the next planning conference in December 1933 included: "The list of tested creatively sound [*polnotsennyi*] film directors, who, under the reduced program, from the point of view of their qualifications and abilities, can be trusted to produce a feature film in 1934." It listed seventy-one names.[71] The December plan was organized largely by title and director.[72]

The next planning conference, in July 1934, was marked by yet another step away from content planning. Several commentators, including Shumiatskii, questioned whether the term "thematic," still widely used in reference to planning, reflected Soviet cinema's actual practices. Since screenplays and directors

---

68. RGALI, f. 2497, op. 1, d. 98, ll. 24–26.

69. See, e.g. "Zheleznyi khrebet templana," *Kino*, January 4, 1933, 1; Mikhail Shneider, "Real'noe poniatie ili rechevaia fiktsiia?" *Kino*, June 28, 1933, 1.

70. Glavnoe upravlenie kino-foto-promyshlennosti, *Korennye voprosy sovetskoi kinematografii.*

71. RGALI, f. 2456, op. 1, d. 76, ll. 15–17.

72. RGALI, f. 2456, op. 1, d. 76.

were now planned without themes, *Kino* wrote, the "thematic plan" was an obsolete holdover from the agitprop days. Borrowing the concept from the Mezhrabpomfilm Studio, *Kino* proposed to call the annual program "the repertory plan."[73] Rejecting this term as more suitable for distribution and citing Stalin's words that the "plan is real people, it is you and me," Shumiatskii proposed the term "production plan" instead.[74]

For the next three years, Shumiatskii and his associates were more likely to refer to planning as "production" rather than "thematic." This was not just a matter of language. To plan content rather than talent would have been a Soviet innovation. In contrast, Shumiatskii's production plans became a management tool, moving the Soviet practice closer to the Western model.[75] By promoting production planning, Shumiatskii skipped the thematic step almost entirely. After 1932, the annual plan resulted from what the industry called "drift" (*samotek*), a largely spontaneous inflow of proposals from screenwriters and directors.[76] Instead of planning content, Shumiatskii "planned" creative workers. Shumiatskii's Soviet innovation was the prominence of the director. Although in Hollywood, for instance, stories were found for directors as much as directors were found for stories and stars, in Soviet Russia the director was primary. In 1931 the Moscow film studio reported that to secure the production of twenty feature films assigned to it during preliminarily planning, it had signed contracts for eighty screenplays; nevertheless, everything depended on the "quantity and quality of directors."[77] Even at Mezhrabpomfilm production was organized around the director. Savchenko, who worked at Mezhrabpomfilm, wrote in 1934 that *he* had a personal "repertory plan," which contained four titles.[78] Apparently following the lead of the studios, Shumiatskii believed that "if no director was found right away, the project (screenplay) was as good as done for," and this became an industry-wide norm.[79] This too was a move

73. "Za repertuarnyi plan!" *Kino*, July 16, 1934, 1; B. M. Migalov, "Repertuarnyi plan," *Kino*, June 16, 1934, 1; Ia. Zaitsev, "Ot tem k repertuaru," *Kino*, June 28, 1934, 1.

74. Boris Shumiatskii, "Proveriaem gotovnost'," *Kino*, July 16, 1934, 1. The quote is from "Vykhod iz proryva—tverdyi plan," *Kino*, March 22, 1933, 1. What Stalin actually said was, "The reality of our program is real people, it is you and me." Iosif Stalin, "Novaia obstanovka—novye zadachi khoziaistvennogo razvitiia," *Pravda*, July 5, 1931, 1.

75. The "businesslike" nature of Shumiatskii's planning was specifically heralded at this time. B. V—V, "Konkretnost' i delovitost'," *Kino*, July 28, 1934, 2.

76. Richard Taylor and Ian Christie translate *samotek* as "individual initiative" (Taylor and Christie, *Film Factory*, 243).

77. N. Kiva, "Uslovnyi plan moskovskoi fabriki," *Kino*, October 16, 1931, 4.

78. I. Savchenko, "Moi repertuar," *Kino*, July 10, 1934, 1.

79. Anderson et al., *Kremlevskii kinoteatr*, 476.

away from thematic planning: whereas screenplays were devoted to specific themes, directors rarely were.

Mezhrabpomfilm was the only studio that did not have a full package of screenplays prior to the July 1934 conference. *Kino* reported that this was because planning at Mezhrabpomfilm started with a number of films, their "themes and genres," and their directors.[80] Indeed, by 1934 it was also becoming more common throughout the industry to plan production around genres. This was related to Shumiatskii's general push for genre diversity (*zhanrovoe raznoobrazie*), in addition to a general thematic scope. Shumiatskii's objective was to produce not just mass hits but also features in traditional entertainment genres, and the Central Committee only encouraged him. In the mid-1930s Shumiatskii too often talked about "themes and genres," as well as genre specialization among directors and the need to develop such genres as comedy, satire, science fiction, adventure, and children's film. Accordingly, studios started to divide their production programs not only by the large thematic category but also by genre. For instance, the Mosfilm proposal for the July conference included "thirteen dramas, thirteen comedies, three epics, three poems, four tragedies, and five fairytales." As for the thematic breakdown, which Mosfilm also provided, these films contributed to the following themes:

- Epics about the heroes of the Soviet Union
- Construction
- Agriculture
- War films
- Culture and everyday life
- Historical films
- Travelogues
- Science-fiction films
- Children's films[81]

An equivalent list from Ukrainfilm consisted of the following headings:

- "People of socialist industry"
- Agriculture
- National politics
- Culture and everyday life

---

80. Migalov, "Repertuarnyi plan."
81. R. Zverina, "Potylikha," *Kino*, July 16, 1934, 2.

- Defense films
- Children's films
- Literary classics[82]

As these lists suggest, in the mid-1930s thematic categories became equivalent to genre and subgenre designations. The defense/war film, the children's film, the historical film, the science-fiction film, and the literary adaptation were well-established international genres. The agricultural comedy, melodrama, or musical and the industrial drama or epic were Soviet-specific subgenres. Films about industrial construction and agriculture stipulated certain generic settings, characters, storylines, and tones as much as they stipulated certain Soviet-specific themes, such as struggle for plan fulfillment, collective labor, technological progress, or the role of the party.

Indeed, when Konstantin Iukov, Shumiatskii's deputy in charge of feature production, discussed the 1935 "production" plan in the press after the planning conference of January 1935, he warned against thinking exclusively in themes. Iukov said, "Today we are trying to avoid dividing up the plan's thematics into schematic sections: industry versus collective farms. When we speak of collective-farm construction or of new people of socialist industry, we need to take into account that, as we create well-rounded characters, we necessarily incorporate a number of themes into one screenplay." A collective-farm film, he continued, should incorporate the themes "the party and its leading role," "the impact of industry on the growth and development of our agriculture," and "formation of the mentality of the Soviet collective farmer."[83] Thus thematic thinking was certainly not abandoned. Yet by 1935 a short list of broad subject-themes needed had become largely standardized. The desired thematic scope of Soviet cinema became so general it could no longer serve as a planning tool, for it could no longer specify any particular project. *All* projects were expected to contribute to all the broad themes. Something else had to distinguish among films, and genre became a suitable alternative.

By the next planning conference in December 1935 and under the influence of Shumiatskii's Hollywood travels, thematic thinking had been further diluted by the emergence of the term "story" (*siuzhet*). Instead of referring to film projects as themes, film professionals started to also call them stories. To quote Shumiatskii, cinema's task was to attain high quality "in screenplays, their thematics

---

82. V. Katinov, "Ukrainfil'm," *Kino*, July 16, 1934, 2.
83. K. Iukov, "Proizvodstvennyi plan 1935 goda," *Sovetskoe kino* 2 (1935): 9. Iukov, who worked for Shumiatskii's administration in 1933–1936, was purged and executed in September 1938.

(*tematika*), stories, and genres."[84] Meanwhile, the content goals of Soviet cinema became ever more general. As summarized by Piotrovskii, they were: "To show the remarkable growth of the Soviet country and create heroic characters of new people, who, under the leadership of the Communist Party, in the cities and in collectivized villages, on the seas and in the air, fight for the glory and happiness of the proletarian state."[85] This thematic field dictated no specific stories. Films did not have to be about party leadership or agriculture as such. They were merely supposed to reflect these notions along with heroism, romanticism, glory, optimism, and other delights of Soviet life. All arts and media were working in this broad propagandistic vein. Thus the Lenfilm "thematic plan" for 1936, a list of screenplays and proposals, was divided up into the following categories:

- The party
- Historical-revolutionary films
- Socialist deeds and people
- Social utopia or fantastic films
- Literary adaptations
- Biopics
- Children's films
- Collective-farm films

Piotrovskii reported that his studio was working on two to eight film projects in each of the first seven genres, but no good screenplays on collective farms were available at Lenfilm.[86]

By December 1935 Shumiatskii's planning conferences had turned into nothing short of industry-wide creative congresses. More than two hundred industry professionals participated, including central administration and studio executives, leading directors, writers, playwrights, screenwriters, composers, actors, cameramen, and art designers.[87] Many of them spoke at the conference, and to accommodate all the exchanges and speeches the December 1935 conference lasted for nine days. Delegates representing party organizations, the public, and various interest groups were also present. For example, at the conference Shumiatskii promised a delegation of railway workers a film about the railroads.[88]

---

84. B. Z. Shumiatskii, "Puti sorevnovaniia," *Kino*, December 11, 1935, 1. Story-based thinking too was a practice at Mezhrabpomfilm (see Zaitsev, "Ot tem k repertuaru").

85. A. Piotrovskii, "Plan realizuem!" *Kino*, December 11, 1935, 2.

86. TsGALI, f. 257, op. 12, d. 21, ll. 2–13.

87. Mikh. D., "Bol'shaia sovetskaia kinematografiia," *Komsomol'skaia pravda*, December 14, 1935, 4.

88. Anderson et al., *Kremlevskii kinoteatr*, 308.

The conference was one of the high points of Shumiatskii's success. In late 1934 and 1935 he released some major hits, several of which were praised by Stalin. As detailed in chapter 1, Shumiatskii was also planning a Soviet Hollywood and a radical industry reform. Restructuring film industry planning was part of his proposals.[89]

When Shumiatskii's reform ideas were abandoned in 1936, "thematic" terminology saw a comeback. As part of the antiformalism campaign, cinema was attacked for lacking in thematics: there had been no films about the railway workers, ethnic minorities, and women.[90] Shumiatskii was invited to the Central Committee to report on his film-production plan for 1936. Before the meeting Shumiatskii and representatives from the Committee on Arts Affairs and the Central Committee Propaganda Department had already adjusted the plan proposed by Shumiatskii, but the Central Committee asked to additionally "supplement the thematics of motion pictures in 1936 with screenplays (for 1936–1937) addressing the following themes:

- the people of Soviet transport,
- the Stakhanovites of industry,
- the struggle of collective farms to harvest seven to eight billion poods of wheat,
- the Red Army,
- socialist construction in national republics and regions,
- the role of young people in socialist construction,
- the Soviet woman."[91]

This directive was communicated to the studios and the list was published in *Kino*.[92] Notably, however, the 1937 thematic plan included only one project, *Chest'* (*Honor*, Evgenii Cherviakov, 1938), that seems to have been developed in response to this mandate. It dealt with "the people of socialist transport," Soviet railway workers. Moreover, in preparing this film, Shumiatskii was perhaps following not on Central Committee's orders, but on his own promise to the railway workers made in 1935. Indeed, several films produced in 1937–1938 were compatible with the themes listed in the resolution, but it is hard to attribute them to the resolution alone, as they addressed topics that had been identified

89. Fomin, *Letopis' rossiiskogo kino, 1930–1945*, 353.

90. Anderson et al., *Kremlevskii kinoteatr*, 306–311.

91. Anderson et al., *Kremlevskii kinoteatr*, 319–320.

92. [Platon] Kerzhentsev, "Postanovlenie no. 39 Vsesoiuznogo komiteta po delam iskusstv pri SNK SSSR," *Kino*, August 4, 1936, 1.

as required far earlier. Pyr'ev's *Bogataia nevesta* (*The Rich Bride*, 1937), set on a Ukrainian collective farm, for example, was about the struggle for the harvest, everyday life in the national republics, and the Soviet woman.

The renewed focus on "themes" to the detriment of "genres" and "stories" did not, however, change the planning practices. At a planning meeting in May 1936 Aleksandr Shcherbakov, the head of the Propaganda Department and Shumiatskii's primary critic, observed, "There is no such thing that cinema poses to screenwriters a series of core problem themes and actively orients screenwriters toward them. So far the unshakable order of things has been that screenwriters come, propose a theme that they are working on or want to work on, these proposals are written down, and then pronounced to be the plan. This order of things has to change." The Central Committee asked that Shumiatskii combat the disorganized "drift" of proposals and focus his planning on the screenwriter.[93]

Shumiatskii held the next planning conference at the Soviet Writers' Union. He told the writers he needed screenplays for major motion pictures to mark the twentieth anniversary of the revolution in 1937.[94] Following these contacts, the Union newspaper, *Literaturnaia gazeta*, wrote: "whereas before a successful screenplay may not have been accepted simply because no available or interested director had been found to film it, these days the plan is being compiled such that film ideas (*zamysly*) from both directors and writers are equally taken into account."[95] When studios discussed their portfolios for 1937, they talked of them in terms of screenplays, and only some of the projects had a director attached.[96]

The published plan for 1936, still titled the "production" plan, was organized by studio and contained no thematic designations. It was a list of projects identified by title, screenwriter, director, and release date.[97] Screenplays were referred to as themes, partially because some projects included in the plan had no finalized screenplays or titles and their theme was used as their shorthand identifier. Such projects were also called "conditional" and were equivalent to the themes without screenplays that used to appear in the pre-1931 plans. Furthermore,

93. [Aleksandr] Shcherbakov, "Dramaturgi dolzhny pomoch' GUKF," *Kino*, May 17, 1936, 1.
94. Fomin, *Letopis' rossiiskogo kino, 1930–1945*, 401; "Soveshchanie v Soiuze pisatelei," *Kino*, May 17, 1936, 1.
95. A. Kamennogorskii, "Pisateli i kino," *Literaturnaia gazeta*, April 20, 1936, 6.
96. "Stsenarnyi portfel' GUKF," *Kino*, May 17, 1936, 1.
97. "Plan proizvodstva khudozhestvennykh fil'mov na 1936 god," *Biulleten' Vsesoiuznogo komiteta po delam iskusstv pri SNK Soiuza SSR* 1/2 (1936): 20–23.

film titles in the 1936 plan were likely to be thematic summaries. Mosfilm's plan for 1936, for example, included *Partiinyi bilet* (*The Party Card*), *Zakliuchennye* (*The Convicts*), *Muzhestvo* (*Courage*—the film's eventual title was *Na Dal'nem Vostoke/In the Far East*), *Rodina zovet* (*Motherland Calls*), and *Izobilie* (*Plenty*, which became *Chudesnitsa/The Miracle Worker*).[98] Thus started a trend where rather than being clever or playful, many Soviet film titles described the film's central thematic concern.

An attempt at divorcing planning from directors also manifested itself in changes in the nature of planning conferences. The May 1936 conference at the Writers' Union was followed in July by a conference with studio "planners" (screenplay editor-censors) and in August 1936 with a conference "on plan fulfillment." Central Committee Propaganda Department staffers, top executives of major studios, and secretaries of studio party committees attended the latter.[99] These were no longer "creative" conferences. And the focus of the next planning conference, in January 1937, was also on planning accountability. Yet all the films projected for 1937 release had both screenplays and directors attached, and the emphasis was on the promising director–screenplay combinations, indicating that Shumiatskii never gave up on his preference for directors.[100] The final planning conference of Shumiatskii's tenure in June 1937 combined the tasks of monitoring plan fulfillment with planning for 1938. The press referred to the gathering as "a conference of studio directors and party committee secretaries."[101] No film directors were present.

Shumiatskii's fall from favor solidified the return to a thematic lexicon. Shumiatskii's 1937 conferences were referred to as "thematic" or "production-thematic" in reports. Shumiatskii's replacement, Semen Dukel'skii, used the word "thematic" exclusively in reference to planning. Yet Shumiatskii's "production" legacy and director-centered approach lingered on. Starting in 1938 the industry used both terms, to identify two different plans. The list of screenplays and film proposals that the studios planned to produce was called the "thematic plan," whereas the list of screenplays accepted for production and

---

98. "Plan proizvodstva khudozhestvennykh fil'mov na 1936 god," 20. Stalin may have contributed to this titling tendency by telling Shumiatskii that Ivan Pyr'ev's film, originally titled *Anna* based on the protagonist's name, be renamed *The Party Card*. Maiia Turovskaia, "Fil'my i liudi," *Kinovedcheskie zapiski* 57 (2002): 257; Anderson et al., *Kremlevskii kinoteatr*, 1044; Kenez, *Cinema and Soviet Society*, 132.

99. See coverage in *Kino*, August 22, 1936, 4; *Kino*, September 4, 1936, 1–2.

100. V. A. Usievich, "Plan 1937 goda," *Kino*, February 4, 1937, 2.

101. "Plan iubileinogo goda," *Kino*, June 11, 1937, 1; E. Kuznetsova and A. Amasovich, "Temy i fil'my 1938 goda," *Kino*, June 11, 1937, 2.

assigned directors was the "production plan." The list of screenplays ("themes") was the industry's "thematics," its official face. The list of directors' projects was its internal production schedule.

Planning under Semen Dukel'skii (1938–1939)

Dukel'skii came to cinema straight from the People's Commissariat of Internal Affairs (the NKVD, a predecessor to the KGB), and his appointment was an attempt to bring order to the film industry. Dukel'skii took three steps to reorient the film industry toward content planning: he distanced film directors from screenwriting and planning, introduced the formal submission of the industry production plan to the Central Committee, and encouraged the writing of screenplays on contemporary themes. Dukel'skii realized (or was told by the party ideologists above him) that to increase control, screenplays and not directors should determine thematics. One of his major decisions was that no project would be included in the plan without a complete and censored screenplay regardless of the status of the director associated with it.[102] Directors were also discouraged from writing original screenplays, the practice already in decline under Shumiatskii. A director wishing to film his own screenplay could do so only with permission from Dukel'skii. Dukel'skii's planning conference in September 1938 was with studio screenplay editors.[103]

In December 1938 Dukel'skii decreed that studios prohibit the production of films whose author or coauthor had been involved in the planning process, formally distancing filmmakers from planning. By the same decision, he instituted a new structure of compensation. Under Shumiatskii, directors and screenwriters received royalties as long as their film was in distribution. Dukel'skii ended this system, ruling instead that both directors and screenwriters would be compensated only once at the end of production. Directors were to be paid a lump-sum bonus of 6,000 to 50,000 rubles (in addition to their annual salaries of 14,000 to 24,000 rubles). In contrast, screenwriters would be paid a contract fee of up to 40,000 rubles per screenplay, as well as 50 percent (200 prints) to

---

102. V. Molotov and N. Petrunichev [and Semen Dukel'skii], "Ob uluchshenii organizatsii proizvodstva kinokartin," *Pravda*, March 24, 1938, 1 (translated in Babitsky and Rimberg, *Soviet Film Industry*, 297). The document was signed by Viacheslav Molotov as the head of the Soviet government, but it was written by Dukel'skii (see Anderson et al., *Kremlevskii kinoteatr*, 487–488).

103. Fomin, *Letopis' rossiiskogo kino, 1930–1945*, 574–575; S. Dukel'skii, "Vazhneishie zadachi stsenarnykh otdelov," *Kino*, September 29, 1938, 2–3.

200 percent (more than 1,000 prints) of that fee depending on the number of prints made of the film.[104] This system placed screenwriters of highly acclaimed films ahead of directors in per-film earnings, a preference that Bol'shakov would reverse.[105]

Soon after coming to office, Dukel'skii officially submitted the thematic plan for 1938 to the Central Committee (Shumiatskii also sent his plans to the Central Committee, but this was not made public).[106] The submitted plan contained eighty-eight projects, but, as Dukel'skii admitted, it did not cover all the subjects it should have. Two weeks later the Central Committee signed a resolution approving a shortened version of the plan, fifty-one titles. Dukel'skii had this plan published in *Pravda* and *Kino*. In contrast to Shumiatskii's plans, the 1938 plan contained a list of screenplays organized by the thematic-generic category. (The insistence on using the word "theme" was perhaps Dukel'skii's attempt to counteract the essentially generic nature of the list.) No director names or studios were included. The categories were:

- "Historical themes"
- "Historical-revolutionary themes"
- "Themes based on the classics"
- "Themes on the struggle with the agents of international fascism"
- "Defense themes"
- "Anti-fascist themes"
- "Themes on the Stakhanovite movement"
- "Themes on socialist construction"
- "Children's themes"
- "Ethnographic themes"
- "Comedies"[107]

The Central Committee instructed Dukel'skii to provide in three months an "additional thematic plan" covering the following subjects: Defense, the Red

---

104. "O poriadke oplaty tvorcheskikh rabotnikov kinematografii," in *Sovetskaia kinematografiia: Sistematizirovannyi sbornik zakonodatel'nykh postanovlenii*, ed. A. E. Kossovskii (Moscow: Goskinoizdat, 1940), 294–295; "Novaia sistema oplaty truda tvorcheskikh rabotnikov kinematografii," *Kino*, January 5, 1939, 3.

105. Under Bol'shakov, the screenplay fee rose to 80,000 rubles, while director bonuses (*postanovochnye*), which were based on the number of prints, ranged from 50,000 to 100,000 rubles. To put these fees in perspective, in 1940 the average annual wage in the USSR was 4,000 rubles, and in 1946 a car cost 15,000 rubles.

106. Anderson et al., *Kremlevskii kinoteatr*, 489–490.

107. "Tematicheskii plan," *Pravda*, April 3, 1938, 3.

Army, air force and border guards, antifascist themes, "the struggle with the agents of international fascism," the Stakhanovite movement, socialist construction in the national and autonomous republics, "friendship among peoples," ethnographic themes, women, family, sports, comedies, "and so forth." The text of the Central Committee resolution was almost a copy of the text submitted by Dukel'skii as a proposal, suggesting that these thematic categories were Dukel'skii's own.[108]

Dukel'skii's mandate was to focus on contemporary subjects. He cancelled a number of literary adaptations, historical films, and children's films in the 1938 program, announced to the filmmakers that only films on contemporary themes would be made from then on, and held an open competition for screenplays on contemporary subjects.[109] The Central Committee approved without change Dukel'skii's additional plans for 1938 and 1939. However, it proved difficult to supply screenplays on all the desired subjects. The September list included one film about "the woman" and six films "on socialist construction and friendship among peoples." No films dealing with ethnography or the military were listed. The December plan projected four films "about the woman, family, young people, and children" and two on construction and peoples' friendship. Nine new comedies were also planned.[110] Despite his initial push for contemporary subjects, during his short tenure Dukel'skii nonetheless proposed a score of new titles in the historical and biographical variety.[111] Although Dukel'skii justified his actions by the historical film's evident popularity with audiences, it is likely that the reason for the inclusion of historical films was that he had a good number of reliable screenplays to work with in this category.[112]

108. Anderson et al., *Kremlevskii kinoteatr*, 493–494 (and compare to 489–490).

109. Semen Dukel'skii, "Povorot kino k sovremennosti," *Pravda*, April 26, 1938, 4; Mikhail Romm, *Ustnye rasskazy* (Moscow: Kinotsentr, 1989), 66; Anderson et al., *Kremlevskii kinoteatr*, 489–490, 493–494; "Ob organizatskii konkursa na kinostsenarii," *Kino*, June 17, 1938, 1; Fomin, *Letopis' rossiiskogo kino, 1930–1945*, 574.

110. "27 novykh kinofil'mov," *Pravda*, September 22, 1938, 4; Anderson et al., *Kremlevskii kinoteatr*, 507–512, 531–532; "O tematicheskom plane proizvodstva polnometrazhnykh khudozhestvennykh kartin na 1939 god," *Kino*, January 29, 1939, 1.

111. Anderson et al., *Kremlevskii kinoteatr*, 539–541; M. Ia. Dubrovskii and L. N. Cherniavskii, eds., *Ezhegodnik sovetskoi kinematografii za 1938 god* (Moscow: Goskinoizdat, 1939), 144–149.

112. It appears that planning was better organized in technical and educational films than in fiction films, although it is difficult to ascertain how closely the former planning was followed in practice. A large proportion of the topics were entered into the plan at the request of various government agencies. Komitet po delam kinematografii pri SNK SSSR, *Tematicheskii plan proizvodstva nauchnykh i uchebno-tekhnicheskikh fil'mov na 1939 god* (Moscow: Goskinoizdat, 1939).

Dukel'skii lasted as the top cinema executive for only a year and a half. He was not in charge long enough to reboot Soviet screenwriting or implement thematic planning proper. New writers "revealed" by his very successful screenplay competition did not get integrated into the film industry. Meanwhile, emphasizing the screenwriter over the director greatly offended Soviet film directors and made Dukel'skii's "bureaucratic" leadership, as they called it, unacceptable to them.[113] In fact, it is likely that Dukel'skii's disregard of the interests of the "masters" cost him his position (albeit his new position, the People's Commissar for the Navy, was certainly no worse). Shumiatskii was right that in the Soviet film industry it was the director who was ultimately responsible for film production. This was Bol'shakov's position as well.

Planning under Ivan Bol'shakov (1939–1953)

Ivan Bol'shakov became the chief industry executive in June 1939. His approach to planning started with the screenplay-centered model promoted by Dukel'skii but then evolved toward Shumiatskii's director-based approach and creative counterplanning. In August 1939 Bol'shakov sent for approval to the Central Committee the thematic plan for 1939–1940, which included many of the titles Dukel'skii had already proposed.[114] The plan's format was again reorganized. It contained two sections: "Themes (Screenplays) to Be Developed" and "Themes Based on Existing Screenplays." The latter was a list of titles organized by thematic section and based on authors' proposals. The thematic/genre sections were the same as in Dukel'skii's plans: historical films, defense films, antifascist films, children and young people's films, fairy tales, and comedies. No directors or studios were listed.[115] The 1940–1941 plan the Central Committee approved in November 1939, however, was no longer organized by genre or theme.[116] Starting then, all the Bol'shakov thematic plans were lists of titles with names of screenwriters attached. Sometimes comedies were singled out into a separate category, and after the war color and black-and-white films were also distinguished. Also, in an apparent compromise between the Shumiatskii and Dukel'skii models, Bol'shakov titled his plans "the thematic plan for the production of. . . ." "Theme" was now formally synonymous to "screenplay."

---

113. Anderson et al., *Kremlevskii kinoteatr*, 500–502.

114. Compare Anderson et al., *Kremlevskii kinoteatr*, 550–561 to 539–541.

115. Anderson et al., *Kremlevskii kinoteatr*, 550–561.

116. "Tematicheskii plan proizvodstva polnometrazhnykh khudozhestvennykh kinokartin na 1940–1941 gg," *Kino* 1939, November 11, 1939, 4.

Bol'shakov's screenplays easily divided into familiar genre categories, and he also reintroduced Shumiatskii's prestige film as a type. *Kino* broke the 1939 film output up into the following sections:

- "Major works of [cinema] art"
- "Defense themes"
- "The Stakhanovite movement"
- "Life of our collective-farm village"
- "Soviet comedies"
- "Films for children and young people"
- "Films produced at the national studios"
- "Newsreel-and-documentary films"[117]

The "major works" section was categorized by type rather than theme and included films in different genres: the collective-farm comedy *The Tractor Drivers*, the collective-farm drama *Member of the Government*, the historical-revolutionary film *Shchors*, and the historical epic *Minin and Pozharskii*. Other designations were either Soviet subgenres or international genres. The additional plan for 1940–1941 Bol'shakov published contained the following genres: "Defense themes," "on socialist construction and the Stakhanovite movement," "collective-farm construction," "the life of peoples of the USSR," "new way of life and socialist culture," and "children and young people's thematics."[118] This generic focus continued for the rest of Bol'shakov's tenure. Moreover, in direct parallel with Shumiatskii in 1934–1935, after the war Bol'shakov called for genre diversity as well as for the exploration of new genres: films about scientists, adventure films, science fiction, and sports films.[119] Even if for the rest of the Soviet period genre was often dismissed as a Western (bourgeois, pure entertainment, etc.) concept to which "theme" offered an ideologically superior alternative, themes never replaced genres in practice.[120]

Bol'shakov's tenure also heralded a move back to Shumiatskii-type attention to the director-masters. In March 1940 Bol'shakov ordered five major studios to form Artistic Councils comprising leading creative workers. As we

---

117. "Sovetskaia kinematografiia uspeshno vypolnila plan 1939 goda," *Kino*, January 5, 1940, 1.

118. "Dopolnitel'nyi tematicheskii plan proizvodstva khudozhestvennykh kinokartin na 1940–41 god," *Kino*, June 17, 1940, 2.

119. I. Bol'shakov, "Nashi blizhaishie zadachi," *Iskusstvo kino* 1 (October 1945): 3.

120. Dawn Seckler has argued that despite all the denial of genre-based thinking, post-Stalin thematic planning was based on genres. Seckler, "What Does *Zhanr* Mean in Russian," in *Directory of World Cinema: Russia*, ed. Birgit Beumers (Bristol, UK: Intellect, 2010), 28–33.

shall see in chapter 3, this policy made the responsibility for film quality the explicit domain of the film directors. Moreover, in direct reversal of Dukel'skii's rules, Bol'shakov made overseeing the studio thematic plans one of the Artistic Councils' primary responsibilities.[121] Bol'shakov also restored creative planning conferences. He gathered filmmakers to discuss comedy in November 1939 and historical films in February 1940. Aleksandrov was the keynote speaker in November and Eisenstein in February.[122] The latter conference was immediately followed by the celebration of the twentieth anniversary of Soviet cinema, and, as under Shumiatskii, filmmakers received an official greeting from the Central Committee to mark that date.[123] At other conferences during Bol'shakov's first few years in office, the participants discussed film planning in terms of general themes, specific titles, and directors. Yet when speaking of their studio plans, studio executives prioritized directors. For example, the interim director of Mosfilm, Nikolai Kiva, noted in 1940 that no screenplays were available for Eisenstein, Aleksandrov, Medvedkin, Raizman, Macheret, Dzigan, and five other Mosfilm directors.[124]

Under Bol'shakov, studios continued to plan their work primarily around directors. When Mosfilm's Artistic Council discussed Semenov's prestige titles for the 1942 plan, many of these had a director attached. Vishnevskii was writing a screenplay about Moscow "for" Dzigan, and Kapler was writing a screenplay about Dzerzhinskii "tentatively for" Romm. In addition, members of the Artistic Council discussed both Mikhail Dubson and Aleksandr Faintsimmer as candidates to film *Kotovskii* (Dubson had wanted to make the film for a very long time, but it was given to Faintsimmer, who was deemed more experienced), which is probably why *Kotovskii* was listed without a director in Mosfilm's plan.[125] Mosfilm's "thematic" plan for 1941 was a list of projects and directors, although most projects had a specific screenwriter as well. The list also included generic units (e.g., "a musical film"), and one item, "the conditional twelfth," envisioned

121. "Polozhenie: O khudozhestvennykh sovetakh pri direktorakh kinostudii khudozhestvennykh fil'mov," *Biulleten' Komiteta po delam kinematografii pri SNK Soiuza SSR* 6 (1940): 20.
122. "Tvorcheskoe soveshchanie po voprosam kinokomedii," *Kino*, November 23, 1939, 3; "Tvorcheskoe soveshchanie po istoricheskomu i istoriko-revoliutsionnomu fil'mu," *Kino*, February 11, 1940, 1.
123. "Privetstvie TsK VKP(b) i SNK SSSR rabotnikam sovetskoi kinematografii," *Kino*, February 15, 1940, 1.
124. "Obraztsovo podgotovit'sia k 1941 godu," *Kino*, August 2, 1940, 4.
125. RGALI, f. 2453, op. 2, d. 506, ll. 1–8; RGALI, f. 2453, op. 2, d. 507; RGALI, f. 2453, op. 2, d. 508; RGALI, f. 2453, op. 2, d. 97, l. 19. This screenplay was by Kapler, but a screenplay on Kotovskii by Aleksei Tolstoi assigned to Dubson was in Lenfilm plans as early as in 1936.

one of three screenplays or an adaptation of a classic. One item was identified as "a comedy" by Aleksandrov and another as "a color film" by Eisenstein. Eisenstein and Aleksandrov were top masters and were expected to write or find screenplays for themselves.[126]

It is possible to describe Bol'shakov's planning approach as mixed, for he took into account everything that mattered: directors, screenplays, subject matter, and genres. And nominally, planning started with a screenplay, whether directors found screenplays or screenplays were found for them.[127] Nevertheless, to use the strong language of the screenplay editor Vasilii Katinov, under Bol'shakov thematic plans continued to be "bastard plans" (ubliudochnye plany) because ultimately everything depended on directors. Actual production, Katinov said, was based not on the officially accepted plan but on the readiness of screenplays, on and off the planned list.[128] Indeed, a large proportion of screenplays originally projected in the plans did not pan out. They were not delivered, rejected by censorship, or cancelled as no longer relevant by the time they were completed. Only one screenplay was planned for a specific director at a time. If that screenplay was rejected, no replacement was immediately available, and the director stood idle, sometimes for months or years in a row. Moreover, as Katinov also said, planning screenplays was pointless: in practice screenplays were realizable only if directors were interested in them.[129] This was why under Shumiatskii and Bol'shakov, major directors were involved in planning, and why, as figure 2.1 keenly suggests, the director had authority above the screenwriter.

By 1940 it was clear that the party-state leadership also associated the well-being of Soviet cinema with individual directors and screenwriters. When Zhdanov met with filmmakers in May 1941, eighty-one professionals were present, and the majority (fifty-four) were screenwriters and directors.[130] At the meeting Zhdanov said that quality required "two conditions: a high-quality screenplay and a tested master."[131] Shumiatskii and Bol'shakov knew this already: it was best to focus on screenplays by prestige authors assigned to leading directors. Yet the plans continued to be called "thematic."

---

126. RGALI, f. 2453, op. 2, d. 509, ll. 1, 2.

127. Some directors applied to produce screenplays that were available at their studios (see, e.g., RGALI, f. 2453, op. 2, d. 97, l. 20).

128. RGALI, f. 2453, op. 2, d. 97, ll. 23–24.

129. RGALI, f. 2453, op. 2, d. 97, l. 24.

130. Anderson et al., Kremlevskii kinoteatr, 622.

131. Iumasheva and Lepikhov, "Fenomen 'totalitarnogo liberalizma,'" 134.

FIGURE 2.1   Konstantin Eliseev, "Director," *Krokodil* 30–31 (1943): 8. The caption reads: "Director: If I so fancy, I would love. If I so fancy, I would strike. If I so fancy, I would cut. If I so fancy, I would stall. Most likely, I would fancy nothing." The folders to the right of the director read "Screenplay."

When in August 1940 the Central Committee banned *The Law of Life*, Zhdanov attacked thematic planning as no guarantor of quality. He observed, "What do they [the cinema administration] give the Central Committee when they submit the thematic plan? They give a tiny annotation on what [the film] would be about, on intention. But there is a huge distance between the thematic plan and a good screenplay." He added that thematic plans should not be the basis of production, especially provided the film industry felt pressured to implement them. According to Zhdanov, no ideological control was possible with such plans, and he was quite right. Worse yet, Zhdanov complained, by signing off on these plans, the Central Committee inadvertently approved future failures, as

The Law of Life had been.[132] It must have been as a result of these comments that Bol'shakov started submitting not just plans but also screenplays to the Central Committee Propaganda Department. Even the best-intended thematic formulations tended to morph unrecognizably in screenplays. Moreover, as Zhdanov realized, there was a great difference between a projected screenplay and the final cast, shot, and edited film. This is why after the ban on *The Law of Life*, the Central Committee started to formally censor completed films itself and mandated that its Propaganda Department sign off on all annual plans.

The Propaganda Department always found Bol'shakov's plans unsatisfactory. The most common problem was the thematic scope, and specifically too few contemporary themes. Georgii Aleksandrov, head of the Propaganda Department, criticized the plan for forty-five features in 1941 for containing twelve historical and historical-revolutionary films, but only one film each on socialist construction, collective farms, and the Soviet intelligentsia. The preliminary plan for 1942 was even worse from Aleksandrov's point of view. No screenplays on Soviet youth, five screenplays on Soviet industry and the Stakhanovite movement, and an overwhelming thirty-one screenplays for biographical and historical films were being projected.[133] Aleksandrov recommended that five screenplays from the 1941 plan be excluded, but his recommendation was largely ignored. Three of the five films were in production three months later, and one was eventually made (*Anton Ivanovich serditsia/Anton Ivanovich Is Angry*, Ivanovskii, 1941).[134]

The war period changed little in the system of planning. As for genres, it created a greater supply and demand for war dramas, making the planning process a bit more congenial. Here is how Aleksandrov described the genre makeup of the plan for thirty-one features in 1943:

- Films about the [Great] Patriotic War (12)
- Historical films (5)
- On the people of the Soviet rear (3)
- Biographical films (1)
- Musical films (4)
- Comedies (3)
- Children's films (3)

132. Anderson et al., *Kremlevskii kinoteatr*, 608, 613.
133. Fomin, *Kino na voine*, 24–28.
134. Fomin, *Kino na voine*, 42.

Complaining that, as before, the thematic makeup of the plan was "haphazard," Aleksandrov said the cinema administration was making no effort to prepare a large number of films about the Soviet rear. Neither were films about collective farms, the heroism of Soviet women in the rear, nor the "heroic struggle of Soviet people for coal, metal, and oil" included in the plan. Aleksandrov recommended excluding several contemporary titles from the plan, of which one was made nevertheless (*Nebo Moskvy/Moscow Skies*, Raizman, 1944).[135]

In 1944 as the war was nearing an end, Bol'shakov ruled that the plan would now represent only the minimum program the industry could deliver. He said that although earlier planning had been organized around "themes" (i.e., screenplay proposals) rather than screenplays, starting then the plan would be based on "real capacity, real director, and real screenplay and studio." No one prevented the studios from expanding the plan at any time, he said, but such expansion could only happen if completed screenplays and specific directors were proposed.[136]

The thematic scope Bol'shakov established for 1945 consisted of the following categories:

- The military and moral destruction of fascism
- The reconstruction of territories formerly under the Nazi occupation and the rear
- Comedy and musical films
- Films about the Soviet youth
- Classics and historical-biography films[137]

However, when the Scenario Studio prepared a draft plan for 1945 containing forty-five screenplays, it expanded Bol'shakov's last entry into four separate genres: historical-revolutionary, historical, historical-biography, and literary adaptations.[138] As with Dukel'skii, this was the Studio's way of adjusting to the screenplay supply: the authors were more willing to write on historical subjects than on postwar themes. In 1945 only ten screenplays prepared by the Studio were accepted for production.[139]

---

135. Anderson et al., *Kremlevskii kinoteatr*, 652–654; Fomin, *Kino na voine*, 370–372. See also Anderson et al., *Kremlevskii kinoteatr*, 674–680.

136. RGALI, f. 2456, op. 1, d. 1080, l. 11.

137. RGALI, f. 2456, op. 1, d. 1080, ll. 13–17.

138. RGALI, f. 2372, op. 11, d. 45, ll. 1–8.

139. Anderson et al., *Kremlevskii kinoteatr*, 721.

By 1946 it was clear that thematic planning was not working as expected. It did not guarantee the desired content of Soviet film output. Films on contemporary themes were always lacking, and the plan did not reliably predict output from year to year in quantitative or qualitative terms. In a secret report received by Zhdanov, an informer reported that Mosfilm's screenplay editor Il'ia Vaisfel'd had said, "The thematic plan is a document that only exists on paper and is only needed as a basis for the functioning of the studio. In reality everything will proceed in an unplanned fashion (*samotekom*)."[140]

Nevertheless, the planning practice continued. In April 1946 Zhdanov and Bol'shakov held another conference to discuss the thematic plan for the following few years. Forty individuals were present, among them leading directors, screenwriters, and cinema and propaganda executives. Zhdanov gave the keynote address, in which he described the thematic needs of the state. His first point was that historical films were certainly still acceptable, despite what the Propaganda Department's Aleksandrov might have indicated, but contemporary themes and genre pictures were in much greater demand. As for the specific themes, he encouraged filmmakers to work on the following: contemporary Soviet people who fought and won against the fascists, or how the ideology of friendship won over the ideology of "beastly misanthropy"; friendship among nations; cultural and technical advancement of Soviet workers and peasants (Zhdanov suggested that comedy would be particularly suitable here); and ordinary Soviet people doing heroic things.[141]

In 1946 the industry thematic plan for the first time underwent major changes while under consideration by the Central Committee. In May 1946 Bol'shakov submitted to the Central Committee a plan for 1946–1947 containing forty-six titles (ten of which had already been completed and were awaiting approval). Zhdanov and Aleksandrov sent it to Stalin for his signature. They recommended excluding fifteen titles that were either ideologically useless (literary adaptations, filmed concerts, or fairy tales) or had poor screenplays. They proposed replacing these with nineteen different screenplays also offered by Bol'shakov. In addition the document specified thirteen new themes to be developed into screenplays for 1947.[142]

Thus the first operation performed by Zhdanov and Aleksandrov was to simply select a different grouping of screenplays from those Bol'shakov had on offer. The more significant operation was the inclusion of new themes, as this was a rare example of a direct order from above. Moreover, Stalin personally edited

140. Anderson et al., *Kremlevskii kinoteatr*, 721.
141. Anderson et al., *Kremlevskii kinoteatr*, 724–729.
142. Anderson et al., *Kremlevskii kinoteatr*, 732–737.

this list. He crossed out two "themes": "Fictional documentary on the destruction of German troops near Moscow in December 1941" (perhaps because a documentary film on this topic, *Moscow Strikes Back*, had already been made in 1942) and an item about postwar reconstruction of the Stalingrad Tractor Factory (perhaps foreshadowing the banning of *A Great Life*, part 2). The eleven "themes" that Stalin left untouched were as follows:

- On the destruction of German troops in Stalingrad
- On the destruction of German troops in Leningrad
- On the destruction of German troops in Crimea
- Technology innovators
- Oil workers
- Metal workers
- Former partisans rebuild their collective farm in a territory freed from German occupation
- A Georgian collective farm cultivates citruses
- Uzbek cotton growers
- The mother-hero
- Taras Shevchenko ("proposed by the Ukrainian Central Committee")[143]

With the exception of the last subject, it is hard to know who proposed these ideas. What matters, however, is there was little new in these Stalin-approved themes: contemporary heroes, industry, collective farms, women, and biopics had been the staples of thematic planning for years.

The true novelty here was the films about the military milestones of the Second World War. The inclusion of Stalingrad, Leningrad, and Crimea in the thematic plan of 1946–1947 launched a new Soviet genre: the "fictional documentary" about the war. Several films were subsequently made in this genre: *Tretii udar* (*The Third Blow*, Savchenko, 1948), about the Crimean operation; *Stalingradskaia bitva* (*The Battle of Stalingrad*, Vladimir Petrov, 1949); and *Padenie Berlina* (*The Fall of Berlin*, Mikhail Chiaureli, 1949). However, it is not clear that, as Grigorii Mar'iamov reports, the idea to create a series of ten such films belonged to Stalin.[144]

---

143. Anderson et al., *Kremlevskii kinoteatr*, 736.

144. Mar'iamov writes: "Stalin dictated to Bol'shakov his plan for the creation of a cycle of feature documentary films under the general title of *Ten Blows* that crushed Hitler's military machine" (Mar'iamov, *Kremlevskii tsenzor*, 105). At the meeting of the Scenario Studio editorial board with writers and screenwriters on May 11, 1945, someone mentioned that Stalin told major general Nikolai Talenskii, the head of the Artistic Council's screenplay commission, only that war films were needed (RGALI, f. 2372, op. 10, d. 87, l. 23). Grigorii Mar'iamov worked as the Cinema Ministry senior editor under Bol'shakov.

It is more likely these war themes developed within the film industry. At the very least, a project called *The Brandenburg Gate* about the Soviet entry into Berlin in 1945 (screenplay by Mikhail Svetlov for the director Boris Babochkin, unrealized) had already been listed in the thematic plan for 1946.[145] Moreover, of the four films in this series included as embryonic ideas in the Zhdanov-Aleksandrov-Bol'shakov plan, Stalin crossed out one, offering no alternative.[146]

Plans for subsequent years also went through Stalin's office, but the screenplays available to the cinema administration largely dictated their thematic makeup. Critics and party officials continued to complain that the thematic content and genre assortment of Soviet cinema was far from satisfactory. Not enough comic and dramatic narratives were produced on contemporary Soviet morals, conflicts, ethics, achievements, women, youngsters, collective farmers, managers, and party members, and too many historical epics and literary adaptions were planned.[147] Early in 1948 at the Central Committee meeting on the plan, Zhdanov proposed to gather a thematic conference of directors and screenwriters to determine what *they* were interested in working on. Have them tell us what they could offer, and we would select what we like, he said.[148] Appealing to talent, however, was what Bol'shakov had been doing all along.

The plans for 1948 through 1951 were either accepted without change or with deletions. No alternative lists were proposed and no new themes were ordered.[149] According to the head of the Propaganda Department Dmitrii Shepilov, in 1948 some titles were excluded because Stalin made derogatory comments about many of the films planned.[150] The 1952 plan contained several titles crossed out by Malenkov. Apparently even the Central Committee had run out of ideas. Also, by the end "thematic" and "production" plans merged. The 1952 plan included titles, screenwriters, and annotations, as well as studios, directors, and production dates.[151] The final 1953 plan of the Stalin period contained no deletions. In fact Stalin, who personally edited this plan, reversed an earlier decision, probably by the Propaganda Department staff, to cancel four projects already in production. Stalin also changed the titles of half of the films proposed. In this plan, the director was listed prominently and before the screenwriter.[152]

145. Anderson et al., *Kremlevskii kinoteatr*, 769; see also 716–717.
146. Anderson et al., *Kremlevskii kinoteatr*, 736.
147. See, e.g., "Itogi 1947 goda," *Iskusstvo kino* 1 (January–February 1948): 1–4.
148. Anderson et al., *Kremlevskii kinoteatr*, 799.
149. Artizov and Naumov, *Vlast'*, 635–637, 647–648, 661–662, 668–669.
150. Shepilov, "Vospominaniia," 24–25, also cited in Artizov and Naumov, *Vlast'*, 789.
151. Anderson et al., *Kremlevskii kinoteatr*, 883–885.
152. Anderson et al., *Kremlevskii kinoteatr*, 904–908.

Conclusion

It has been argued that Soviet planning limited filmmakers' choices to themes that benefited the party, and that this alone made it an instrument of control.[153] In any film industry, production plans reflect industry goals. In the Soviet film industry, a major goal was to support the regime. This, however, did not mean the regime controlled what the industry produced. The Stalin regime did not dictate film content from the top down, but delegated thematic planning to film practitioners. Through a variety of feedback, including from Stalin himself, the industry formed a short list of general thematic categories, genres, and film types that the leadership wanted. Actual production planning adhered to this broad framework only very generally and with a lot of noise. Moreover, there was a big difference between the desired topic headings and the actual stories, characters, and tones enacted by the filmmakers.

Soviet film planning was "thematic" in that it catered to exhibition and distribution pressures only in a weak sense. What mattered more was what subject matter would mobilize the audiences. Films about contemporary Soviet people—the cardinal theme of Soviet cinema—were in great demand not because they distributed well but because Soviet party ideologists believed that viewers emulated film characters. Few correct new films about contemporary Soviet people were made, however, for the Soviet film industry lacked a mechanism of top-down content development and therefore could not easily plan propaganda content. With some exceptions, planning amounted to selecting and approving a sample of film projects generated at the studio level, and the screenwriters, writers, screenplay editors, and directors constantly failed to meet the expectations of the party-state leadership.

The concept of thematic planning was an oxymoron. Predictable output is difficult to achieve in any artistic endeavor. It is even more difficult to plan content. The 1932 transition from thematic planning to production counterplanning based on specific directors and screenplays was the industry's attempt to control its risks and enhance its offerings. Although the new approach improved predictability, output decline was a major side effect. As the plan dwindled numerically, so did the pool of filmmakers and screenwriters. Risks were reduced, but thematic coverage, genre diversity, and prospects of expansion diminished along with them.

---

153. Miller, *Soviet Cinema*, chap. 4.

THE MASTERS

The Director-Centered Mode of Production
and the Tradition of Quality

> One consolation to cinema workers:
> **"Governing bodies come and go; art remains."**
>
> —Vladimir Mayakovsky

Although the functioning of Soviet cinema was in theory determined by the demands of the party-state, in practice film output was shaped by executives, directors, and screenwriters.[1] Film production was organized around the director in particular, and the centrality of directors, especially those considered masters, was a deliberate policy for most of the Stalin period. Most filmmakers were not propagandists but artists, and this made a difference in terms of what kinds of services they were able to render to the regime. The Stalinist environment not only severely restricted their creative practice but also enabled them to maintain some autonomy. This is not to deny that Stalin-era filmmakers had "crippled biographies" but to say that, as circumscribed as they were individually and as diverse as they are in their personal stories, filmmakers also functioned as a group, and this group represented something larger than their individual successes and failures.[2]

This chapter discusses the impact the director-centered mode of production had on the failure of the Soviet film industry to meet the goals of the regime. It considers how Soviet filmmakers responded to Stalin's cultural policy as a community of professionals working within an institutional environment that

1. The lines that serve as the epigraph for this chapter were written by Mayakovsky when his screenplay, praised by Kuleshov and Shklovsky, was rejected by the Sovkino governing board as inaccessible to the masses. Vladimir Mayakovsky, "Karaul!" *Novyi LEF* 2 (1927): 25.

2. Herbert Marshall, *Masters of the Soviet Cinema: Crippled Creative Biographies* (London: Routledge & K. Paul, 1983).

determined both their possibilities and constraints. Soviet film directors under Stalin were a privileged cultural elite and performed a variety of roles, including as executives and censors.[3] Not unlike other members of the intellectual class, they negotiated and shared authority with the regime.[4] This put Soviet filmmakers in a position to pursue their own agenda that developed in parallel with Stalin's cultural policy under the pull of such powerful endogenous influences as the Soviet filmmaking tradition and Sergei Eisenstein. Their agenda was artistic and professional, and it was never entirely subsumed by Stalinism. Many filmmakers worked before Stalinism and survived it, and they were at least as much a part of Stalinist culture as they were a part of the world cinema process.[5] Moreover, Stalin's policy of delegating filmmaking to a select and professionally close-knit group of director-masters allowed this artistic agenda to endure.

The fundamental precondition to the enabled director was the director-centered mode of production. The Soviet film industry did not have producers, and only directors had the creative and technical expertise to make films. This unique expertise, which was hard to replicate, put directors in a formidable position vis-à-vis the party-state.[6] The director-masters expected strong authorship rights, considered themselves entitled professionals, and—regardless of party membership—were politically passive. They were not an ideal group to rely on to mount a controlled mass propaganda cinema.

The Director-Centered Mode of Production

Stalinist intolerance of imperfection precluded industry modernization and solidified what I call the director-centered mode of production. In Hollywood,

---

3. Ian Christie, "Canons and Careers: The Director in Soviet Cinema," in Taylor and Spring, *Stalinism and Soviet Cinema*, 142–170; and Natacha Laurent (*L'œil du Kremlin*) have written about the status of the director. Both describe the joint contributions of the directors and the party-state as coauthorship.

4. On the relationship between the intellectuals and the party-state under Stalin, see Katerina Clark, *Petersburg: Crucible of Cultural Revolution* (Cambridge, MA: Harvard University Press, 1998); Nikolai Krementsov, *Stalinist Science* (Princeton, NJ: Princeton University Press, 1997); Kiril Tomoff, *Creative Union: The Professional Organization of Soviet Composers, 1939–1953* (Ithaca, NY: Cornell University Press, 2006); Serhy Yekelchyk, "Diktat and Dialogue in Stalinist Culture: Staging Patriotic Historical Opera in Soviet Ukraine, 1936–1954," *Slavic Review* 59, no. 3 (2000): 597–624; Sheila Fitzpatrick, "Introduction," *Stalinism: New Directions*, ed. Sheila Fitzpatrick (London: Routledge, 2000), 6–7.

5. For similar arguments in regard to writers, see Lazar' Fleishman, *Boris Pasternak i literaturnoe dvizhenie 1930-kh godov* (St. Petersburg: Akademicheskii proekt, 2005); Sarah Pratt, *Nikolai Zabolotsky: Enigma and Cultural Paradigm* (Evanston, IL: Northwestern University Press, 2000).

6. The mechanism of power through expertise has been described for intellectuals in general by Jerome Karabel, "Towards a Theory of Intellectuals and Politics," *Theory and Society* 25, no. 2 (1996): 220, and for Soviet experts in particular by Francine Hirsch, *Empire of Nations*.

for example, film production underwent several successive organizational systems, starting with the "director" system (1907–1909) and "director-unit" system (1909–1914) when directors were in charge of everything from organization to editing and there were no producers. As the complexity and volume of production grew, the Hollywood mode of production switched to the "central producer" system (1914–1931), which introduced a studio producer and limited the director's responsibilities to executing the shooting script. In the 1930s this system expanded into the "producer unit," when each studio had multiple specialized producers, and in the mid-1950s the producer unit evolved into the "package unit," when films were financed on a film-by-film basis.[7]

In the Soviet film industry, in contrast, the mode of production never evolved beyond the director-unit system. Starting in the 1920s, the director was in control of all aspects of production, often initiating the screenplay and frequently in charge of executing the final cut.[8] Soviet cinema did not operate on the incentive of profit, and no producer—or manager responsible for the efficient allocation of studio resources, who could challenge the authority of the director—was ever introduced. The process that led to the Soviet domestic and international successes of the 1920s was not a Hollywood-style mass production and division of labor but the "artisanal" mode largely inherited from the prerevolutionary period. Moreover, the people who made Soviet film famous in the 1920s were film directors, not writers, stars, producers, or studios. In the 1930s, due to underinvestment in the workforce and institutions, Soviet cinema retained director-centered production, an approach where film production was staked almost entirely on successful directing talent.

From 1933 when Shumiatskii introduced his director selectivity policy, the film industry was largely limited to the pool of talent that emerged from the avant-garde 1920s or immediately thereafter. Such figures as Eisenstein, Dovzhenko, Pudovkin, Barnet, Kozintsev, Trauberg, and Ermler—all the 1920s "greats" with the exception of Abram Room, Lev Kuleshov, and Dziga Vertov, whose participation did become less pronounced—remained industry leaders in the 1930s and 1940s. This

---

7. David Bordwell, Janet Staiger, and Kristin Thompson, *The Classical Hollywood Cinema: Film Style and Mode of Production to 1960* (New York: Columbia University Press, 1985), parts 2 and 5. These types of labor arrangements have been used to describe other filmmaking environments. For example, Colin Crisp has shown that, in contrast to Hollywood, the system that dominated the French film industry since the 1920s was the package unit. Colin Crisp, *The Classic French Cinema, 1930–1960* (Bloomington: Indiana University Press, 1993), chap. 6.

8. Kristin Thompson has written about this lack of a division of labor in the Soviet film industry in the 1920s. Kristin Thompson, "Early Alternatives to the Hollywood Mode of Production: Implications for Europe's Avant-Gardes," *Film History* 5 (1993): 396–401.

first "Soviet" generation was closely tied to the second generation—Romm, Aleksandrov, Iutkevich, Gerasimov, the Vasil'evs, Raizman, Savchenko, Lukov, Aleksandr Stolper, and Konstantin Iudin—and most directors in both groups made their first films between 1924 and 1934. These individuals became the backbone of Soviet film production for the duration of the Stalin period, while many other film directors active in the early 1930s could no longer get film projects.[9]

After 1933 there were too many directors working in the industry at any given moment (compared to the volume of production). In addition, in 1938 the cinema administration ranked all feature directors "directors" (90 individuals), "second directors" (85 individuals who were a type of assistant director without the right for independent production), and "assistant directors" (270 individuals). Those in the first group were further assigned three categories: "highest," "first," and "second."[10] Since then, only those in the "highest" category (about 20 directors) were considered trusted "masters."[11] Periodically, those who were not directing "quality" films got fired, demoted, or moved to nonfiction filmmaking.[12]

The possibility of entry by new talent was severely restricted. According to Pudovkin, out of 143 individuals who graduated from the directing department of the State Cinema Institute (VGIK) between 1936 and 1951, only 23 were able to get directing work.[13] Given that film production shrank over time, new entrants' chances of being assigned a feature were extremely low. Out of 54 nonchildren's features produced and released between 1948 and 1952, only one was directed by a complete newcomer: the 1944 VGIK graduate and Eisenstein's student Boris Buneev. Young directors also had few chances to make short films to launch their careers, for the production of shorts had been curtailed as well.[14]

Being granted the right to work on independent productions only made the position of the select group of masters stronger. Together these directors—many of

9. John Rimberg reports that in the period between 1918 and 1952, 58 percent of all Soviet films were made by only 18 percent of Soviet film directors (Rimberg, *Motion Picture in the Soviet Union*, 121). Also see Christie, "Canons and Careers," 166; Iumasheva and Lepikhov, "Fenomen 'totalitarnogo liberalizma,'" 128. For a list of directors who made the most films between 1921 and 1931, the "pre-Soviet" generation that preceded Eisenstein's, see Youngblood, *Movies for the Masses*, 40.

10. Kossovskii, *Sovetskaia kinematografiia*, 295–296. The numbers (as of 1941) are from Iumasheva and Lepikhov, "Fenomen 'totalitarnogo liberalizma,'" 128 and 143 n.21; and Anderson et al., *Kremlevskii kinoteatr*, 618.

11. Anderson et al., *Kremlevskii kinoteatr*, 617.

12. For such a move at Mosfilm in 1940, see RGALI, f. 2453, op. 1, d. 1, ll. 26–29. The same or similar document (RGALI, f. 2456, op. 4, d. 69, ll. 26–32) is cited in Fomin, *Letopis' rossiiskogo kino, 1930–1945*, 687–688. See also Anderson et al., *Kremlevskii kinoteatr*, 500.

13. Pudovkin, *Sobranie sochinenii*, 2: 383–384. See also, Miller, *Soviet Cinema*, 146–147.

14. On this, see Al. Dovzhenko, "Odin iz glavnykh voprosov," *Pravda*, October 20, 1936, 4; Dubrovskii, "O 'predelakh' i vozmozhnostiakh sovetskoi kinematografii," 23–27.

whom were still in their thirties in the 1930s—brought their filmmaking practices and artistic convictions into the Stalin period. Among these was the expectation that the director was the principal creative force behind the film and also its principal author. As shown in chapter 2, by the end of the 1930s directors were much less likely to write their own screenplays, but they continued to actively find subjects and screenwriters to work with. If a film failed to satisfy official opinion, the director personally was blamed for the failure. This "director hegemony," as the screenwriter Mikhail Bleiman and others have called it, made it difficult to impose thematic planning, for directors were reluctant to produce material that was not theirs.[15]

Shumiatskii's master-centered policy, as discussed in the previous chapters, emerged under the influence of Stalin's general policy toward the technical and creative intelligentsia. In 1934 Stalin, and after him Zhdanov, also "anointed" Soviet writers, and by implication all artists, "the engineers of human souls." Artists had the power to inspire the masses and were expected to use this power to help the party leadership transform Soviet society into a communism-inspired civilization. Accordingly, Soviet artists had the status of an elite group, comparable to that of the party apparatus and to the country's top engineers and scientists. They were expected to manage their own affairs and develop their own content. This idea that artists were "engineers of human souls" explains why the Soviet leaders encouraged self-governance in cinema and other arts and why their expectations of the artistic elite were unrealistically high. It also explains why failures by artists were poorly tolerated and why the party leadership launched periodic campaigns to remind artists of their role.[16]

Shumiatskii's addition to the director-centered mode and talent stagnation was to establish patronage relationships with several directors who had access to him over the heads of their more immediate superiors, such as studio heads.[17]

---

15. M. Bleiman, "Podriadchik ili organizator?" *Kino*, March 4, 1933, 3; B. Alpers, "Kinodramaturgiia i rezhissura," *Kino*, July 10, 1933, 2. See also Youngblood, *Soviet Cinema in the Silent Era*, 168.

16. See, e.g., Katerina Clark, "Engineers of Human Souls in the Age of Industrialization: Changing Cultural Models, 1929–1941," in *Social Dimensions of Soviet Industrialization*, ed. William G. Rosenberg and Lewis H. Siegelbaum (Bloomington: Indiana University Press, 1993), 248–263. Clark offers another, related explanation of self-governance: according to the Bolshevik doctrine, in a classless society, the state was expected to "wither away" at some point. Katerina Clark, *The Soviet Novel: History as Ritual* (Bloomington: Indiana University Press, 2000), 18–19.

17. As Joan Neuberger showed in her talk, "Making *Ivan the Terrible*" (the Society for Cinema and Media Studies Conference, Seattle, March 22, 2014), the relationship between the filmmaker and the top cinema executive was often one of patronage. On patronage under Stalin see, e.g., Sheila Fitzpatrick, "Intelligentsia and Power: Client-Patron Relations in Stalin's Russia," in *Stalinismus vor dem Zweiten Weltkrieg: Neue Wege der Forschung*, ed. Manfred Hildermeier and Elisabeth Muller-Luckner (Munich: Oldenbourg, 1998), 35–54; Kirill Tomoff, "'Most Respected Comrade . . .': Patrons, Clients, Brokers, and Unofficial Networks in the Stalinist Music World," *Contemporary European History* 11, no. 1 (2002): 33–65.

FIGURE 3.1   Boris Shumiatskii with the stars of *Jolly Fellows*, friends, and family, c. 1934. *Seated, from left*: Liia Shumiatskaia, Shumiatskii's wife; Liubov' Orlova; Fania Mal'skaia (Guseva), a family friend; and Boris Shumiatskii. *Standing, from left*: Vladimir Nil'sen, Leonid Utesov, and Nora Shumiatskaia, Shumiatskii's daughter. I am grateful to Boris Lazarevich Shumiatskii for helping me identify Shumiatskii's relatives and the friend. RGALI, f. 2753, op. 1, d. 65, l. 8. Used with permission.

Despite his famous disdain for Eisenstein in particular, which was completely mutual, Shumiatskii patronized several major filmmakers and was close friends with Ermler, Aleksandrov, and Vladimir Vainshtok (see figure 3.1).[18] Starting with *Counterplan* (Lenfilm, 1932), Shumiatskii and his deputies personally supervised major prestige productions through direct contact with directors and singled out Lenfilm in particular for their patronage. Shumiatskii's deputy Sutyrin spent months at Lenfilm working with the crew of *Counterplan*, the film later widely considered the immediate precursor to *Chapaev*, and Shumiatskii traveled to Leningrad to watch and support the film at its first studio screening.[19] Direct access to Shumiatskii gave directors greater operational freedom and better resources. In September 1936, for example, Aleksandr

18. See, e.g., Anderson et al., *Kremlevskii kinoteatr*, 462–477.
19. Sh. Akhushkov, ed., *Vstrechnyi: Kak sozdavalsia fil'm* (Moscow: Kinofotoizdat, 1935), 42, 167.

Medvedkin wrote to Shumiatskii inviting him for some fish soup on location of *Chudesnitsa* (*The Miracle Worker*) and requesting 3,000 meters of foreign-made film stock that "you with V. A. Usievich allotted to me during our last meeting." In his friendly response, Vladimir Usievich, Shumiatskii's deputy, wrote that the stock had been sent.[20] Shumiatskii's favoritism also meant he trusted the judgment of some directors, giving them a lot of free reign in their productions.

Indeed, from 1936 on the whole of Soviet film production was run from Moscow as essentially one studio. The heads of the Soviet cinema administration, Shumiatskii, Dukel'skii, and Bol'shakov—key intermediaries between the filmmakers and the party-state—acted as quasi-central producers. With the help of their staff, they personally signed off on screenplays and launched and released every film. However, since actual productions under them were distributed among over a dozen studios, each with its own process, it was impossible for the chief administrator to execute operational control over every production. Dovzhenko suggested in 1941 that one reason why Soviet cinema had such low output was because a single person was entrusted with supervising all films and that person could not handle more than forty titles per year.[21]

At the studios, productions were executed by production units (*s"emochnaia* or *tvorcheskaia brigada, gruppa*, or *kollektiv*) headed by a film director (or a two-member director team). The director was the only permanent member of director-units, but many directors tended to work with the same people: cameramen, assistant directors, production administrators, actors, screenwriters, and so forth.[22] Although studios had their own top executives, these served as midmanagers rather than powerful producers, and many decisions were made in negotiation between the film director and the center, bypassing or with the agreement of the studio head.

Studio chief executives were generally party appointees with little cinema experience who had to rely on their subordinates and film directors to make

---

20. Gosfilmofond Archive, f. 3, op. 2, d. 2770, ll. 38 ob and 41.

21. Iumasheva and Lepikhov, "Fenomen 'totalitarnogo liberalizma,'" 133–134.

22. Alternatively, Vladimir Nil'sen wrote somewhat self-servingly: "The basic unit of the Russian cinema system is the team of Director and Cinematographer. They work together as co-producers jointly supervising every detail of production from story to scoring and sharing in the film's profits." Vladimir S. Nielsen, "Director-Cameraman Team Basis of Soviet System," *The Film Daily*, August 15, 1935, 9. Reports indicate that directors sometimes lured cinematographers to work on productions with them by promising to share their royalties, paid informally. N. Naumov-Strazh, "Svoevremennoe meropriiatie," *Kino*, January 15, 1939, 3. This extended "authorship" to the cinematographer. On Soviet cinematographers as auteurs, see Philip Cavendish, *The Men with the Movie Camera: The Poetics of Visual Style in Soviet Avant-Garde Cinema of the 1920s* (New York: Berghahn Books, 2013).

decisions.[23] This diminished their standing in the eyes of both the filmmakers and the central leadership in Moscow. Efim Dzigan reported in *Pravda* in 1936: "Studio [heads] are nearly always incapable of independently resolving even the simplest of issues. Under today's system, the [studio head] is not a responsible one-man manager but some kind of a relay entity, devoid of personality, will, right, or responsibility. As a matter of fact, he is responsible neither for the screenplay nor for the selection of the major creative personnel to make a film. Neither can he manipulate the raw materials—the film stock allotted to the studio. He has no right to even produce a film advertisement poster. The Main Cinema Administration [GUK] passes, approves, and disperses everything."[24]

Heading a Soviet studio was no enviable job. The central cinema administration and republic officials constantly attacked studio executives for failing to produce good films and fulfill the plan. Not surprisingly, the turnover among studio heads was extremely high. Here is how Mikhail Romm described his experience with Mosfilm studio executives while making his first film, *Boule de suif* (*Pyshka*, 1934): "I began filming *Boule de suif* in August 1933, but in October a new studio chief was appointed and he shut down the picture. Soon he was replaced, but the new studio chief did not resume the shooting. I had to wait some more. Studio chiefs then changed often. This top executive too was replaced. The picture was reinstated and I completed it successfully in June 1934."[25] High turnover in the mid-1930s resulted from the shortage of managers throughout the Soviet economy.[26] In the later 1930s the problem was exacerbated by the arrests of party-member managers under the Great Terror.

In 1936 several top directors voiced the idea of completely independent management by directors: to eliminate GUK and studios and establish instead a system of director-headed independent production enterprises.[27] A semblance of this idea was realized in the 1960s in the form of "creative units" (*tvorcheskie ob"edineniia*), production units headed by directors and semi-independent from their host studios. In fact it can be argued that the Soviet version of director-centered auteur cinema (*avtorskoe kino*) originated under Shumiatskii.

---

23. The situation was similar in other industries. Hiroaki Kuromiya, "Edinonachalie and the Soviet Industrial Manager, 1928–1937," *Soviet Studies* 36, no. 2 (1984): 185–204.

24. E. Dzigan, "Prikazy vmesto rukovodstva," *Pravda*, October 15, 1936, 4.

25. Romm, *Besedy o kino*, 14.

26. David Hoffman writes that according to some reports, in 1936 70 percent of factory top managers served in their positions for no longer than two years (Hoffmann, *Stalinist Values*, 63).

27. I. O., "Bol'nye voprosy kino," *Izvestiia*, December 9, 1936, 4; Anderson et al., *Kremlevskii kinoteatr*, 373.

The Rise and Fall of the Film Producer, 1931–1938

In the 1930s an attempt was made to introduce producers to reshape the director-centered mode. From the 1920s to 1931 director units were directly responsible to the studio artistic (or production) director, an administrator in charge of productions and deputy to the studio head. From 1931 to 1938 Soviet studios also used a version of a "producer-unit" system, in which several director-units were unified under one "producer" into the so-called artistic-production units, the KhPOs (*khudozhestvenno-proizvodstvennye ob"edineniia* or *kusty*).[28] This innovation was introduced to promote the production of mass fiction films, to keep the director in check, and to answer Stalin's call for one-man management. Ten KhPOs were formed at the future Mosfilm in 1931, at least four operated at Lenfilm in 1934, and three at the Kiev studio in 1933. The KhPOs were organized by the type of film its units tended to produce. For example, in 1931 one of the KhPOs at Mosfilm specialized in the defense film, another in the technical-instructional film, and yet another in animation. Most other KhPOs worked on a variety of features. They affiliated screenwriters and trained apprentices.[29] Under this system, the studio head and the KhPO producers along with the film directors were responsible for the film before the central cinema administration.

The KhPO producer, *direktor* in Russian, was different from the *direktor kartiny* (production administrator), a post that existed throughout the Soviet period and was an administrative position within the director-unit equivalent to the modern-day production manager or line producer.[30] The production administrator was in charge of scheduling and budgeting, as well as of coordinating

---

28. I use the term "producer" here to differentiate the Russian KhPO *direktor* from studio heads, film directors, and production administrators. The term, rendered as *prod'iuser*, *produser*, and *produsser* in Russian, was used to apply to the heads of KhPOs in 1935–1938 only sporadically. Yet it was certainly well-known by then. Moisei Aleinikov, a long-standing member of Mezhrabpomfilm leadership, considered himself a producer. See also Lev Anninskii, "Iz zhizni prodiusera," *Kinovedcheskie zapiski* 79 (2006): 41–120, and 80 (2006): 6–109 on Aleksandr Anninskii, who administered KhPO #4 at Mosfilm. I am grateful to Natalie Ryabchikova for sources on both Aleinikov and Anninskii.

29. E. Kuznetsova, "Ne stroit' na peske," *Kino*, February 21, 1933, 2; E. K. "Nakanune stsenarnogo proryva," *Kino*, May 28, 1933, 2; Fomin, *Letopis' rossiiskogo kino, 1930–1945*, 218–219. The screenwriter Aleksei Speshnev worked in the producer-unit that joined together Aleksandr Macheret, Iulii Raizman, Mikhail Romm ("unofficially"), and the screenwriters Boris Lapin and Zakhar Khartsevin (RGALI, f. 2372, op. 14, d. 59, l. 99). See also Babitsky and Rimberg, *Soviet Film Industry*, 83–87.

30. The term *administrator*, used in the 1920s and early 1930s, was replaced by *direktor gruppy* and then *direktor kartiny* in the late 1930s. Multiple administrators worked on a film, especially if it was a prestige production: the KhPO head had a deputy, and so did the production administrator. Anninskii, "Iz zhizni prodiusera," *Kinovedcheskie zapiski* 79.

the work of the unit with various studio departments and with local authorities in case outside resources were used. It was desirable that the production administrator was a party member (i.e., someone capable of performing censorship functions as well), but such cadres were in very short supply.[31] The power dynamic between the director and the production administrator depended on the individuals involved, but as a rule the latter answered to the former. It turned out that the same happened to the KhPO "producers" as well. When describing production flow at the studios in the 1930s, Paul Babitsky writes: "[The director's] duties began as soon as a scenario was approved by the studio and the organs of censorship. First the film director drew up for approval a financial plan, a filming schedule, and suggested drawings and models. After work started, although every [production unit] was theoretically headed by its own chief, in practice the film director retained complete and direct control over every operation of every group under his general supervision."[32]

According to the Lenfilm studio head at the time, Leontii Katsnel'son, KhPOs were created to address the problem of the "extreme deficiency" in production administrators by adding an additional supervisor to the production unit. He explained that production administrators were "predominantly purely operational workers with executive functions, who had neither the organizational ability nor sufficient cultural level and political authority to become genuine one-man managers and unit production organizers, especially in units headed by major masters." However, he said, the KhPO producers also failed to live up to expectation: "At this moment [1936] it may be considered firmly established that the organization of KhPOs does not solve this problem, as KhPO [producers] are unable to control the production life of all of their pictures and, as a result, work organization inside production units and even work discipline itself in many cases have deteriorated." He warned that Lenfilm was facing the elimination of the KhPO producers and reverting back to a system in which key administrative responsibility rested with the production administrator. He concluded, however, that for it to work this time around, the studio needed workers to reinforce the managerial ranks.[33] Ivan Kudrin, the head of Ukrainfilm, reported in 1933 that there were "no people" to head the Kiev studio's three KhPOs. He added that his attempts to find at least one person who could supervise film production had failed.[34]

31. Allentina I. Rubailo, *Partiinoe rukovodstvo razvitiem kinoiskusstva: 1928–1937* (Moscow: MGU, 1976), 172–173.

32. Babitsky and Rimberg, *Soviet Film Industry*, 83.

33. TsGALI, f. 257, op. 13, d. 29, ll. 9–10.

34. RGALI, f. 2456, op. 1, d. 86, l. 10. For Shumiatskii's repeated requests for additional managers for all levels of the industry, see Anderson et al., *Kremlevskii kinoteatr*, 207, 244.

In 1938 the KhPOs were abolished and the mode of production reverted back to the director-unit system. The lack of qualified personnel must have been a key factor in this change. Under the conditions of shrinking output, it also made more sense to continue to rely on directors than to train new cadres of genuine producers. It did not help that with the demise of Shumiatskii and his Hollywood-inspired reforms, the concept of the "producer" came under suspicion as "kowtowing" to the West and director hegemony continued.

Studio heads, their staff, and production administrators were the three administrative control layers of weaker managers between the director and the center. There were also strictly party supervisors: local party officials outside the studio and the head of the studio party cell. However, the multiplicity of supervisors and their lack of specialization diminished the authority of each individual one, forcing the directors to look for reliable guidance and patronage further up the hierarchy. Under Stalin, in lieu of the producer-driven model, film directors and the leadership of the central cinema administration jointly managed film production. In addition to patronage and a weak division of labor, the director-centered mode incorporated the institution of director self-governance.

Director Self-Governance

From the 1920s on, in addition to the director-unit structure of production, Soviet studios incorporated a body—depending on the period, the artistic bureau, creative board, creative section, directors' board, or artistic council—that advised the studio head and evaluated the studio product before it was shown to outsiders. These peer-criticism institutions emerged thanks to the principle of collectivism at the workplace (socialist ideology presupposed unionization and employee self-governance), but they played a particularly sizable role in filmmaking due to the lack of producers.

In the early 1930s these studio advisory bodies comprised a variety of professionals. For instance, when in 1934 the Lenfilm artistic bureau discussed Iosif Prut's screenplay *Zolotoi pesok* (*Golden Sand*), those present included Lenfilm's artistic director Adrian Piotrovskii, the studio head's assistant for production B. Obnorskii, the film directors Leonid Trauberg, Il'ia Trauberg, and Dubson, the screenplay editors Messer and Krinkin (or Krynkin), the director of KhPO No. 2 Aleksandr Gorskii, and a certain Slepkov.[35] By the mid-1930s Mosfilm and Lenfilm also formed directors' boards, which, apart from film directors, included

---

35. TsGALI, f. 257, op. 10, d. 18, l. 19.

representatives of other creative professions as well. For instance, in February 1936 Lenfilm paid the following individuals for serving on its directors' board: the directors Ermler, Georgii Vasil'ev, Leonid Trauberg, Il'ia Trauberg, Iutkevich, Vladimir Petrov, and Pavel Petrov-Bytov, the actor and director Vladimir Gardin, the set designer Evgenii Enei, the cameraman Andrei Moskvin, and the screenwriter Bleiman.[36] By the later 1930s meetings of the Lenfilm artistic bureau seem to have been replaced by meetings of the directors' board. Piotrovskii and Messer were typically present, but administrators were no longer invited.[37]

Despite his bureaucratic inclinations, Shumiatskii's successor, Semen Dukel'skii, kept the style of personnel management practiced by his predecessor. After assuming office, he met with representatives of every director-unit (the director and the production administrator) from Mosfilm and likely other studios as well.[38] Dukel'skii also took steps to expand creative-worker self-governance to the central level. In January 1939 he instituted a Screenplay Council attached to his office to help him manage screenplay selection. The prominent screenwriters Vishnevskii and Petr Pavlenko, the directors Mikhail Chiaureli, Il'ia Trauberg, Romm, and Pudovkin, as well as the writer and prominent literature functionary Aleksandr Fadeev staffed the Council.[39] Apparently Dukel'skii also planned to form a central Artistic Council, an idea that was only realized in 1944.[40] Moreover, in August 1938 studios started to recruit directors into executive positions: Lenfilm, for example, formed a Sector for Artistic Management with producer functions and appointed Sergei Vasil'ev deputy studio director for artistic affairs.[41]

Ivan Bol'shakov went further. In March 1940 he ordered the creation of the Artistic Councils at five major studios—Mosfilm, Lenfilm, Kiev Studio, Tbilisi Studio, and Soiuzdetfilm—"to engage creative workers' active participation in artistic-creative work of studios."[42] The studio Artistic Councils were composed of members of the creative professions and were dominated by film directors. For instance, as of November 1940 the Mosfilm Artistic Council included all

36. TsGALI, f. 257, op. 12, d. 43, l. 33.

37. TsGALI, f. 257, op. 12, d. 43.

38. Romm, *Besedy o kino*, 60.

39. "O sostave stsenarnogo soveta KDK," *Biulleten' Komiteta po delam kinematografii pri SNK Soiuza SSR* 4 (1939): 12. The Cinema Section of the Soviet Writers' Union proposed that this council be created in February 1936 (RGALI, f. 962, op. 3, d. 67, l. 16).

40. Anderson et al., *Kremlevskii kinoteatr*, 501.

41. "Sektor khudozhestvennogo rukovodstva," *Kino*, August 5, 1938, 4; also cited in Fomin, *Letopis' rossiiskogo kino, 1930–1945*, 568.

42. "O sozdanii khudozhestvennykh sovetov pri direktorakh kinostudii khudozhestvennykh fil'mov," *Biulleten' Komiteta po delam kinematografii pri SNK Soiuza SSR* 6 (1940): 19–20.

the studio's leading talent: the directors Eisenstein, Romm, Raizman, Pyr'ev, Pudovkin, Aleksandrov, Dzigan, Grigorii Roshal', and Aleksandr Macheret, the screenwriter Kapler, the cameramen Boris Volchek, the set designer Boris Dubrovskii-Eshke, and others. Similarly, among the members of the Lenfilm Artistic Council were the directors Ermler, Sergei Vasil'ev, Georgii Vasil'ev, Kozintsev, Trauberg, Petrov, Zarkhi, Kheifits, Gerasimov, and Rappaport, the screenwriter Bleiman, the set designer Nikolai Suvorov, and the composer Dmitri Shostakovich.[43] The Artistic Councils met weekly and their responsibilities included consideration and approval of the studio's thematic plans, literary scenarios, director's scenarios, rushes, and rough cuts.[44]

In addition, after the banning of *The Law of Life* in August 1940, Bol'shakov approached the Central Committee and received permission to appoint prominent directors as artistic directors (*khudozhestvennye rukovoditeli*) of major studios. Soon Eisenstein became the artistic director of Mosfilm, Ermler of Lenfilm, Iutkevich of Soiuzdetfilm, Dovzhenko of the Kiev Studio, Chiaureli of the Tbilisi Studio, and Amo Bek-Nazarov of the Erevan Studio.[45] At the same time Bol'shakov appointed Romm artistic director of the cinema administration's Feature Production Department.[46] If we conceive of Soviet feature production as one operation run from Moscow, as I have suggested we might, these appointments amounted to Romm sharing the central-producer functions with Bol'shakov and six top directors becoming unit-producers.

These moves must have been partly instigated by a letter on the dismal situation in the industry, which Leonid Trauberg, Sergei Vasil'ev, Romm, Ermler, Aleksandrov, and Kapler sent to Stalin in the summer of 1940. Writing on behalf of all filmmakers, they blamed the industry's poor performance on the extreme centralization of cinema leadership, where neither they nor their studios, the agents and institutions that actually made films, were trusted to make decisions. Asking for greater independence, given their mandate, and frustrated with the growing risk aversion at the center, they wrote: "Those who make pictures of the greatest political importance and who are called to solve great artistic and political questions in art find themselves under conditions of petty tutelage and

43. Fomin, *Letopis' rossiiskogo kino, 1930–1945*, 686.

44. RGALI, f. 2453, op. 2, d. 505, ll. 4–5.

45. Fomin, *Letopis' rossiiskogo kino, 1930–1945*, 683.

46. Romm was subordinate to the head of the Feature Production Department (*Glavnoe upravlenie po proizvodstvu khudozhestvennykh fil'mov*, GUPKhF, or the Main Administration for Feature Film Production, a unit within the cinema administration), who was subordinate to Bol'shakov. Bol'shakov also applied to appoint Ermler his deputy, but this request was rejected (Fomin, *Letopis' rossiiskogo kino, 1930–1945*, 681).

haughty mistrust and consequently are deprived of the opportunity to fully realize themselves creatively."[47]

By appointing directors to executive positions Bol'shakov "solved" the problem of the perpetual shortage in experienced managers. Notably, however, directors were essentially appointed to manage themselves. In June 1941, acting as a studio producer stealing talent from a competitor, as well as someone responsible for all of Soviet cinema, Eisenstein invited Lenfilm's top directors Kozintsev and Trauberg to Moscow to work at Mosfilm, and with him specifically. He proposed that Kozintsev take upon himself responsibility for Mosfilm's actors and that Trauberg tackle Mosfilm's screenwriting. He said, "We would love and pamper you, but more important we would work on the great, serious, and real task. We can get done literally anything (*mozhno sdelat' bukval'no vse*). We are limited only in ability and people."[48]

Scholars have referred to the Bol'shakov self-governance policies as a curious instance of "totalitarian" or "timid liberalism."[49] Clearly, receiving more decision-making power from the party-state felt liberating to the creative personnel.[50] However, although this policy pursued cooperation from the filmmakers, the main impulse behind it was not to give them license to rule themselves. The objective was to put them in the leadership's shoes, forcing them to see their practice from the party-state's perspective. Here is how Romm reflected on the self-governance policy: "Many thought that the organization of the Artistic Councils and the appointment of artistic directors would lead to a certain 'golden age,' meaning directors would be freed from any norms, regulations, and so on. The opposite turned out to be the case. The creative workers who were recruited into executive positions grasped their responsibility before the state and started to actively fight for creative discipline. Today we witness a fundamental destruction of the years-entrenched psychology in some directors, who consider themselves 'free artists' unbound by deadlines, money, or plans."[51]

Much of Romm's responsibility as artistic director for feature production at the Cinema Committee, and his peers as artistic directors of studios, became to manage "deadlines, money, or plans." Yet director-executives were asked to

---

47. Artizov and Naumov, *Vlast'*, 446–448; Fomin, *Letopis' rossiiskogo kino, 1930–1945*, 673–674.

48. Fomin, *Kino na voine*, 82–84.

49. Iumasheva and Lepikhov, "Fenomen 'totalitarnogo liberalizma'"; Fomin, *Kino na voine*, 36–37.

50. See, e.g. Iumasheva and Lepikhov, "Fenomen 'totalitarnogo liberalizma,'" 131–32.

51. "Soveshchanie aktiva rabotnikov khudozhestvennoi kinematografii," *Za bol'shevistskii fil'm*, April 16, 1941, 1.

make censorship decisions as well.[52] At the end of 1940, having just become the artistic director of Mosfilm, Eisenstein took a risk-averse position when discussing which director, Dubson or Faintsimmer, should be entrusted with the prestige biopic *Kotovskii* (Faintsimmer, 1942): "The tragic fate of this year has shown that every director needs guidance. The story of this year has assigned to us a colossal responsibility. We should give productions only to those directors who present less risk. We should listen more to the doubts 'contra' than to the doubts 'pro.' If I have this responsibility, I would think that [Dubson, a less experienced director] should not be given this assignment."[53]

Director self-governance continued through and after the war. Romm stayed as the Cinema Committee artistic director for feature production until 1943. The film director Mikhail Kalatozov replaced Romm until 1946 and then served as Deputy Minister of Cinema from 1946 to 1948.[54] As for the studio artistic directors, they continued to play their executive roles, but did not become managers, bureaucrats, or censors. Moreover, their identity as directors, and as peers to the people they were supposed to manage, interfered with their executive obligations. In 1946 Sergei Vasil'ev, then the artistic director of Lenfilm, said to his colleagues, "What does this mean to be artistic director of a studio where such directors as Trauberg, Ermler, and so forth work. Each of them is his own artistic director. It'll be all the same. You'll do what you want."[55] The artistic director was one among equals, hardly the strong censor-producer the party-state needed.

By establishing self-governance in the early 1940s, Bol'shakov diluted his own authority but gained little in film quality. In September 1944, to reinforce self-censorship, Bol'shakov created the Cinema Committee Artistic Council, which was sometimes called the Big Artistic Council to differentiate it from those at the studios. The Resolution on the Artistic Council stated that it was created "to attract creative workers in the field of cinema to the functioning of the Committee for Cinema Affairs." All but four of the Big Artistic Council's twenty-nine members were major film directors (nine), actors, writers, theater directors, and composers. The four noncreative members, other than Bol'shakov, were the secretary of the Soviet Writers' Union and former Propaganda Department official

52. Laurent, *L'œil du Kremlin*, 253. Laurent's book offers an excellent account of the Artistic Councils.

53. RGALI, f. 2453, op. 2, d. 506, l. 5.

54. Kalatozov was partly appointed due to his tenure in Hollywood (1943–1944) as a Soviet cinema representative, on which see Valerii Golovskoi, "Mikhail Kalatozov—poltora goda v Gollivude," *Kinovedcheskie zapiski* 77 (2006): 271–298; Fomin, *Kino na voine*, 586–620.

55. TsGALI, f. 257, op. 16, d. 1354, l. 158.

Dmitrii Polikarpov, and the major generals and military historians Mikhail Gal-aktionov and Nikolai Talenskii.[56] The Artistic Council met bimonthly to discuss and order changes to screenplays, competed films, and thematic plans, and to review rushes, film scores, and screen tests. Bol'shakov chaired the Artistic Council, and the only authority that could overturn a decision by the Artistic Council was the Central Committee. In 1946 the second composition of the Artistic Council—now under the newly established Ministry of Cinema—presented a reduced version of the trend toward creative self-governance: ten out of thirty-four members were film directors, eighteen were other creative workers, and three—besides Bol'shakov (the chair), Galaktionov, and Talenskii—were highly positioned bureaucrats.[57]

The involvement of party officials, and Stalin and Zhdanov personally, in film affairs is often seen as an example of totalitarian control. However, the party-state's persistent attempts at delegating industry supervision to top experts through self-governance show that the party leadership's involvement was supposed to be minimal. Indeed, after the Central Committee attack on literature in 1946, when Soviet writers asked Zhdanov to appoint a leader to supervise them, Zhdanov reportedly responded, "In your works you teach us how to govern, you show us both bad and good party workers, so you yourselves should supervise and advance your own professional affairs." Bol'shakov informed filmmakers that same year that Stalin had told him the exact same thing about cinema governance.[58]

Only after 1946 did creative-worker self-governance erode. The 1947 composition of the reconstituted Artistic Council comprised no filmmakers, and Bol'shakov was no longer a member. Only two film directors—Savchenko and Chiaureli—as well as Bol'shakov were members of the 1949 and 1951 versions.[59] Even in the absence of filmmakers, however, the Artistic Council could fail to censor correctly, and the Central Committee banned two films approved by the Council in 1947, two in 1948, and one in 1949. The only person who could get it "right" every time was Stalin. This is why in the late Stalin period, Stalin became the best patron a director could have. Although only Chiaureli found himself in this "ideal" patronage situation—Stalin systematically read the screenplays to

56. Fomin, *Kino na voine*, 430–432.
57. Artizov and Naumov, *Vlast'*, 557–558.
58. Parfenov, *Zhivye golosa kino*, 377.
59. Anderson et al., *Kremlevskii kinoteatr*, 610; Artizov and Naumov, *Vlast'*, 620–621, 788 n.35.

his films—the surest way to get a film released was by getting access to Stalin, bypassing Bol'shakov and the Artistic Council.[60]

The Masters' Lobby

Access to Stalin was granted infrequently and only to a very few. Eisenstein, Aleksandrov, and Dovzhenko met with Stalin several times throughout Stalin's reign, and for years Dovzhenko considered Stalin his personal patron.[61] Stalin also changed Eisenstein's fate at least once. When, after the banning of *Bezhin Meadow* (1937), Shumiatskii told Stalin that Eisenstein should not be allowed to work as a director, Stalin reversed this decision and instructed Shumiatskii to give Eisenstein a film (which became *Aleksandr Nevskii* in 1938).[62] There were also occasions where filmmakers found themselves in a position to negotiate with Stalin and got their way to some degree. It is well known that Stalin personally communicated to Eisenstein why he did not like *Ivan the Terrible*, part 2 (1945). It is also well known that Eisenstein did not change his conception, and the film remained banned during Stalin's life. Eisenstein was not the only director capable of standing up to Stalin in at least some way. Romm reported that around 1952 he refused when the head of Mosfilm told him he was being assigned *Aleksandr Nevskii*, a new film, now in color, on the subject of Eisenstein's film. The executive "grew pale" and said, "Don't you understand who made this request? . . . Write the letter yourself. I won't commission myself with passing on your reply." Romm wrote to Stalin. He said that *Ivan the Terrible*, part 2, was criticized for its makers' ignorance about Ivan's historical period. Likewise, he knew the period of Aleksandr Nevskii poorly. Two weeks later Bol'shakov offered Romm a film about Mikhail Kutuzov and Napoleon and told him that Stalin found his reasons meritable, saying, "If he knows Russian history starting with the eighteenth century, let him make *Kutuzov and Napoleon*."[63] We will never know whether it was possible to negotiate further. These events took place soon before Stalin's death, and the project to remake

---

60. The notorious NKVD Chief Lavrentii Beria was also Chiaureli's patron.

61. Stalin's involvement with individual films and filmmakers is well described. See Mar'iamov, *Kremlevskii tsenzor*; Evgenii Gromov, *Stalin: Vlast' i iskusstvo* (Moscow: Respublika, 1998). On Dovzhenko in particular, see Vance Kepley, Jr., *In the Service of the State: The Cinema of Alexander Dovzhenko* (Madison: University of Wisconsin Press, 1986); George O. Liber, *Alexander Dovzhenko: A Life in Soviet Film* (London: BFI, 2002).

62. Anderson et al., *Kremlevskii kinoteatr*, 417–420, 424–425.

63. Romm, *Besedy o kino*, 281. *Aleksandr Nevskii* was included in the 1953 film industry plan; Aleksandr Ivanov was listed as the director (Anderson et al., *Kremlevskii kinoteatr*, 904). It was never made.

historical-biography films in color died with Stalin. Yet the episode suggests that at least some Soviet directors had enough authority to occasionally negotiate even with Stalin. Although Eisenstein and Romm were clearly exceptional in this regard, the possibility reflected the elite status of the Soviet director more generally.[64]

The strength of Soviet filmmakers was not only in their patronage relationships with Stalin, Shumiatskii, and Bol'shakov, in their status as select masters and "engineers of human souls," and in their unique creative and organizational expertise in film production. It was also that despite whatever personal dislikes they had, they acted as a group and could present a unified front when this was necessary to protect their profession. In December 1935 twenty-nine directors, screenwriters, and cinematographers, including Dovzhenko, Pudovkin, Ermler, Romm, Barnet, Iutkevich, and Protazanov, signed an appeal "To all workers of Soviet cinema" to demonstrate their support for Shumiatskii and Soviet Hollywood. Calling themselves "cinema activists," the filmmakers argued on the pages of the central newspaper *Izvestiia* that without an upgrade Soviet cinema was not ready to fulfill the task set before it on the world stage. "What ought to be and what will be our place in world art?" they asked. Their answer was that the international status of Soviet cinema impelled it to produce eight hundred films, diverse in purpose and genre but sincere and high in quality. To achieve this goal, Soviet cinema was to overcome its primitive technology and organization and develop an army of screenwriters, film actors, and managers.[65]

Shumiatskii did his part in promoting Soviet filmmakers' international identity. During the December 1935 conference, he arranged for such Hollywood luminaries as Charlie Chaplin, Lewis Milestone, Frank Capra, and Cecil B. DeMille to send them their greetings.[66] Shumiatskii's demise did not stop the filmmakers from exchanges with Hollywood. In 1939 the newspaper *Kino* publicized a telegram that Eisenstein and over forty leading Soviet filmmakers had sent to Chaplin on the occasion of his fiftieth birthday, as well as Chaplin's response.[67] Eisenstein stayed in contact with several of his Hollywood peers throughout his life.[68] Eisenstein, of course, was an international celebrity and,

---

64. According to Romm, he also refused to make a biopic about Ivan Pavlov, whose screenplay he consulted (Romm, *Ustnye rasskazy*, 93–94). *Academician Ivan Pavlov* was made by Grigorii Roshal' in 1949.

65. Vsevolod Vishnevskii et al., "Boevye zadachi sovetskogo kino," *Izvestiia*, December 6, 1935, 4.

66. "Moskva. GUKF. Tov. Shumiatskomu," *Kino*, December 16, 1935, 1.

67. Eisenstein et al., "SShA. Gollivud. Charli Chaplinu," and "Khello, Charli!" *Kino*, April 17, 1939, 2; "Charli Chaplin—sovetskim kinematografistam," *Kino*, April 23, 1939, 3.

68. Sergei Kapterev, "Sergei Eisenstein's Letters to Hollywood Film-Makers," *Studies in Russian and Soviet Cinema* 4, no. 2 (2010): 245–253.

as Katerina Clark has suggested, considered himself (rightly) part of the world cultural process.[69] This too must have helped his status and perhaps survival domestically.

The lobby also got together to protect the profession in December 1938. In a letter to Molotov, the nominal head of the Soviet government, twenty-seven directors wrote to protest Dukel'skii's new compensation system. They opposed the reform because it stripped them of authorship fees (*avtorskie otchisleniia*), which, as they said, amounted to denying them authorship rights. They proposed equalizing screenwriters and directors in terms of authorship. Otherwise, they argued, the director might be viewed as a mere technician, and that went against "the interests of Soviet art."[70] Although this appeal did not prevent Dukel'skii from implementing the change, the complaint was a strong statement from the profession that helped directors to reconfirm their status and perhaps allowed them to negotiate a better compensation package than what Dukel'skii had originally intended.[71]

The directors' successful lobbying efforts and direct access to Stalin were outcomes of the institutional structures discussed above: the director-unit system, talent stagnation, weak management, and director self-governance. Stalin's structural role as the ultimate patron, as well as his uncompromising expectations, earned Stalin, erroneously, the reputation as the chief "producer" of Soviet cinema.[72] Stalin did not act as a producer in any systematic sense, and his interactions with the filmmakers were quite limited. Yet Stalinist policy did enable a select group of masters to act on their international status, unique expertise, and the perceived role as "engineers of human souls," thus allotting directors a surprisingly large role in the course of Soviet cinema compared with other, nominally freer contexts, such as Hollywood. This institutionally enabled director, however, was a particularly poor match to the ideological goals of the party-state, for the backgrounds and convictions of Soviet directors conflicted with Stalinist agenda, making it difficult for the directors to deliver on Stalin's wishes.

---

69. Katerina Clark, *Moscow, the Fourth Rome: Stalinism, Cosmopolitanism, and the Evolution of Soviet Culture, 1931–1941* (Cambridge, MA: Harvard University Press, 2011), 31.

70. Anderson et al., *Kremlevskii kinoteatr*, 516–519.

71. Dukel'skii reported that once the filmmakers knew what their actual compensation would be, they accepted it (Anderson et al., *Kremlevskii kinoteatr*, 520–523).

72. Fomin, "Sovetskii Gollivud," 98. On Stalin as patron, see also Sarah Davies, "Stalin as Patron of Cinema: Creating Soviet Mass Culture, 1932–1936," in *Stalin: A New History*, ed. Sarah Davies and James Harris (Cambridge, UK: Cambridge University Press, 2005), 202–225.

The Masters and the Standard of Quality

It is possible that Soviet filmmakers operated as a group because it was far safer: it was less likely that all of them would be arrested at once for a collective misdeed. However, what also allowed the filmmakers to act as a group was their identification with a cause independent of the Stalin party-state: the Soviet filmmaking tradition. Even if they considered themselves Soviet artists working under Stalin, they also remained loyal to the 1920s venerable tradition of revolutionary art that had an international reputation of its own. To paraphrase Yuri Tsivian, to these filmmakers cinema was architecture; Stalinism was furniture.[73] The masters continued to view their practice in formal and artistic terms even as their films contributed to the Soviet political moment. Such institutions as ARRK (the Association of Workers of Revolutionary Cinema, 1924–1935), thematic conferences, Artistic Councils, the newspaper *Kino*, the journal *Iskusstvo kino*, VGIK, and the Moscow and Leningrad Houses of Cinema (*Doma kino*), where they met regularly, all served as productive forums.[74]

Mikhail Kalatozov once said, "A creative worker, Stalin's contemporary, has to be a philosopher-Stalinist. He has to be a Bolshevik in the form and spirit of his mentality."[75] Philosopher-Stalinists most Soviet film directors (and other filmmakers) were not. Politically the leading directors were only the regime's sympathizers. They were traditional intellectuals rather than political activists. A 1931 Soiuzkino report on the ideological standing of Soviet directors stated that only 10 percent of all directors, "from the political, social, and industrial points of view, [were] fully qualified to meet the requirements of Soviet cinema during the reconstructive period," whereas the rest were "fellow travelers" (*poputchiki*).[76] Although over time many leading directors became party members—membership was often required to hold administrative positions and to travel abroad—by 1930 only Ermler was a card-carrying Communist. Their singular preoccupation was cinema.[77] As Petr Bagrov writes, even Ermler liked to say that he had three "births": his literal birth in 1898, joining the party

---

73. Speaking about cultural explanations for cinematic phenomena, Tsivian writes, "Cinema is architecture; culture is its wallpaper." Yuri Tsivian, "New Notes on Russian Film Culture Between 1908 and 1919," in *The Silent Film Reader*, ed. Lee Grieveson and Peter Krämer (London: Routledge, 2004), 347.

74. On ARRK in particular see Natalie Ryabchikova, "ARRK and the Soviet Transition to Sound," in *Sound, Speech, Music in Soviet and Post-Soviet Cinema*, ed. Lilya Kaganovsky and Masha Salazkina (Bloomington: Indiana University Press, 2014), 81–99.

75. RGALI, f. 2456, op. 1, d. 1339, l. 6.

76. RGALI, f. 2497, op. 1, d. 48, ll. 175–176.

77. For some it was probably easier to identify as an artist than as a Stalinist.

in 1919, and becoming a film director in 1923, and that "art and not the party was his final station."[78]

Not surprisingly, throughout the Stalin period film directors displayed unsure judgment when ideology was concerned. In 1933 Shumiatskii said that the creative cinema workers were receptive to party policy, but confused by it. "A humongous political-education effort is required if, given the extraordinary limited number of qualified masters, we are to produce by their hands entertaining, ideological, and artistically high-quality pictures."[79] Indeed, in Shumiatskii's view some filmmakers were "hopeless" and could never be reeducated.[80] Eisenstein topped Shumiatskii's list of the hopeless, but in 1934 his office also wrote that Kuleshov was a "glaring representative of dying cinema Bohemia"—who worked in Soviet cinema "insincerely" and who was incapable of "reorienting himself toward properly Soviet thematics."[81]

None of this was true of course. It was only that Eisenstein, Kuleshov, and their peers put art above politics and, as such, were formalists. That, despite Shumiatskii's frustration, these fellow travelers and formalists were entrusted with the fate of Soviet cinema made a difference in terms of what this cinema became. As long as Eisenstein was watching their films, Soviet filmmakers could not completely abandon the tradition of innovation he helped establish in the 1920s. Moreover, they did not have to. It was not only that for Eisenstein and his peers the Soviet film canon, to use Ian Christie's terminology, never changed, but also that, thanks to their unique institutional status, they *were* the canon.[82] This indispensability of the filmmaking old guard prevented Soviet cinema from deteriorating artistically.

It is common to associate the end of avant-gardism and outright "formalism" in Soviet cinema with 1934. That year the Writers' Union Congress established socialist realism as the "method" of Soviet artistic production, and Georgii and Sergei Vasil'evs made *Chapaev*, a film often considered a turning point toward

---

78. Petr Bagrov, "Zhitie partiinogo khudozhnika," *Seans* 35/36 (2008), http://seance.ru/n/35-36/jubilee-ermler/zhitie-partiynogo-hudozhnika.

79. Anderson et al., *Kremlevskii kinoteatr*, 207.

80. Shumiatskii referred to Eisenstein and Pudovkin this way in 1936 (Anderson et al., *Kremlevskii kinoteatr*, 396).

81. RGALI, f. 2456, op. 4, d. 10, ll. 138–141, cited in Fomin, *Letopis' rossiiskogo kino, 1930–1945*, 303.

82. Christie, "Canons and Careers." I also agree with John Rimberg, who said, objecting to the view that Eisenstein was "in a class by himself": "It would be more correct to consider Eisenstein an extreme case of a personality structure common to most talented artists" working during this period. Rimberg, *Motion Picture in the Soviet Union*, 213.

socialist realism in Soviet cinema.[83] The filmmaking community, however, did not see *Chapaev* as an interruption. Instead the filmmakers used *Chapaev*'s success and the rhetoric of the moment to reaffirm their film tradition and develop a principle compatible with both their own convictions and socialist realism: artistic quality.

Chapaev was a story about the civil war commander Vasilii Chapaev (1887–1919). As opposed to some 1920s masterpieces such as *Potemkin*, *Chapaev* had a conventional plot focused on well-rounded characters and was both heroic and entertaining in tone. Stalin personally hailed *Chapaev* as a great achievement, signaling that Soviet cinema was entering the right socialist-realist path. The filmmaking community, however, viewed *Chapaev* as both a fortunate accident and a logical development on its past history.[84] Eisenstein in his article "At Last!" said that *Chapaev* opened the new, fourth five-year period in the history of Soviet cinema. This period synthesized—at last!—the best achievements of the second (1924–1929) and the third periods (1930–1934) by merging these periods' opposing preoccupations: poetry and prose, epic ethos and character psychology, plotlessness and story-bound plotting, and stylization and emotion, respectively. Almost equating the film with the April 1932 Central Committee resolution on the literary organizations, Eisenstein wrote that *Chapaev* put an end to the feud of periods in cinema.[85] Eisenstein, Shumiatskii, and others charted the genealogy of *Chapaev* to *Potemkin*, which was its "grandfather," *Mother* (1926), which was its "grandmother," and *Counterplan* (1932), which was its "father."[86]

Chapaev was very popular, and by 1934 the avant-gardists knew that to succeed domestically they needed to attract popular audiences. According to Eisenstein's definition, the 1930–1934 period was the training ground when Soviet cinema learned to engage Soviet audiences. Iutkevich, one of the directors of

---

83. *Chapaev* had a number of "socialist-realist" precursors. On this, see Vincent Bohlinger, "Compromising Kino: The Development of Socialist Realist Film Style in the Soviet Union, 1928–1935" (PhD diss., University of Wisconsin–Madison, 2007).

84. Sergei Iutkevich reported that when the Vasil'evs took on the project, Lenfilm treated it "with much skepticism." When the semi-completed film was screened for the Lenfilm artistic board, its members concluded that the rushes "were gray and visually uninteresting" and left "little hope for a major picture." It was only when the Lenfilm community saw the completed picture that they were "stunned" by it. Sergei Iutkevich, *Kino—eto pravda 24 kadra v sekundu* (Moscow: Iskusstvo, 1974), 223. Viktor Shklovsky wrote retrospectively, "*Chapaev* appeared logically, but all of a sudden." Viktor Shklovsky, *Za 60 let: Raboty o kino* (Moscow: Iskusstvo, 1985), 241.

85. Sergei Eisenstein, "Nakonets!" *Literaturnaia gazeta*, November 18, 1934, reprinted in Eisenstein, *Izbrannye proizvedeniia v shesti tomakh*, vol. 5 (Moscow: Iskusstvo, 1968), 48–52.

86. RGALI, f. 962, op. 3, d. 66, l. 7. It needs to be noted that the Vasil'evs themselves did not agree with this ancestry and saw only their own films, and specifically *Lichnoe delo* (*A Personal Affair*), as *Chapaev*'s precursors. Zil'ver, *Za bol'shoe kinoiskusstvo*, 102–116.

Counterplan, who belonged to the second generation of Soviet filmmakers, admitted that his early films fell flat with the audiences because all he wanted was to satisfy the masters of the first generation, including Eisenstein. As if apologizing for his departures from avant-gardism in *Counterplan*, he said that he made the film the way he did because of his overwhelming "thirst" for a popular audience.[87] The Vasil'evs were Eisenstein's students and learned their craft reediting foreign films for Soviet distribution in the 1920s. Partly thanks to this pedigree, in contrast to *Counterplan*, *Chapaev* was treated not as a retreat but as a step forward without abandoning the past. According to Eisenstein, with *Chapaev* Soviet cinema entered its "classical period," where "classical" stood for the highest possible *quality* in artistic work.[88]

Chapaev's "classical" mixture of mass appeal and artistic sophistication, however, proved extremely difficult to achieve, as could be seen in the peer reception of *Chapaev*'s close counterpart and another Lenfilm production, *Yunost' Maksima* (*The Youth of Maksim*, 1935). *The Youth of Maksim*, a biography of a "typical" Bolshevik, partially inspired by the figure of Shumiatskii himself, was completed a month after *Chapaev* and became another surprise hit.[89] The film was directed by Kozintsev and Trauberg, leading avant-gardists from the 1920s, and it was seen as their step away from their roots toward socialist realism. Although the majority of peers saw this transition as welcome, some believed that, not unlike *Counterplan*, *The Youth of Maksim* went too far, betraying the tradition. At a discussion organized by the newspaper *Kino* and attended primarily by writers and critics, Kozintsev and Trauberg were accused of eschewing their good taste and stylistic purity, producing a cold and didactic film, and making major artistic sacrifices in order to achieve realism.[90] Dovzhenko reported that he had heard that "the directors had made a spectacularly bad picture that excited no one" (an opinion with which he disagreed).[91] Some even believed *The Youth of Maksim* meant Kozintsev and Trauberg "were lost for Soviet cinema."[92] Trauberg himself admitted that the film was "a living canvas of a civil war between Kozintsev and Trauberg and Kozintsev and Trauberg."[93]

87. Zil'ver, *Za bol'shoe kinoiskusstvo*, 82.
88. Zil'ver, *Za bol'shoe kinoiskusstvo*, 22–49, 160–165.
89. Grigorii Kozintsev, "Glubokii ekran," in *Sobranie sochinenii v piati tomakh*, vol 1. (Leningrad: Iskusstvo, 1982), 208.
90. BETA, "V sporakh o tvorcheskom metode," *Kino*, December 22, 1934, 2. See also RGALI, f. 2923, op. 1, d. 1a, l. 2.
91. Zil'ver, *Za bol'shoe kinoiskusstvo*, 74.
92. RGALI, 2923, op. 1, d. 1a, ll. 31–32.
93. Zil'ver, *Za bol'shoe kinoiskusstvo*, 51.

Filmmakers discussed the virtues of both films during the January 1935 cinema conference called to celebrate the fifteenth anniversary of Soviet cinema. The anniversary of the 1919 cinema nationalization decree was actually in 1934, but Shumiatskii delayed the festivities until after *Chapaev* and *The Youth of Maksim* had been completed.[94] The conference was devoted to the future of Soviet cinema, but the executives and the filmmakers who spoke at the conference had slightly different visions of this future. Although everyone was expected to express their commitment to socialist realism, hardly anyone other than party officials and film executives mentioned the term. Most filmmakers spoke about what interested them: professional issues, art, and form. They agreed that future cinema was to serve the nation and that this service amounted to accessibility. But accessibility was to include such aesthetic notions as simplicity, expressivity, and beauty. In fact, the filmmakers used the conference to reconcile *Chapaev*'s audience-engagement strategies with the avant-garde tradition of formal mastery, and validated both.

Simplicity (*prostota*) was particularly singled out as a concept that could bridge old experimentalism and new accessibility. Leonid Trauberg noted, "My utmost dream is that no one can see how something was shot. This does not mean rejecting good-quality shooting. Yet utmost mastery is achieved when neither the set designer nor the cameraman are noticeable."[95] The cameraman Andrei Moskvin, Kozintsev and Trauberg's frequent collaborator, said simplicity was not "simplification" but "a certain more perfect form." Using Iutkevich's term for simplicity, "streamlined form," he added that this form was "law-based," "precisely calculated," and difficult to achieve. Simplicity also required cinema to harmoniously merge the efforts of the screenwriter, director, cameraman, actor, and everyone else.[96]

The filmmakers were speaking of a kind of classicism that required great mastery and effort, and in his closing address Eisenstein made this explicit.[97] In addition to masterful simplicity, they agreed it was time to replace episodic storytelling practiced in the 1920s with more accessible and mature plot-based forms. Greater attention to the screenplay was to help in this effort. They decided that the editing-based (montage) aesthetic was only one of the means of cinematic expressivity, and that other means—acting, plotting, cinematography, staging, and sound—were to be employed in the future. Yet everything had to answer to

---

94. *The Youth of Maksim* was released on January 27, 1935, but many present at the conference had seen it prior to release.

95. Zil'ver, *Za bol'shoe kinoiskusstvo*, 57.

96. Zil'ver, *Za bol'shoe kinoiskusstvo*, 151–152.

97. Zil'ver, *Za bol'shoe kinoiskusstvo*, 160–165.

the standard of quality established by the 1920s masterpieces. If anything, artistic quality was to advance.[98]

What emerges from these discussions is a collective anxiety that socialist realism and a greater emphasis on politically appropriate themes would lead to the loosening of formal mastery, and this should be prevented. As we saw in chapter 1, however, the language of quality and high artistic standards was also part of the official discourse. According to the Central Committee's 1931 resolution, the objective of Soviet cinema was to reflect "the heroic struggle for socialism and the heroes of this struggle; the historical path of the proletariat, its party, and its unions . . . in works of exemplary high art" (*v vysokikh obraztsakh iskusstva*).[99] The Central Committee's address to the 1935 conference read in part: "The Central Committee impels the workers of cinema to not rest content with what has been achieved, to fight for highly artistic (*vysoko-khudozhestevnnye*) pictures that educate the masses in the spirit of socialism, are loved by the masses, and are intelligible to them."[100] "Artistic" here meant accessibility and polish, while "high" connoted both ideological commitment *and* formal craftsmanship. At the conference Shumiatskii's deputy Iukov said: "We understand simplicity in art not as a striving to do away with high artistic technique or with any work with form . . . ; on the contrary, we summon you to great highly qualified work with the form of a film."[101] As Gorky insisted, however accessible to the masses and politically propagandistic, Soviet art had to be high art.[102]

Whether or not the filmmaking community used the language of quality strategically, this language adhered to the filmmakers' own standards. In fact it is possible that the influence went the other way. As Katerina Clark has argued, Soviet artists and intellectuals' "native" culture was high culture, and to secure their participation the Soviet party-state had to not only speak the language of high culture but also believe in it.[103]

Whatever the underlying logic, the discourse of quality became the common ground on which the party-state and the filmmakers could agree, and the effect of

98. Zil'ver, *Za bol'shoe kinoiskusstvo*.

99. Anderson et al., *Kremlevskii kinoteatr*, 156.

100. TsK VKP(b), "Rabotnikam Sovetskoi kinematografii," in *Partiia o kino*, ed. Nikolai Lebedev (Moscow: Goskinoizdat, 1939), 98 (originally in *Pravda*, January 11, 1935).

101. Zil'ver, *Za bol'shoe kinoiskusstvo*, 131–132.

102. Fleishman, *Boris Pasternak i literaturnoe dvizhenie*, 246. On the conceptual history of the Bol'shevik attitude to art, including the evolution of the notion of "artist" and "mastery," see Ben Brewster, "The Soviet State, the Communist Party and the Arts, 1917–1936," *Red Letters* 3 (Autumn 1976): 3–9.

103. Clark, *Petersburg*, 305.

this convergence was the preservation of the Soviet filmmaking tradition. Once established in the first half of the 1930s, the quality rhetoric made it possible for filmmakers to continue to justify their work—even if commissioned—on artistic grounds, thus maintaining their professional (and perhaps moral) integrity. As Savchenko said of Soviet filmmakers: "we are propagandists who work by means of art."[104] When the Central Committee banned Eisenstein's *Bezhin Meadow* as "politically bankrupt" *and* "antiartistic," the intention was to prevent political dissent, but the linking of art and politics had the effect of validating both.[105] Moreover, since the appeal to artistic quality was expressed in vague terms, the filmmakers had room for articulation. Finally, as we have seen, the inclusion of artistic quality in what constituted socialist realist art preserved the masters by encouraging the cinema administration to maintain individuals with a record of quality on staff at Soviet studios.

The Masters and the 1936 Campaign against Formalism

The language of quality and the preservation of the masters presented a major handicap in the Soviet party-state's handling of culture, as both constantly threatened to shift the balance between high art and propagandistic utility toward the former. The threat of formalism never went away, prompting Stalin and Kerzhentsev to carry out a campaign against formalism and naturalism in 1936. The campaign took many by surprise because it seemed to contradict artistic standards. What was widely recognized to be "good" (Shostakovich), *Pravda* pronounced to be "bad." The artistic community almost universally supported *Pravda* in public statements (as expected), but the secret police reported dissension. The writers, critics, and composers quoted by the secret police believed that by attacking Shostakovich the campaign attacked true art and artistic freedom. Others stated confusion and frustration with the arbitrary, amateur judgments of those in power. Some were sure the articles were *Pravda*'s overzealous mistake, which would soon be rectified by the party leadership. Yet others thought that attacking formalism was a waste of effort. A natural bedfellow of high art, formalism was indestructible.[106] Although this tiny sampling of negative opinion could not be considered representative, it suggests the Soviet artists held a certain

---

104. Fomin, *Kino na voine*, 733–734.

105. Anderson et al., *Kremlevskii kinoteatr*, 406.

106. Artizov and Naumov, *Vlast'*, 290–295; Arlen Blium, ed., *Tsenzura v Sovetskom Soiuze, 1917–1991: Dokumenty* (Moscow: ROSSPEN, 2004), 240–251.

universal artistic standard they felt was threatened by the campaign, and this made them more likely to disavow it.

In cinema the campaign produced reactions similar to those in the other arts. Behind the scenes there was a lot of confusion and anxiety. As Dovzhenko related, filmmakers were wondering if the campaign was not a return to the pre-April 1932 push for proletarian and simplified works, a new clamping down, a strike against the best art and artists, or a prohibition on all experimentation and novelty.[107] This anxiety transpired at the meetings at the Moscow House of Cinema organized to reflect on the *Pravda* initiative. Kuleshov said, for example: "When the articles in *Pravda* appeared I did not understand them and they made an unpleasant impression on me."[108] Both Kuleshov and others were surprised some of their peers were labeled formalists, although they agreed that the problem—which they took to be a failure to connect with audiences due to formal and compositional difficulty—was real.[109]

The film community was less willing than the literary community to name formalists or publicly support the articles. This task was left primarily to cinema executives, such as Shumiatskii and Grigorii Vovsy, the editor of *Kino*.[110] *Pravda* reported that at a meeting at the Committee for Arts Affairs, filmmakers "strangely" defended cinema and refused to engage in sufficient self-criticism.[111] In Leningrad the meetings organized to reflect on the campaign were inadequately attended, prompting a *Kino* journalist to conclude: "The *Pravda* articles did not receive a proper response among Leningrad filmmakers."[112] It is clear that the campaign did not have many ardent supporters. Yet it had to be reconciled with, and the reconciliation track chosen by the film community was similar to that employed during the 1935 conference. Everyone agreed that art had to serve the state. As for the formal approach, given that naturalism was often interpreted to mean poor taste and quality, it was decided that by rejecting formalism and naturalism, *Pravda* advocated for greater artistic merit.[113]

---

107. RGALI, f. 962, op. 3, d. 67, ll. 1–1 ob.

108. RGALI, f. 962, op. 3, d. 69, l. 20.

109. RGALI, f. 962, op. 3, d. 66; RGALI, f. 962, op. 3, d. 69.

110. [Boris Shumiatskii], "Iz doklada B. Z. Shumiatskogo," *Kino*, March 6, 1936, 1; G. Vovsy, "O formalizme," *Kino* 10, February 21, 1936, 3.

111. "Soveshchanie kinorabotnikov vo Vsesoiuznom komitete po delam iskusstv," *Pravda*, February 27, 1936, 4; also, "Pervye itogi," *Kino*, March 11, 1936, 1.

112. Ark. Kin., "Obsuzhdenie prodolzhit'," *Kino*, March 16, 1936, 2.

113. See articles under the general title "Protiv formalizma i naturalizma" in *Kino*, March 6, 1936, 1; March 16, 1936, 2; March 21, 1936, 3; and March 26, 1936, 2.

The groundwork for this interpretation was laid by the first article on the topic, Vladimir Nil'sen's "'Simplicity' and Simplicity." Echoing 1935 discussions, Nil'sen warned that appeals to simplicity (or, in his department, "transparent" cinematography) "could lead to simplification of the visual form of our films and to the destruction of the rich visual culture that has been accumulated by Soviet cinema throughout the years of its existence." To avoid this, he advocated for true simplicity, which, according to Nil'sen, required great mastery: "There could exist simplicity of a different kind, that which is a result of high mastery and creative perfection, a simplicity that strikes the viewer with the intelligibility and clarity with which it conveys the work's theme, images, and ideas. Achieving such simplicity is a problem of great difficulty, requiring immense artistic culture, professional experience, and a tremendous amount of work over every shot."[114]

The difference here was between surface, stylistic "simplicity" and deeper, emotional and thematic clarity, an interpretation that fit the campaign well. Moreover, in a clever preemptive move, Nil'sen's language coincided almost entirely with the language that concluded *Pravda*'s attack on cinema, the article against Ivan Kavaleridze's historical epic *Prometheus* (*Prometei*, Ukrainfilm, 1935), which was published two days later. The film dealt with the Russian imperialist policy and local revolutionary movement in the Caucasus, and it was accused of misrepresenting history. *Pravda* wrote: "[Kavaleridze] ignored the principal requirements of socialist realism. Every work of art, including a feature film, needs to be truthful, intelligible, and produced with great simplicity, which results only from high mastery."[115] Nil'sen even coined a term that combined "great simplicity" (*bol'shaia prostota*) and "high mastery" (*vysokoe masterstvo*): "artistic simplicity" (*khudozhestvennaia prostota*).[116] Shumiatskii picked up this compromise expression in his obligatory response to *Pravda* when he said that Soviet art was "the art of great artistic simplicity."[117] *Pravda* itself then used a variation on the expression by defining the goal of Soviet art as "high simplicity" (*vysokaia prostota*).[118]

---

114. Vladimir Nil'sen, "'Prostota' i prostota," *Kino*, February 11, 1936, 3.

115. "Grubaia skhema vmesto istoricheskoi pravdy," *Pravda*, February 13, 1936, 4.

116. Nil'sen, "'Prostota' i prostota."

117. [Boris Shumiatskii], "Iz doklada B. Z. Shumiatskogo," 1.

118. Iu. Iuzovskii, "O shablone i prostote," *Pravda*, February 27, 1936, 4. It is very likely that Nil'sen's and Shumiatskii's responses were coordinated, since the two were collaborators (on a book about American cinema, which was never completed), and that Shumiatskii knew the details of *Pravda*'s attack against Kavaleridze ahead of time.

Following Nil'sen's, Shumiatskii's, and *Pravda*'s formulations, the filmmaking community concluded that the ideal postcampaign works had to be useful, accessible, *and* artistically accomplished. In response to *Pravda*, Dovzhenko pledged he would produce *Shchors*, his current project, "with maximum calculation, without reducing the artistic quality of the picture, and using language that would be maximally accessible to many millions."[119] Iutkevich noted, "I understood the *Pravda* articles as an appeal to high mastery, as a war against middling works."[120] Kuleshov admitted that his primary mistake prior to the campaign was that for him "theme often served as only an excuse to put [his] creative devices into practice." His adjusted position was: "Our art, of course, needs impeccable devices. Only these devices need to be subservient to the idea of the work."[121] Artistic simplicity or intelligible quality was a mandate to produce well-made and expressive works with clear ideas and politically appropriate themes.

In 1940 Romm concluded that the change heralded by the 1936 campaign was a change in priorities: Before, the director was the priority, and after, the theme became dominant. Yet artistic standards continued to guide filmmaking practice. Romm wrote:

> Our art is far from perfect even in its best examples. The poetics of sound cinema, its specific language, has not yet been found even in our most significant films. And at this stage a number of directors often resort to forgoing much of their search for distinctive styles in favor of the most precise, clear, and unambiguous presentation of ideological tasks, while the latter [those tasks] have grown humongously. I consider this phenomenon undoubtedly progressive; yet we all know that in a perfect work of art the artist expresses himself to the end, and he should be to the end organic and completely free in his language. The problem is that we have yet to produce perfect works of art.[122]

As a result of the antiformalism campaign, by 1940 the emphasis on theme had been firmly incorporated into the practice of Soviet filmmakers, but the masters' concern over the deterioration of Soviet film quality, which resulted from this change, had also became palpable.

---

119. RGALI, f. 962, op. 3, d. 67, l. 3 ob.
120. B. Chernyi, "Diskussiia v Dome kino," *Kino*, March 6, 1936, 1.
121. Chernyi, "Diskussiia v Dome kino."
122. Mikhail Romm, "Rezhisser i fil'm," *Iskusstvo kino* 1/2 (1940): 34–36.

When in 1945 the political climate improved, the filmmakers rushed to rein-state their standards. Invigorated by the relative relaxation of the war years, they expected even greater creative freedom after the war. Nothing reflected this enthusiasm more than the first postwar issue of *Iskusstvo kino*, published in October 1945. In its lead article, Bol'shakov outlined the grand program for post-war Soviet cinema, setting the target to one hundred films a year, many of them comedies and color films.[123] Bol'shakov also discussed the quality of Soviet films, appealing for greater mastery and formal innovation in particular. He wrote:

> Our directors should definitively abandon the direct, declarative, and in-your-face resolutions of their themes. They should with great atten-tion and seriousness consider the problems of mastery and work with actors with great care and thoroughness. Our screenwriters and direc-tors should strive to make plot-based films that give our actors ample opportunities to create memorable and expressive performances and profound characterizations. Bold and insistent quest in the area of artis-tic form, summoned to represent with utmost clarity and complete-ness the idea of modernity, should be carried on in all creative branches of our cinema. Only by way of tireless perfection and mastery can we approach the creation of new outstanding works of film.[124]

Bol'shakov's piece was followed by Eisenstein's article "In Close-Up," which was entirely devoted to formal mastery. Eisenstein used the three shot scales, the long shot, the medium shot, and the close-up, as metaphors for the three critical lenses through which all Soviet films should be viewed. The "long shot" was the general sociopolitical evaluation given to films in the central newspapers. This view evaluated the film's theme, contemporary relevance, ideological position, mass accessibility, and mobilizational quality. The "medium-shot" perspective was that of the average audience member, who acknowledged the theme but was primarily interested in the story, drama, and characters. This evaluation focused on plot, acting, mood, and verisimilitude, and was something reviewers wrote about in the popular press. The "close-up" was professional criticism: the peer evaluation of the details, including the nuts and bolts of construction, editing, camerawork, dialogue, rhythm, timing, and accents. The professional critique was the domain of the specialized press (and *Iskusstvo kino* in particular) and of

---

123. Bol'shakov, "Nashi blizhaishie zadachi," 2–5.
124. Bol'shakov, "Nashi blizhaishie zadachi," 4.

the peers and experts. This close-up evaluation was primary, Eisenstein argued, but it was also the evaluation that had been relaxed in the years prior (since the closure of ARRK in 1935, he said). Yet without it, the growth and development of Soviet cinema were impossible. Moreover, it was no longer acceptable to forgive technical problems and lapses in artistic judgment because of the film's official and audience success. Let us be ruthless in our close-up evaluation of works, Eisenstein wrote, and let us not fear those who would accuse us of separating out form and content only because we point to differences in quality between theme and its representation in images. "True unity of form and content require[d] a unified perfection in both."[125]

In September 1946, on the wave of new bans, including on Eisenstein's *Ivan the Terrible*, part 2, *Pravda* attacked *Iskusstvo kino* for practicing uncritical (close-up) criticism and for publishing Eisenstein's article. It called the article erroneous and formalist for its separation of ideological content from artistic achievement, and said that the article amounted to the propagation of art for art's sake.[126] As in 1935 then, Eisenstein and the editors of *Iskusstvo kino*—Pyr'ev was the editor and Eisenstein was on the editorial board for the 1945–1946 issues—used Bol'shakov's rhetoric of mastery and quality to forcefully promote their own priority: to do everything they could to maintain and improve the formal quality of Soviet films. As if no time had passed since 1936, Pyr'ev said in 1946 that filmmakers had forgotten to be aware of formalism. Formalism, he clarified, was when a film was masterfully made but "false, fake, and harmful" in terms of ideas.[127]

Reflecting on the situation filmmakers faced after 1946, Kozintsev wrote in his memoirs:

> We had a difficult time making sense of the demands that started to be made of the screen by people who understood little about art. . . . The areas of a film director's work became increasingly narrow. Sound track became primary. Yet it was not I who was supposed to add the sound track—they wanted to add a sound track to me. The task (and I was very bad at it) was that the movements of my lips coincide with someone else's text. . . . A filmmaker of the 1920s generation, I am no longer able to select a camera position. I do not know how to edit two shots together. I am incapable of helping the performer.[128]

---

125. Sergei Eisenstein, "Krupnym planom," *Iskusstvo kino* 1 (October 1945): 6–8.
126. "Reklama vmesto kritiki," *Pravda*, September 15, 1946, 2.
127. RGALI, f. 2456, op. 1, d. 1339, l. 16.
128. Kozintsev, "Glubokii ekran," 345–346.

In terms of their professional value system, Soviet filmmakers of the 1920s generation maintained their professional standards despite the introduction of socialist realism and periodic attacks on formalism. By 1946 when it became obvious that the political demands would continue to grow, these masters started to withdraw from film production. Vsevolod Merkulov, the People's Commissar for National Security, reported to Zhdanov in 1946 that "using every excuse, [Soviet film directors] prefer being idle, working in theater, and writing screenplays to carrying out their direct responsibilities."[129] Citing secret records of conversations within the film community, he pointed to frequent complaints about impossible work conditions; yet clearly many directors were also wary of the enormous risk involved in actually working.[130] As head of the Scenario Studio, the writer Dmitrii Eremin summed up the situation in 1946: "In today's era masterpieces and artistic geniuses are impossible because speaking about what one wants to is prohibited and the confines of what is allowed are so narrow that within them no one can create anything worthy. In recent years not a single exceptional screenplay has been written. All film works are devoid of the quality of high art."[131]

Elevating the old masters in the early 1930s reinforced the tradition of quality. In 1936 and every other time when the masters felt under attack, they retreated and produced less. The tradition, however, persevered and found an unexpectedly influential expression in another institution of Soviet cinema: peer criticism. With film directors in executive-censor positions, in the 1940s decisions were influenced not just by the party-state's ideological or economic needs but also by the aesthetic preferences of the director-masters.

The Quality Standard and Peer Criticism

An artwork has at least two audiences: the artwork's consumers and the artist's peers. In the context of Soviet cinema, the consumer was split between the actual Soviet audiences and the party ideologists, including Stalin. However, before the party officials, critics, and the public viewed them, most Soviet film underwent an internal evaluation, when their makers' peers assessed the films' merits. When Iutkevich said in 1935 that he had worked not for audience approval but for the masters' praise, he was describing a common phenomenon. Peers provide a particular kind of pressure on artists. As David Bordwell reminds us, "the desire

---

129. Anderson et al., *Kremlevskii kinoteatr*, 718.
130. Anderson et al., *Kremlevskii kinoteatr*, 718–722.
131. Anderson et al., *Kremlevskii kinoteatr*, 722.

to surpass one's peers often prods artists to innovate."[132] Thanks to such peer institutions as the studio Artistic Councils, during the Stalin period peer assessment was not just informal or reputational but also a matter of record and consequence, and the desire to impress such masters as Eisenstein, who lived to 1948, continued to influence filmmaking practice.[133] Given that factors determining official success were often unpredictable, the professional peer evaluation was not only the first but also the most reliable indication of a film's merit. The primacy and greater institutionalization of the peer evaluation in the Soviet film industry made it far more important as compared to that in other, more commercial contexts. Soviet filmmakers tended to make their films for one another as much as they did for the state (and the audience). This made it only more difficult for the party-state to force filmmakers to focus on message over form.

Between 1940 and 1944, before the formation of the central Artistic Council, the studio Artistic Council was a peer-criticism institution making principal decisions on most films. As the studio head Nikolai Lotoshev told members of the Lenfilm Artistic Council soon after its creation, they were to act as "the studio bosses and the bosses of the rushes under review."[134] This was particularly the case when the Council considered costly but failing productions that needed to be salvaged. The studio head was always present and actively participated in the Council meetings, but decisions were made jointly. The decisions were passed on to Bol'shakov for approval, but Bol'shakov's opinion was highly contingent on the Artistic Council's judgment (or these opinions tended to converge). Moreover, on occasion Bol'shakov's staff approached the Mosfilm Artistic Council to consider films made by studios that did not have Artistic Councils, as was the case with the controversial and ultimately banned Tashkent Studio production *Veselei nas net* (*We Are the Merriest*, Aleksandr Usol'tsev-Garf, 1940).[135] In the absence of producers, members of Artistic Councils were asked to perform producer functions—to administer productions, cut costs, improve rough cuts, doctor scripts, censor, test-screen, and critique the studio's films. However, in practice they acted primarily as peer critics with a "close-up" perspective, for

---

132. David Bordwell, *On the History of Film Style* (Cambridge, MA: Harvard University Press, 1997), 222.

133. Lev Anninskii writes that a film always received two evaluations: the official one, "as mandated," and the unofficial but real one, meant only for the insiders. Anninskii, "Iz zhizni prodiusera," *Kinovedcheskie zapiski* 80: 28. The institutions of peer criticism, however, allowed the latter to seep through.

134. TsGALI, f. 257, op. 16, d. 919, l. 92.

135. RGALI, f. 2453, op. 2, d. 507, l. 41.

most of their comments fell under the rubric of artistic and professional evaluation, and they had less to say on the film's political relevance.

Take, for example, Barnet's *The Old Jockey* (1940, screenplay by Nikolai Erdman and Mikhail Vol'pin), a comedy set on a collective farm that raised racehorses. The film portrays an aging jockey who feels that his old age (sixty) has made him professionally useless, but who finds a new calling as a jockey trainer. *The Old Jockey* was banned by the Central Committee as "false and ideologically harmful" with the following justification: "[The film] portrays Soviet reality in a perverted manner, and is a slander against the collective-farm system and the Soviet people. The film mocks everything that characterizes the new collective village (the physical-education culture, radios, cars, etc.). Decent Soviet people in the picture are shown to be emphatically stupid and are given the vile qualities of greed, competitiveness, envy, and petty-bourgeois mentality. The collective farm is shown as a haphazard mob of eccentrics—who lead an idle existence."[136]

When the Mosfilm Artistic Council reviewed the film's rushes at 70-percent completion, hardly any of these flaws were noted. Instead the Council members and Barnet's peers worried about the film's rhythm and pacing, casting and acting, haphazard compositions, empty backgrounds, insufficient expressiveness, excessive footage, and limited shot-scale coverage. They did not recognize Barnet's masterful hand in the rushes, thought he was working in a hurry, and recommended that Barnet, who was present, "work on raising the visual aspect of the picture to a high level." That said, the Council members were supportive of the film and expressed confidence it would end up exciting, funny, and fresh. Raizman specifically noted that although the screenplay's eccentric characters had alarmed him, in the rushes he saw "the people of today." Only glimpses of the future problems surfaced during the discussion. Pudovkin noted that all the characters seemed to have a lot of free time, and there was "something not quite normal about this." Semenov, the head of Mosfilm's screenplay department, also asked Barnet to be careful not to turn some of the film's characters into simpletons.[137]

Bol'shakov later lamented that the Mosfilm Artistic Council did not do its job to prevent the banning of Barnet's film.[138] Yet the banning was difficult to predict, especially once the film was already in production. As was often the case with film bans, the problems were with the very premise of the project. Although

136. Fomin, *Letopis' rossiiskogo kino, 1930–1945*, 698.
137. RGALI, f. 2453, op. 2, d. 169.
138. RGALI, f. 2456, op. 1, d. 710.

we do not know with absolute certainty why the Central Committee banned *The Old Jockey*, the reasons could have ranged from how the Soviet people were represented (as officially stated), to the film's emphasis on horseraces (a "bourgeois" leisure preoccupation not worthy of Soviet citizens), to Stalin's self-consciousness about his age.[139] As Vladimir Zabrodin suggests, Stalin turned sixty in 1938 and the idea of a "useless" sixty-year-old might have seemed offensive to him.[140]

Members of the Artistic Council were no different from Barnet himself in determining the political safety of the screenplay, and there was little reason to expect greater foresight from them. As the actor (and star of *The Youth of Maksim*) Boris Chirkov once noted, filmmakers believed their task was to give pleasure to audiences, and there were other people who were in charge of making sure that everything was correct politically.[141] The only job Soviet filmmakers could accomplish successfully was to give peer support and artistic evaluation. This maintained the artistic norms of Soviet cinema, but did not help the films' censorship future.

Indeed, a system of decision-making that relied heavily on the opinions of filmmakers promoted those projects that the filmmakers liked for artistic reasons and hindered those that might have been politically useful but were not artistically promising. In May 1940 the Lenfilm Artistic Council supported the comedy *Muzykal'naia istoriia* (*The Musical Story*, 1940). Gerasimov, Ermler, Zarkhi, and Arnshtam were all very pleased with the film, and Kozintsev called it a "first-rate picture." Lotoshev noted that it was expertly edited and welcomed the film's screenwriters, the writers Evgenii Petrov and Georgii Munblit, to the Lenfilm family. Trauberg, who liked *The Musical Story*'s tempo and dialogue, said "the authors discovered quite a lot from the point of view of cinema."[142] The film was directed by two top experts: Aleksandr Ivanovskii, who started making films in 1918 under the tutelage of Protazanov, and Gerbert Rappaport, who immigrated to Soviet Russia in 1936 at Shumiatskii's invitation and had previously worked in Europe as assistant director to G. W. Pabst. Yet Zhdanov later criticized *The Musical Story* (which was not banned), along with other films, for simplifying Soviet reality and cultivating frivolous attitudes to labor among the Soviets.[143]

---

139. Viktor Shklovsky mentioned the totalizator (or betting more generally) as the reason for the ban. Milena Musina, "'Tut Barnet pereklikaetsia s siurrealizmom!' Stenogramma zasedaniia sektsii teorii i kritiki pri Dome kino, May 28, 1945," *Kinovedcheskie zapiski* 57 (2002): 146.

140. V. V. Zabrodin and E. A. Misalandi, "'Sovetskaia komediia—eto svetlyi put' Barneta,'" *Kinovedcheskie zapiski* 45 (2000): 108. On the film, see also Anna Kovalova, "Kinodramaturgiia Nikolaia Erdmana," in Nikolai Erdman, *Kinostsenarii* (St. Petersburg: Masterskaia Seans, 2010), 28–32.

141. RGALI, f. 2456, op. 1, d. 1238, l. 34.

142. TsGALI, f. 257, op. 16, d. 919, ll. 138–149.

143. Fomin, *Kino na voine*, 21.

In contrast, when ten days earlier the Lenfilm Artistic Council discussed Matvei Tevelev and Semen Polotskii's screenplay *Molodoi chelovek* (*A Young Man*), directors rejected this politically promising screenplay because it was below average artistically. Lotoshev and the editor-censors Nikolai Kovarskii and Zhezhelenko thought the screenplay contained some useful ideas. Zhezhelenko, who reported on the screenplay, said that Marx had shown that bourgeois society had split the human being into the citizen and the private individual, with the emphasis on the latter. Most Soviet screenplays too emphasized the private individual, whereas *A Young Man*, in contrast, showed people as heroes and citizens. The response of the directors was the opposite. In Kozintsev's words, "It was torture reading [the screenplay] to the end, and I thought literally in horror: What if a film based on it is actually made? This is deadly dull and hackneyed." Trauberg too was categorically against the screenplay, while Arnshtam said it had little to do with art. Lotoshev decided to reject the screenplay, though acknowledging its "very good theme."[144]

A similar pattern of filmmaker-censor discrepancy reproduced itself in the Big Artistic Council. Since the majority of the 1944 Council members and one-third of the 1946 Council members were filmmakers, the Artistic Council, although often highly critical in details, on the whole tended to protect film directors, undermining its censorship role. In 1946 the Central Committee banned or reprimanded *Ivan the Terrible*, part 2, *A Great Life*, part 2, *Prostye liudi* (*Ordinary People*, Kozintsev and Trauberg, 1945), and *Bliznetsy* (*Twins*, Konstantin Iudin, 1945) on ideological grounds.[145] Yet all four had passed Artistic Council review and were deemed major artistic achievements by executives and peers. When the Council met to ruminate on its "mistakes" in judgment, it was admitted that, in Pyr'ev's words: "While thoughtfully and comprehensively discussing the formal-artistic and narrowly professional qualities of films, we have begun to forget and have paid insufficient attention to what *matters most*—their ideological direction, their ideological purpose. We have begun to forget the agitation-educational significance of each of our films for our people and their propaganda importance for the whole world."[146]

Kozintsev and Trauberg's *Ordinary People* provides an excellent example of how the Big Artistic Council evaluated films and why it so often failed ideologically. The discussion of *Ordinary People* was full of praise for the film's artistic merits. The film told the story of an airplane factory in the Central Asian rear

---

144. TsGALI, f. 257, op. 16, d. 919, ll. 118–126.

145. Anderson et al., *Kremlevskii kinoteatr*, 732.

146. RGALI, f. 2456, op. 1, d. 1339, l. 13 (emphasis in the source).

during the war, interweaving it with the personal stories of the factory employees affected by the war. At the start of the Artistic Council meeting, one of its members, the actor-director Boris Babochkin (the star of *Chapaev*), related his subcommission's evaluation of the film.[147] The subcommission found that "on the whole" the film was "undoubtedly" "a talented and engaging work," but identified several flaws that could be easily corrected. The recommended corrections, however, ranged from minor (to eliminate Stalin's signature under the order to produce a plane ahead of schedule and to reshoot or eliminate a speech by the factory director) to quite major: To rewrite and reprint most titles (they were "boring" and technically poorly executed), to reconceive or delete a central scene where the factory director learns that his wife will live (the scene was too "melodramatic"), to correct the confusion of what seemed like a double ending, and to readjust the performances or replace two actors playing side characters. The response of the artist-members (Romm, Sergei Vasil'ev, Aleksandrov, Chirkov, the actor Nikolai Okhlopkov, and Simonov) to this evaluation was strongly negative. They found the recommendations bureaucratic and taste-based. They said the film was artistically strong, extraordinarily moving, and masterfully acted, with some of the actors giving performances yet unmatched in Soviet cinema. They believed the film was also unusually brave and honest: it showed ordinary people and their actual hardship during the war. They wanted *Ordinary People* to be released as soon as possible. The meeting took place on November 9, 1945, and there was some concern that, since the war had ended, the film might quickly lose relevance. They had their own list of the film's blunders, which they wanted acknowledged for the record but considered forgivable.

The nonartist members of the Council pushed back. In response to the others' praise, they mounted new critiques, which together, according to Galaktionov, "possibly call[ed] into question the film as such." Why, they asked, was the film called *Ordinary People* when it centered on a factory director? Was this really how a factory functioned under war conditions? Was this indeed "our highly principled system of leadership?" Why did the film not show collective decision-making? Why were the work processes so primitive and chaotic? What if the film is shown abroad? What would it show? That Soviet people have enthusiasm but no skill or manufacturing culture? Why could the factory director and technical experts not agree? Are conflicts between leadership and experts a reality in the Soviet Union? The criticism of nonartists operated on the level of policy and politics, in stark contrast to the artistic concerns of the creative members.

---

147. Babochkin made his first film, *Rodnye polia* (*Native Fields*), in 1944.

Bol'shakov spoke last. He noted that the film harbored "deep contradictions" and several "false spots," but was devoid of major "political mistakes." Based on this last opinion, it was decided that Kozintsev and Trauberg should think about ways to improve the picture.[148] After additional deliberations, Bol'shakov approved *Ordinary People* for release, and the film, still containing all the scenes and characters criticized by the Artistic Council, received a distribution license on December 19, 1945.[149]

In the end it turned out that the instincts of the noncreative council members were spot on from the party-state perspective: *Ordinary People* was banned for "giving a false representation of the life of the Soviet people during the war."[150] A review prepared by the Central Committee Propaganda Department stated other reasons as well—all similar to the concerns expressed by the nonartist members of the Artistic Council (the review's author had access to the transcript of the Council's meeting). First, the film failed to reflect that the movement of the Soviet manufacturing base to the rear during the war was a large-scale and organized effort carried out by many state bodies. The factory manufacturing process, as shown in the film, was primitive and disorganized, making it unclear how the factory could actually make airplanes. Second, the film tried to convince the viewer that the factory operated thanks to the factory director and not the collective. The chief engineer and the regional party secretary were presented incorrectly; both had to be shown as integral to the success of the factory. Third, the film falsely represented the work force: new workers arrived haphazardly, training was primitive, and work went on under harsh weather conditions, which could damage the machinery. Fourth, half of the action was based on the fact that the director and his wife, who escaped from the Germans, happened to end up in the same city. This was a coincidence, and it had nothing to do with the picture's theme. Fifth, many episodes designed to incite hatred of the Germans had become obsolete. The review concluded by stating that the opinions of the

---

148. RGALI, f. 2456, op. 1, d. 1067.

149. Margolit and Shmyrov, *Iz"iatoe kino*, 93. The version released on DVD contains all these scenes, even though Kozintsev reported that the film was reedited for release by a party unknown to him (93). See also Laurent, *L'œil du Kremlin*, 152–154.

150. Anderson et al., *Kremlevskii kinoteatr*, 732. See also E. Koval'chik, "Fal'shivyi fil'm," *Kul'tura i zhizn'*, July 20, 1946, 6. The film was released in 1956. Mar'iamov writes that *Ordinary People* was added to the list of condemned films in August 1946 by Andrei Zhdanov, who disliked Kozintsev and Trauberg since *The Youth of Maksim* (Mar'iamov, *Kremlevskii tsenzor*, 83). However, Aleksandr Ptushko reported that "comrade Zhdanov said that it was a fabulous film, I heard that myself, and that it was hijacked not because it was bad but because it needed additions, and Romm alone said that it was bad" (RGALI, f. 2372, op. 12, d. 79, l. 34).

Artistic Council members and of viewers at test screenings were negative, without acknowledging the overwhelmingly positive responses of the filmmakers.[151]

As the case of *Ordinary People* suggests, the gap between the filmmakers and the ideologists was insurmountable. The Council's self-assessment after the 1946 bans was that it was too liberal, too soft, and ineffective. The filmmakers dominated discussions and nonfilmmaker members' objections, although more predictive, were ignored. It was not surprising, however, that the filmmaker members tended to be lenient: they often liked one another's films and/or did not want to hurt one another's feelings. As Kalatozov said, the Council had become "a society for mutual praise."[152] This must have been why the Artistic Council was restructured in 1947 and all filmmakers were relieved of their membership duties.

Conclusion

In combination with the shrinking production program, the director-centered mode became a major impediment to the development of mass propaganda cinema under Stalin. No significant generational shift occurred during the Stalin period, and a select group of director-masters was allowed to consolidate over time. Convinced that a privileged group of creative workers should be capable of managing themselves, the party-state supported significant director contributions to creative and administrative decision-making. Their status as a self-governing elite, their reputations as world-class artists, their peer institutions, and their professional identity helped this select group of directors to maintain artistic integrity.

It is customary to associate the Stalin period with artistic stagnation. As this chapter suggests, however, the filmmaking community, and specifically film directors, never gave up on the standard of artistic mastery. They listened to the signals sent by the Soviet leadership, but then incorporated these into their own professional value system, which developed in the 1920s outside of the direct purview of the state. Using the state's discourse of quality and their peer institutions, they enforced their own shared norms of artistic merit. These norms

---

151. Fomin, *Kino na voine*, 376–377. Margolit and Shmyrov (*Iz"iatoe kino*, 93) report that the response at a House of Cinema screening was positive. Although the case of *Ordinary People* seems to show that the film was banned purely because of censorship, I hope that chapters 4 and 5 will clarify why I think censorship does not explain everything in such a case. For now, let me just note that all of the film's problems could have been resolved but were not resolved at the scripting stage.

152. RGALI, f. 2456, op. 1, d. 1339, l. 8.

often overshadowed the filmmakers' concern for the state's political agenda and made it difficult for them to conform in practical terms.[153] When in 1936 Stalin and his ideologists reminded the filmmakers that creating politically utilitarian content was their primary obligation, they could not adjust and started to stall. The complete mismatch between the task at hand—propaganda cinema—and the group of experts with authority to fulfill it—the enabled artistic elite—led to a major impasse in Soviet film output. As the next two chapters show, the director-centered mode also had a profound influence on the failures in Soviet screenwriting and censorship.

---

153. Cf. Jan Gross's assertion that the Soviet state was a "spoiler state," which prevented the association of citizens to anything but itself, as well as any forms of collective life that were not to its benefit. A spoiler state, he writes, "eradicate[d] peer pressure and the constraint of group norms except as they [we]re state sponsored." Jan T. Gross, *Revolution from Abroad: The Soviet Conquest of Poland's Western Ukraine and Western Belorussia* (Princeton, NJ: Princeton University Press, 2002), 116.

SCREENWRITING
Lack of Professionalization and
the Literary Scenario

No other area of Soviet filmmaking discourse generated as many metaphors as screenwriting. One of the most poignant metaphors of the period was the "iron" scenario. This idea perfectly captured the period's zeitgeist: It referenced both the constructivist fascination with precision machinery and Stalinist industrial construction, and it even gestured to Stalin himself, for the iron scenario was also referred to as the "steel" scenario.[1] Given the seeming fittingness of this metaphor, it is easy to assume that Soviet screenplays were indeed iron: thoroughly censored, fixed, and precisely followed. As we shall see in this chapter, however, the iron scenario was never implemented, and another set of metaphors, far less suitable to the zeitgeist—butter, margarine, and rubber—better describes what actually happened. "Butter" were original screenwriting masterpieces authored by a single author, the type pursued by the Soviet film industry but very difficult to attain. "Margarine" were well-made scripts written by multiple authors, the type that fueled Hollywood and was antithetical to Soviet cinema. To propose a Soviet variation on margarine, a butter substitute, but avoid the concept's unfavorable connotations, Grigorii Zel'dovich proposed the third option: rubber. Synthetic rubber (*kauchuk*), Zel'dovich argued, was no worse than natural rubber, and Soviet cinema too had room for any good screenplay, single-authored or not.[2]

---

1. *Stal* is the root of *stal'* (steel), from which the name *Stalin* is derived.
2. G. Zel'dovich, "Stsenarnoe khoziaistvo," *Sovetskoe kino* 11 (1935): 26–27.

In 1936 Soviet cinema rejected margarine screenplays, but instead of butter or steel it ran on endlessly flexible rubber.

The goal of mass cinema required thousands of screenplays, but such quantities were never available under Stalin. On the contrary, throughout this period cinema experienced a "scenario crisis" (*stsenarnyi krizis*), a perpetual shortage of suitable screenplays. Scholars have identified a shortage of screenwriters and censorship as the key factors responsible for the scenario crisis.[3] Yet there was no shortage in potential writers and stories. The more fundamental problem, once again, was institutional. Soviet screenwriting lacked a mechanism that could allow studios to convert potential stories into solid, censorship-proof scripts.

As in other film industries, Soviet screenwriting was split into two basic stages: the literary screenplay (the prose treatment of the film's story) and the shooting script (the shot-by-shot breakdown of the screenplay). In contrast to more industrialized contexts, however, both stages remained underdeveloped in that only the original author(s) could complete the first stage, and only the film director could write the shooting script. As a result, the Soviet screenwriting formula included only the author, the editor-censor, and the director. There was no further division of labor and authorship, and no other writing professionals could adjust the screenplay to meet censorship, thematic, or quality requirements.

This institutional arrangement was too thin to support a consistent output of ready-made screenplays on desired topics. It also made the Soviet screenplay a vulnerable format. In the absence of in-house writers, there was no one to keep the screenplay intact while it was being negotiated with the censors. Once the censors accepted the screenplay, it was subjected to a new reworking by the director, who added his own take to the material. The director's involvement meant that creative work on the story continued during and even after filming, ultimately compromising both the screenwriter's authorship and screenplay censorship. Nevertheless, since the author and the director were to be respected, instead of strengthening the screenplay by inviting specialized professionals to rewrite it, all the effort went into censoring the original. A complex censorship apparatus grew to compensate for the weak screenplay, yet censors, authors, and directors had different stakes in the format. Because it remained only an approximation of the film and was always available for more revisions, the weak screenplay became a major bottleneck in Soviet filmmaking. As figure 4.1 nicely visualizes, the Soviet screenplay itself was in crisis. It could never become a reliable contract guaranteeing the film's quality and success.

---

3. Babitsky and Rimberg, *Soviet Film Industry*; Youngblood, *Soviet Cinema in the Silent Era*.

FIGURE 4.1 M. Khrapkovskii, "Uzkoe mesto" [Bottleneck], *Kino*, October 16, 1931, 4. On the left, there are "500 Films." On the right, the banner reads "Soiuzkino Thematic Plan." The scroll in the middle reads "Screenplay."

This chapter details the practices of Soviet screenwriting and three solutions the film industry considered to solving the scenario crisis: Hollywood-style multiple authorship, the iron scenario, and the authored literary scenario. These were roughly associated with the three cinema executives: Shumiatskii, Dukel'skii, and Bol'shakov, respectively. By the end of the 1930s the industry abandoned the first two solutions in favor of the authored literary scenario. This, however, only worsened the crisis, since the authored scenario did not generate midlevel screenwriters or improve screenplay quality but further reduced the number of screenplays available. I conclude by suggesting that the ideology-driven insistence on individual authorship was the main cause for this counterproductive policy choice.

Lack of Professionalization and the Defective Author

On the brink of the 1930s there was no shortage of screenplays or individuals willing to write for Soviet cinema. Screenplay supply remained substantial in the 1930s and, as discussed in chapter 2, studios received hundreds of unsolicited submissions through the process of "drift" (*samotek*). The screenplay drift was in theory a positive phenomenon. As one industry report stated, it "ought to be considered a mass manifestation of public initiative toward the thematics of our cinema."[4] Very few of the screenplays submitted through *samotek*, however, were ideologically appropriate and ready for production. According to Pavel Bliakhin, the head of the state censorship agency Glavrepertkom, of 169 screenplays submitted by studios to Glavrepertkom in 1929 none were "best works," 2 percent were "better than average both artistically and ideologically," 49 percent were average but "generally acceptable Soviet products," and another 49 percent were either "hardly acceptable" (20 percent) or banned (29 percent).[5]

These ratios should not be surprising in a system where the majority of screenplays were unsolicited and screenwriters were freelancers or amateurs. In the 1910s, under similar conditions, American film companies were processing up to 1,000 script submissions per week, and all but 1 percent of them were rejected.[6] What is surprising is that the film industry expected most screenplays to be best or better than average upon submission rather than focusing on the 49 percent—over eighty screenplays for the RSFSR alone, a healthy number—that were average and could potentially be perfected.

This was because the Soviet film industry had no established personnel to convert average screenplays into suitable ones. By the 1930s Hollywood screenwriting was organized around such personnel. The major Hollywood studios incorporated story departments with several story scouts who systematically looked for stories in newly published literature. Studios also ran writing departments that were staffed by journalists and other members of the writing profession, whom

---

4. RGALI, f. 2496, op. 1, d. 32, l. 10 ob.
5. TsGALI, f. 257, op. 6, d. 19, l. 13.
6. Janet Staiger, "'Tame' Authors and the Corporate Laboratory: Stories, Writers and Scenarios in Hollywood," *Quarterly Review of Film Studies* 8, no. 4 (1983): 40.

Janet Staiger calls "tame" writers, as they did not necessarily receive authorship credit for their work.[7] The (published and unpublished) material that studios purchased to be developed into screenplays was assigned to either outside writers (for prestige productions) or staff writers (for ordinary titles). Writing departments both composed screenplays and turned completed screenplays into standardized shooting or "continuity scripts," as they were called. When specialized writing experts developed, Hollywood directors were largely relieved of screenwriting responsibilities.[8] In other words, in Hollywood a small army of writing professionals could convert promising stories into solid screenplays and multiple authorship was common. There was a clear division of labor: film conception (screenplays) and film execution (the filming) were separate processes carried out by different groups of experts.[9]

There were several reasons why specialized story and writing departments developed in Hollywood. The large volume of production required for studios to stay afloat necessitated the consistent generation of hundreds of stories. Under the pressure of mass production, it was cheaper and easier for Hollywood firms to produce stories through studio-integrated departments staffed with dozens of writers. Prestige authors could bring fame, but could also— through delays, for instance—interfere with the production process. There was also no guarantee that outside authors would not sell their screenplay to another higher-bidding studio. With in-house writers and writers on long-term contract, Hollywood firms could have a steady supply of stories tailored to their particular strengths: stars, directors, genres, and budgets. In addition, taking the writing of the shooting script from the director and placing it in the hands of specialized experts contributed to standardization and efficiency in planning and production.[10]

One reason why specialized screenwriting never emerged at Soviet studios was that many of the pressures of Hollywood were absent in Russia. The volume of production was always low and falling, and, since studios were state-run,

---

7. Staiger, "'Tame' Authors," 33–45.

8. Naumburg, *We Make the Movies*, 1–52; Janet Staiger, "Blueprints for Feature Films: Hollywood's Continuity Scripts," in Balio, *American Film Industry*, 173–192; Bordwell, Staiger, and Thompson, *Classical Hollywood Cinema*.

9. Steven Maras, *Screenwriting: History, Theory, and Practice* (London: Wallflower Press, 2009). See also Bordwell, Staiger, and Thompson, *Classical Hollywood Cinema*; Vladimir Nil'sen, "Organizatsiia proizvodstva fil'mov v SShA," *Iskusstvo kino* 4 (1936): 56–61. On multiple authorship in the French film industry, see Crisp, *Classic French Cinema*, 300–307.

10. Staiger, "'Tame' Authors"; Staiger, "Blueprints for Feature Films"; Bordwell, Staiger, and Thompson, *Classical Hollywood Cinema*.

financing and profitmaking were less of an issue. Standardization was also unimportant, as production was organized around directors and the mode of operation in their units. As a result, Soviet screenwriting was never industrialized and was run *kustarno*, in a disorganized and amateurish manner.[11] In Hollywood screenwriting duties were divided into theme and story scouting, synopsis and screenplay writing, fact checking and censorship rewrites, and the preparation of the shooting script. Because of the nonindustrial mode of Soviet film production, in Soviet cinema some of these duties were marginalized to the point where almost no writers were available to perform them.

Since the 1920s screenplays were largely conceived as inseparable from their authors. Therefore it was not the imperfect screenplay but the imperfect author that needed fixing. According to the critic Ippolit Sokolov writing in 1930, the Soviet scenario crisis had two causes: one "social" and the other "production-related." The social problem was that the existing pool of screenwriting talent was unprepared to work under the new thematic requirements. The industrial problem was that studio screenplay-department staffs were failing to provide these screenwriters with helpful guidance.[12] A year earlier, the cinema executive Moisei Rafes referred to this personnel conundrum as a "historical defect," where those with a writing talent were ideologically unprepared and those who were ideologically savvy lacked artistic instincts or writing experience.[13]

Conceived as a "defect" of the individuals rather than the system, the personnel problem remained largely in place through the end of the Stalin period. In 1948, reflecting on the failures of screenwriting in the previous year, the Scenario Studio's Eremin said that the failures were caused not by the writers' lack of skill or knowledge of cinema specificity but by their "insufficiently deep ideological and political direction." He added, "We lack authors-thinkers, authors-politicians, and authors who think in state terms, both theoretically and practically."[14] This focus on fixing the ideologically "defective" screenwriter channeled the industry thinking toward authors and away from screenplays, to the detriment of screenwriting.

In the absence of writing departments or any other efficient system of improving scripts, the industry could not expect a large quantity of perfect screenplays. However, instead of multiplying screenwriters, the industry multiplied the censors.

---

11. Zel'dovich, "Stsenarnoe khoziaistvo": 26–34.
12. Ippolit Sokolov, "Reorganizovat' stsenarnoe delo," *Kino*, March 1, 1930, 2–3.
13. TsGALI, f. 257, op. 6, d. 19, l. 53.
14. RGALI, f. 2372, op. 14, d. 59, l. 3.

The Screenplay Department and Its Editor-Censors

Soviet screenwriting was organized around the author, the editor–censor, and the film director. Screenwriters were freelancers operating essentially as agents would in a free-market environment. Authors submitted "proposals" (*zaiavki*) to studios and studios contracted them on a project-by-project basis to write screenplays. The screenplay fee ranged from 5,000 rubles in the early 1930s to 100,000 rubles by the end of the Stalin period. The studio unit that processed the proposals and screenplays was the screenplay department.[15] Between 1938 and 1941 authors also submitted work directly to the Screenplay Department (*Stsenarnyi otdel*) of the Cinema Committee in Moscow. However, this was a minority practice: In the last three months of 1938, Iakov Cherniak, chief editor of the Screenplay Department, processed sixty-eight manuscripts, only two of which came directly from authors; studios submitted the rest.[16] Starting in 1941 screenplay proposals were submitted both to the studios and to the Cinema Committee Scenario Studio.[17]

With few early-1930s exceptions, screenplay departments employed no writers in a writing capacity. At all levels they were staffed by political editors (*politredaktory*) or consultants (*konsul'tanty*), who did not develop content but only sifted through what authors sent them. This gatekeeping function turned screenplay departments into censorship units. Their primary role was to vet proposals for substance, theme, and political errors. The editors either rejected screenplays or accepted them. In either case, they were legally obligated to issue a review (*zakliuchenie*), a written justification of their decision, which contained recommendations for improvement. In accordance with the standard screenwriting agreement, the screenwriter was responsible for the revisions.[18]

Throughout the Stalin period, screenplays were first censored at studio screenplay departments. The studios then forwarded accepted screenplays to the central cinema administration, where, if approved, the top executive signed off on

---

15. It appears that studio screenplay departments were briefly disbanded around 1933 and their staffs were incorporated into director-units. E. K. "Nakanune stsenarnogo proryva," *Kino*, May 28, 1933, 2. They were reinstated in 1935. Ark. Kin., "Neispol'zovannye vozmozhnosti," *Kino*, February 6, 1936, 1. During the war, the Scenario Studio functioned as the screenplay department of TsOKS (1941–1944).

16. RGALI, f. 2208, op. 2, d. 605, ll. 4–6.

17. With the creation of the Scenario Studio, the Cinema Committee Feature Production Department absorbed the Committee Screenplay Department.

18. A. E. Kossovskii and V. G. Dorogokupets, eds., *Kinofotopromyshlennost': Sistematicheskii sbornik zakonodatel'nykh postanovlenii i rasporiazhenii* (Moscow: Kinofotoizdat, 1936), 161.

them.[19] In the early 1940s the Central Committee Propaganda Department also started reviewing those screenplays approved by Bol'shakov, submitting some of them further to Zhdanov or another Central Committee member for review. At each of these levels—the studio, the cinema administration, and the party apparatus—multiple individuals censored screenplays, and the number of these grew over time. At the studio level, following screenplay-department evaluation, screenplays were reviewed again by the artistic board or its equivalents in the 1930s and the studio Artistic Council from 1940 to 1953. At the administration level, political editors from the Feature Production Department read screenplays. In 1939–1940 the administration's chief executive was aided by the Screenplay Council. In the 1940s this Council morphed into the Screenplay Commission of the Cinema Ministry Artistic Council. With the establishment of the Scenario Studio, the Studio's editorial board and chief editor also reviewed screenplays. Additionally, editors at each level, including the Propaganda Department, solicited outside expert opinions to inform their decisions.

Thus by the 1940s each screenplay faced at least two-dozen editor-censors. The multiplicity of censors was a direct consequence of the single-author policy. Since only the original author was expected to rewrite the screenplay, editor-censors focused on consulting the author on improvements.[20] The industry was very aware this system was inefficient, overwhelming to authors, and destructive to screenplays. Every few years, it blamed the scenario crisis on the "multiplicity of authorities" (*mnozhestvennost' instantsii*) and made calls to concentrate screenplay censorship in the hands of one or two individuals. Despite this, the number of censors only increased over time because screenplays were not getting better and screenplay editors were growing increasingly uncertain of what to censor for.

The individuals who staffed screenplay departments generally had one of two backgrounds. Chief editors were likely to have some writing credentials or literary training. Cherniak, Messer, Kovarskii, Vaisfel'd, Katinov, Efim Dobin, Grigorii Chakhir'ian, and Fedor Levin were critics. Rank-and-file editors, among whom there was great turnover and about whom very little is known, did not have creative qualifications, yet they outnumbered the intellectuals. For

---

19. Studios in the Soviet republics also submitted screenplays to the cinema administrations in their republics.

20. On the politico-economic logic behind the multiplicity of monitoring bodies, see Andrei Markevich, "How Much Control Is Enough? Monitoring and Enforcement under Stalin," *Europe-Asia Studies* 63, no. 8 (2011): 1449–1468; János Kornai, *The Socialist System: The Political Economy of Communism* (Princeton, NJ: Princeton University Press, 1992), 99.

example, in 1939 the Mosfilm screenplay department employed nine editors, and only the head, Il'ia Trauberg, and his deputy, Vaisfel'd, belonged to the creative professions.[21]

Screenwriters tended to despise most editors. They believed editors only cared about ideology and lacked taste, competence, education, and awareness of cinema as a medium. The writer Lev Slavin reported in 1936 that the screenplay department of the Kiev studio asked him to fix the dialogue in two screenplays scripted by others.[22] The dialogue in the first screenplay, in his opinion, was excellent. The second screenplay was so poor that any changes to the dialogue could not redeem it. Slavin concluded that the Kiev studio's editorial staff was incompetent.[23] The screenwriter Katerina Vinogradskaia wrote in 1933: "Cinema leadership informs us of Central Committee resolutions and of government actions and decisions, but instead of helping the screenwriter translate all of this from newspaper language to cinema language, they translate the screenwriter from cinema language to newspaper language."[24] In 1938 she wrote: "As one witty person said of such 'editors': 'in cinema rabbits are the scariest animals: they can kill.'"[25] Screenwriters believed that editorial recommendations, if adopted, forced them to produce "stillborns" instead of scripts and "dull bastards" (skuchnye ubliudki) instead of characters.[26] Shklovsky compared censored screenplays to dogs jumping from under the streetcar and censors to the ironing ladies at the Moskva hotel.[27]

It did not help either that censors could disagree among themselves and issue conflicting instructions. According to Gennadii Fish, one of the screenwriters for the comedy Devushka s kharakterom (The Girl with Character, 1939), ten editors reviewed this film's screenplay and all had different recommendations. It was hard to ascertain whose recommendations the filmmakers were to follow, and, Fish added, part of the problem was that some of the reviewers lacked a sense of humor.[28] Nor were the editors always effective in catching crucial mistakes.

---

21. RGALI, f. 2456, op. 1, d. 577, l. 11.

22. As I discuss below, dialogue doctoring and other services were sometimes contracted to writers other than the original author, but these services too were performed by established writers and freelance screenwriters.

23. RGALI, f. 631, op. 2, d. 173, l. 63.

24. Katerina Vinogradskaia, "Zven'ia razryvov," Kino, June 4, 1933, 2. See also "Obeshchaniia i deistvitel'nost'," Kino, December 17, 1936, 3; RGALI, f. 2456, op. 1, d. 324.

25. Katerina Vinogradskaia, "Avtor, rezhisser, redaktor," Kino, September 17, 1938, 2.

26. Oleg Leonidov, "O bol'shikh strastiakh, utrachennom dare i dozirovke talanta," Kino, February 10, 1933, 2. Leonidov wrote screenplays for several dramas between 1926 and 1934. After 1934, all of his successful screenplays were for children's films.

27. Parfenov, Zhivye golosa kino, 247.

28. RGALI, f. 2456, op. 1, d. 324, ll. 28–29.

Aleksandr Rzheshevskii and Vladimir Skripitsin's screenplay *Rubinovye zvezdy* (*Ruby Stars*) for Usol'tsev-Garf's 1940 comedy *We Are the Merriest*, which I have already mentioned in chapter 3, was rewritten at least five times and vetted repeatedly by the Tashkent studio, the central cinema administration, and three directors acting as editors.[29] The film told the story of a distinguished Russian family traveling to Uzbekistan to attend the wedding of their son, a border guard, who was marrying an award-winning Uzbek cotton grower. Many problems were found and many were corrected. Censors worried about how the screenplay represented Soviet notables, but said little about the attitude of the Russians to the Uzbeks other than that the Uzbeks were exoticized.[30] Upon seeing the film, Zhdanov, however, was appalled that the censors missed such "elementary" things as "Russian chauvinism." In the finished film, Uzbekistan was once referred to as *u cherta na rogakh* or "Timbuktu." The film was banned for its dishonorable presentation of Soviet notables and its chauvinistic portrayal of the Uzbeks.[31]

Not only were the editors perceived to be incompetent but their recommendations could also not be trusted. Nonetheless the authors had to address at least some of the editors' suggestions. The way to negotiate was to selectively incorporate some censorship demands and see if the revised screenplay would be rejected, returned, or passed nevertheless. This strategy was often effective, especially given that future revisions by the director after the screenplay was approved were envisioned anyway, making the review process always incomplete.

The majority of editors' recommendations were proscriptive. Editor-censors were primarily concerned about how the party representative, the ordinary citizen, and the enemy were portrayed. Common reasons for rejection included: insufficient emphasis on the role of the party in the story; lack of "Soviet content," that is, Soviet society was represented as no different from bourgeois societies; degrading or negative portrayals of Soviet people, officials, or institutions; attractive enemies; moral and political ambiguity; excessive pessimism and brutality; and the lack of "typicality," that is, representations of negative phenomena, which censors invariably judged "atypical." As Vinogradskaia suggested in her reference to "newspaper language," many editors mentioned recent policy pronouncements in their reviews. A perpetual request, for instance, was to build up the role of the masses or the collective in a screenplay, and when making this request in 1939, an editor added, "this needs to be done in the spirit

---

29. Gosfilmofond Archive, f. 2, op. 1, d. 2082.
30. Gosfilmofond Archive, f. 2, op. 1, d. 2082, l. 2.
31. Fomin, *Kino na voine*, 28–30, 33–34.

of formulations in *The Short Course.*[32] *The Short Course on the History of the VKP(b)* was a programmatic 1938 text on Bolshevik history written by Stalin.

Prescriptive recommendations were also common. In some cases, when editors were concerned about story coherence, respectful treatment of worthwhile causes, good taste, and basic morality, the recommendations did not fundamentally differ from what a Hollywood censor might have demanded. Take, for example, Il'ia Nabatov's comedy screenplay *Prizyvniki* (*Conscripts*, 1940) from the Odessa Studio. At a Cinema Committee screenplay conference in June 1939, the editor Tokareva noted that it was inappropriate for the female characters to take a ride with the male characters before mutual introductions. The editor Georgii Avenarius said that some events of the story were unmotivated and that one character overplayed his pretend madness. These were routine and productive comments meant to improve an already successful screenplay. Editors thought that *Conscripts* was an excellent comedy, comparable to a good Western screenplay. Censors also gave the film the green light because it addressed such topical themes as the Red Army, patriotism, and conscription. Nevertheless, Bol'shakov discontinued the production in the aftermath of *The Law of Life*'s ban, for an ideological reason, also mentioned in editorial discussions, but apparently not considered decisive. The film had a faulty premise: too much screen time was devoted to ways in which Soviet young men avoided conscription.[33]

Given the multiplicity of censors, their eagerness to critique, and their divergences in opinions, it was difficult for screenplays to pass review, and the vast majority of screenplays were rejected. This was true not only for screenplays by unknown authors but also for those written by accomplished professionals. To give just one example, in the mid-1930s Shklovsky wrote the screenplay *Stepan Razin* for the Mosfilm directors Olga Preobrazhenskaia and Ivan Pravov. He was asked to revise it. He revised it three times, but the screenplay was not accepted for production. Preobrazhenskaia and Pravov made *Stepan Razin* in 1939 based on a screenplay they cowrote with Aleksei Chaplygin, the author of a 1927 novel about Razin. The same happened with the screenplays Shklovsky wrote for Lenfilm's Erast Garin and Khesia Lokshina and for Mosfilm's Esfir' Shub. At least six additional screenplays Shklovsky wrote in the 1930s were rejected.[34] None of the thirteen screenplays Shklovsky wrote during the war (for which he received a total of 200,000 rubles in advance payments) were produced.[35]

---

32. RGALI, f. 2456, op. 1, d. 485, l. 121.
33. RGALI, f. 2456, op. 1, d. 485, ll. 33–37; RGALI, f. 2450, op. 4, d. 35, ll. 21–24.
34. "Obeshchaniia i deistvitel'nost'," 3.
35. Parfenov, *Zhivye golosa kino*, 324.

The Scenario Studio did not alter the principles of Soviet screenwriting. As already suggested in chapter 2, rather than producing in-house scores of ideologically correct stories on subjects the party-state wanted, it organized its efforts around authors (and directors). By 1943, two years into the Studio's operation, the Propaganda Department's Aleksandrov complained to the Central Committee that the Studio made no difference in solving the scenario crisis and that the screenplays it prepared were poor in theme and content and had primitive and repetitive plots, characters, and styles.[36] In 1943 the staff of the Studio changed and Bol'shintsov left. By 1946, under the leadership of Astakhov and Eremin, the Studio had become just another clearinghouse, a centralized censorship body equivalent to studio screenplay departments.[37] Shklovsky complained in 1945 that the Studio employed only a dozen individuals, whereas it should have hired hundreds. He was also right to suggest that the Studio's focus should have been on stories, "five hundred to seven hundred a year," not on screenplays and authors.[38]

In contrast to Hollywood, Soviet screenplay departments did not write screenplays but selected and censored submissions. This made their functioning restrictive from the start. It also tended to turn screenwriters against editor-censors. Soviet screenwriting, however, harbored an additional problem. Since the majority of screenplays required repeated rewrites by the original, often reluctant author, screenplays were never ready-made for production, and the process of rewriting continued after the screenplay was accepted. At this point, the screenplay was passed on to the director, who converted the censored literary original into the shooting script. At this stage, the divergence between screenwriters and censors was compounded by authorship conflicts between screenwriters and directors.

The Director's Scenario and the Crisis of Control

Due to the director-centered mode and the absence of writers and producers at Soviet studios, only the director could rewrite the original censored screenplay into a shooting-ready script. Fittingly, these scripts were called the "director's scenarios" (*rezhisserskii stsenarii*). Soviet directors did not mind preparing their own director's scenarios. In fact, it was inconceivable to them that it could be otherwise. Even if the literary scenario they received did not require major

---

36. Anderson et al., *Kremlevskii kinoteatr*, 676.

37. See, e.g., RGALI, f. 2372, op. 8, d. 75; RGALI, f. 2372, op. 12, d. 76; Anderson et al., *Kremlevskii kinoteatr*, 721.

38. RGALI, f. 2372, op. 10, d. 87, l. 26.

rewriting of the literary prose into a numbered shot-by-shot format of the director's scenario, they made a point of rewriting it just to make it their own. Eisenstein wrote: "When checking the literary scenario against the director's scenario we can immediately determine whether we are dealing with a servile shot breakdown (*rabskaia raskadrovka*) or with a new creative elevation of the material, which, after having been authored by the screenwriter, has passed through the creative consciousness of the director."[39]

Converting screenplays into director's scenarios was therefore not just a matter of professional habit and technical necessity but also a way of shifting authorship over the final product from the screenwriter to the director. In his 1938 textbook on screenwriting, Valentin Turkin wrote that the two stages of the Soviet screenplay—the literary scenario and director's scenario—were comparable to the two stages in Hollywood: the treatment and the shooting continuity script, respectively. Turkin welcomed the precision of the Hollywood shooting script, but, echoing Eisenstein's sentiments, noted: "Except we cannot agree that turning the treatment into the shooting script is purely technical work. In the [Russian] shooting script, the work of shaping the artwork is finalized, the breakdown and progression of action is elaborated, and the details are developed."[40] The practice of adjusting the film's form, theme, and character in the director's scenario, after the screenplay had already been censored, was an industry-wide norm.[41]

Three additional factors contributed to the cavalier attitude on the part of the Soviet directors to the original literary scenarios. First, many directors either wrote their own screenplays or considered themselves capable screenwriters. Therefore they felt free to tweak the original material as they pleased when writing a director's version. Perhaps the most famous example of this behavior in the 1930s was *Tsirk* (*The Circus*, 1936). The director Grigorii Aleksandrov introduced so many changes to the screenplay that its authors, Il'ia Il'f and Evgenii Petrov, asked for their names to be removed from the film.[42] Additionally, directors had a financial incentive to earn screenwriting credit, since this allowed them to receive additional royalty payments.[43]

---

39. Sergei Eisenstein, "Po mestam!" *Kino*, March 10, 1933, 3.

40. V. K. Turkin, *Dramaturgiia kino* (Moscow: VGIK, 2007), 48.

41. For a discussion of contemporary Soviet screenplay theory, as developed in screenwriting manuals, textbooks, and theoretical works on screenwriting, see Anke Hennig, "Obobshchenie kinodramaturgii: Ot kinodramaturgii do dramaturgii iskusstv," in *Sovetskaia vlast' i media: Sbornik statei*, ed. Hans Günter and Sabine Hänsgen (St. Petersburg: Akademicheskii proekt, 2006), 430–449.

42. See, e.g., Salys, *Musical Comedy Films of Grigorii Aleksandrov*, 132.

43. Kossovskii and Dorogokupets, *Kinofotopromyshlennost'*, 164. This factor is also discussed by Babitsky and Rimberg, *Soviet Film Industry*, 97, and Youngblood, *Soviet Cinema in the Silent Era*, 237.

Second, directors continued to believe that films were created not in the script but during shooting and editing.[44] Eisenstein, for one, apparently subscribed to the following metaphor, coined by Isaak Babel': "writing a screenplay is like inviting a midwife to the conjugal night."[45] Directors preferred loose, oversized, and even bad screenplays, as these allowed them to shoot a lot of footage and have choices during editing.[46] Soviet film editors (*montazhery* and *montazhnitsy*) worked for the directors.

Finally, directors believed that screenplays written by writers in particular were either their professional refuse (*otbrosy*), the material that the writers could not use in prose writing, or quality material presented in a raw form that had nothing to do with cinema.[47] Directors believed writers did not understand cinema, did not take screen work seriously, and only engaged in it for the money. According to the writer Mikhail Zoshchenko, many of his peers indeed felt this way.[48] This produced a disrespectful attitude toward screenplays and necessitated substantial "cinematization" of the original material by directors. As one commentator described it, this was a vicious circle: "the director rewrites screenplays because they are [only] raw material, and screenwriters lack motivation because they are supplying [only] raw material."[49]

Neither did film directors consider director's scenarios to be exact approximations of their future films. The actress Elena Kuz'mina left the following record of Boris Barnet, her first husband, working with a film script in the mid-1930s: "He never kept to the original screenplay. He would write out each shot painstakingly and stick these pieces of paper one after another to make a long scroll. Then he would unroll this on the ground and get down on his knees to search for the shot he was about to do. And in the end he would shoot something quite different, improvising on the spot. This is the reason for the 'freedom' in his films."[50] Jay Leyda, who participated in the making of Sergei Eisenstein's *Bezhin Meadow* (1937), made the following entry in his diary: Eisenstein's preparatory sketches "are as loose and elastic as the scenario will remain to the last

44. See Thompson, "Early Alternatives to the Hollywood Mode of Production," 397.

45. Rostislav Iurenev, *Sergei Eizenshtein: Zamysly, fil'my, metod*, vol. 2 (Moscow: Iskusstvo, 1985), 193.

46. B. Alpers, "Kinodramaturgiia i rezhissura," *Kino*, July 10, 1933, 2.

47. A. Macheret, "Tvorcheskaia podopleka iuridicheskikh nepoladok," *Kino*, March 10, 1933, 3; RGALI, f. 2456, op. 1, d. 324.

48. Parfenov, *Zhivye golosa kino*, 239.

49. S. Bugoslavskii, "Stsenarist—rezhisser—kompositor," *Kino*, April 4, 1933, 3.

50. Bernard Eisenschitz, "A Fickle Man, or Portrait of Boris Barnet as a Soviet Director," in Taylor and Christie, *Inside the Film Factory*, 153.

shot. I have seen more than one filming day pass without E. [Eisenstein] referring once to the script—so reliant is he upon the firm mental images he keeps
with him."[51]

Directors assumed that as long as they were the primary authors behind their
films, they could continue to reshape their works all the way to the final cut.
This is underscored by the fact that the director's scenario was also called the
"working scenario" (*rabochii stsenarii*) and the "editing scenario" (*montazhnyi
stsenarii*), and that some directors believed the director's scenario could only be
completed at the end of shooting—presumably to then assist in the editing.[52]
Trying to distinguish among these scripts, Kuleshov once said that for him, the
director's scenario was an official document that ought to be censored, whereas
the film ought to be shot using a different, "working" or "editing" script, an
internal working document for the director and the crew.[53] This distinction was
never implemented.

Each director had his or her own way of using the director's scenario during production, making this text only a raw approximation of the finished film.
Directors' scenarios ranged from the original prose broken down into numbered shots to completely new renditions of the original. Their format, however,
remained basically the same throughout this period. It was a shot-by-shot rendition of the film, including, in most cases, shot numbers, settings, shot scales,
shot footage, and descriptions of action and sound (figure 4.2). The important
distinction, relative to the Hollywood continuity script, was that footage for each
shot was designated in advance. It is difficult to know exactly why footage estimations were included. Certainly the tradition of thinking in montage (rhyth-
mic) terms, on the one hand, and in terms of reels and programming units, on
the other hand, might have been responsible. My guess is this practice also developed to account for imported film stock, which was a scarce resource in Soviet
cinema in the 1920s and 1930s. By including footage estimations in the director's scenario, the directors could start negotiating the stock allotment before
the shooting started.

Yet the footage estimations and stock limits did not mean very much in practice. Filmmakers present at the 1938 conference devoted to the shooting script
noted that the footage numbers in the director's scenario were anywhere from
approximate to meaningless.[54] Indeed, footage estimations sometimes had little

51. Leyda, *Kino*, 328.
52. Evg. Iavorskii, "Ubytki i montazhnyi stsenarii," *Kino*, March 28, 1933, 3.
53. RGALI, f. 2450, op. 2, d. 31, l. 1 ob.
54. RGALI, f. 2450, op. 2, d. 31.

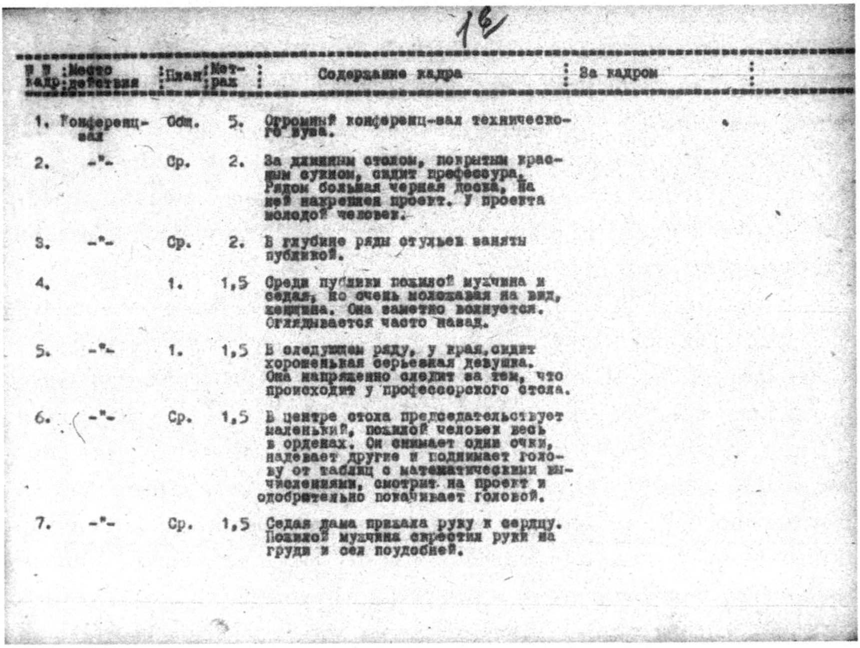

№ кадра / Место действия	План	Мет-раж	Содержание кадра	За кадром
1. Конференц-зал	Общ.	5.	Огромный конференц-зал техническо-го вуза.	
2. -"-	Ср.	2.	За длинным столом, покрытым крас-ным сукном, сидит профессура. Рядом большая черная доска, на ней начерчен проект. У проекта молодой человек.	
3. -"-	Ср.	2.	В глубине ряды стульев заняты публикой.	
4.	1.	1,5	Среди публики пожилой мужчина и седая, но очень моложавая на вид, женщина. Она заметно волнуется. Оглядывается часто назад.	
5. -"-	1.	1,5	В следующем ряду, у края, сидит хорошенькая серьезная девушка. Она напряженно следит за тем, что происходит у профессорского стола.	
6. -"-	Ср.	1,5	В центре стола председательствует маленький, пожилой человек весь в орденах. Он снимает одни очки, надевает другие и поднимает голо-ву от таблиц с математическими вы-числениями, смотрит на проект и одобрительно покачивает головой.	
7. -"-	Ср.	1,5	Седая дама прижала руку к сердцу. Пожилой мужчина скрестил руки на груди и сел поудобней.	

FIGURE 4.2 A page from the director's scenario for *Svet nad Rossiei* (*Light over Russia*, Iutkevich, 1948). The columns are: Shot Number, Setting, Shot Scale, Footage (in meters), Content, and Off-screen [Sound]. RGALI, f. 2453, op. 2, d. 279, l. 1v.

to do with the footage eventually filmed or used. Savchenko, the director of *Garmon'* (*Accordion*, 1934), reported that a scene written up in the director's scenario as lasting 4 meters (or 10 seconds) became 40 meters long (or a minute and a half) in the finished film. It was a dance scene between the two principal characters and it was filmed with sync sound. The music sounded so good, he explained, that they kept filming, deciding on the spot that the scene should be much longer than scripted.[55]

The discrepancy between the shooting script and the final footage here was unintentional. As Savchenko admitted, he did not take music into account when writing the director's scenario—it was his first feature and first sound film.[56] However, experienced directors knowingly planned one length of footage and filmed another, or decided in postproduction how long the scene would last.

55. Gosfilmofond Archive, f. 2, op. 1, d. 429, l. 66.
56. Gosfilmofond Archive, f. 2, op. 1, d. 429, l. 66.

Pudovkin's original director's scenario for *Admiral Nakhimov* (1946) was 4,500 meters (15,000 feet) long; that is, Pudovkin was planning a 164-minute film. He was asked to shorten the script, which he did. However, when his revised version was approved for production, it was still too long and had to be cut to 2,870 meters (105 minutes).[57] It is not that Pudovkin did not realize that 4,500 meters was far too long for a feature-length film. Rather, he wanted to have more footage to work with in the editing process. He wanted to have not just takes but entire scenes to choose from.

As *Kino* reported in 1940, filmmakers believed that "to make one good film one had to shoot two bad ones."[58] The total length of Aleksandrov's *Spring*, as it exists today, is 2,850 meters. Aleksandrov, however, shot 1,300 meters of footage for just one scene: a stage performance featuring one of the film's protagonists. The scene was shot on location at Moscow's Bolshoi Theater. When Aleksandrov showed the footage to his colleagues, its excessive length appalled them. Aleksandrov responded that he planned to use no more than 300 meters of this footage in the film, but he needed to have available over four times as much. This way he could find moments in the recorded performance to parody the theater as an institution.[59] The scene does take about 10 minutes (or under 300 meters) in the film, but only portions of it use the Bolshoi footage, and much in rear projection, making the filming of 1,300 meters an extravagance indeed.

The director's-scenario practice produced another inefficiency. For most of the Stalin period, the film was considered "in production" after the studio screenplay department and the central cinema administration approved the literary original. Although in the 1940s and early 1950s shooting scripts were also censored, even then films were typically launched into production prematurely—before all story, character, setting, and ideological-message issues were settled. The reason for this practice was both the planned nature of Soviet film production and the director-centered mode. Because of writing, revision, and censorship delays, studios always had fewer production-ready screenplays than they needed. In order to come closer to the annual goals, studios often began production on screenplays that still needed work. "To be corrected in the director's scenario" or "while filming" was a ubiquitous notion often found at the end of many screenplay approvals. The assumption was the director would incorporate the required changes as he or she worked on the film.

---

57. RGALI, f. 2453, op. 2, d. 3, ll. 1–2.
58. "Navedem poriadok v studiinom khoziaistve," *Kino*, February 11, 1940, 4.
59. RGALI, f. 2453, op. 2, d. 14, l. 23.

Here is one example. When the screenplay of *Na otdykhe* (*On Vacation*, 1936) by the acclaimed children's writers and satirists Nikolai Oleinikov and Evgenii Shvarts was discussed at Lenfilm, it was found far from ready. According to Leonid Trauberg, the screenplay "made a pleasant impression," contained "very nice portions as far as humor and ingenuity," and was "very well thought out as far as sound design." Yet it had no plot, its events were unmotivated, its message was unclear, and its characters were not sufficiently "Soviet." Despite this, the meeting's participants decided that, since the screenplay read well and the director was experienced, it should be put into production.[60] The film was shot by Eduard Ioganson and almost banned for all the reasons mentioned during the Lenfilm discussion. Although Ioganson was only in his forties when he made the film, it was his last. He died in 1942.

As the following example shows, ten years later, the situation was the same. Aleksandrov's *Vesna* (*Spring*, 1947) was based on a screenplay by Aleksandr Raskin and Moris Slobodskoi and started production on August 2, 1944. In a letter of July 27, 1944 to the Cinema Committee Feature Production Department, Mosfilm's chief executive Vladimir Golovnia asked that the screenplay be submitted for Bol'shakov's approval, adding, "all the necessary changes (incorporating the comments you gave at the studio Artistic Council meeting) will be introduced by comrade Aleksandrov directly in the director's scenario."[61] Ten months later, Mosfilm requested that the satirists Nikolai Erdman and Mikhail Vol'pin (Aleksandrov's previous collaborators) rework the dialogue and make other changes. Another six months later, the film still did not have a shooting script. Actors had been hired, sets had been built, expensive costumes had been tailored, and 2 million rubles (one-sixth of the total projected budget) were spent, but the filming had not started and it was not clear whether the sets would be used.[62]

Launching productions before the director's scenario was finalized was a wasteful practice. But as long as the directors wrote the director's scenario, it too remained a flexible, open-ended format. At the end of the Stalin period, Gerasimov, writing an entry on directing in a 1952 book on Soviet film craftsmanship, described the director's scenario as the director's initial rendition of the literary screenplay, which does not and should not "anticipate the future film in every detail." Moreover, he proposed that the question of how much the director's scenario determined the future film was not a technical question, but a matter

60. TsGALI, f. 257, op. 12, d. 43, ll. 1–7; TsGALI, f. 257, op. 16, d. 471, l. 40.
61. RGALI, f. 2453, op. 2, d. 17, ll. 1, 30.
62. RGALI, f. 2453, op. 2, d. 17, ll. 23, 30, 44, 46.

of how one understood "the nature of film art." He wrote: "Directors for whom film construction, the composition of every shot, and the editing-and-rhythmic form are primary, see in the director's scenario a precise and exhaustively detailed blueprint of the film. Directors who above all value the live creative work of actors and who understand film creation to be a complex creative process having a number of stages and phases, see in the director's scenario nothing more than a plan for creative work, a construction scheme."[63] According to Gerasimov, there was a difference between true creators and technicians in how they used the director's scenario. The latter did not create, but "technically execute[d] the film that had been fixated on paper," eschewing creative inputs from the actors and other collaborators. Such an approach "inevitably" made the film artificial, schematic, and lifeless. He concluded that his own practice had shown that the best time to write the director's scenario was not in preproduction but after the film had been thoroughly rehearsed with actors.[64]

Sometimes scripting flexibility worked to the film's advantage. The second, supposedly final, preproduction version of the director's scenario for *Chapaev* contained fifty-seven scenes. In the finished film, twenty-one of these scenes were completely excluded (some after having been filmed) and eleven entirely new scenes were created from scratch. More than half of the eighty-two-page director's scenario was either completely rewritten or significantly revised. These changes made the film's characters crisper and its plot more focused.[65] At other times flexibility threatened the fate of the film. When 75 percent of Aleksandrov's *Spring* was shot, the Cinema Ministry Artistic Council reviewed the rushes and found the film lacking in ideas and politically indifferent. According to the Council, Aleksandrov's changes only aggravated the "depravities" already present in the screenplay, such as the "slavish imitation of bourgeois film examples" and "false representation of Soviet society." Aleksandrov and Mosfilm insisted that the film could be corrected, but the Council suspended the production and ordered that Aleksandrov and the screenwriters rewrite the screenplay.[66] The film, with some scenes rewritten and reshot, was finally released in 1947. Its positive reviews mentioned that it was a vast improvement over the screenplay.[67]

---

63. S. Gerasimov, "O professii kinorezhissera," in *Voprosy masterstva v sovetskom kinoiskusstve*, ed. B. Kravchenko (Moscow: Goskinoizdat, 1952), 23.

64. S. Gerasimov, "O professii kinorezhissera," 22–25.

65. D. Pisarevskii, "Stsenarnye chernoviki *Chapaeva*," in Gornitskaia, *Iz istorii Lenfil'ma*, 3: 230–272.

66. Elena Dolgopiat, "'V sovetskom gosudarstve—liudi-dvoiniki.' Iz istorii sozdaniia fil'ma *Vesna*," *Kinovedcheskie zapiski* 57 (2002): 242–244.

67. Tat'iana Tess, "*Vesna*," *Izvestiia*, July 13, 1947, 3.

In the Soviet film industry, screenplay revisions, which a Hollywood studio would, ideally at least, complete in preproduction, were routinely carried out during production and even in postproduction. According to Iutkevich, the reason filmmakers put so much faith in the editing was because nothing was ever fully planned in advance.[68] Nevertheless, as late as 1948 censorship continued to focus on the literary original, and the director's scenarios were only censored "when necessary."[69] Yet given that the Soviet shooting script was the director's own version of the original, the discrepancy between the screenplay and the finished film continued to be a problem. In 1954 *Literaturnaia gazeta* complained that among the directors "there still exists a deeply erroneous attitude to the literary scenario as a kind of supplementary material, based on which a 'real' director's scenario will be written."[70] On top of discouraging screenwriters from collaboration, the director's scenario made screenplay censorship ineffective; films had to be censored again upon completion and film bans were a constant threat.

Failed Solutions: Soviet Hollywood and the Iron Scenario

The scenario crisis persisted throughout the Stalin period. In 1936 no Soviet director who had completed a film had his or her next screenplay ready for filming.[71] This meant no director was employed in his or her primary capacity throughout the year. The preliminary thematic plan for 1946 envisioned fifty new films, but only ten approved screenplays were available at the start of the year.[72] As a result, in 1946 as well, most directors had nothing to work on. In 1947 when the Soviet leadership wanted to organize film production in Germany, including at the flagship UFA studio captured during the war, Deputy Cinema Minister Konstantin Kuzakov told Zhdanov that such an initiative would be "unnecessary" since film production in the country was constrained not by studio capacity but by "the shortage of sound [*polnotsennyi*] screenplays."[73] In 1952 a *Pravda* editorial reported that Soviet cinema's only limitation was screenwriting.[74] Only after

68. [Sergei Iutkevich], "Deklaratsiia pervoi khudozhestvennoi masterskoi pod khudozhestvennym rukovodstvom S. Iutkevicha," in Gornitskaia, *Iz istorii Lenfil'ma*, 4: 128–137.

69. Artizov and Naumov, *Vlast'*, 635.

70. "Preodolet' nedostatki kinematografii," *Literaturnaia gazeta*, July 1, 1954, 1.

71. See, e.g., N. A., "Bez stsenariev," *Kino*, January 30, 1936, 3; Ark. Kin., "Neispol'zovannye vozmozhnosti," *Kino*, February 2, 1936, 1.

72. Anderson et al., *Kremlevskii kinoteatr*, 721.

73. Fomin, *Letopis' rossiiskogo kino, 1946–1965*, 62–63.

74. "K novomu pod"emu sovetskogo kinoiskusstva," *Pravda*, August 28, 1952, 3, also cited in Babitsky and Rimberg, *Soviet Film Industry*, 108.

Stalin's death, when a new generation of screenwriters entered the film industry and the intolerance of imperfection was relaxed, did the scenario crisis end.

This is not to say that the Soviet film industry did not try to solve the crisis. Three solutions were in circulation in the 1930s: Hollywood-type studio-integrated screenwriting, the iron scenario, and the scenario as an authored literary work. The Hollywood solution was to establish story and writing departments at Soviet studios. The iron-scenario idea, which originated back in the 1920s, was to introduce a fixed script that could not be changed during production. And the scenario as an authored literary work was to attract legitimate writers to cinema work. All three were designed to introduce a better division of labor in screenwriting, strengthen the screenplay, constrain the director, make censorship more productive, and ultimately solve the scenario crisis. The first two solutions, which had the potential of reforming Soviet screenwriting, were abandoned for ideological reasons, and the third solution—focusing industry efforts on the literary scenario and its author—only exacerbated the problem.

One of the reforms Shumiatskii proposed as part of the Soviet Hollywood project was to introduce a division of labor in screenwriting by establishing Hollywood-style story departments at Soviet studios. Shumiatskii was very impressed by the story departments he observed during his trip to Hollywood. He called them "the temples of dramaturgy" and said they were the hearts of every studio. He described how wonderfully equipped these departments were. They had a library, a reference section, a screening room, stenographers, and secretaries. He was impressed that highly renowned writers were sometimes employed there. Of course he maintained there was a difference in the kinds of stories Hollywood writers produced. In Russia, he said, life was "wonderful" and all Soviet screenwriters needed to do was to "reflect it." In contrast, bourgeois Hollywood artists could not represent real American life, as their task was to distract the audience from reality. Yet he insisted that the division of screenwriting into story selection, dialogue writing, comedy writing, and so forth produced excellent results: "More often than not, [American] story departments prepare solid and thoroughly developed scripts, true artworks that execute the 'social commission' of capitalists with sophistication and skill."[75] If only the abundance of Soviet stories could be combined with the kind of staff and support offered by the Hollywood story departments, Shumiatskii thought, the Soviet film industry would solve the scenario crisis.

---

75. Shumiatskii, *Sovetskaia kinematografiia segodnia i zavtra*, 22–23. See also Ippolit Sokolov, "Amerikanskii stsenarii," *Kino*, October 4, 1937, 3.

Under Shumiatskii's reform plan, some screenplays would be written by one screenwriter from beginning to end, in accordance with the existing single-author practice. However, since very few screenwriters were capable of supplying ready-made screenplays, the majority of screenplays, like in Hollywood, would be written by multiple authors, each specializing in some aspect of screenwriting.[76] Shumiatskii's longer-term plans for Soviet Hollywood in the south included story and writing departments staffed with eighty writers, thirty-two dialogue experts, and twelve literary editors, and he envisioned that staff writers would develop screenplays.[77] Sergei Tret'iakov had proposed differentiating screenwriting into outline, material, screenplay, and shooting script, all written by different specialized professionals as early as in 1925.[78] By the mid-1930s, the industry (and Mezhrabpomfilm in particular) had had experience with writers integrated into studios and units, and studios had on numerous occasions contracted partial writing services, such as dialogue doctoring, to writers other than the original author.[79] Shumiatskii had the administrative authority to extend these practices into full-fledged screenwriting reform based on the Hollywood example.

To implement his reform, on January 1, 1936 Shumiatskii organized what appears to have been a pilot story department (*siuzhetnyi otdel*) at Mosfilm. The Mosfilm department included many of the components of a Hollywood-style unit. It accepted not screenplays but stories (*siuzhety*). If the author of a promising story was unable to produce a screenplay based on it, the department purchased the story (for 1,000 to 5,000 rubles) and was tasked with finding a different writer to develop it. If someone brought in interesting material or an episode without a story, this was also purchased (for 500 to 2,000 rubles) and then passed on to a story specialist (*spetsialist-siuzhetchik*). Two individuals were reportedly employed to browse through new fiction. Someone was searching for stories in the press and someone else reviewed screenplay submissions. It appears, however, that other than the story specialist, the others employed in this department were not writing professionals. The *Kino* article announcing the Mosfilm unit urged that it assemble an active group of screenwriters to avoid becoming just another clearinghouse for outside submissions.[80]

76. Shumiatskii, *Sovetskaia kinematografiia segodnia i zavtra*, 54–55.

77. Glavnoe upravlenie kinematografii, *Osnovnye polozheniia planovogo zadaniia*, 21–22.

78. Sergei Tret'iakov, "Stsenarnoe khishchnichestvo," in *Kinematograficheskoe nasledie: Stat'i, ocherki, stenogrammy vystuplenii, doklady, stsenarii*, ed. I.I. Ratiani (St. Petersburg: Nestor-Istoriia, 2010), 62.

79. N.S. Gornitskaia, "Dokumenty, materialy," in Gornitskaia, *Iz istorii Lenfil'ma*, 3: 130–131; S. Ermolinskii, "Stsenarii i fil'ma," *Kino*, March 16, 1933, 2; A. Tin, "Sozdavat' stsenarii na proizvodstve," *Kino*, October 17, 1935, 2.

80. A., "Davaite siuzhety," *Kino*, January 11, 1936, 4.

It turned out this warning was well warranted. Without writers on staff, the Mosfilm story department had trouble fulfilling its new duties. *Kino* reported that after a month and a half of operation the department purchased only five stories, three of which it outsourced to the stories' authors, passing the two remaining ones to writers Isaak Babel' and Nikolai Virta. The work of the three experts who reviewed fiction generated no story ideas.[81] (Compare this to a concurrent report from the same newspaper that in the first nine months of 1935 Hollywood studios generated 679 stories, or an average of seventy-five stories a month.)[82] Another three months later, the writers' newspaper *Literaturnaia gazeta* wrote about the Mosfilm story department in the past tense. The newspaper stated that the department had not become an intermediary between the authors and the studio, and that its functions had lapsed to passing or rejecting submissions.[83] Both observations confirmed that the department failed to become the Hollywood-style story powerhouse Shumiatskii had envisioned. By 1938 Mosfilm's screenplay work was again concentrated at the screenplay (*stsenarnyi*) department employing only five to six editors.[84]

Why did Shumiatskii fail? As with other reforms he attempted, it appears that Shumiatskii did not have the personnel he needed. Shumiatskii instructed other Soviet studios to also organize Hollywood-type story departments, but these plans remained on paper due to lack of personnel. The Kiev studio, for instance, reported that its existing screenplay department employed six individuals, but no fewer than twenty-three were required for the new story department to operate.[85] The same fate befell Shumiatskii's other innovation, also at Mosfilm: a director's-scenario department (*biuro rezhisserskogo* or *rezhissersko-montazhnogo stsenariia*) headed by Moisei Aleinikov (formerly a Mezhrabpomfilm executive). This unit was to monitor the shooting scripts prepared by the director-units from the technical point of view.[86] Shumiatskii also proposed replacing the director's scenario with the editing scenario and taking editing entirely out of the director's hands. All these innovations, however, required new qualified staff, which was not available.[87] When he came to office, Dukel'skii too attempted to implement a division of labor in which the screenwriter functioned independently of the director, and

---

81. "V siuzhetnom otdele," *Kino*, February 21, 1936, 4.

82. Br. Shelestovy, "Stsenarnyi golod," *Kino*, January 30, 1936, 4.

83. A. Kamennogorskii, "Pisateli i kino," *Literaturnaia gazeta*, April 20, 1936, 6.

84. A. Orlovskii, "Udvoit' vypusk fil'mov," *Kino*, December 22, 1937, 3.

85. N.A., "Bez stsenariev," *Kino*, January 30, 1936, 3.

86. I. Vaisfel'd, "Nekotorye predlozheniia," *Za bol'shevistskii fil'm*, April 13, 1936, 2.

87. Shumiatskii, *Sovetskaia kinematografiia segodnia i zavtra*, 30–31; Boris Shumiatskii, *Puti masterstva: Stat'i i doklady* (Moscow: Kinofotoizdat, 1936), 111–118.

the studio screenplay departments, instead of accepting-rejecting, generated stories for the entire film industry.[88] Dukel'skii's innovations also failed and for the same staffing reasons.[89]

The second solution to deal with the weak screenplay was to require that each film had a strong screenplay or an iron scenario—a type of script fully developed prior to production. This idea too was related to the Hollywood continuity script, but as opposed to the story and writing departments advocated by Shumiatskii, it did not entail multiple authorship. For the majority of commentators, the iron scenario was simply a finalized director's scenario: "The iron scenario is a preliminary working out of all the production details and editing in the film. Nothing is superfluous; nothing is left to chance. The film ought to be literally assembled in advance, before the filming begins. . . . Prior to filming, the director ought to see the entire film in his mind; he ought to have run it in his head, shot by shot, dozens of times."[90] As such, the iron scenario was to serve as a reliable contract between the censors and directors.

The closest the film industry ever came to realizing the iron scenario was in 1938–1939 during Dukel'skii's short tenure. Dukel'skii introduced mandatory censorship of directors' scenarios.[91] One of his rulings prohibited studios from making changes in the directors' scenarios after they were approved by the cinema administration unless permission was obtained from the chairman himself.[92] It would be incorrect to assume, however, that after Dukel'skii's ruling the iron grip of censorship over Soviet cinema was complete.[93] The same ruling also ratified two existing screenwriting practices: the director's scenario (i.e., the shooting script written by the director) and the single-author policy. What Dukel'skii's rules did accomplish was to make it more likely that directors followed their own directors' scenarios while filming.

Moreover, as soon as Bol'shakov replaced Dukel'skii, the business of preproduction censorship of screenplays took a step back to the usual dysfunction. Bol'shakov shifted the focus of censorship back to the literary original.

88. Molotov, Petrunichev [and Dukel'skii], "Ob uluchshenii organizatsii proizvodstva kinokartin"; Semen Dukel'skii, "Za bol'shevistskii poriadok v kinematografii," *Kino*, April 23, 1938, 3.

89. See, e.g., Anderson et al., *Kremlevskii kinoteatr*, 527.

90. Ippolit Sokolov, *Kino-stsenarii: Teoriia i tekhnika* (Moscow: Kinopechat', 1926), 68. See also Ippolit Sokolov, "Khoroshii stsenarii," *Kino-front* 9–10 (1926): 11.

91. Directors' scenarios were censored before 1938, but only selectively, for high-profile films.

92. Molotov, Petrunichev, [and Dukel'skii], "Ob ulichshenii organizatsii proizvodstva kinokartin." Film files contained at the Gosfilmofond Archive offer evidence that Dukel'skii's personal signature was required even for minimal changes (see, e.g., Gosfilmofond Archive, f. 2, op. 1, d. 2812).

93. Kenez, *Cinema and Soviet Society*, 129.

The project to standardize the director's scenario, ordered by Dukel'skii, was abandoned. According to Kuleshov, who took up the project at VGIK, script standardization had soon gained the reputation as "a formalist contrivance or nonsensical raving of dry, uncreative people."[94] As we have seen, from the point of view of the Soviet director, the director's iron scenario was a bit of a conceptual oxymoron. Besides, as long as censorship focused on the literary original, the pressure to make the director's version "iron" abated, along with the disappearance of that term.

The Triumph of the Authored Literary Scenario

The iron scenario debate harbored a minority opinion, according to which screenwriters, not directors, were to write iron scenarios. As opposed to Hollywood, however, where screenwriters wrote many versions of each screenplay, this idea, proposed by Vladimir Sutyrin in 1929, entailed that the original literary screenplay would be written *as* iron, eliminating the need for other screenplay stages, including the director's scenario.[95] The leading analogy here was the play. In theater, the play was considered an independent literary work that was produced multiple times and in multiple renditions, but such productions did not alter the original play.[96] Moreover, in theater there was no equivalent to the director's scenario.[97] Although commentators vastly exaggerated the independence of the play in theatrical practice, this theatrical conception of screenwriting (the Russian term for the trade was "film dramaturgy," *kinodramaturgia*) dictated the film industry's orientation toward single authors. Even if Sutyrin's idea went radically against the director's authority and was unrealistic as a practical matter, it was attractive because it fulfilled the pervasive expectations that all screenplays would be perfect to start with and that single authors would be in charge. Thus Sutyrin's far-fetched iron literary scenario became the basis for the third and final solution to the scenario crisis: the screenplay as an authored literary work.

Before the authored literary scenario matured under Bol'shakov, it took a detour that became known as the "emotional scenario." Not unlike Sutyrin's literary scenario, the emotional scenario was associated with literary skill. It was

---

94. Lev Kuleshov, "Kul'tura rezhisserskogo tvorchestva," *Iskusstvo kino* 3 (March 1941): 11–12.

95. V. Sutyrin, "O stsenarii i stsenariste," *Sovetskii ekran*, April 16, 1929, 8.

96. Sutyrin, "O stsenarii i stsenariste." See also, M. Shneider, "Avtorskii stsenarii," *Iskusstvo kino* 3 (1941): 30–34.

97. "Preodolet' nedostatki kinematografii," *Literaturnaia gazeta*, July 1, 1954, 1.

an independent literary work marked by formal mastery, powerful imagery, and emotional force. As opposed to Sutyrin's scenario, however, it was not an exact blueprint for the film but a literary stimulant that encouraged the director to produce a masterful and emotionally powerful work. Still, in both the emotional scenario and the literary scenario, the author's conception was to be so original that it could not be altered in any requisite rewriting. As such, the emotional and iron literary scenarios were "strong" enough that they would be treated with respect. Unfortunately, several attempts at adapting emotional scenarios in the 1930s showed that this strength was an illusion. When Eisenstein's *Bezhin Meadow*, based on a prominent emotional scenario by Aleksandr Rzheshevskii, was banned in 1937, the emotional scenario lost its ground. The literary scenario as an independent work of literature survived, however, since it promised to combine artistic merit with untouchability.[98]

Hollywood-style story departments and multiple authorship required training and retraining of personnel. Specialized screenwriting and iron scenarios entailed a radical reconceptualization of current screenwriting practices. These factors made these solutions unattractive. The industry was under pressure to produce more and better films immediately. The quality-literary-scenario option did not necessitate any investment in personnel or time or major departures from the existing author-focused practice. It required only attracting "better" authors to cinema work, and this is what the film industry decided to do. The country already had a large number of legitimate writers who were both talented and ideologically grounded, and some of them already occasionally wrote for the screen. In addition, Stalin invested time and effort into shaping up literary professionals through the Soviet Writers' Union, formed in 1932. What could better guarantee quality than the prestige and presumed ideological savviness of the members of the Soviet Writers' Union?

The "writer injection" (*pisatel'skaia privivka*), as one contemporary dubbed this policy, became the focus of the Soviet screenwriting approach from about 1933 to the end of the Stalin period.[99] To give legitimate writers an incentive, the screenplay was officially elevated to the status of an independent work of

---

98. For more on the iron and the emotional scenarios, see Maria Belodubrovskaya, "The Literary Scenario and the Soviet Screenwriting Tradition," in *A Companion to Russian Cinema*, ed. Birgit Beumers (Hoboken: John Wiley & Sons, 2016), 251–269.

99. Mikhail Shneider, "Stilevye tendentsii kinodramaturgii 1934 goda," *Kino*, November 22, 1933, 2. This was certainly not the first time that Russian cinema appealed to the writers. As early as in the 1910s Russian film producers recruited the writers Aleksandr Kuprin, Fedor Sologub, and Dmitrii Merezhkovskii to work for the screen. Anna Kovalova, *Kinodramaturgiia N. R. Erdmana: Evoliutsiia i poetika* (Candidate diss., St. Petersburg State University, 2012), 23.

literature and screenplays started to be published in literary journals and screen-play collections. The screenwriter now appeared before the director in a film's opening credits. The elevation of the screenplay to the status of an independent literary work gave authors well-defined authorship rights. According to the Standard Screenwriting Agreement (*Tipovoi stsenarnyi dogovor*) introduced in 1939, the author could be asked to revise the screenplay no more than twice and no third party could be brought in to rewrite the screenplay without the author's agreement.[100] Indeed, the writer-injection policy initially convinced more writers to author screenplays. However, because the policy was not matched by corresponding changes in censorship or directing and because it collapsed the already author-centered effort into the figure of a prestige writer, it only exacerbated the scenario crisis.

First, the focus on the established author confined the pool of screenwriters to the existing writers willing to write for the screen. The number of professional screenwriters remained very small: the number cited in 1946 was ten to fifteen professional screenwriters, unchanged since 1929.[101] To compare, in 1938 Hollywood's four largest studios had 238 screenwriters under contract, meaning these screenwriters worked full time for these studios and did not have to split their time with fiction, play, or essay writing.[102] The writer injection undermined professionalization and barred new, inexperienced screenwriters from entering the profession. Of a total of eighty screenwriters who graduated from VGIK between 1934 and 1945, only seven worked as screenwriters.[103] This shrank the number of screenplays available only further. In 1941 the director Nikolai Shengelaia said that directors were no longer the bosses (*khoziaeva*) of cinema; the real boss was the Soviet Writers' Union.[104] Similarly, as Eisenstein once said, without screenplays the directors were like "planes without fuel."[105]

The insistence on the screenplay as an original literary work also discouraged the use of preexisting material for screenplays, reducing the story source base. Although by the late Stalin period more screenplays were based on preapproved plays, short stories, and novels, original screenplays were valued far more. At the same time, turning someone else's story into a screenplay was not considered creative work unless the new author altered the original. In 1936 Turkin

---

100. Kossovskii, *Sovetskaia kinematografiia*, 222–225.
101. TsGALI, f. 257, op. 6, d. 19, l. 50; Anderson et al., *Kremlevskii kinoteatr*, 721–722.
102. Balio, *Grand Design*, 83.
103. Anderson et al., *Kremlevskii kinoteatr*, 741.
104. RGASPI, f. 77, op. 1, d. 919, l. 51, cited in Iumasheva and Lepikhov, "Fenomen 'totalitar-nogo liberalizma,'" 127.
105. Sopin, "'. . . Idem na soveshchanie v TsK.'" 303.

described with disdain how a chief editor once gave him a book with a note, "To Comrade Turkin. Break down into shots. Urgent." Reflecting a widespread attitude, Turkin said that such a mechanistic approach was unacceptable, and literary adaptation too had to guarantee authorship.[106] Compare this to Hollywood where, in the 1930s for instance, 50 percent of all stories were adapted and typically by writers other than the original author.[107]

The screenplays authored by writers also did not live up to the expectation of perfection. In 1952 Ivan Bol'shakov complained that, more often than not, screenplays submitted by writers were "weak in ideological and artistic terms, lacking in plot, and showing Soviet people superficially and schematically."[108] One reason for this was a lack of practice. Given Soviet cinema's low output, by the 1940s each individual writer or screenwriter had very few opportunities to practice his or her skills. The low production volume eliminated competition, while veteran screenwriters lacked the incentive to produce, as the likelihood that any of their screenplays would be accepted was extremely low. It did not help that studios only commissioned as many screenplays as were listed in their plans and discouraged submissions of multiple screenplays on the same topic. The writer Boris Gorbatov reported that he wanted to write a screenplay about miners, but when he approached the cinema administration about it he was told that there already was a screenplay on miners, and two would be too many.[109] As Pyr'ev commented, "If three or four screenplays proved inadequate—a natural thing in creative work—there was no reserve from which to draw." Without a reserve, he added, inadequate screenplays had to be rewritten, and the writer, "instead of getting pleasure from work, experienced trauma."[110]

The risk associated with writing for the screen was also enormous. Although to my knowledge no writer was arrested for an inadequate screenplay as such, a banned film threatened a loss of status, job, and freedom of movement, as well as exclusion from the profession, which is what happened to Aleksandr Avdeenko after the ban on *The Law of Life*.[111] As for the reward, by the time the writer

---

106. V. Turkin, "O kinoinstsenirovke literaturnykh proizvedenii," in *Kak my rabotaem nad kinostsenariem*, ed. I. F. Popov (Moscow: Kinofotoizdat, 1936), 108–109.

107. Balio, *Grand Design*, 99–100.

108. I. Bol'shakov, "Prichiny otstavaniia kinodramaturgii," *Literaturnaia gazeta*, September 2, 1952, 2, also cited in Babitsky and Rimberg, *Soviet Film Industry*, 108.

109. Boris Gorbatov, "Bol'she fil'mov," *Literaturnaia gazeta*, September 2, 1952, 2.

110. Ivan Pyr'ev, "Tam gde net tvorcheskoi atmosfery," *Literaturnaia gazeta*, September 2, 1952, 2, also cited in Babitsky and Rimberg, *Soviet Film Industry*, 109.

111. For reasons behind the execution of Isaak Babel', who wrote a version of the screenplay for Eisenstein's banned *Bezhin Meadow*, see Benedikt Sarnov, *Stalin i pisateli: Kniga chetvertaia* (Moscow: EKSMO, 2011), 5–216.

injection was implemented, working in cinema was no longer as financially attractive as before. The system of royalty payments that depended on the film's box office was discontinued by Dukel'skii. Whereas the earlier system allowed screenwriters to draw royalty payments as long as the film was in distribution, the new system typically provided a one-time payment, which, although substantial, did not guarantee a stable income. According to Romm, the prominent writer and occasional screenwriter Aleksei Tolstoi joked that his family had not experienced a financial blow comparable to the Dukel'skii royalty system since the abolition of serfdom in 1861.[112] In addition, by 1946 film directors had received fifty-one Stalin Prizes for films, whereas screenwriters had been awarded only eight.[113]

Finally, the director continued to be seen as *the* film's author, and directors continued to treat literary scenarios as raw, auxiliary material. When in 1943 film executives reminded filmmakers that Dukel'skii's 1938 rules about following the director's scenario were still in force, Romm pointed out that these rules did not dictate that directors follow the literary scenario.[114] Literary scenarios written by legitimate writers were too literary to be immediately filmable, and directors continued to spend time rewriting them, investing them with their authorship and changing them during shooting. The December 1946 Central Committee resolution complained that Soviet film directors continued to have "little consideration" for the screenplays approved by central film authorities and "willfully altered the approved screenplays."[115] In 1954, referring to this as a "bad tradition," *Iskusstvo kino* lamented that because of planning pressures, studios continued to knowingly place unfinished screenplays into production, expecting the director to fix them in the director's scenario.[116]

Suggesting directors' scenarios should be censored instead of the literary ones, Mark Donskoi said that the only "honest" way for the director to commit to

---

112. Romm, *Ustnye rasskazy*, 71.
113. Anderson et al., *Kremlevskii kinoteatr*, 729, 742.
114. Fomin, *Kino na voine*, 459.
115. Anderson et al., *Kremlevskii kinoteatr*, 785.
116. "Za rastsvet kinodramaturgii!" *Iskusstvo kino* 9 (September 1954): 3–10, also cited in Babitsky and Rimberg, *Soviet Film Industry*, 110–111. In a 2011 interview, Andrei Konchalovskii reports that this continued to be the case throughout the Soviet period: "In the Soviet Union you could shoot a movie that was nothing to do with the script, and no one was going to watch over your shoulder. My second film was banned, but no one was checking my dailies because film was cheap and the state didn't care that they spent this money." He adds that when he got to Warner Brothers, he was "shocked" when a producer told him to move his camera. Alistair McKay, "Andrei Konchalovsky: I Want My Films to Leave a Little Wound in the Psyche," *London Evening Standard*, January 14, 2011, http://www.standard.co.uk/goingout/film/andrei-konchalovsky-i-want-my-films-to-leave-a-little-wound-in-the-psyche-6555996.html.

an outcome was to rehearse the film with actors based on the literary scenario, then write the director's scenario and submit it for approval.[117] Yet censorship continued to focus on the literary scenario, leading to absurd outcomes. In 1943 the Propaganda Department chief Aleksandrov reported to the Central Committee on the problematic films of that year, among which was Leonid Trauberg's *Aktrisa* (*Actress*, 1943). Aleksandrov found the film so "false" and "unintelligent" that he was shocked the cinema administration produced it.[118] In his response to this attack, Bol'shakov noted that Aleksandrov himself had read and approved Erdman and Vol'pin's screenplay for the film.[119] The multiplicity of censors certainly helped to avoid more censorship pitfalls in the finished films. Still, without an independent writing department or a censored iron scenario, Soviet screenplay censorship was bound to be flawed.

The Authored Literary Scenario as an Ideological Choice

The choice to invest in the authored literary scenario over multiple authorship and the iron shooting script was in many respects counterproductive. In addition to the lack of institutional will and time pressure, the authored scenario also triumphed for ideological reasons. As in other areas of policy, the decision to adopt it followed shortsighted Stalinist logic, according to which it was preferable to stimulate the talented individuals rather than to reform the institution.

In their travelogue of the United States, the writers Il'ia Il'f and Evgenii Petrov, who visited the United States in 1936, write of the then newly constructed Boulder Dam (now Hoover Dam) on the Colorado River. They talk with anticipation about the dam throughout the book, and when they finally see it, they ask: Who built it? Their guide has trouble answering the question and instead gives the name of the joint venture that built the dam on the government's commission, adding: "Engineers here in America are not well known. We only know the company names." Il'f and Petrov find this to be very odd. In response to their guide's explanation that we live in a world where individual achievement is no longer celebrated, as everyone contributes to technological progress as best one can, the visitors object that in the Soviet Union there are engineers and workers

---

117. Fomin, *Kino na voine*, 459.

118. Anderson et al., *Kremlevskii kinoteatr*, 674. See also, "Ob ideinosti v kinoiskusstve," *Pravda*, September 29, 1943, 3. The audiences, in contrast, loved the film (Kovalova, "Kinodramaturgiia Nikolaia Erdmana," 33).

119. Anderson et al., *Kremlevskii kinoteatr*, 682.

who are famous and whose portraits are printed in newspapers. They conclude that capitalism has denied individuals their right to fame and has replaced fame with a paycheck.[120]

Similarly, Soviet screenwriting policy pursued and celebrated individual achievement and authorship and refused to assign the work of writing screenplays to nameless scribes. This position was part of the official government rhetoric of Soviet superiority, and this sentiment was shared by screenwriters. A later formulation of this rhetoric can be found in the notorious *Pravda* critic David Zaslavskii's famous 1958 article against Boris Pasternak's Nobel Prize in Literature:

> The false bourgeois legend that socialism is hostile to the individual, that it erases the individual and deprives individuals of individuality and that it hinders the creative development of original people and original character, has long been refuted by deeds. On the contrary, it is precisely under socialism, precisely in the atmosphere of socialist collectivism that conditions of every kind are created for the fullest possible development of the creative individual, for the flourishing of original and distinctive thought.[121]

Using similar language, Bol'shakov, speaking about screenwriting, wrote in 1948 that in the Soviet Union all conditions were created "for the realization of the individual abilities of every artist," and that "creative daring, initiative, and innovation marked almost all the major works of Soviet film dramaturgy."[122] These statements reflect how Stalinist culture wished to see itself and suggest why original screenplays, quality, and film masterpieces (as opposed to just censorship and restrictions) were so high on the Stalinist agenda. They also imply that as long as individual screenwriters were entrusted with producing content in Soviet cinema, they had to be treated with respect, and not only rhetorically.

Whether out of genuine conviction or out of self-protection, many Soviet screenwriters believed in and propagated this ideal of creative freedom and originality for the chosen few. They too were "engineers of human souls," and theirs was a tall order. In parallel to directors, who responded to the rhetoric of quality, writers were encouraged by this stance and supported the literary scenario. Many

---

120. Il'ia Il'f and Evgenii Petrov, *Odnoetazhnaia Amerika* (Moscow: AST-Zebra E, 2009), 288–289.

121. David Zaslavskii, "Shumikha reaktsionnoi propagandy vokrug literaturnogo sorniaka," *Pravda*, October 26, 1958, 4.

122. Ivan Bol'shakov, *Sovetskoe kinoiskusstvo v gody velikoi otechestvennoi voiny (1941–1945)* (Moscow: Goskinoizdat, 1948), 27.

filmmakers maintained that the screenplay was a "special kind of artistic work" to be performed by authors with talent, not by "punchers of ideology" (the Soviet extreme) or "contrivers of 'stories' and 'plots'" (the Western extreme).[123] To highlight its investment in originality and individual authorship, the literary scenario was also often referred to as the authored scenario (*avtorskii stsenarii*). Moreover, the literary scenario (and the authored scenario of the post-Stalin era) was seen as the final stage in the evolution of the Soviet screenplay. According to Ivan Popov's easy taxonomy, in the silent period there was the technical scenario. Then came the iron scenario and the emotional scenario. The iron scenario threatened creativity. The emotional scenario took creativity too far. Finally, the writer had come to cinema. The authority and the name of the writer protected the screenplay from both censors and directors, and Soviet cinema got the creative authored screenplay Soviet cinema deserved.[124]

Even though it was important to compete with Hollywood in terms of film output, the character of this output and the talent recruited to produce it was to be superior to Hollywood's. Bol'shakov wrote:

> The task of American films is to distract the toilers from urgent social issues, to dull their consciousness and direct it away from political awareness toward amorality and apologetics for the beastly mores of capitalist society.
>
> Soviet cinema faces entirely different tasks. It is to assist the Soviet state and the Bolshevik Party in educating our people in the spirit of communism and in raising its political battle-readiness.[125]

This ideological position of superiority and difference affected how Soviet screenwriters themselves perceived Hollywood screenwriting and made them less interested in adopting Hollywood methods. Many screenwriters believed Western screenwriting was an uncreative and nameless process, resembling an assembly line. Vishnevskii and Dzigan, a screenwriter-director team, visited European film studios in 1936. The Western screenwriting process, they said, reminded them of the conveyor belt in Charlie Chaplin's *Modern Times* (1936). Their colorful description merits quoting at length:

---

123. The first two conceptions are from the April 2, 1929 issue of *Kino* cited in Fomin, *Letopis' rossiiskogo kino, 1863–1929*, 656. The third quote, in Russian "pridumyvateli 'fabul' i 'intrig,'" is from Sutyrin, "O stsenarii i stsenariste," 8.

124. I. F. Popov, "Kremnistyi put'," *Kino*, January 11, 1935, 3.

125. Bol'shakov, *Sovetskoe kinoiskusstvo v gody velikoi otechestvennoi voiny*, 26.

A greedy, rushed entrepreneurial gang makes a sweatshop, line-dashing toil out of a joyous creative process. In the West they do not shy away from tearing, mutilating, and mangling . . . not only works by contemporaries but even classic masterpieces. In Hollywood *Anna Karenina* was turned into an adultery drama. The cynicism of this system goes so far that in the pursuit of money and success the screenplay is put together like a pair of pants. They take the idea from one person, another person concocts the "plot," the third one writes the dialogue on the run, the fourth one sprinkles all of this with humor, and the fifth one "inserts" the gags. This system provokes deep disgust and protest. . . . It is strange that among our cinema workers there are some who recommend adopting this cutter-conveyor system.[126]

At a different venue Vishnevskii also proclaimed: "The Soviet writer is a self-sufficient figure. He is a writer of a new society, he is a Bolshevik, whether a party member or not. He is a person who is accustomed to answering for his work without reservations. . . . We will never agree to 'piece-' and 'cut-out' work as faceless quarter-screenwriters."[127]

For the screenwriters the debate over screenwriting was a battle for authorship and identity cast in ideological terms. They resisted Hollywood-style integrated screenwriting and multiple authorship, as these could lower their special status and self-esteem. Some considered it a disgrace that in Hollywood so few screenplays were original.[128] Citing celebrated American screenwriters, such as Ben Hecht, they maintained that even in Hollywood true artworks were scripted by well-known authors.[129] *That* was a Hollywood model their film industry should follow.

In contrast to screenwriters, directors welcomed the idea of Hollywood story departments. They understood that more and better stories could be developed there. Dovzhenko said: "In American cinema, for instance, we always see: based on the novel by such-and-such, screenplay by two or three screenwriters, then the author of dialogues. In other words the cinema artwork is executed by a number of people with various specialties who, like bees, contribute their honey

---

126. Vsevolod Vishnevskii and Efim Dzigan, "Po kinostudiiam Evropy," *Pravda*, July 26, 1936, 3.
127. RGALI, f. 631, op. 2, d. 173, l. 5.
128. RGALI, f. 2372, op. 14, d. 59, l. 51.
129. O. Afanas'eva, "Stsenarii, siuzhet, dialog," *Kino*, January 26, 1936, 3. See also Sokolov, "Amerikanskii stsenarii," 3. These commentators did not realize or failed to acknowledge that even Hecht often worked with coauthors and doctored many screenplays for money without receiving credit. William MacAdams, *Ben Hecht: The Man Behind the Legend* (New York: Scribner, 1990).

to the same honeycombs, and a beautiful and useful work emerges." Soviet directors, Dovzhenko added, had to deal with untouchable authors.[130]

Yet directors objected to the iron scenario because it could impinge on their authorship, hinder creativity, and turn them into mere technicians. Raizman said in 1940: "The process of the birth of a film is a deeply creative process, as opposed to the theory making the rounds these days, according to which the filming process is only an execution of a creative task thought out in advance."[131] Having the freedom to choose their screenplays, to write shooting scripts, and to edit their own films was a matter of pride and identity. And the Soviets were not unique in believing that Russian screenwriting was better. One American, writing about Soviet cinema for *Cinema Quarterly* in 1934, anticipated that American filmmakers would soon start moving to Russia, where directors had creative freedom and there were no producers.[132]

The authored literary screenplay solution suited both the ideological rhetoric of the Soviet state and the authorship concerns of screenwriters and directors. As it happened, however, this happy convergence precluded the Soviet state from achieving its controlled mass cinema goals.

Conclusion

The image of a director on his knees, looking for the right shot, not finding it, and improvising on the spot, or the sight of another director never referring to the script while shooting, might seem strange under Stalinist conditions. The idea of improvisation and "freedom" that Kuz'mina invokes seems utterly out of place in an environment that we think of as redundant, restrictive, and ruthless. Yet there is nothing out of the ordinary in Barnet's and Eisenstein's approaches. Although these examples are extreme manifestations of the Soviet mode of production, not adhering to the screenplay, improvising, and experiencing freedom on the set were just as much a part of filmmaking under Stalin as was multilayered censorship.

Soviet film production was organized around the director, while most screenwriters worked outside of the industry. Stalinist ideology celebrated original authorship and encouraged individual achievement. These institutional and ideological factors dictated that prestige authors should write screenplays. The screenplay was conceived as a quality literary work and screenwriters as agents

---

130. Iumasheva and Lepikhov, "Fenomen 'totalitarnogo liberalizma,'" 126.

131. RGALI, f. 2453, op. 2, d. 64, l. 7.

132. Helen Schoeni, "Production Methods in Soviet Russia," *Cinema Quarterly* 2, no. 4 (1934): 210–214.

free to create without pressures from producers or profit. As a result, Hollywood had "tame" writers, whereas the Soviet film industry did not. In the absence of producers and midlevel writing staffs, the screenplay was a contested format open to a variety of influences, not a reliable contract on the finished film. No mechanism was ever developed for the large-scale procurement and rewriting of stories that could be changed at the will of the censors. In combination with the director-centered mode, the authored literary scenario led to censorship compromises at the screenplay stage and resulted in "imperfect" films. Yet as long as the Stalin government continued to believe screenwriters and directors were the elite responsible for content, it was impossible for industry censors to counterbalance this authority.

CENSORSHIP

Industry Self-Censorship and
Extreme Uncertainty

Since the Soviet film industry lacked effective mechanisms for production control, it had to rely on censorship to ensure conformity. In what is probably the most remarkable inconsistency between the Stalinist control project and the institutional structure of Soviet cinema, however, under Stalin responsibility for film censorship was assigned to the film industry itself. When industry self-censorship proved unsuccessful, Stalin, the Central Committee, and the Propaganda Department intervened. The party corrective, the outcome of which was hard to predict, introduced extreme uncertainty and lack of responsibility to the already compromised self-censorship, making it only less productive.

Before the Soviet archives opened in the 1990s, scholars could only discuss censorship in general terms.[1] Today we have access to vast collections of documents from the period and many long-forgotten banned films have been catalogued and described.[2] However, we still lack an account of how censorship was

---

1. Valery S. Golovskoy, "Film Censorship in the USSR," in *Red Pencil: Artists, Scholars, and Censors in the USSR*, ed. Marianna Tax Choldin and Maurice Friedberg (Boston: Unwin Hyman, 1989), 117–143; Kenez, *Cinema and Soviet Society*, 127–134; Sidney Monas, "Censorship, Film, and Soviet Society: Some Reflections of a Russia-Watcher," *Studies in Comparative Communism* 17, no. 3/4 (Fall/Winter 1984–1985): 163–172.

2. The best source on banned films is Margolit and Shmyrov, *Iz"iatoe kino*. See also, Evgenii Margolit, "Budem schitat', chto takogo fil'ma nikogda ne bylo," in Mamatova, *Kino*, 132–156; Ekaterina Khokhlova, "Forbidden Films of the 1930s," in Taylor and Spring, *Stalinism and Soviet Cinema*, 90–96.

conducted. Who were the censors? How did they function? What was the level of Stalin's involvement in censorship? Why were bans common? This chapter offers an account and suggests why despite its intent the transition to industry-party censorship failed to secure satisfactory film production. The cinema administration could not censor effectively because in addition to entitled directors and screenwriters, it faced a conflict of interests. As both the censor and the producer, it could not censor itself effectively, for the effort to prevent bans clashed with the pressure to fulfill the plan. As Joseph Berliner observed in the 1950s, as long as the control personnel are part of the organization they control, they cannot be effective.[3] In addition, the industry censors never had a complete sense of which guidelines to apply, and there was always a chance that party censors would reverse industry decisions, making industry self-censorship not only uncertain but in some instances pointless.

Party censorship was introduced to fill the gaps in self-censorship. Yet rather than addressing the causes of censorship failures, the leaders attacked filmmakers through bans. The industry responded with extreme caution and a decrease in productivity. In an explicitly ideological environment, which necessitated prescriptive censorship and clear guidelines, the party leadership failed to provide the film industry with sophisticated censorship tools. It was not the strength of censorship, but its weaknesses that made it impossible for Soviet cinema to properly function.

From State Censorship to Industry Censorship, 1929–1933

On the brink of the 1930s, the party had no direct role in censoring individual films. Soviet film censorship comprised two sets of players: state censors and film-industry censors. State censors worked at the state censorship agency for public performances and spectacles, the Main Repertory Control Committee (Glavrepertkom, *Glavnyi repertuarnyi komitet*), which, as part of the Commissariat of Education (Narkompros), was independent from the film industry. When originally created in February 1923, Glavrepertkom was only responsible for licensing films for distribution in the RSFSR. Republic studios submitted films

---

3. Joseph S. Berliner, *Factory and Manager in the USSR* (Cambridge, MA: Harvard University Press, 1957), 325.

to Repertory Control Committees in their own republics at the same time they sent them to Moscow, and a film could be in distribution in the home republic before Glavrepertkom approved it for the RSFSR.[4] Glavrepertkom also started to censor screenplays in 1926.

Glavrepertkom employed nearly a dozen censors, many of whom had creative backgrounds. Pavel Bliakhin, who headed the Film Section, was a screenwriter. Another head of the Film Section was Aleksandr Katsigras, and he, along with the senior political editor Nikolai Ravich, and the top Glavrepertkom officials Konstantin Gandurin and Osaf Litovskii were writers by trade. The editor Karl Krumin was a theater director. Industry censors worked at the studio screenplay departments and at the central cinema administration in Moscow. Both studio and central industry censors engaged in preproduction censorship of screenplays and postproduction censorship of completed films. Between state and industry censors there was a clear hierarchy: Glavrepertkom made the final decisions.[5]

Glavrepertkom censors met regularly to screen and review films. Several Glavrepertkom employees were usually present, as well as officials from a variety of other organizations, including the OGPU, the secret police. After each screening, one of the employees filled out a form record (*protokol prosmotra*), in which he or she described the film, stated the decision—to release or not, to which kind of screens, and for how long—and substantiated it. Sometimes the record included minutes of the postscreening discussion (*preniia*). Each form had a number, and subsequent decisions on the same film were recorded in it. Based on this record Glavrepertkom issued film distribution licenses (*udostovereniia*). It was not uncommon for Glavrepertkom to reject a film's cut with the understanding that a different cut, incorporating recommended changes, could be resubmitted. The language Glavrepertkom used was always that the film was rejected "in the version submitted" (*v predstavlennoi redaktsii*). Glavrepertkom employees informed the cinema administration and the

---

4. In 1930–1933 Glavrepertkom was part of the Arts Sector within the RSFSR People's Commissariat of Education.

5. The independence of Glavrepertkom from the industry was not absolute, since some of its personnel traveled between the two domains. Bliakhin headed the Production Department of Soiuzkino in 1931 and was back at Glavrepertkom in 1932. Trainin, the first director of Glavrepertkom, was a Sovkino executive in 1925–1929 and head of the Moscow Studio (Mosfilm) in 1930. Ravich was senior political editor at Glavrepertkom in 1928–1929 and political editor at Soiuzkino by 1931. Later he wrote the screenplay for Pudovin's *Suvorov* (1940). Krumin codirected *Rodina zovet* (*Call to Arms*, 1936) with Aleksandr Macheret. He was purged and executed in 1937.

studios of a rejection in a letter, which typically repeated the wording of the numbered record. Sometimes Glavrepertkom employees also met with the director of a problematic film to advise him or her on corrections, of which a note was made in the record.[6]

Although among filmmakers Glavrepertkom had a reputation for being strict, overall it was a lenient censor, for it was much more likely to license a film than to ban it. Glavrepertkom accepted up to three repeat submissions of new screen-plays and films, and it almost always passed resubmissions as long as the new version addressed the censors concerns. Glavrepertkom also used a very flexible system of film ratings ("categories"), which determined the duration and scope of distribution. The categories ranged from one to five. Category one was given to artistically and ideologically "perfect" films, which were granted unlimited release. Category five was assigned to artistically and ideologically "semiliterate products" that were often distributed "to commercial/central cinemas only" (cin-emas in urban centers, serving the write-collar and equivalent clientele).[7] This sophisticated system of film ratings allowed Glavrepertkom to release most films, but to limit the exposure of worker and peasant audiences to those considered politically imperfect.[8]

Glavrepertkom acted in the interest of the state and the average viewer first, and in the interest of the studios second, which is probably why it had a repu-tation for strictness in the industry. For example, it banned Ivan Kavaleridze's *Shturmovye nochi* (*Storm Nights*, 1931) despite Odessa Studio's claims that the film was its major achievement. *Storm Nights*, the story of a backward peasant who becomes a socialist, was a striking avant-garde experiment with a completely incoherent plot. Glavrepertkom said the film contained "crude political mis-takes" while its open formalism made it inaccessible to the mass audience.[9] Here, however, is an example that illustrates just how flexible Glavrepertkom could be. In October 1929 Glavrepertkom received for review Aleksandr Solov'ev's film

---

6. Some Glavrepertkom papers can be found at the Gosfilmofond Archive in Moscow.

7. Prior to 1929 Glavrepertkom only used four categories, and the films in the fifth category were banned. Pavel Bliakhin, "K itogam kino-sezona 1927–1928 goda," *Kino i kul'tura* 2 (1929): 3–16.

8. It was routine for Glavrepertkom to place films in the lower (higher-number) categories. As reported by Bliakhin, out of 111 films Glavrepertkom reviewed in 1929, seventy-one were in the two lowest categories (four and five). It was common for films in the lower categories to also receive a distribution end date, which usually was within one year. Soiuzkino, *10 fil'm i pol-itprosvetrabota vokrug nikh* (Moscow: Soiuzkino, 1931); Narkompros RSFSR, *Repertuarnyi ukazatel', tom 3, Kinorepertuar*; Babitsky and Rimberg, *Soviet Film Industry*, 87–88).

9. Gosfilmofond Archive, f. 2, op. 1, d. 1065, ll. 1–3, 12, 13; see also Margolit and Shmyrov, *Iz"iatoe kino*, 28.

Piat' nevest (*Five Brides*), also made by the Odessa Studio. The film tells the story of a small Jewish village in Ukraine during the civil war. The village is taken over by White troops, who demand the villagers provide five young women ("brides") for their pleasure. The film then deals with the drama of the young women. In the brief last shot of the film and at the very last moment narratively, the Red troops arrive to save the women.

Studio executives found the film "very good both artistically and ideologically" and probably expected it to receive a high category rating from Glavrepertkom.[10] Glavrepertkom, however, rejected *Five Brides* on several grounds, including that the class composition of the villagers was not transparent in the film and that the interest of the film centered on whether the brides would be sexually victimized. The version of the film that survives contains shots in which a heavy villager, whose size and costume mark him as a representative of the upper class, strangles a young man who wants to help the brides. The young man does not figure anywhere else in the film, which leads one to presume that this scene was included to satisfy Glavrepertkom's demand for showing class struggle. Nothing could be done about the brides' plotline, however, since it was essential to the film. Whatever changes were made, they did not satisfy Glavrepertkom when it reviewed the film again in February 1930. In May 1930, when the film was submitted for the third time, it received a license, despite the fact that just about everyone present at the Glavrepertkom screening found the film still lacking in multiple respects. Glavrepertkom probably passed the melodrama because it knew it could give it the lowest, fifth, category rating, limiting its release to urban commercial theaters, which is what it did. Nevertheless, six months later it had to withdraw the film from distribution "in view of public protest."[11] According to *Kino*, political activists among the public found *Five Brides* to be anti-Semitic and believed rape was not a proper subject for Soviet art.[12]

Even as it protected state interests, the logic of censorship practiced by Glavrepertkom was to ensure the release of as many films as possible. The censors made their political prescriptions to studios—such as to show class struggle in *Five Brides*—but were willing to be flexible. The focus of the system was on prevention: Glavrepertkom told filmmakers what to do to avoid problems, and bans were rarely necessary. When they were, bans were issued mostly on artistic

---

10. RGALI, f. 2769, op. 1, d. 340, l. 4.

11. Gosfilmofond Archive, f. 2, op. 1, d. 775, ll. 2–31 (13).

12. A. Stepanov et al., "Vreditel'stvo na ideologicheskom fronte" and "Otkrytoe pis'mo Feliksu Konu," *Kino*, November 27, 1930, 2.

grounds: when the presentation was too experimental to carry any plot (as was the case with *Storm Nights*) or was too incompetent. In other words, Glavrepertkom was a liberal political censor, and soon this came to the attention of the party leadership.

In March 1930 the Central Committee for the first time found it necessary to directly interfere with Glavrepertkom's activities. Weeks after Glavrepertkom gave Aleksandr Dovzhenko's *Zemlia* (*Earth*, 1930) a distribution license, the press reported that the prominent party-approved poet Dem'ian Bednyi called the film pornographic and ideologically flawed. (There is a scene in the film where the female protagonist is in grieving agony and happens to be also nude.) After several similar reports appeared, the Central Committee ordered the suspension of the film and instructed the Propaganda Department to excise "its pornographic elements and other elements that contradict[ed] Soviet policies."[13] This wording was a direct hit at Glavrepertkom, as two of the items it was supposed to censor were anti-Soviet agitation and pornography.[14]

In the summer of 1930 Glavrepertkom was also relieved of its responsibility to review screenplays. The move was instigated by the film industry, which wanted to streamline and shorten the screenplay review process.[15] However, it was also part of the general policy shift spearheaded by the Propaganda Department to reinforce political censorship through self-censorship by moving preproduction censorship from state agencies to the production entities themselves.[16] For cinema, this meant Glavrepertkom "plenipotentiaries," political editors and consultants, at the film studios on the film-industry payroll now performed screenplay censorship.

The move from preproduction state censorship to preproduction industry censorship was not supplemented with a significant increase in the number of censors. Whereas representatives of Glavlit (the Main Administration for Literary and Publishing Affairs), the censor of the printed text, numbered in the thousands, only a handful of individuals at each studio and at the central cinema administration censored cinema. The political editors were required to have only

---

13. Fomin, *Letopis' rossiiskogo kino, 1930–1945*, 25–29; Anderson et al., *Kremlevskii kinoteatr*, 117. Bednyi's poem about the film ("Filosofy"), originally published in *Izvestiia* (April 4, 1930, 2), is reprinted in Iu. A. Belousov, "Dem'ian Bednyi—kritik *Zemli*," *Kinovedcheskie zapiski* 23 (1994): 149–162. See also Kepley, *In the Service of the State*, 75–84.

14. Blium, *Tsenzura v Sovetskom Soiuze*, 32–33.

15. RGALI, f. 2497, op. 1, d. 2, ll. 56, 104, 109, 115; RGALI, f. 962, op. 10, d. 6, l. 96; Fomin, *Letopis' rossiiskogo kino, 1930–1945*, 37.

16. On similar policies developed for Glavlit, see Artizov and Naumov, *Vlast'*, 54–55.

one qualification: party loyalty. It was even better if they represented the primary target audience: the worker and peasant population. There is evidence that studios made an effort to employ just such individuals. The Lenfilm studio reported in July 1931 that it hired as political editors some "upward-moving workers" (*vydvizhentsy*) "straight from the factory floor."[17] As we have seen, the studios, however, employed editor-censors with creative backgrounds as well, as these were more attuned to creative issues.

Both types of backgrounds, proletarian and intellectual, had misgivings. Censors with working-class credentials lacked sophistication, and directors did not take them seriously. In 1931, after many months of trying to get the film *Pesni* (*Songs*, not realized) approved, Ermler finally learned from a political editor at his Leningrad studio that his screenplay was "useless, nonparty, and non-Soviet." Ermler objected. The editor dropped these labels, but refused to pass the screenplay on the grounds that it was mystical. Only after a public discussion of his screenplay at the authoritative Communist Academy found that Ermler's project was indeed full of "crude methodological errors" did the director become convinced. He decided to take a year off of cinema and brush up on his "communist methodology."[18] Censors with intellectual backgrounds may have had the filmmakers' trust, but were more likely to forgive political errors to directors and screenwriters whose work had artistic value. Worse of all, when the political editor became part of the studio, he or she became part of the team, so to speak, and each censorship case was now more personal than had been the case with Glavrepertkom. This lowered the overall effectiveness of censorship, especially because industry censor-editors were under pressure from executives to pass screenplays and films to fulfill production plans.

For two years following the temporary suspension of *Earth*, party ideologists kept an eye on cinema, but refrained from direct involvement in censorship. In April 1933 the Central Committee was again alerted of a problematic film. The Propaganda Department chief Aleksei Stetskii complained about Glavrepertkom's "liberalism" in passing *Moia rodina* (*My Motherland*, Zarkhi and Kheifits, 1933), which Stetskii's agency then banned.[19] The film was set on the Chinese border and focused on a teenage Chinese laborer who adopted Soviet Russia as his spiritual motherland through an encounter with a friendly Soviet border

---

17. RGALI, f. 2497, op. 1, d. 37, l. 23. *Vydvizhentsy* were workers and peasants without specialized education promoted to administrative positions for their activism.

18. RGALI, f. 2497, op. 1, d. 48, ll. 168–169.

19. Anderson et al., *Kremlevskii kinoteatr*, 190.

172   **CHAPTER 5**

patrol. Shumiatskii personally green-lighted the film for Glavrepertkom review and, in February 1933, Bliakhin as Deputy Head of Glavrepertkom, personally signed the film's release documents.[20] The day after the film received its license, Shumiatskii reviewed it in the newspaper *Komsomol'skaia pravda* as "one of the major films of the season."[21] Another positive review followed on March 2.[22] The March 4, 1933 issue of *Kino* contained no less than six pieces praising the film. Then on April 3, 1933 *Pravda* reported that the film was banned. Glavrepertkom reviewed it for the second time a day earlier and ordered it out of distribution. Bliakhin again signed the document.[23] *Komsomol'skaia pravda* immediately responded with an editorial stating that *My Motherland* "presented an incorrect, distorted representation of our Red Army, its force, and its people."[24] Shumiatskii's own denunciation, "A Harmful Picture," followed the editorial.[25]

What prompted these individuals to publicly change their minds? According to Kheifits, Stalin ordered the film banned at the film's screening by reportedly saying, "We will respond to warmongers with a blow three times their strength. [This film fails to show such a response]; this is Tolstovianism."[26] In his account, Shumiatskii reported that Stalin watched the film and found it "fundamentally erroneous," saying that it propagated "passive [military] resistance."[27] The border guards, and therefore the Soviet Union, were portrayed as too weak. There is also evidence that the film was ordered banned by the Central Committee member and People's Commissar for the Army and Navy Kliment Voroshilov, who likely was the first to learn about its failings.[28] Soiuzkino sent the film for review not only to Glavrepertkom, but also to the USSR Revolutionary Military Council, the highest executive military authority in the country, headed by

20. TsGALI, f. 257, op. 9, d. 36, ll. 2–4; Gosfilmofond Archive, f. 2, op. 1, d. 1349.

21. Boris Shumiatskii, "Mnogo zanimatel'nosti, bodrosti i iarkikh krasok," *Komsomol'skaia pravda*, February 17, 1933, 4. The review's headline included this praise: "*My Motherland* is Komsomol's gift for the fifteenth anniversary of the Red Army" ("Van nakhodit svoiu rodinu," *Komsomol'skaia pravda*, February 17, 1933, 4.)

22. V. Zalesskii, "Van naidet svoiu rodinu," *Vecherniaia Moskva*, March 2, 1933, 3.

23. Gosfilmofond Archive, f. 2, op. 1, d. 1349; Margolit and Shmyrov, *Iz"iatoe kino*, 34.

24. "O kartine *Moia rodina*," *Komsomol'skaia pravda*, April 6, 1933, 4.

25. Boris Shumiatskii, "Vrednaia kartina," *Komsomol'skaia pravda*, April 6, 1933, 4; also in *Kino*, April 10, 1933, 3.

26. Anderson et al., *Kremlevskii kinoteatr*, 201.

27. Boris Shumiatskii, "Stalin o kino," in Anderson et al., *Kremlevskii kinoteatr*, 85–86.

28. Avel' Enukidze, then head of the USSR Central Executive Committee, who was close to Stalin, wrote to Voroshilov on April 10, 1933 thanking him for banning the film (Anderson et al., *Kremlevskii kinoteatr*, 201).

Voroshilov.[29] Voroshilov could have learned about the film and then discussed it with Stalin. For what it is worth, Kheifits learned of Stalin's reaction from a military official.

Whatever the actual sequence of events, it is easy to see how the film could have alarmed anyone from a low-level military officer to Stalin. In the film, Soviet patrolmen are periodically killed while on duty, but they do not respond because the filmmakers and industry censors both thought that the Soviet policy on the Chinese border was one of nonengagement. Soviet troops also give shelter to the Chinese man without suspicion. Again, the assumption was that as long as the man was poor, he could not be an ideological enemy. When the studio was alerted that this image of the Soviets in the film could be a problem, the alert was apparently ignored. The consultant M. Slavin, who reviewed the screenplay, told the studio that the character of the Soviet commander was weaker than the enemy and thus did not meet standards.[30] Indeed, to those up-to-date on Stalin's thinking, the Soviet border guards' behavior in the film amounted to weakness. As Ekaterina Khokhlova writes, the film's ban happened soon after "Stalin's speech . . ., in which he asserted the Army's strength. Against this background, a film in which Red Army soldiers actually died was regarded as a very crude mistake."[31]

The banning of *My Motherland* illustrates that already by 1933 successful industry self-censorship had become a difficult task. It was not clear which recommendations required implementation and which were simply cautionary. Also, it typically took Soviet filmmakers many months to produce a film. If a policy change occurred during the film's production, it was hard to incorporate this change. Glavrepertkom was fully aware of these difficulties and did not ban films simply because they were slightly out of date. Stalin and other party censors, who treated films as equivalents to current policy statements, however, considered such liberalism unacceptable. The problem of not being able to respond to changes efficiently, or not having reliable information on current policy, would haunt the film industry for the rest of this period.

As for Glavrepertkom, the ban of *My Motherland* effectively ended its tenure as the country's primary film censor. From then on, Glavrepertkom's independent

---

29. TsGALI, f. 257, op. 9, d. 36, l. 3.
30. TsGALI, f. 257, op. 8, d. 40, ll. 99–103.
31. Khokhlova, "Forbidden Films of the 1930s," 94. It is also likely that the ban was a consequence of a concurrent policy turn from internationalism to nationalism and defense, on which see David Brandenberger, *National Bolshevism: Stalinist Mass Culture and the Formation of Modern Russian National Identity, 1931–1956* (Cambridge, MA: Harvard University Press, 2002).

responsibilities with regard to film were reduced to censoring and purging Soviet and foreign films already in distribution and approving Soviet films for export.[32] Films still received physical distribution licenses for RSFSR from Glavrepertkom, but these were only rubber stamps, and the final censorship responsibility for preparing new releases was given to the film industry. Although the film industry was owned by the state, I here reserve the label "industry" rather than "state" for the cinema administration because of how its interests were aligned. Being an entity independent from the film industry, Glavrepertkom protected the interests of the party-state, even if it did so imperfectly. The cinema administration, in contrast, had its own industry-specific interests. It wanted to contribute to the Soviet regime as best it could, but it also needed to protect itself and support its crucial cadres, the film directors.[33]

To aid the newly independent cinema administration, in 1933 the Central Committee appointed a Film Commission, headed by Stetskii, to supervise screenplays and approve "all" films for release. The Commission comprised a dozen members, most of whom were Propaganda Department officials, as well as Shumiatskii and his deputy Sutyrin.[34] For the next two years, the industry had to share censorship responsibility for both screenplays and films with the party, which was what film executives had been asking for.[35]

Industry Censorship, the Propaganda Department, and Joseph Stalin, 1933–1935

Between June and November 1933 the Central Committee Film Commission reviewed more than fifty film projects at various stages of development. Commission members read screenplays and reported on them at Commission meetings. Based on these reports, the Commission, which never found any project entirely satisfactory, made recommendations to excise, add, or rewrite specific scenes, themes, and plotlines, and then expected to reconsider the new version.

---

32. Glavnoe upravlenie po kontroliu za zrelishchami i repertuarom, *O kontrole za zrelishchami i repertuarom* (Moscow: Narkompros RSFSR, 1935), 3–45; Golovskoy, "Film Censorship in the USSR," 122–126. In 1933–1936 Glavrepertkom (later GURK) continued to be part of the RSFSR People's Commissariat of Education. On the "purges" of distribution, see Khokhlova, "Forbidden Films of the 1930s," 90–96.

33. On the industry-regime divide in interests, see Paul R. Gregory, *The Political Economy of Stalinism: Evidence from the Soviet Secret Archives* (Cambridge, MA: Cambridge University Press, 2004).

34. Anderson et al., *Kremlevskii kinoteatr*, 190–191, 201, 205–209.

35. RGALI, f. 2497, op. 1, d. 37, ll. 96–114.

Many of the screenplays under the Film Commission's review were already being produced, suggesting that Shumiatskii used the Commission to obtain ongoing editorial feedback or external validation. In addition to reading screenplays, members of the Commission met with screenwriters and directors and reviewed film rushes. It is fair to say that the Commission vetted every film project in the second half of 1933.[36]

It is difficult to ascertain the consequences of the Commission's involvement, however. What we know is that soon Lenfilm made *Chapaev* and *The Youth of Maksim*. Even though the Commission was not enthusiastic about either screenplay, it may have steered these projects away from mistakes. The Commission also prevented some questionable films from being completed, and the number of bans in 1933 and 1934 dropped substantially as a result. Both of these developments boosted film industry morale by showing it could be useful and productive again. On the flip side, the Commission insisted on selectivity. Out of twenty-eight screenplays it considered, it rejected twelve.[37] Shumiatskii later told his subordinates that he learned from the Commission that "as soon as there is any doubt, all work should be stopped without hesitation."[38] Since few project raised no doubts, output could not but suffer.

The Commission and Shumiatskii did not always see eye to eye, and both used Stalin and other members of the Central Committee to arbitrate their differences. When Stetskii objected to Ol'ga Preobrazhenskaia and Ivan Pravov's contemporary drama *Odna radost'* (*The Only Joy*, 1933), blaming Shumiatskii, Shumiatskii asked Stalin to watch the film. Stalin apparently did, siding with Stetskii (the film was banned).[39] This showed that the industry was incapable of providing preventive censorship to the party's satisfaction and should have prompted the Central

36. RGALI, f. 2456, op. 1, d. 92. The minutes have been published (with omissions) by Viktor Listov, "'Nazvanie kazhdoi kartiny utverzhdaetsia Komissiei Orgbiuro,'" *Kinovedcheskie zapiski* 31 (1996): 108–130. An early version of the list of projects reviewed by the Commission is preserved in the Central Committee files (RGASPI, f. 17, op. 114, d. 362, ll. 147–150) and is mentioned in Anderson et al., *Kremlevskii kinoteatr*, 209. The complete list is contained in GUKF files (RGALI, f. 2456, op. 1, d. 76, ll. 24–31).

37. Anderson et al., *Kremlevskii kinoteatr*, 225.

38. Anderson et al., *Kremlevskii kinoteatr*, 462–463.

39. Anderson et al., *Kremlevskii kinoteatr*, 221–226, 228. On December 8, 1933 Shumiatskii issued an order "in relation to establishing due process for especially closed film screenings" at GUKF headquarters in central Moscow (RGALI, f. 2497, op. 2, d. 19, l. 7). Since these must have been screenings for Stalin, it is possible that this episode had prompted Shumiatskii to encourage Stalin to request such screenings. Before 1934 screenings for Central Committee members were held at GUKF. In the fall 1934 the screenings were moved to the Kremlin.

Committee to scale up the party's involvement. Instead, after having given the Propaganda Department only six months to supervise the film industry closely, on December 7, 1933 the Central Committee cut party censorship back to only ten major films.[40] The responsibility for censoring screenplays for the rest of the 1934 program was delegated back to the industry.

The reason this solution was chosen could have been Stalin's growing willingness to watch films himself, which rendered some of the Commission's services unnecessary. Stalin made this point to Shumiatskii in January 1935: "[My watching films] is better than any Commission!"[41] Curiously, according to Shumiatskii, only months earlier Stalin was unaware of the Commission. At the screening in May 1934 he asked, "Who permits such films to be made?" and, upon hearing about the Commission, displayed ignorance.[42] Getting direct access to Stalin—his best test audience, patron, and advisor under the circumstances—and bypassing the Propaganda Department was exactly what Shumiatskii wanted.

We have a pretty good idea as to when Stalin first started watching films. According to Shumiatskii, who had every reason to exaggerate Stalin's involvement, Stalin saw only very few films in the early 1930s. Shumiatskii reported it was in 1934 that Stalin's interest grew to the point where he began ordering "brilliant instructions" on how to improve particular films.[43] Shumiatskii's detailed notes on screenings with Stalin, which start in May 1934 and end in March 1936, confirm this interest. They also show how over the period of two years, Stalin grew increasingly more comfortable in the shoes of a decision-maker. At first he acted as a mere test audience, simply commenting on being bored by lengthy scenes and slow story progression. By the end, he asked Shumiatskii to bring him rough cuts and offered explicit suggestions. Even so, Stalin had more to say about documentaries and newsreels than fiction films. Moreover, in the case of nonfiction, Stalin gave precise instructions on which shots to include and where. In the case of fiction features, his critical comments mostly targeted better clarity of action.[44]

Shumiatskii's notes show that Stalin's censorship functions during this period were very partial. A smart politician, Shumiatskii used his position as a

40. Anderson et al., *Kremlevskii kinoteatr*, 228, 232–233.
41. Anderson et al., *Kremlevskii kinoteatr*, 986.
42. Anderson et al., *Kremlevskii kinoteatr*, 928.
43. Shumiatskii, "Stalin o kino," 84–89.
44. Anderson et al., *Kremlevskii kinoteatr*, 919–1053.

mediator between Stalin and Soviet screens to show Stalin only the best of the products his industry prepared, giving Stalin a falsely favorable picture of the industry performance. Stalin, for his part, did not seem interested in watching every film. Instead, he opted to watch *Chapaev* at least thirty-eight times, reducing to absurdity his own contention that each film should be watched more than once.[45] In fact it appears that at least during the 1930s Stalin considered his screenings entertainment rather than work and was happy to see the light fare Shumiatskii offered.[46] It is also clear that in 1934 Stalin sided with Shumiatskii, at the expense of the Film Commission, on the kinds of films to support. One example was Stalin's response to Aleksandrov's boisterous musical comedy *Jolly Fellows* (1934).

The Film Commission found *Jolly Fellows* to be "good-for-nothing, rowdy, and false all the way through," as well as "counterrevolutionary," and asked for scenes to be deleted. It instructed the Main Administration for Repertory Control (GURK, *Glavnoe upravlenie po kontroliu za zrelishchami i repertuarom*), the successor to Glavrepertkom, to deny the film its release documents for the International Film Festival in Venice.[47] In contrast, Stalin and other Central Committee members' response to the film was unambiguously positive. According to Shumiatskii, Stalin laughed hard at every antic in the film and after the screening said: "Nice. This picture allows one to relax in an interesting, entertaining way. We all feel as if after a weekend. For the first time I feel this way after seeing one of our films, among which there have been very good ones."[48] Using this response as his trump card in the conflict with Stetskii, indignant Shumiatskii officially appealed to Stalin, Kaganovich, Zhdanov, and Voroshilov for help.[49] *Jolly Fellows* performed well in Venice in the summer of 1934 and was successfully released at home in December 1934, becoming a major feather in Shumiatskii's and Soviet cinema's cap.

Despite cases such as *Jolly Fellows*, prior to 1936 Stalin left the primary censorship responsibility to the industry censors. Yet already then, and *Jolly Fellows*

45. Anderson et al., *Kremlevskii kinoteatr*, 920, 1024.

46. Stalin's daughter, Svetlana Allilueva, confirms this in her memoirs, adding that before the war it was not customary to criticize the films. Svetlana Allilueva, *Dvadtsat' pisem k drugu* (Moscow: Sovetskii pisatel', 1990), 137.

47. Anderson et al., *Kremlevskii kinoteatr*, 246–247; Nikolai Sidorov, "*Veselye rebiata*—komediia kontrrevoliutsionnaia," *Istochnik* 3 (1995): 72–75; Richard Taylor, "*Veselye rebiata/The Happy Guys*," in *The Cinema of Russia and the Former Soviet Union*, ed. Birgit Beumers (London: Wallflower Press, 2007), 86.

48. Anderson et al., *Kremlevskii kinoteatr*, 946.

49. Anderson et al., *Kremlevskii kinoteatr*, 246–248.

is a case in point, his presence introduced the possibility of arbitrariness into the system. If Stalin liked a film, all the censorship decisions still outstanding were annulled, and no one but Stalin could be absolutely sure the film was politically acceptable. For the moment, however, based on Stalin's commentary at his screenings, Shumiatskii had a pretty good sense of what Stalin wanted. Moreover, the successes of *Chapaev* and *The Youth of Maksim* in November–December 1934 demonstrated to Stalin that Shumiatskii knew what he was doing. At a November 1934 screening Stalin said: "As long as Shumiatskii is trusted to make films, he should be freed from petty guardianship."[50] The Film Commission was disbanded on December 17, 1934.[51] To formalize his censorship role, on December 31, 1934 Shumiatskii established his own commission on film approval (*komissiia po priemke*), comprising administration executives and the editor of *Kino*.[52]

Shumiatskii's peak years as the central producer were 1934–1935. Stalin's support encouraged Shumiatskii to take risks and allowed the film industry to feel able to make its own censorship decisions. As a result, Soviet cinema experienced a brief relaxation that some scholars have suggestively called the first thaw, in reference to the post-Stalin thaw of the 1960s.[53] But the thaw did not last. After the newly restructured Propaganda Department, which now included a Film Section, turned its attention to cinema in the second half of 1935, it found that from the forty films produced earlier in the year only "four or five" were "relatively satisfactory" and even so greatly inferior to *Chapaev*. The rest were "ideologically helpless and unpersuasive."[54] Whereas only four films produced in 1934 were banned, sixteen of those made in 1935 ended up on the shelf.

Preventive Industry Censorship and Reactive Party Censorship, 1936–1937

As we have seen, in 1936 Stalin recognized the Soviet arts were not transitioning to socialist realism as readily as he had hoped. With only four or five "relatively

---

50. Anderson et al., *Kremlevskii kinoteatr*, 954.
51. Anderson et al., *Kremlevskii kinoteatr*, 252.
52. Kossovskii and Dorogokupets, *Kinofotopromyshlennost'*, 24–25.
53. Naum Kleiman, "'Drugaia istoriia sovetskogo kino,' Lokarno, 2000 g.," *Kinovedcheskie zapiski* 50 (2001): 70–71; Nina Dymshits (VGIK lecture, 2002). The first person to designate the era as a thaw was probably Grigorii Kozintsev, who called 1932–1936 "the second utopia." In Peter Bagrov, "Soviet Melodrama: A Historical Overview," *KinoKultura* 17 (July 2007): http://www.kinokultura.com/2007/17-bagrov.shtml.
54. Anderson et al., *Kremlevskii kinoteatr*, 308.

satisfactory" films a year, cinema was undoubtedly a culprit, and this was made clear when *Pravda* attacked Kavaleridze's *Prometheus*. Unlike *Jolly Fellows*, Shumiatskii never supported *Prometheus*. As GUKF's Voloshchenko emphasized in a letter to Ukrainfilm in August 1934, GUKF approved Kavaleridze's screenplay only under pressure from the "authorities." Across the copy of this letter preserved at Gosfilmofond, Shumiatskii wrote with a red pencil, "Tell Central Committee Secretariat that ODSK [The Society of Friends of Soviet Cinema, an activist organization for propagating cinema, 1925–1934] forced us. GUKF is against it. The screenplay is depraved (*porochnyi*)."[55] When the first version of the film was finished in September 1935, Shumiatskii reviewed it negatively in *Izvestiia*.[56] Yet as Shumiatskii reported to Stalin, the Propaganda Department and even Molotov recommended only that Kavaleridze make changes. Ukrainfilm sent a new version to Shumiatskii in November 1935.[57] Shumiatskii showed the film to Stalin at Stalin's request on February 7, 1936, and on February 13, 1936 *Pravda* attacked it for its "formalist" treatment of history.[58]

In the aftermath of the antiformalism campaign, the party leadership put more pressure on Shumiatskii to prevent wrong films from being produced. When in 1936 GUKF was subordinated to the Arts Committee, GURK, the state censor, also became part of the Arts Committee and was thus promoted to all-Union status. Moreover, in June 1936 the Central Committee made a decision to officially reintroduce party censorship. The decision read: "Films accepted by GUKF [GUK] for release are to be screened and approved by the Propaganda Department in collaboration with the Committee for Arts Affairs before they are shown to the public or enter distribution."[59] In other words, censors outside of Shumiatskii's administration were again given final censorship rights over competed films. However, Shumiatskii was still in charge of censorship up to the final cut. An amendment specified, "Put GUK in charge of screenplay approval, control during filming, and the release of films throughout Soviet cinema."[60] Given that the composition of the industry censorship

55. Gosfilmofond Archive, f. 2, op. 1, d. 1975. For more information on the censorship of *Prometheus*, see this Gosfilmofond file, as well as Margolit and Shmyrov, *Iz"iatoe kino*, 43–45.

56. Boris Shumiatskii, "Talant i ucheba," *Izvestiia*, October 21, 1935, 4.

57. In 1934 the Film Commission also passed the screenplay of the film. Gosfilmofond Archive, f. 2, op. 1, d. 1975.

58. Anderson et al., *Kremlevskii kinoteatr*, 1041–1042; "Grubaia skhema vmesto istoricheskoi pravdy," *Pravda*, February 13, 1936, 4.

59. Anderson et al., *Kremlevskii kinoteatr*, 320.

60. Anderson et al., *Kremlevskii kinoteatr*, 321.

staff remained the same as it was in the early 1930s, preventive censorship of screenplays continued to be weak. When the Propaganda Department personnel watched films, they were dissatisfied with the results: seven films were banned in 1936 and five in 1937.

The surviving protocols of the Propaganda Department film screenings cover the period from January 1936 to December 1937. The first record is numbered fifteen, however, suggesting at least fourteen such screenings were held in 1935.[61] They show that every film approved by GUK went through the Propaganda Department screenings.[62] The group of individuals at the screenings varied, but four individuals were almost always present: the head of the Propaganda Department Aleksei Angarov, the head of the Propaganda Department Film Sector E. M. Tamarkin, the head of GURK Osaf Litovskii, and Shumiatskii or one of his deputies. The decisions made at the screenings were either to release or to reject the film. The positive decisions, the vast majority, were followed by a specification of "circulation" (tirazh), or how many prints to make. The number of prints ranged from 150 to 300; the better, more politically useful the film, the more prints. Sometimes a few recommendations for cuts, changes, and additions were also included with the positive decision. The negative decisions were almost always substantiated and followed by a suggestion that GUK rework the film.[63]

The protocols suggest that the antiformalism campaign did not change film censorship requirements. Like screenplay editors, Propaganda Department officials and the Central Committee always watched for the image of the party, the image of the Soviet person, and the image of the enemy.[64] They wanted the characters of communists to be unambiguously positive, impressive, steady, and proper. The Only Joy was banned because its protagonist did not possess these qualities. Party censors wanted the Soviet person to be attractive, dignified, and

---

61. Protocol number sixteen, of February 15, 1936, refers to protocol number eight dated September 5, 1935; both discussed Prometheus.

62. For instance, the surviving protocols from 1936 (thirteen out of twenty-four) reveal that the Propaganda Department group made decisions on twenty-nine films. Even if only one film was screened at each of the eleven meetings that remain undocumented, this means that during 1936 the group saw at least forty features.

63. RGALI, f. 962, op. 10, d. 7a; 962, op. 10, d. 313; 962, op. 3, d. 324.

64. Liliia Mamatova has argued that many 1930s films contained three stock characters—the ordinary Soviet person, the party representative, and the wrecker—and their plots followed a model where the party representative uplifted the ordinary person while the ordinary person unmasked the wrecker. Liliia Mamatova, "Model' kinomifov 30-kh godov," in Mamatova, Kino, 52–78. On a similar analysis of the socialist-realist master plot, see Clark, Soviet Novel.

deserving. To give a later example, among the complaints voiced by the censors against Aleksandrov's *Svetlyi put'* (*The Radiant Path*, 1940), the story of a peasant girl, Tania, who works her way up to become a deputy to the Supreme Soviet, was that Tania achieved her successes too easily. The critic and editor Fedor Levin wrote: "The film shows the path of a Stakhanovite incorrectly. . . . By showing this picture one cannot foster the love of labor or the will to overcome obstacles."[65] Censors required the Soviet person be stronger and smarter than the enemy—the character traits that the makers of *My Motherland* had ignored. The enemy also could not be more compelling than the Soviet protagonists, yet he or she had to be realistic.[66]

Even if it was common (in the surviving protocols at least) for the Propaganda Department to justify its rejection by saying that a film was "antiartistic" or "weak," it is clear from other evidence that the problem was always the film's politics and message. Here is what the screening protocol of February 20, 1936 said about Mezhrabpomfilm's comedy *O strannostiakh liubvi* (*About the Oddities of Love*, Protazanov, 1936), which was banned: "The film is antiartistic, plotless, extraordinarily weak in its direction and performances, and vulgar in some episodes. . . . In this version it cannot be released. Suggest to Mezhrabpomfilm to rework the film."[67] This response does not tell us much about the characters. However, here is what we read in Mikhail Nikanorov's internal industry review of the film's screenplay: "It is hard to determine what the positive significance of the future film for the viewer could be *as far as its content*. It is clear that the characters are Soviet people and the action takes place in the Soviet country. But this is only clear to the Soviet viewer. It is clear thanks to the Russian names, the shape and cut of the clothes, and a number of other *external* indicators. Internally, however, organically, this does not emerge from the content. The entire plot is based on deeply personal, 'intimate,' sides of the characters' lives. Their connections and relationships do not extend beyond the relationships of flirting, love, and jealousy. The causes and consequences of their actions are only linked to these same 'pure' relationships of love. [The events and story of the screenplay could have happened] outside of the Soviet country. This separation of the theme, plot, story, and characters from Soviet reality or, rather, of Soviet

65. Sidorov, "*Veselye rebiata*," 78.

66. See, e.g., Zhdanov's 1941 comments on flawed films, in Fomin, *Kino na voine*, 470–472, as well as my film examples below.

67. RGALI, f. 962, op. 10, d. 7a, l. 17.

reality from the characters is the main *ideological* depravity of the screenplay."[68] All presumed attempts by Mezhrabpomfilm to make the picture more Soviet failed to satisfy the party censors. Notice, however, that the film made it to the Propaganda Department screening, which means despite this clearly negative screenplay review, the film had Shumiatskii's personal approval. This was likely because *The Oddities* director was a venerable master and the film was a delightful comedy.

The Propaganda Department's hands were tied by its lack of access to the film while it was in production and in Shumiatskii's control. Propaganda officials could only respond reactively to the completed films, at which point banning was the only option and a drastic one. This explains why so many politically questionable films were allowed to be made, why a sizable proportion of them was subsequently banned, and why bans were sometimes accompanied by emphatic shaming campaigns. A great example of how industry self-censorship functioned and why it failed to protect a film from being banned is the case of Medvedkin's *The Miracle Worker* (1936), a story of a milkmaid and one of the most original films of the period.

Medvedkin submitted the screenplay for *The Miracle Worker*—titled *Chudesnitsa-devchonka* (*Izobilie*)/*The Miracle Girl* (*Plenty*)—to Mosfilm in April 1936.[69] Mosfilm's leadership considered the screenplay on May 3, 1936, and the decision, signed by the deputy head of the studio Elena Sokolovskaia, stated that the screenplay contributed to several important themes—socialist agriculture, women collective farmers, and Stakhanovism—and presented these themes in an optimistic comedy filled with humor. While giving a realistic picture of today's agriculture, the statement said, the screenplay reflected Medvedkin's unique stylistic interest in the fairytale form. The characters and situations, it added, were "typical," "truthful," "convincing," "vivid," and originally drawn. In other words, the screenplay was thematically topical and politically useful, while at the same time artistically accomplished—the sought-after formula.

Despite these "major achievements," the Mosfilm decision recommended that Medvedkin execute six improvements in plot structure and characterization. Specifically, Medvedkin was asked to emphasize the heroine's mastery of "the new socialist culture" and the hero's "healthy tendency toward heroism," to

---

68. Gosfilmofond Archive, f. 2, op. 1, d. 1619, ll. 3–4 (emphasis in the original).
69. An untitled literary screenplay contained in the Gosfilmofond Archive file is dated April 1936 (Gosfilmofond Archive, f. 3, op. 2, d. 2770).

intensify plot development by introducing a theme of competition among collective farms, to lyricize the romantic subplot, to enhance the folk quality of dialogues, and to replace excessive literariness of the text with more "plastic expression." The resolution insisted, however, that because Medvedkin's project was Mosfilm's only comedy on collective farming in 1936, the studio would appeal to GUK to approve the literary screenplay, allow Mosfilm to execute the revisions in the director's scenario, and launch the film into preproduction.[70]

Evidently Mosfilm had few reservations about Medvedkin's film or at least thought the virtues of its subject paired with the director-master guaranteed the film's future. Two days later Mosfilm submitted the screenplay to GUK. On May 20, 1936 Shumiatskii's deputy Usievich and the inspector (yet another name for the editor-censor) of GUK's Feature Production Department Zel'dovich (the same Zel'dovich that supported "rubber" screenplays in 1935 but denounced Shumiatskii in 1938), responded to Mosfilm with a very encouraging letter, albeit stating that the screenplay was unfinished and recommending seven pages of their own detailed revisions along the lines of the studio's recommendations. Nonetheless, GUK granted Mosfilm permission to launch the film.[71]

Less than a month later, on June 15, 1936, Mosfilm approved and forwarded to GUK the second version of Medvedkin's director's scenario, titled *Izobilie (Plenty)*. Mosfilm also allocated 40,000 rubles to the film's preproduction, ordered the drawing of the production's financial plan, schedule, and art design, and approved some of the cast. At GUK Usievich asked Zel'dovich to send the director's scenario to Shumiatskii. The archival file does not contain Shumiatskii's response, but it is likely that Usievich needed Shumiatskii's opinion because, according to the review of the director's scenario signed by Zel'dovich and the acting head of the Feature Production Department Isaak Kogan, Medvedkin had failed to implement GUK's directives.[72] Whatever Shumiatskii's reaction was, he did not interrupt the production.

70. "Postanovlenie po literaturnomu stsenariiu *Chudesnitsa-devchenka* [sic] (*Izobilie*), avtor A. Medvedkin," Gosfilmofond Archive, f. 3, op. 2, d. 2770 (Document titles are included here because Gosfilmofond files lack continuous pagination).

71. V. Usievich and G. Zel'dovich, Letter to Mosfilm, May 20, 1936, Gosfilmofond Archive, f. 3, op. 2, d. 2770.

72. I. Kogan and G. Zel'dovich, Review of the Director's Scenario *The Miracle Worker*, June 19, 1936, Gosfilmofond Archive, f. 3, op. 2, d. 2770.

On July 7, 1936 Medvedkin submitted to Mosfilm a sort of statement of intentions for the film titled *The Miracle Worker*, confirming his commitment to a new, more realistic approach to storytelling, to the approved director's scenario as written, and to character "typicality."[73] At the end of August GUK was already viewing the first rushes, and there is little doubt that Shumiatskii supported Medvedkin's project at this point. As mentioned in chapter 3, Medvedkin wrote to Shumiatskii in September 1936 requesting foreign-made stock to film night scenes. The stock was provided and Medvedkin promised to finish the film by the Union Congress (November 25).[74] The production schedule of only five months (July to November) was extraordinary for Soviet filmmaking at the time and could not but have pleased Shumiatskii.

GUK screened the rough cut of the film on November 28, 1936. Shumiatskii, several other GUK officials, the head of Mosfilm Boris Babitskii, Sokolovskaia, Medvedkin, and the film's production administrator Lev Indenbom were present at the screening. According to the screening report, the cut was not satisfactory in the least. The primary problem was that Medvedkin showed the collective farm not as a "new socialist village" but in an "exaggerated manner" and "in a style of the old village, with elements of idiotism." Placing the collective villagers in this dated environment, the report said, "clearly depraved (*porochit'*) [the film's] ideological basis." In addition, many character portrayals were "failures," and the majority of performances were of low professional quality. The tempo was also "impermissibly slow," the dialogues were too lengthy, and the language was simplified to the level of elementary agitation. The report concluded that Medvedkin willfully (*samovol'no*) approached the film in a way that went contrary to GUK's recommendations.[75]

GUK recommended cuts, deletions of scenes and characters, and dialogue revisions. At the meeting that accompanied the screening, however, Shumiatskii acknowledged with regret that GUK so often had to act against the director and his studio. Moreover, he said, *The Miracle Worker* was an improvement over Medvedkin's previous *Happiness* (1934), if only because *Happiness*, which showed the country "thoroughly negatively," was a complete failure. It was also

---

73. Aleksandr Medvedkin, "*Chudesnitsa*: Rezhisserskaia eksplikatsiia," Gosfilmofond Archive, f. 3, op. 2, d. 2770.

74. GUK Review of the Rushes for *The Miracle Worker*, August 31, 1936, Gosfilmofond Archive, f. 3, op. 2, d. 2770.

75. GUK Review of the Rough Cut of *The Miracle Worker*, November 26, 1936, Gosfilmofond Archive, f. 3, op. 2, d. 2770.

an improvement over the screenplay *Okaiannaia sila* (*The Accursed Force*), which Medvedkin proposed between the two films and which GUK rejected.[76] Clearly referring to his conversations with Stalin, Shumiatskii also mentioned that the country's leadership was unhappy that GUK was making few comedies.[77] Apparently because Shumiatskii believed in Medvedkin, as well as to acknowledge his record-breaking production speed and allow Mosfilm to complete its only collective-farm comedy of 1936, GUK continued supporting the film it considered ideologically flawed.[78]

On December 11 GUK reviewed Medvedkin's "corrections" to the film and concluded that the director followed some recommendations and ignored others.[79] After some additional changes were apparently introduced, on December 28, 1936 GUK approved the film for release, having made this decision at a regular screening with Propaganda Department officials. The film was to be released in two hundred prints, including one hundred for rural screens.[80] GUK applied for a GURK license on December 31, 1936 and received it without a hitch on January 4, 1937. The GURK evaluation stated: "The film is made unevenly. The landscape is shown well. There are many lyrical episodes and comic situations. However, socialist competition is shown not as well. Intertitles and dialogue lines concerning the competition are too prosaic, simply dry, and in places stylistically negligent. Some gags are superfluous. Pass for distribution for two years."[81] The film was officially released (in Moscow and at least in some other territories) on February 11, 1937, and it received largely positive reviews.[82] Reportedly,

---

76. Medvedkin objected to this by pointing out that *Happiness* was still successfully playing in theaters and was especially favored by collective farm workers, an objection that greatly angered Shumiatskii. "Stenogramma soveshchaniia u nachal'nika GUK, tov. Shumiatskogo, po obsuzhdeniiu fil'ma *Chudesnitsa*," Gosfilmofond Archive, f. 3, op. 2, d. 2770, ll. 31–34.

77. "Stenogramma soveshchaniia u nachal'nika GUK," 14–26.

78. On Medvedkin's career and comedy prior to 1936, see Richard Taylor, "A 'Cinema for the Millions': Soviet Socialist Realism and the Problem of Film Comedy," *Journal of Contemporary History* 18, no. 3 (1983): 439–461.

79. GUK Discussion of Corrections for *The Miracle Worker*, December 11, 1936, Gosfilmofond Archive, f. 3, op. 2, d. 2770.

80. RGALI, f. 962, op. 10, d. 313, l. 3; GUK Note to the Printing Department, January 7, 1937, Gosfilmofond Archive, f. 3, op. 2, d. 2770. A document dated February 20, 1937 in the same Gosfilmofond file stated that GUK ordered the printing of *The Miracle Worker* in 250 prints, Mosfilm's *The Convicts* in 250 prints, and Ukrainfilm's *Konduit* (*Conduit*, Boris Shelontsev, 1935) in 200 prints. Since *Conduit* was released in May 1936 and *The Convicts* in December 1936, this may have been an additional print run order for all three.

81. GURK Protocol No. 501, Gosfilmofond Archive, f. 3, op. 2, d. 2770.

82. M. Shevchenko, "Na puti k realizmu," *Iskusstvo kino* 2 (1937): 48–52; N. Klado, "*Chudesnitsa*," *Kino*, January 17, 1937, 2.

Kerzhentsev, Chairman of the Arts Committee, speaking at the January industry conference, called the film an overall success despite some flaws.[83]

Medvedkin's supervisors, peers, and official critics could see that the film had problems, yet nobody in the film community anticipated it would be banned. At an internal January discussion at Mosfilm, the film was evaluated as having both succeeded in some ways (stylization and production speed) and failed in others (acting, plotting, dialogues, and sound). In the words of Sokolovskaia, *The Miracle Worker* was a step forward in Medvedkin's path even if not the end of this path. However, when Shumiatskii gave the film only very reserved praise at the January industry conference, Mosfilm was enraged.[84] Despite their many specific criticisms—which were a mandatory part of any discussion—Medvedkin's peers at the House of Cinema gave the film a "very warm," "interested," and "lively" reception.[85]

Notably, the central newspapers (*Pravda* and *Izvestiia*) did not review the film. On April 24, 1937 *Izvestiia* published a short "Letter to the Editor" demanding, in the words of two individuals who signed it, that the film be immediately taken off the screens. The reasons were the film's "gross perversion" of Soviet collective-farm reality and Medvedkin's "obtuseness" in his treatment of it. The letter specifically objected to two scenes. According to the authors, the scene of the farm fire showed a weak response from the farmers. Far worse, the letter said that the ending, where the film's champion milkmaid Zinka participates in a meeting with the country leaders at the Kremlin, had no business appearing in a film this "perverse."[86] GURK had already called the picture "for immediate rereview" on April 21, 1937.[87]

It is not clear from the archival record what spurred the reconsideration of the film (*Izvestiia* did not have to go ahead with the letter whatever its provenance). It is likely that the banning of Eisenstein's *Bezhin Meadow*, a collective-farm drama from Mosfilm, by the Central Committee in March 1937 attracted renewed attention to *The Miracle Worker*. It is also possible that *Izvestiia* or another newspaper, having received a letter of the sort that *Izvestiia* published, alerted GURK or GUK. What is clear is that by allowing the production of Medvedkin's film and by releasing it, Shumiatskii, GUK, and Mosfilm had taken a major risk. Between

83. Anderson et al., *Kremlevskii kinoteatr*, 397.
84. Boris Babitskii, "Mosfilm," *Kino*, January 29, 1937, 3.
85. "Na obsuzhdenii *Chudesnitsy*," *Kino*, January 11, 1937, 2.
86. S. Stemasov and N. Naumov, "Pis'mo v redaktsiiu," *Izvestiia*, April 24, 1937, 4.
87. GURK Protocol No. 501, Gosfilmofond Archive, f. 3, op. 2, d. 2770.

the call for rereview at the end of April and the ban at the end of May, a small avalanche of negative commentary asking for the film's withdrawal descended on both GURK and GUK. It is possible the commentary, which came in the form of telegrams from distribution officials on the ground, was solicited by GURK to justify the ban: all telegrams date from May 1937, as if they were a response to a call for evidence. Nevertheless, the readiness and unanimity of the commentary's scorn is striking. For example, in the earliest such correspondence filed at Gosfilmofond, officials from the Crimea wrote that the film "vulgarized" collective farms and that the ending at the Kremlin was "impermissible and politically damaging."[88] All other notices, from Ukraine, Tatarstan, Khabarovsk, Kirov, Leningrad, and Sverdlovsk, mentioned "perversion of collective-farm reality." Some also wrote that the public was protesting the release of the picture, perhaps suggesting a genuine grass-roots response.

The basic conclusion of the review GURK issued on April 22 was that Medvedkin still occupied a "depraved formalist stance," which caused him to "distort Soviet reality" in his film. Specifically, Medvedkin deployed a fire, a grave event in the life of any collective farm, which "more often than not is an act of class hatred," for comedy. He also made fun of the inadequacy of the firefighters and treated the hero's heroic actions during the fire ironically.[89] The scene of the fire was flagged as problematic during many of the film's discussions. Yet at the discussion of the rough cut at GUK, Medvedkin was specifically told that it was fine to satirize the firefighters (since his were not "typical" firefighters), and it did not apparently occur to anyone then that the fire ought to be treated as arson.[90] (Arson was a major dramatic event in *Bezhin Meadow* as well.) Three more elements of the film were judged "absolutely impermissible" by GURK: Cows read the newspaper celebrating the heroic actions of the protagonist during the fire, an intertitle says "All girls dream of becoming milkmaids," and a local prosecutor makes decisions based on whether or not he has a toothache. The review concluded that the film needed to be taken off the screens.[91] On

---

88. Screening Certificate from Simferopol', Gosfilmofond Archive, f. 3, op. 2, d. 2770.

89. GURK Review of *The Miracle Worker*, April 22, 1937, Gosfilmofond Archive, f. 3, op. 2, d. 2770. The signature under the document looks like that of the GURK official Konstantin Gandurin, but it is difficult to discern.

90. "Stenogramma soveshchaniia u nachal'nika GUK," l. 3.

91. GURK Review of *The Miracle Worker*, April 22, 1937.

May 16 the head of GUK's distribution office, apparently under pressure from the ground, appealed to Usievich as well to ban the film.[92] GURK banned *The Miracle Worker* on May 26, 1937.[93]

The story of *The Miracle Worker* shows that Mosfilm, GUK, and Shumiatskii personally were responsible for censoring Medvedkin's film. The final censorship decision, to release it, was made jointly by Shumiatskii and Usievich, representing GUK, and Angarov and Tamarkin, representing the Propaganda Department. There is no evidence that Angarov and Tamarkin recommended or introduced any changes. In other words, the Propaganda Department and its head, Angarov, approved of GUK's censorship. Yet Angarov's passing the film for release in effect also granted *The Miracle Worker* a party-state stamp of approval. GURK went along with this decision. Only when GURK officials received signals from outside that the film being exhibited and therefore under their purview was problematic did they act to ban it. Moreover, if GURK indeed solicited negative responses from its local affiliates, then it needed evidence to make its case for the ban, possibly against Shumiatskii's continued patronage of the film. GURK officials made copies of the entire negative correspondence they received and forwarded these to the Arts Committee and the Propaganda Department, putting GUK on the spot for its "blunder."[94]

The story also shows that as late as 1937 the industry continued to push the envelope on censorship and took risks with sensitive subjects. By supporting *The Miracle Worker* despite its problems, Shumiatskii aligned himself in favor of the director, the studio, and the industry and against the state, as he did often. (*Bezhin Meadow* was an exception here. In March 1937 when Shumiatskii arranged for the ban on *Bezhin Meadow* by showing it to Stalin, Shumiatskii's patience with Mosfilm and Eisenstein had apparently run out.[95] It did not help *Bezhin Meadow*'s case with Shumiatskii that the Propaganda Department,

92. Letter from Head of Rossnabfil'm Bineman to Usievich, May 16, 1937, Gosfilmofond Archive, f. 3, op. 2, d. 2770.

93. GURK Protocol No. 501, Gosfilmofond Archive, f. 3, op. 2, d. 2770. For an analysis of *The Miracle Worker*, see Emma Widdis, *Alexander Medvedkin* (London: I. B. Tauris, 2005).

94. A handwritten note marked classified (*oglasheniiu ne podlezhit*) from Deputy Head of GURK to Angarov and Tamarkin, not dated, and other documents from May 1937, Gosfilmofond Archive, f. 3, op. 2, d. 2770.

95. Shumiatskii's destructive approach to *Bezhin Meadow* was colored by his confrontation with both Eisenstein and Mosfilm's then leadership, Babitskii and Sokolovskaia, who had repeatedly challenged his authority over the film. See Anderson et al., *Kremlevskii kinoteatr*, 389–406, 409–411.

Izvestiia, and other authorities took Eisenstein's side against Shumiatskii.)[96] Moreover, even after *The Miracle Worker* was banned, Mosfilm apparently believed it could be shown. A year later, Mosfilm—no longer under Babitskii and Sokolovskaia, both of whom had been arrested as "wreckers"—attempted to reinstate the picture to the screens. Based on an application from Mosfilm, on June 20, 1938 GURK reconsidered the film for distribution once more, but reconfirmed the ban.[97]

The stories of both *The Miracle Worker* and *Bezhin Meadow* also suggest that the Propaganda Department was not a "vigilant" enough censor and could not serve as the ultimate guarantor of ideological purity. Indeed, not unlike what happened with *Jolly Fellows* in 1934, in 1936–1937 there continued to be cases when films that received negative responses from the Propaganda Department and GURK were, to Shumiatskii's delight, supported by Stalin, and vice versa. According to Shumiatskii, Stalin liked *Sluchainaia vstrecha* (*A Chance Encounter*, Savchenko, 1936), *Zakliuchennye* (*The Convicts*, Evgenii Cherviakov, 1936), and *Devushka speshit na svidanie* (*Late for a Date*, Mikhail Verner and Sergei Sidelev, 1936), whereas Angarov, Tamarkin, and Litovskii did not. Stalin and his associates criticized *Pokolenie pobeditelei* (*Generation of Victors*, Vera Stroeva, 1936) as "ideologically false," whereas Angarov, Tamarkin, and Litovskii considered it "ideologically and artistically perfect."[98] Incidentally, Pyr'ev reported that his peers at Mosfilm were "disgusted" by his *Partiinyi bilet* (*The Party Card*, 1936), but Stalin liked it.[99] Central Committee members, and specifically Stalin, were the only authority in the country that could make reliable censorship decisions. This was tragically emphasized when both Angarov and Tamarkin were arrested in the summer of 1937 and subsequently executed, perhaps allowing Shumiatskii to hope for a moment that, since his opponents were "the enemies of the people," he would be spared.[100]

---

96. Artizov and Naumov, *Vlast'*, 351–352, 357–358; Anderson et al., *Kremlevskii kinoteatr*, 409–411. Aleksandr Rzheshevskii, the screenwriter for *Bezhin Meadow*, reported that he felt the support of Angarov, Tamarkin, and Kerzhentsev and that he could go and talk to them about his creative plans anytime (RGALI, f. 631, op. 2, d. 173, l. 43). Shumiatskii also included Sergei Dinamov, a major Writers' Union functionary, among his opponents.

97. GURK Protocol No. 501, Gosfilmofond Archive, f. 3, op. 2, d. 2770.

98. RGALI, f. 2456, op. 4, d. 26, ll. 5, 8 ob. See Anderson et al., *Kremlevskii kinoteatr*, 364–365, for other examples.

99. RGALI, f. 2453, op. 2, d. 9, l. 26.

100. In a letter to Central Committee Secretary Andrei Andreev of July 29, 1937, Shumiatskii complained that *Izvestiia* was publishing articles against his administration using Angarov's arguments. He asked Andreev to investigate how the ideas of an enemy of the people could appear in the central press (RGALI, f. 2456, op. 4, d. 26, l. 12). See also Anderson et al., *Kremlevskii kinoteatr*, 442–443.

Stalin's actions in 1936–1937—the antiformalism campaign and his seemingly arbitrary preference for some films over others (which would continue)—were extraordinarily disruptive to the film industry. These actions had the effect of disorienting most professionals. When Dem'ian Bednyi's opera *Bogatyri* (*The Warriors*) was banned in November 1936 as "antihistorical," everyone realized that even the highest-placed cultural authorities, in this case Kerzhentsev and Litovskii, both of whom passed the opera, were neither personally safe nor professionally trustworthy.[101] This was confirmed in 1937–1938 with the arrests of Shumiatskii, Angarov, and Tamarkin (Kerzhentsev and Litovskii were spared). What Stalin believed was not entirely clear, however, and that was because communications of his preferences, which included editorials, awards, campaigns, bans, arrests, phone calls, and rumors, were intermittent, cryptic, or crude. In this vacuum of reliable information, no one ultimately knew what to do.[102] Neither for that matter did Stalin: "the chief spectator" knew which films he wanted, but he only knew them when he saw them.[103] Yet as long as he was watching the films, his opinion could change everything.

The division of censorship labor arrived at by the end of Shumiatskii's tenure—conflicted industry self-censorship focused on the screenplay and reactive party censorship focused on the completed film—became the final censorship arrangement under Stalin. It made sense for the party to censor completed films because, as we have seen in the previous chapters, directors adjusted the censored screenplays during production and there was a substantial time lag between the screenplay and the final cut. However, as the 1933–1934 episode of screenplay censorship by the Propaganda Department demonstrates, it would have been far more efficient for the party to censor the screenplays than to censor the films. As it was, the director-centered mode, the weak screenplay, and the weakness of industry self-censorship forced the party to move the censorship effort to the final cut, resulting in an outsized number of banned films.

---

101. See Artizov and Naumov, *Vlast'*, 333–341.

102. On Eisenstein's references to being surprised and initially confused by Stalin's decisions in the 1940s, see Sopin, "'. . . Idem na soveshchanie v TsK,'" 307, 309, 310. On Stalin's approach to the management of literature, the approach that Leonid Maksimenkov calls "voluntaristic," "subjective," and ultimately "uncontrolled" (10), see Leonid Maksimenkov, ed., *Bol'shaia tsenzura: Pisateli i zhurnalisty v strane Sovetov 1917–1956* (Moscow: Materik, 2005). On why Stalin's personal decision-making made the system fundamentally "unstable," see, e.g., Yoram Gorlizki and Oleg Khlevniuk, *Cold Peace Stalin and the Soviet Ruling Circle, 1945–1953* (Oxford: Oxford University Press, 2004).

103. This label has been used by Margolit, "Budem schitat', chto takogo fil'ma nikogda ne bylo," 154; and Fomin, "Sovetskii Gollivud," 98.

Stalin's presence as the unpredictable final arbiter not only created extreme uncertainty in the censors' work but also undermined their responsibility as decision-makers. By the end of the 1930s industry censors learned to write their reviews such that the decision to pass or reject could be resolved either way. Contemporaries described this method as the "both-yes-and-no formula."[104] No screenplay or film was ever just approved; rewrites and reedits were always recommended. This was the censors' way of protecting themselves and passing the responsibility to their superiors. The later period only exacerbated uncertainty and lack of responsibility. The growth in censorship layers in response to uncertainty further diluted responsibility while censorship recommendations piled up. Yet no one but Stalin had real veto power.

Industry Self-Censorship and the Party, 1938–1953

When in March 1937 the Central Committee for the fourth time in the 1930s issued a resolution on a particular film, this time *Bezhin Meadow*, it realized that screenplay censorship did not prevent mistakes. The resolution instructed Shumiatskii to make sure that future productions conformed precisely to the screenplays, dialogues, and production plans he approved.[105] In 1938, as we have seen, Dukel'skii attempted to realize this objective. He also cut the program for 1938 by half because many films already in production had no finalized screenplays.[106] Some of the films Dukel'skii stopped were almost complete. This preemptive purge of risky films explains why only one film was banned in 1938 and 1939 each.

In addition to placing a former NKVD officer in charge of cinema, the party also enhanced its own reactive censorship functions. In February 1938 the Central Committee transferred final censorship responsibility ever higher: from the Propaganda Department to a new three-member commission comprising the Central Committee member Andrei Andreev, the new chairman of the Arts Committee Aleksei Nazarov, and Dukel'skii.[107] It promoted the cinema administration

---

104. A. Zelenov and A. Lin, "Kritika 'ne podlezhashchaia oglasheniiu,'" *Kino*, February 5, 1938, 3. Leonid Heller has called it "the uncertainty principle." Geller, "Printsip neopredelennosti."

105. Anderson et al., *Kremlevskii kinoteatr*, 406.

106. Anderson et al., *Kremlevskii kinoteatr*, 487–496, 523–528.

107. Anderson et al., *Kremlevskii kinoteatr*, 486. Nazarov replaced Kerzhentsev as head of the Committee for Arts Affairs in January 1938.

to the ministry level and freed it from the Arts Committee's direct supervision. GURK, formerly a division of the Arts Committee, was split into two organizations. The part responsible for cinema (now titled URK, *Upravlenie po kontroliu za kinorepertuarom*, Administration for Cinema Repertory Control) became part of the Cinema Committee, that is, part of the industry, thus completing its trajectory of diminishing authority first started in 1930.

In August 1940 the Central Committee banned *The Law of Life*. Mosfilm and the Cinema Committee passed the film on May 23, 1940, URK issued it a license several days later, and *Izvestiia* and other newspapers published positive reviews.[108] The film's screenplay was repeatedly censored, and three versions of the literary scenario and at least two versions of the director's scenario were written between January 1939 and January 1940. The screenplay was twice sent to the Komsomol Central Committee for review, and the directors Stolper and Ivanov reportedly secured screenplay approval from none other than Andrei Vyshinskii.[109] At every stage the film raised major objections, and its "political depravity," "libel against Komsomol," and potential for a ban were all mentioned. It appears that the Cinema Committee pursued the material only because Komsomol was a highly coveted subject and the screenplay's author, Aleksandr Avdeenko, came with a stamp of party-state approval. Indeed, the head of the Cinema Committee Screenplay Department Lev Cherniavskii, who had approached Avdeenko about the screenplay, blamed the author for the film's chief mistake: the young characters' lack of vigilance in exposing their corrupt leader.[110] It was the incorrect balance in sophistication, attractiveness, and strength between the enemy and the ordinary young Soviets that doomed the film. In Stalin's words, "The problem is not that Avdeenko shows the enemy as a decent man, but that he leaves our people in the shadows."[111]

In early September 1940 Avdeenko and other prominent writers were summoned to the Kremlin to discuss the film's ban with Stalin, Zhdanov, and Andreev. The failures of the film were apparently so glaring that Stalin felt compelled

---

108. E. Gavrilov, "*Zakon zhizni*," *Izvestiia*, July 26, 1940. It needs to be noted, however, that newspaper reviewers depended in their evaluations on what the Cinema Committee told them. Georgii Aleksandrov reported in 1941 that newspapers asked Bol'shakov whether the film had been positively received by the Central Committee and wrote reviews based on his response (Fomin, *Kino na voine*, 23). This was, of course, how Soviet criticism functioned since the late 1930s.

109. RGALI, f. 2450, op. 2, d. 634; Nevezhin, "Fil'm *Zakon zhizni* i otluchenie Avdeenko."

110. RGALI, f. 2450, op. 2, d. 634, l. 7.

111. Anderson et al., *Kremlevskii kinoteatr*, 597.

to deliver the message personally. The matter needed attention also because Avdeenko was a promising young writer and the meeting could potentially teach a lesson to both cinema and literature.[112] Simultaneously with *The Law of Life*, the Central Committee banned Leonid Leonov's play *Metel'* (*The Blizzard*) because of its negative communist protagonist and inadequate portrayal of the Soviet people. The same fate befell Anna Akhmatova's poetry collection *Iz shesti knig* (*From Six Books*) and Nikolai Borisov's novel *Vygovor* (*Reprimand*) in October 1940.[113]

This ban or subsequent bans did not, however, prompt the Central Committee to intervene in industry censorship with any sophistication, and party censorship, including that by the Propaganda Department, continued to be reactive and supervisory. In August 1940 the Central Committee censorship commission was restructured to no longer include industry or culture executives. It now comprised only Zhdanov, Andreev, Malenkov, and Vyshinskii.[114] It is not clear how long into the 1940s this commission functioned (its functioning seems to have been suspended during the war), but in 1940–1941 and then again from 1945 to his death in 1948, Zhdanov was the man who handled cinema on behalf of the Central Committee.[115] Stalin continued to watch films as well; this was his late-night entertainment. Everyone in the industry knew that ultimately, if Stalin saw the film, his opinion could reverse decisions made by the prior censors. Eisenstein had ignored most of the censors' recommendations when *Ivan the Terrible* was being scripted, yet part 1 won Stalin's approval and the Stalin Prize nevertheless.[116]

During the war, self- and party censorship were both partially relaxed because the screens needed films. Several suspended films were rereleased, including those, like Eisenstein's *Aleksandr Nevskii* (1938) or Macheret's *Bolotnye soldaty* (*Peat-Bog Soldiers*, 1938), that had been pulled out of distribution as anti-German

---

112. Anderson et al., *Kremlevskii kinoteatr*, 573–604. According to Zhdanov, the meeting was called because by early September the *Pravda* article against the film produced no reaction from Avdeenko.

113. Artizov and Naumov, *Vlast'*, 449–460.

114. Oleg Khlevniuk, ed., *Stalinskoe Politbiuro v 30-e gody: Sbornik dokumentov* (Moscow: AIRO, 1995), 73; Artizov and Naumov, *Vlast'*, 448, 778.

115. In practice Zhdanov's opinions always echoed Stalin's. As Kees Boterbloem shows, Zhdanov, including during what has been misnamed *zhdanovshchina* (1946–1948), was only an executioner of Stalin's wishes. Kees Boterbloem, *The Life and Times of Andrei Zhdanov, 1896–1948* (Montréal: McGill-Queen's University Press, 2004). During the war years the Propaganda Department reported on cinema to the Central Committee Secretaries Andreev, Malenkov, and Shcherbakov; after Zhdanov's death Malenkov curated cinema.

116. Joan Neuberger, *Ivan the Terrible* (London: I. B. Tauris, 2003), 14.

after the Soviet-German nonaggression pact of August 1939.[117] By 1943 the Propaganda Department was reading screenplays approved by Bol'shakov and giving Bol'shakov official permissions to start production on every film.[118] This did not mean, however, that censorship worked: eight films completed in 1942 and five films produced in 1943 were banned. The only practice that could reduce or eliminate bans was greater risk aversion: no films were banned in 1944 and two in 1945, but, compared with 1940 or 1941, only half as many films were produced in each of these two years.

Party censorship also remained primarily reactive during the war. The Propaganda Department's Aleksandrov wrote to the Central Committee in July 1943 that the screenplays Bol'shakov provided were "completely unsuitable." Suggesting his task was only supervisory, Aleksandrov lamented, "due to the Cinema Committee's inactivity, the Propaganda Department is forced to carry out work (reviewing and editing screenplays, speaking to directors and screenwriters, compiling screenplay plans, and so forth) that is actually Bol'shakov's responsibility."[119] In his rebuttal, Bol'shakov responded that bad screenplays resulted from the fact that all of Soviet fiction was lagging behind requirements.[120] And as long as Bol'shakov successfully produced some screenplays Aleksandrov objected to, while others Aleksandrov approved resulted in "failures" (as was the case with Trauberg's *Actress*), Bol'shakov had little reason to trust Aleksandrov's judgment.[121]

By the time the Central Committee attacked several films in the summer of 1946, it was again clear that the film industry could not effectively censor itself, but no fundamental change in censorship followed.[122] The December 1946 Central Committee resolution on the flaws in feature film production confirmed that screenplays were to be censored by Bol'shakov and the Ministry Artistic Council, while the Central Committee was to watch and approve the finished films. Shifts in personnel concurrent with the resolution showed that an attempt was made to merge Propaganda Department censorship with censorship by the Ministry of Cinema. Rejecting a proposal to replace Bol'shakov, the Central

---

117. For a list, see RGALI, f. 2450, op. 4, d. 38, ll. 1–17. For which films were in distribution in 1940, see Ivlieva, *Repertuarnyi ukazatel' deistvuiushchego fonda kinokartin.*

118. Fomin, *Kino na voine*, 475.

119. Anderson et al., *Kremlevskii kinoteatr*, 678.

120. Anderson et al., *Kremlevskii kinoteatr*, 682.

121. Fomin, *Kino na voine*, 354–370, esp. Fomin's footnote commentary.

122. On the differences between the campaigns of 1940 and of 1946, see Laurent, *L'œil du Kremlin.*

Committee appointed Konstantin Kuzakov, previously one of Aleksandrov's deputies, Bol'shakov's deputy for general questions.[123] At the same time, Aleksei Sazonov, a screenwriter by training and previously chief editor of the Ministry Feature Production Department, became head of the Propaganda Department Film Section.

This party–industry censorship conflation was only a conflation in personnel, however.[124] The real, institutional merger of party censorship and industry censorship occurred in April 1947 with the formation of the "third" central Artistic Council, for it was staffed exclusively by party loyalists. Although the "fourth," 1949 version of the Artistic Council represented a more varied group of interests, from 1947 to 1949, the weight of opinion in the Artistic Council was decidedly on the party's side. Note, however, that institutionally speaking, the Artistic Council was still part of the Ministry of Cinema, and therefore part of the industry. (See appendix 3 for a summary of Soviet censorship institutions.) This meant that not much had changed in the process of censorship. Here is an example of how Konstantin Iudin's war adventure *Smelye liudi* (*Brave Men*, 1950) was censored. The case provides a nice parallel to *The Miracle Worker*.

Brave Men was in production from May 1948 to June 1950. The film told the story of a horse, Buian (Rowdy), and its young trainer, Vasia Govorukhin. When the war comes, Vasia's horse farm is forced to evacuate, while Vasia and Buian uncover a Nazi spy, join the partisans, and prevent a trainload of Russian girls from being taken to Germany. Because of its emphasis on horse riding, deadlines, and adventure, as well as the high-mountain setting (in the North Caucasus), scholars have called the film a Red Western.[125]

Brave Men was scripted by the country's top satirists, Mikhail Vol'pin and Nikolai Erdman, who wrote screenplays for both Aleksandrov's highly successful *Volga, Volga* (1938) and Barnet's banned *The Old Jockey* (1940). The pair spent some of the 1930s in exile for their writings, including antiregime jokes and fables, and in the 1940s found themselves unable to publish substantial work

---

123. Anderson et al., *Kremlevskii kinoteatr*, 783–784, 787.

124. Judging by his subsequent activities, Sazonov did not become a cinema advocate within the Propaganda Department and simply assumed the role of a party supervisor. On the industry side, Bol'shakov continued to be the primary decision-maker, while Kuzakov was absorbed by the film industry. He held his deputy minister position to October 1947 when he was demoted (for reasons unrelated to cinema) and became chief editor at Mosfilm. In 1954–1955 he replaced Bol'shakov as the cinema chief. In his memoirs Romm called Kuzakov "a very good lad" (Romm, *Ustnye rasskazy*, 94). Kuzakov was Stalin's illegitimate son.

125. Sergei Lavrent'ev, *Krasnyi vestern* (Moscow: Algoritm, 2009), cited in Julian Graffy, "Writing about the Cinema of the Stalin Years: The State of the Art," *Kritika* 10, no. 4 (2009): 820.

and living under a constant threat of arrest. Released in September 1950, *Brave Men* became the top film of that year with over forty-one million viewers (many of them Soviet boys who saw the film repeatedly). It rivaled Pyr'ev's *The Kuban Cossacks* (1949), which held second place in popularity in 1950, and became the last film of the Stalin period to attract this many viewers. It received a Stalin Prize, Second Class, in 1951.

Although *Brave Men* was conceived as an ordinary product, not a prestige picture, it underwent repeated scrutiny like any other film. The screenplay, originally entitled *Buian*, was written at the request of the Cinema Ministry. As the head of the Scenario Studio Eremin specified when he submitted the screenplay for Ministry consideration: "The task set before the authors was to create a literary basis for a film in the adventure genre and dealing with Soviet house farms, and to show the beauty and friskiness of Soviet horses, the professional mastery of horse-farm workers, the valor and fearlessness of Soviet people, their strength, dexterity, and wit." Eremin continued that at the recommendation of various individuals whom the authors consulted (including Marshall Semen Budennyi), the authors decided to set the screenplay during the war years, which, he wrote, would require from Iudin, the director for whom the screenplay had been written, "maximum tact in the treatment of certain episodes." Iudin was fully prepared to exercise such tact, Eremin added.[126]

Coming from Erdman and Vol'pin as it did, the original screenplay, however, was neither an adventure nor a valorizing representation of the war. It was an eccentric comedy with zero reverence for the war. In the screenplay the Germans did nothing but steal, the partisans hardly appeared, and the local Russian resistance amounted to mockery of the Germans. The plot focused on a swindle to prevent the elite horse, Buian, from being sent to Germany as a gift to Hermann Göring.[127] Given this, it is not surprising that Eremin, the screenplay's first editor-censor, flagged irreverence toward the war. Notably, however, this did not prompt him to reject the screenplay, likely because it was the Ministry's idea to hire Erdman and Vol'pin for the job.

Another red flag raised in response to the original screenplay by the Cinema Ministry senior editor Grigorii Mar'iamov was the treatment of the spy. In the story, there is a love triangle: Vasia's love interest, Nadia, is romantically involved with Beletskii, who is actually a Nazi spy posing as the farm's new horse trainer.

---

126. RGALI, f. 2456, op. 1, d. 2087, l. 1.
127. RGALI, f. 2453, op. 2, d. 157 (literary scenario *Smelye liudi* [*Buian*], version 1, 1948).

Mar'iamov recommended toning this relationship down and even reversing Nadia's initial friendliness toward Beletskii.[128] This was a standard adjustment to the image of the enemy censors knew to require based on previous precedents, such as *The Law of Life*. Again, however, Mar'iamov recommended that Bol'shakov submit the initial screenplay to the Artistic Council.

Three days later, on June 3, 1948, the Ministry Artistic Council discussed the literary screenplay and rejected it, sending it back to the authors for revisions. According to the Council, the screenplay had three problems: the war was treated too lightly, the relationship between Nadia and Beletskii was incorrect, and the military actions of the partisans were too unambitious.[129] In other words, the Artistic Council too wanted adjustments in the image of the war and the Soviet person (Nadia) and the image of the enemy. (The third typical censorship concern, the image of the party, would come later.) On July 27 Eremin wrote to Bol'shakov's deputy Vladimir Shcherbina to report that he and Scenario Studio chief editor Katinov had worked with Vol'pin, Erdman, and Iudin and had prepared a plan for making the second part of the screenplay—that dealing with the war—less "light-minded."[130] In September, Eremin's replacement, A. Zhuchkov, forwarded to the Feature Production Department a new screenplay version, now entitled *Brave Men*. In a few days, Mar'iamov and the chief Production Department editor N. Rodionov accepted the revised screenplay but recommended ten additional changes. They approved the third version of the screenplay for production in one week and sent it to the Artistic Council.[131]

Between the first and third versions, the literary screenplay underwent a radical revision. A large number of purely comedy scenes and elements were deleted. Beletskii's long, absurd backstory was taken out. Nadia no longer made an effort to attract Beletskii by giving herself a permanent. All the scenes of the German occupation—including jokes referencing three musicals by Aleksandrov—were dropped. The second part of the screenplay, dealing with the war, was entirely rewritten to dramatically raise the stakes of the action by including the partisans and by having Vasia and the horse save Nadia and scores of other women prisoners. The overall effect of these changes was to switch the film's genre from comedy to war adventure and to represent the war with complete tact and respect.

128. RGALI, f. 2456, op. 1, d. 2087, ll. 2–3.
129. RGALI, f. 2456, op. 1, d. 2087, l. 9.
130. RGALI, f. 2456, op. 1, d. 2087, ll. 4–6.
131. RGALI, f. 2456, op. 1, d. 2087, ll. 7–11.

May we conclude that these changes were party-directed censorship changes targeting party-state propaganda? On the surface—of course. A serious war film was more purposeful and patriotic than a comedy about a horse. But in reality the transformation of the screenplay simply made it a better match to the initial goal set before the authors: to write an entertaining adventure about brave Soviet people and horses. That Erdman and Vol'pin were tasked with scripting such a film and wrote an impertinent comedy may be considered a lucky outcome of the shortage of reliable screenwriters. That original had to be adjusted no matter what.

On September 30, 1948 the Artistic Council met to discuss the revised screenplay. David Zaslavskii, the member of the Council, reported on the screenplay. Vol'pin, Erdman, and Iudin were present, and it was mentioned that the authors had not taken the earlier criticisms well. Zaslavskii and other party critics were not satisfied with the revisions: the war was not serious enough and neither were the partisans. The decision was to approve this version of the literary screenplay, allow the filmmakers to execute improvements (strengthen the war part) in the director's scenario, and then review that as well.[132] On October 26, after repeated requests from Mosfilm's top executive Leonid Antonov, Bol'shakov signed the film into preproduction and approved major crewmembers proposed by Mosfilm. Bol'shakov set the production budget limit at 4,800,000 rubles for the film in black-and-white.[133]

Mosfilm sent the Ministry the first version of the director's scenario on January 10, 1949. Mar'iamov and Rodionov acknowledged that the changes made in the director's scenario successfully addressed the recommendations of the Artistic Council. Very few changes were made, however. One important adjustment was to delete the scene that revealed to the audience that Beletskii was a spy before the characters learn this. In the director's scenario and the film, viewers, alongside Vasia and Nadia, have few reasons to suspect Beletskii initially (all we see is that he has a limp and is not a nice person). One result of this change was to provide the audience with a surprise as opposed to suspense, lowering their emotional engagement. Yet the gain from the switch was in the propaganda objective: instead of telling us right away that Beletskii was a spy, the film now required that viewers start doubting Beletskii on their own, therefore, arguably, teaching audiences to be vigilant or rewarding their vigilance.

132. RGALI, f. 2453, op. 2, d. 160, ll. 10–20.
133. RGALI, f. 2456, op. 2, d. 83, ll. 3–6. On the film's initial budget estimation, see RGALI, f. 2453, op. 2, d. 160, ll. 3–6.

The Ministry editors approved the director's scenario, sent it to the Artistic Council, and recommended three additional changes: Nadia's relationship with Vasia had to be clarified, Nadia's arrest by Beletskii had to be better prepared (Nadia stays in the city during the war to aid the partisans, and Beletskii finds her, arrests her, and puts her on a train to Germany to work as forced labor), and the last scene had to be adjusted to represent a more mighty blow on the enemy. In early February the Artistic Council reviewed the second version of the director's scenario and had further complaints about it. The transition to the war had to be strengthened. Nadia and her grandfather had to stay and aid the partisans not out of their own volition but under the instruction of the party. Why Beletskii, a Nazi spy, was sent to the horse farm had to be explained, and so forth. The Artistic Council recommended that Iudin adjust these flaws while filming (which, if we judge by the film, he hardly did).[134]

Later in February, Bol'shakov made a decision to produce *Brave Men* in color: apparently the picture was gaining in status. The budget was recalculated for color and set at 7,716,000 rubles. In March Bol'shakov and the Artistic Council reviewed the screen tests and approved the casting (at some point the choice of the actress for the role of Nadia was left to the director), and Bol'shakov made several arrangements for military equipment to be lent to the film, including two German trophy tanks. By the end of April, Mar'iamov and Rodionov were watching the first rushes. They commented that the actress playing Nadia, Tamara Chernova, had to perform greater "simplicity," while the local party secretary Kozhin (a Caucasian-looking head of the partisan unit played by Nikolai Mordvinov) had to better convey "the menacing breath of the war" in his delivery. Both performances were ordered reshot. (In May Mosfilm approached the Ministry about unavailability of hay for horses on location. The issue was resolved on the level of deputy ministers: Deputy Cinema Minister Nikolai Shitkin arranged with Deputy Minister for Supplies M. D. Shapiro to supply the hay. In August, Shitkin gave permission to the production to spend 5,000 rubles on vodka to warm up the actors and crew in cold temperatures at high-altitude locations.) By late October 1949 the Artistic Council too was screening the rushes.[135]

---

134. RGALI, f. 2453, op. 2, d. 160, ll. 21–22, 24–25. Bol'shakov's signature on the director's scenario is dated February 3, 1949. RGALI, f. 2456, op. 1, d. 2086 (director's scenario *Smelye liudi* [*Buian*], version 2).

135. RGALI, f. 2456, op. 2, d. 83, ll. 30, 38–48, 55, 58, 62, 63, 76; RGALI, f. 2453, op. 2, d. 160, ll. 30, 33.

The film was supposed to be completed on December 24, 1949. On December 23 Mar'iamov screened *Brave Men* and ordered a number of mostly editing changes (to shorten or delete specific shots and parts of scenes).[136] On December 29 the Artistic Council discussed the film. The editor of the literary journal *Ogonek* Aleksei Surkov, who opened the discussion, said the film was good and would serve the young. A plot-based adventure story, it "certainly cultivate[d] (in a lightened way) patriotic feelings in the people," Surkov said. As such, he added, it was a type of film practically absent from Soviet screens since *Krasnye d'iavoliata* (*The Red Imps*, Ivan Perestiani, 1923).[137] Several compared the film to American "cowboy movies," noting that it was well made. Nevertheless, in the opinion of Artistic Council members, the original problems remained: the war was too light, the partisans were too independent from the army leadership, and the Germans were too innocuously stupid (and therefore too easy to defeat). These were serious "depravities" that, in the option of Nikolai Mikhailov, Secretary of the Komsomol Central Committee, lowered the film's political and artistic impact. These were problematic to the Artistic Council especially because if it allowed this film to show war in a sugared way, future films might do the same. Liudmila Dubrovina, head of the Publishing House for Children's Literature, said she was against the film as much as she had been against the screenplay. In her view, the adventure genre was utterly incompatible with the material of the war that was still "smoking of blood" in the memory of the people.[138] In the end the Council members decided the film should undoubtedly be approved for release with a new ending showing the postwar races that Iudin and Bol'shakov had already been developing.[139] Yet they felt it was necessary, in view of some comments, such as those by Dubrovina, and for the record, to state that the film contained "serious flaws."[140] On December 31 Mar'iamov informed URK and Glavkinoprokat that *Brave Men* was approved for release.

The work on the film continued, however. On January 12, 1950 Bol'shakov wrote to Mosfilm's top executive Sergei Kuznetsov and Iudin that the film had "serious flaws," but suggesting only that they rewrite the ending, delete the first scene (which did not contain fast action), add effective shots of riding horses,

---

136. RGALI, f. 2453, op. 2, d. 160, l. 35.

137. RGALI, f. 2456, op. 1, d. 2087, l. 35.

138. RGALI, f. 2456, op. 1, d. 2087, ll. 39–39 ob.

139. The directors' scenario of the new ending is dated January 1950. RGALI, f. 2456, op. 1, d. 2087, ll. 29–33.

140. RGALI, f. 2456, op. 1, d. 2087, ll. 43–44, 65.

and reshoot some close-ups of characters riding against obvious rear-projected backgrounds. Bol'shakov also wrote to the Deputy Agriculture Minister and Marshall Budennyi to request a herd of horses to film additional scenes. Mosfilm requested to see *Padenie roda Dal'tonov, The Daltons Ride Again* (1945), a Western from Hollywood's Universal Pictures, which could serve as a model for how to film riding scenes. The impressive four opening shots of the film, not present in any of the screenplay versions, were scripted at that point. New music for them also had to be written. The overall reshoots were budgeted at more than 600,000 rubles.[141]

And this was not the end either. On March 3, 1950 Kuznetsov wrote to the film's composer Antonio Spadavekkia [Spadavecchia] that *Brave Men* was being subjected to a "radical reworking," which included inviting a new composer to replace Spadavekkia's score.[142] Pyr'ev, who was apparently engaged to bolster the film even further, made that decision. On April 5 Bol'shakov informed the worried Iudin: "The film is treated as being of utmost importance. The Ministry has decided to recruit Pyr'ev to aid you while preserving you as the film's director with complete responsibility for all corrections still outstanding."[143] It is likely that at some point Bol'shakov, as an astute producer, realized the film could become a real hit and a Stalin Prize nominee and decided to continue to perfect it. Notably, however, the improvements were all of an artistic and technical nature—better soundtrack, higher image quality, smoother scene transitions, and crisper plotting. They did not address the "serious flaws" found by the Artistic Council, such as the light treatment of the war, and the uncertainty about these "flaws" must have continued to threaten the picture. It appears that in an atmosphere of unavoidable uncertainty he could not control, Bol'shakov bet that formal qualities and genre would carry the pictures' politics, and he was right.

At the end of April, Mosfilm recruited the preeminent composer Isaak Dunaevskii (*Volga, Volga*) with the fee of 25,000 rubles.[144] Pyr'ev was paid 10,000 for his

---

141. RGALI, f. 2456, op. 1, d. 2087, ll. 25, 46–47; RGALI, f. 2456, op. 2, d. 83, ll. 88, 96, 129; RGALI, f. 2456, op. 1, d. 2084 (literary scenario *Smelye liudi* [*Buian*], version 3, 1948); RGALI, f. 2456, op. 1, d. 2086.

142. RGALI, f. 2456, op. 2, d. 83, ll. 112.

143. RGALI, f. 2456, op. 2, d. 83, ll. 111, 113.

144. RGALI, f. 2456, op. 2, d. 83, l. 117. In the version of the film that survives, Spadavekkia is listed as the composer. It is probable that Dunaevskii provided some musical consultation to Mosfilm: the RGALI file on the film's music (RGALI, f. 2062, op. 1, d. 155) contains some materials that Spadavekkia wrote in collaboration with Dunaevskii.

consultations. Later, apparently on Pyr'ev's advice, additional scenes of riding and rescue, as well as others, were ordered reshot, and better scene transitions and some new riding shots were ordered. The cost of these changes amounted to 490,000 rubles. The film was finally completed and accepted by the Ministry Feature Production Department in June 1950. In July Iudin was paid 62,000 rubles for the film, a sum later reduced by 3,000 rubles because he had gone over budget. In December, because of the film's great success, the 3,000 rubles were reinstated. The screenwriters were originally paid 30,000 rubles each, and when they asked for 10,000 more each in December were given 10,000 total.[145] The director and the screenwriters received an additional 50,000 each in 1951 as Stalin Prize Laureates.

There is no doubt that on *Brave Men* Bol'shakov, as well as editors and executives at Mosfilm and at the Cinema Ministry, all also censors, acted as coauthors. The film was produced and censored by committee, so to speak. On multiple occasions these individuals recommended specific changes, including how to adjust the tone of an actor's performance and how to rewrite or reshoot scenes. Still Iudin, Vol'pin, and Erdman were in charge of executing the revisions, and even Pyr'ev's involvement was advisory. The vast majority of scenes, as well as most of the witty dialogue, appear in the finished film unchanged compared with the final, third version of the literary screenplay.[146] Moreover, many changes were made not for political reasons, but to improve the film as a viewing experience and to meet the original goals set before the film by Bol'shakov.

When the film was released in the United States in 1951 (as *The Horsemen*), *Variety* wrote that it was "devoid of propaganda."[147] This, of course, was not true: the switch from comedy to war adventure made it propaganda. But *Brave Men* was muted, "positive" propaganda, and it was so with the help of the Artistic Council hardliners.[148] As the Propaganda Department staffers before them and in accordance with their official mandate—to "critique" and "evaluate," not ban or destroy—the Artistic Council members acted as advisors telling the

145. RGALI, f. 2456, op. 2, d. 83, ll. 124–126, 128, 147, 157–166; RGALI, f. 2453, op. 2, d. 160, ll. 37–38.

146. RGALI, f. 2456, op. 1, d. 2084.

147. Alst, "Pictures: The Horsemen," *Variety*, February 7, 1951, 18.

148. According to Tony Shaw and Denise Youngblood, "negative" propaganda vilifies the other, whereas "positive" propaganda reaffirms the self. Tony Shaw and Denise J. Youngblood, *Cinematic Cold War: The American and Soviet Struggle for Hearts and Minds* (Lawrence: University Press of Kansas, 2010).

filmmakers what can be objectionable.[149] When Bol'shakov started with such blatant nonpropaganda as a comedy screenplay by Erdman and Vol'pin, authors of anti-Stalin jokes, he deliberately set himself up at a point that was almost impossibly far from "hard-core" propaganda.[150] That was because his goal was to produce an attractive genre film, not propaganda, and he used the alerts from the Artistic Council and his editors as signposts to know where not to overstep ideologically.

The institutional arrangement Bol'shakov faced supported this strategy because it was biased toward the industry. Stalin expected hard-core propaganda but loved Westerns. Most of the censors worked for the industry and not against it. They were there to ensure the film was not going to be banned and, when it became more-or-less clear that it could succeed, to make it even more flawless politically and artistically. When they insisted Soviet people ought to be shown as vigilant, that enemies ought to be shown as unsympathetic, and that even an adventure film ought to respect the memory of the war, the censors of *Brave Men* functioned as censors did in other, less-political film contexts: they were more productive than restrictive. Unless we think all films are supposed to adapt their original screenplays exactly as written—which was hardly the case in any developed film industry—we have to consider Soviet censorship as a partial necessity, and as a practice that would normally be performed by the film's producers.

Censorship Guidelines, the Intolerance of Imperfection, and Extreme Uncertainty

Similarly to Glavlit, the official censor of the printed texts, film censorship guidelines existed but were very general.[151] As of 1934, GURK's general guidelines were to prohibit works that contained propaganda against the Soviet authorities and the dictatorship of the proletariat, divulged state secrets, arouse

---

149. Artizov and Naumov, *Vlast'*, 620. Although the Cinema Ministry banned several films following on the Council's recommendation, the Council did not ban films itself.

150. This is another term used by Shaw and Youngblood in *Cinematic Cold War*.

151. Boris Zaks, "Censorship at the Editorial Desk," in *Red Pencil: Artists, Scholars, and Censors in the USSR*, ed. Marianna Tax Choldin and Maurice Friedberg (Boston: Unwin Hyman, 1989), 155–161. For requirements in literary censorship, see Herman Ermolaev, *Censorship in Soviet Literature, 1917–1991* (Lanham, MD: Rowman & Littlefield, 1997). Glavlit did not read screenplays, as the vast majority of them were not intended for publication.

national and religious fanaticism, were mystical or pornographic, lacked proper ideological stance, or were antiartistic.[152] The first few of these guidelines were clear enough (and there existed additional lists prohibiting depictions of hooliganism and pacifism, romanticized crime, or apologias for drinking and drug use, etc., which were even less specific to the Soviet context).[153] As we have seen, the difficulty was to determine what amounted to an ideologically improper stance and was (therefore) antiartistic.[154] Industry censorship had to proceed by precedent. Under Shumiatskii all GUKF/GUK screenplay and film reviews were collected in monthly volumes entitled "artistic and ideological guides to making films," which were circulated internally among industry censors.[155] This kind of precedent-based collective wisdom and each censor's own experience were the only types of guidance available. This was why bans and Stalin Prizes were two crucial mechanisms for specifying censorship guidelines—they provided major precedents.[156]

As for self-censorship, most screenwriters and directors were not only far less aware of the censorship guidelines than those-in-the-know, like Dukel'skii or Stalin, but also less than an average activist. I have already mentioned the overwhelming negative response from the ground to *The Miracle Worker*, which came as a surprise to most filmmakers. Such citizen pressure, which expressed itself through unsolicited viewer complaints sent to newspapers and authorities, was common under Stalin. It shows that the intolerance of imperfection was not just Stalin's whim but an expectation the activists among the public shared with Stalin. The responses of Stalin and the activist critics were remarkably similar, and it is not clear who was channeling whom. As Evgenii Dobrenko writes, when watching films Stalin put on the mass audience's hat and thought like an

---

152. Golovskoy, "Film Censorship in the USSR," 123.

153. M. V. Zelenov, "'To Prohibit in Accordance with Due Procedure . . .': The Censorship Policy of Narkompros RSFSR, 1926," *Solanus* 21 (2007): 65.

154. A *Kino* editorial explaining the ban of *Bezhin Meadow* asked, "What is politically harmful and therefore artistically inacceptable in this film?" "Usilit' rukovodstvo," *Kino*, March 24, 1937, 1.

155. Zelenov and Lin, "Kritika 'ne podlezhashchaia oglasheniiu.'"

156. Boris Zaks reports that after Stalin read the screenplay for *The Battle of Stalingrad*, a copy of the screenplay appeared on every editor's desk, and everything written on Stalingrad was "checked to see whether or not it was presented the same way as in that script. It became the standard of how one must write about Stalingrad" (Zaks, "Censorship at the Editorial Desk," 157). On the "normative" role of the Stalin Prizes, see Alla Latynina, "The Stalin Prizes for Literature and the Quintessence of Socialist Realism," in *In the Party Spirit: Socialist Realism and Literary Practice in the Soviet Union, East Germany and China*, ed. Hilary Chung and Michael Falchikov (Amsterdam: Rodopi, 1996), 106–127.

average activist.[157] Although the investigation of what Valerii Fomin calls "spectatorial censorship" is beyond the scope of this book, a few examples need to be mentioned.[158]

In 1940 Bol'shakov received a letter from the NKVD lieutenant general Maslennikov, complaining about the recently released films about border guards, *Sovetskie patrioty* (*Soviet Patriots*, Grigorii Lomidze, 1939) and *Na dal'nei zastave* (*At a Distant Outpost*, Evgenii Briunchugin, 1940). Both films, the letter said, "crudely distorted" the reality of how the Soviet borders were guarded and needed to be banned.[159] Both were banned. In 1945 N. N. Garvei, a party member and an employee of the State Cinema Publishing House, wrote a personal letter to Stalin on the degradation of Soviet cinema, citing many contemporary films and calling Abram Room's *Nashestvie* (*The Invasion*, 1944), in particular, "filth."[160] In 1950 Propaganda Department executives reported to the Central Committee on the letters the newspaper *Kul'tura i zhizn'* received from "the toilers" on Chiaureli's war film *The Fall of Berlin* (1949). "The toilers" were unhappy about the protagonist (an ordinary Russian soldier, Aleksei), who, they said, was portrayed as not very bright; about the party leaders (possibly Stalin, as the film included a Stalin character), who were portrayed as too passive; and about the Nazis, who were portrayed as too noble in the face of death.[161]

That even such a prestige picture as *The Fall of Berlin*—now widely considered a quintessential example of what was most inauthentic about Stalinist art and at the time an acclaimed Stalin Prize recipient—could be found profoundly lacking in all the cardinal representations shows how easy it was to make mistakes. No film, even one by Stalin's favorite Chiaureli, was completely uncontroversial. In this atmosphere, choices still had to be made, and Stalin ended up in the role as an arbiter.

Indeed, *The Fall of Berlin* was no exception. Several prestige films of this period—*The Youth of Maksim, We Are from Kronstadt, The Great Citizen, First*

---

157. Evgenii Dobrenko, *Muzei revoliutsii: Sovetskoe kino i stalinskii istoricheskii narrativ* (Moscow: NLO, 2008), 324. See also Yuri Tsivian, *Ivan the Terrible* (London: British Film Institute, 2002), 14.

158. Fomin, *Kino na voine*, 362. On this phenomenon, see also Aleksandr Deriabin, "Vladimir Timin, 'Za bol'shevistskuiu printsipial'nost'' v iskusstve," *Kinovedcheskie zapiski* 57 (2002): 246–250.

159. RGALI, f. 2456, op. 4, d. 68, ll. 11–12; Margolit and Shmyrov, *Iz"iatoe kino*, 68–69; RGALI, f. 2453, op. 1, d. 1, ll. 28–29.

160. Fomin, *Kino na voine*, 406–407.

161. Anderson et al., *Kremlevskii kinoteatr*, 834 and 842–843.

Cavalry Army, Admiral Nakhimov, Michurin, and *Light over Russia,* among others—ran into censorship problems at various stages in their production histories. Kozintsev and Trauberg's screenplay for *The Youth of Maksim* (1934), called *Bolshevik,* was suspended in October 1933 and again in April 1934, both times during filming, because Commissar of Education Andrei Bubnov and later Central Committee member Nikolai Antipov, both of whom reviewed the screenplay along with Stetskii, found multiple flaws in its treatment of a typical Bolshevik.[162] Both times the filmmakers had to rewrite the screenplay before filming could restart.[163] According to one report, the screenplay went through eight or nine revisions.[164] Although the film became a model, produced two sequels, and received a Stalin Prize in 1941, it was twice on the verge of a ban because of its sensitive topic.

Vsevolod Vishnevskii's impressionistic screenplay for *My iz Kronshtadta* (*We Are from Kronstadt,* Dzigan, 1936), another model film of the 1930s, was also criticized by GUKF executives for failing to represent the figure of a party commissar and for underemphasizing the role of the proletariat in the defense of Petrograd.[165] The film dealt with a historical episode in the defense of Petrograd in 1919 when the nearby Kronstadt Navy sent its servicemen to aid the Bolsheviks. Vishnevskii fought back, arguing that his screenplay was not about the party organization but about the sailors. If GUKF wanted a screenplay about the party and the Petrograd workers, he said, they needed a different screenplay. Yet GUKF told Vishnevskii (though some years later Shumiatskii attributed these objections to the Stetskii Commission) the changes were mandatory if the screenplay was to be accepted, forcing him to concede.[166] The film appears to be a compromise: the party representative is central, but the proletariat is missing. Vishnevskii credited Voroshilov with insisting that the film be made.[167] It is possible Voroshilov's support allowed for this successful compromise to be negotiated. Vishnevskii's other project with Dzigan, *First Cavalry Army* (1941),

162. Anderson et al., *Kremlevskii kinoteatr,* 210–212, 217; RGALI, f. 2450, op. 2, d. 1630.

163. Leonid Trauberg, "*Iunost' Maksima*: Kak my rabotali," *Kino,* January 4, 1935, 3.

164. RGALI, f. 2450, op. 2, d. 1630, l. 30.

165. Vsevolod Vishnevskii, "*My iz Kronshtadta.* Poema. Tonfil'm," *Znamia* 12 (1933): 3–25; RGALI, f. 2456, op. 1, d. 76, ll. 246–251; f. 2456, op. 1, d. 78, ll. 157–161; Vsevolod Vishnevskii, *My iz Kronshtadta* (Moscow–Leningrad: Iskusstvo, 1936), 99–101.

166. RGALI, f. 1038, op. 2, d. 544, l. 10; Vishnevskii, *My iz Kronshtadta,* 97.

167. Vishnevskii, *My iz Kronshtadta,* 101.

was ultimately banned even though Stalin, Voroshilov, and Budennyi had supported the screenplay.[168]

Because to its extremely sensitive topic—the murder of the Leningrad party boss, Sergei Kirov—both the screenplay and production of Ermler's *The Great Citizen*, part 1 (1937) experienced persistent delays.[169] Part 2 of *Ivan the Terrible* (1945) was banned on Stalin's orders because Stalin disliked how Ivan the Terrible and his Oprichniki guard were portrayed.[170] Pudovkin's *Admiral Nakhimov* (1946) was suspended in 1946 at the request of the Central Committee to allow Pudovkin to include scenes that reflected Stalin's take on foreign policy at the time.[171] Another Stalin Prize recipient, Dovzhenko's biopic *Michurin* (1948), was heavily censored in part because of Ivan Michurin's association with his controversial student, the geneticist Trofim Lysenko. After many delays and revisions, the film's final version was very different from what Dovzhenko originally conceived.[172] Finally, *Light over Russia* (Sergei Iutkevich, 1948) was strongly disliked by Stalin and banned. It was based on a very successful play *Kremlevskie kuranty* (*The Chimes of the Kremlin*) by Nikolai Pogodin, dealt with Lenin's plans to electrify the country, and included the characters of Lenin and Stalin. According to Iutkevich, Stalin did not like it that Lenin's role in the electrification was presented as greater than his own. *The Chimes of the Kremlin* was then also removed from theaters, as Stalin, who had not seen the play, said that it too must be bad. The filmmakers rewrote the screenplay and reshot the film. Yet the new version was also banned, this time for portraying Soviet Russia as a backward country, among other things. Again, according to Iutkevich, the problem was Stalin's disapproval.[173]

As these short histories show, all the institutions of Soviet cinema together could not guarantee that any film could reach audiences. Stalin's interventions were required precisely because the rest of the system was a poor match to his expectations and had little access to his current views. That an officially acclaimed work, like Pogodin's play, could overnight become banned could

---

168. Nina Chernova and Vasilii Tokarev, "*Pervaia konnaia*: Kinematograficheskii reid v zabvenie," *Kinovedcheskie zapiski* 65 (2003): 280–313; Margolit and Shmyrov, *Iz"iatoe kino*, 74–76.

169. Leyda, *Kino*, 344.

170. See, e.g., Artizov and Naumov, *Vlast'*, 612–619; Anderson et al., *Kremlevskii kinoteatr*, 759, 766.

171. Anderson et al., *Kremlevskii kinoteatr*, 730–731; Davies, "Soviet Cinema and the Early Cold War."

172. Kepley, *In the Service of the State*, 139–140; Anderson et al., *Kremlevskii kinoteatr*, 799.

173. Margolit and Shmyrov, *Iz"iatoe kino*, 98–102.

not but produce extreme uncertainty. With autonomous directors, author-screenwriters, and administrators and censors never certain what the guidelines were the film industry could not function to Stalin's standards without Stalin himself.

Two additional observations are in order. First, note that the problems of all the films discussed in this chapter were content-related and not stylistic. Beyond accessibility and high quality, no specific aesthetic limitations were imposed on Soviet filmmaking. Regarding *Ivan the Terrible*, an openly formalist film, not a word of objection was said about its style. Stalin did say the following: "Ivan the Terrible was a man with will, with character, whereas he [Eisenstein] has some weak-willed Hamlet. This is nothing but formalistics [*formalistika*]. Why should we care about formalism? Give us historical truth."[174] What Stalin seems to have meant by "formalism" here was that Eisenstein had pursued formal goals in disregard of "historical truth," or that the director had given an idiosyncratic and, to Stalin, superficial interpretation of Ivan.

Second, the films that were successfully released were just as subject to the process of endless censorship and revision as the ones that were abandoned or banned. In essence, every Soviet film produced under Stalin ended up somewhere on the scale from acceptable to unacceptable. As Boris Alpers wrote in 1933, "As a rule in the recent years the success of a film is a surprise to everyone in the industry.... Everything here is unknown and unpredictable. And the range of the scale is from complete failure to spectacular triumph."[175] This scale was explicit in Glavrepertkom's ratings, as well as in the Dukel'skii–Bol'shakov system of four categories assigned to films upon release: "excellent" (*otlichno*), "good" (*khorosho*), "satisfactory" (*udovletvoritel'no*), and "a reject" (*brak*). Soviet films were never all masterpieces, and what shifted with time was not the scale but the bar. My final case study, the ban on *A Great Life*, part 2 (1946), illustrates just how volatile and time sensitive the perfection bar had become in the late Stalin period.

Leonid Lukov's film, based on the screenplay by Pavel Nilin, was a sequel to his *A Great Life*, part 1, which came out in 1939 and received a Stalin Prize, Second Class, in 1941. It dealt with the life of the same Donbas coalmine as in part 1, except it was set at the very end of World War II, when the miners returned from the front and decided to revive their coalmine destroyed by the Germans. According to the Central Committee, the film had three major groups of political

---

174. Anderson et al., *Kremlevskii kinoteatr*, 759.
175. B. Alpers, "Kinodramaturgiia i rezhissura," *Kino*, July 10, 1033, 2.

errors. The first had to do with the image of the party-state. The industrial recon-struction in the film was not presented as part of a large-scale party-organized effort, but as a personal initiative of a group of miners. Moreover, the miners were deterred by the regional government: the region's chief industry official believed the effort to reconstruct this particular mine was not worth it, given its state of destruction and the country's need for coal, which was immediate. The Central Committee also objected that the reconstruction was carried out by hand without any mechanization (before the miners could recover the machines bur-ied during the war, they started to mine by hand to show that their mine could deliver coal immediately). The Central Committee said that such an isolated and technologically backward mining initiative clashed with the fully industrialized postwar stage in the country's development.

Second, the depicted cultural level of the young miners was below expecta-tion. They drank, and Stalin and Zhdanov both noted that there were no fewer than seven scenes involving drinking in the film. Furthermore, the characters sang romances, engaged in crude physical labor, and cared about personal affairs over their work (there are three romantic relationships in the film). Also prob-lematic was that one of the lead miners initially objected to his wife's professional training (even if he was proud of its results by the end of the film). This was not how Soviet people acted. Worse yet, these uncultured individuals received lead-ership posts at the mine, an instance of social mobility, which, according to the Central Committee, was common in the early 1930s but not in 1946 when only trained professionals received such posts.[176]

Third, but most consequentially, three individuals in the film worked for the Germans under occupation, but all three were then engaged in the reconstruc-tion process. By the film's logic, this was because no other men were available and because collaboration with the Germans in their cases was either an involuntary act or part of an undercover operation organized by the partisans, two sets of cir-cumstances explicitly articulated in the film. The film clearly established that one of the three "collaborators," Makar Legotin, although a former *kulak*, had proven his loyalty to the regime before the war, during the war, and in the course of the film. Yet Stalin and Zhdanov said those who worked for the Germans, especially in the German police (Legotin), could not be made protagonists in a film. They were appalled that Usynin, one of the three "collaborators" and an otherwise

---

176. In Stalin's mind, the *vydvizhentsy* policy was abandoned in March 1931 (Priestland, *Stalin-ism and the Politics of Mobilization*, 254).

useless but harmless bureaucrat, was not even arrested. The leaders also objected to the film's title—to them there was no evidence of a "great" (*bol'shaia*) life in the film.[177]

In other words, as always, the image of the Soviet person had to be exemplary, and "typical" behaviors and conditions had to be portrayed rather than those that existed in reality. Perhaps deletions of drinking scenes or inclusions of scenes with machinery or with regional party bosses guiding the reconstruction effort would have saved the picture. Yet *A Great Life*'s handling of characters who had worked for the Germans either as "friends" (Legotin) or as inconsequential persons (Usynin) was an extremely moment-specific error, which was much harder to correct. In the atmosphere of the cold war and of paranoia about internal enemies, both of which started to set in in 1946 and both of which defined the late Stalin period, the policy was that all collaborators were potential "enemies."

A Great Life stayed close to the screenplay, and most of Stalin and Zhdanov's objections could have been raised at the preproduction stage.[178] Yet since it was a sequel to a very popular and officially successful film and since industry executives considered the project—a highly topical drama—welcome and urgent, they neglected to thoroughly test if for political soundness. Yet the main problem was that in 1945 no one could predict that the obvious truth about the dismal state of Soviet industry would need to be hidden from film audiences, that drinking and singing—one aspect the film emphasized over the screenplay—could not be shown even though the Soviets had just won a horrendous war, and that after the war Stalin would enact harsh policies against populations on the formerly occupied territories. Only of his approach to rebuilding the mine did Nilin later say that as a communist he should have known better. The problem, he commented, was that he started writing the screenplay when no one could imagine the grand scale of reconstruction to follow.[179]

Timing, that is 1945 versus 1946, made all the difference. Even concurrently with the film's ban, some filmmakers reportedly believed that the Central Committee's attack was a temporary campaign (not unlike how the antiformalism campaign appeared to be in retrospect) and that everything would return to

---

177. Anderson et al., *Kremlevskii kinoteatr*, 747–767; RGALI, f. 2372, op. 12, d. 79. See also Leyda, *Kino*, 390–391. An attempt to release a new version of the film failed in 1949. The film was released in 1958 (Anderson et al., *Kremlevskii kinoteatr*, 757).

178. Pavel Nilin, *Bol'shaia zhizn': Literaturnyi stsenarii v dvykh chastiakh* (Moscow: Goskinoizdat, 1945).

179. Anderson et al., *Kremlevskii kinoteatr*, 754.

normal in a year or two.[180] This was not the case. When Lukov told Stalin, "Allow us to correct [the picture]. These are all mistakes," Stalin responded, "These are not mistakes. We have a difference in understanding."[181] By August 1946 Stalin's perception of the situation in the country had progressed to a point yet unattainable to Soviet filmmakers or censors. If *A Great Life* had been completed earlier, before Stalin had adjusted his positions, it is very likely that its fate would have been more favorable.[182]

After 1946 Soviet filmmakers continued to fail the state. Beyond *Michurin* and *Light over Russia* another biopic, *Fatali-Khan* (Dzigan, 1947), about an eighteenth-century Azeri statesman, was banned in 1948. Screenplays for the biopics *Zhukovskii* (Pudovkin, 1950) and *Composer Glinka* (Aleksandrov, 1952) had to undergo substantial changes. *Velikaia sila* (*The Great Force*, Ermler, 1949), a biopic about a student of Michurin, went through a long revision process after completion. *Ogni Baku* (*The Lights of Baku*, Kheifits, Zarkhi, and Rza Takhmasib), about the development of the Caspian oil industry, with a Stalin character, was banned in 1950. These are just the prestige pictures. The situation with ordinary genre pictures, contemporary dramas and comedies, was only worse. Of the nine film dramas released in 1948, seven were either criticized or had to undergo changes. Two out of five dramas and one out of three comedies in 1949 were considered substandard. One of two dramas and the only comedy of 1951 were identified as failures.[183] Despite enormous effort, Soviet cinema struggled to produce correct films even during the film famine.

Conclusion

It has been argued that Soviet censorship differed from censorship in other periods and contexts in that it was "prescriptive as well as proscriptive."[184] Yet prescriptive censorship came with the territory in the Soviet film industry, and Soviet filmmakers were fully prepared to absorb it. The real problem was that the

---

180. RGALI, f. 2372, op. 12, d. 79, l. 21.

181. Anderson et al., *Kremlevskii kinoteatr*, 761.

182. For more on the film, see Natacha Laurent, "L'interdiction du film 'Une Grande Vie': La reprise en main du cinéma soviétique en août 1946," *Communisme*, nos. 42–44 (1995): 137–153.

183. Margolit and Shmyrov, *Iz"iatoe kino*; Anderson et al., *Kremlevskii kinoteatr*, 816, 837–838; Ivan Bol'shakov, *Sovetskoe kinoiskusstvo v poslevoennye gody* (Moscow: Znanie, 1952). Several of the films mentioned above (*Ivan the Terrible*, part 2, *A Great Life*, part 2, *The Lights of Baku*, *Fatali-Khan*), *The Old Jockey*, *Ordinary People*, as well some other banned films, were released soon after Stalin's death, in 1953–1959.

184. Kenez, *Cinema and Soviet Society*, 130.

film industry was asked to censor itself despite the intolerance of imperfection, the vacuum of information, and strict ideological guidelines. The combination of uncertain industry prescription and reactive party proscription prevented censorship from playing a more productive role in filmmaking. By banning films, the party leadership used proscription as prescription, and that was too blunt a tool for managing censors.

The presence of the authoritative party censors, and most important Stalin, at the top of the censorship hierarchy resulted in extreme uncertainty. Since the ultimate Central Committee reaction was unpredictable, industry practitioners knew that each censor's recommendations might not actually be instrumental for the film's fate. Together with the growing number of censorship institutions, uncertainty had the effect of devaluing each censor's responsibility, making industry censorship less effective. The only way to deal with uncertainty was to kick decision-making up to the superiors. Insecure decision-making, which developed because of Stalin, required Stalin as the final arbiter.

The problem was not that censorship was too strong or too prescriptive, but that it was too institutionally weak, unsophisticated, and unproductive. Katerina Clark and Evgenii Dobrenko write, "Soviet power could be described as a mechanism whereby nothing could function without decisions being made by party bodies."[185] True, but it was only so as a result of unrealistic expectations, weak institutions, and a lack of a long-term development strategy by the party bodies themselves. The party-state wanted Soviet cinema to regulate itself, but when the industry repeatedly failed, it resorted to reactive measures, which not only hurt the film industry but also became detrimental to the party's own effort to foster a cinematic propaganda machine.

---

185. Katerina Clark and Evgeny Dobrenko, eds., *Soviet Culture and Power: A History in Documents, 1917–1953*, trans. Marian Schwartz (New Haven, CT: Yale University Press, 2007), x.

Conclusion

THE FAILURE OF MASS CINEMA UNDER STALIN AND THE INSTITUTIONAL STUDY OF IDEOLOGY

> Even in Stalin's Russia, policy instructions should never be confused with outcomes.
>
> —Sheila Fitzpatrick

Dysfunctional Industry

In its original form, Soviet film policy dictated that cinema was to develop into a "mighty weapon" of mass propaganda designed to not only help the party-state persuade the Soviet population in its favor but to also replace vodka as a source of leisure for the Soviet citizen and a source of income for the state's coffers. In the 1920s film policy pursued competition with foreign films both financially and ideologically. In the mid-1930s when the Soviet Union was no longer importing foreign films, Boris Shumiatskii proposed a plan for boosting cinema's output to Hollywood levels. This plan was rejected, and by the late 1940s Soviet film's annual output fell to single digits and the Soviet leaders accepted that cinema would produce only a few masterpieces per year. The purpose of this book has been to explain this pattern of events. Against the conventional wisdom, I suggest that low output resulted from an unintended institutional failure. To rephrase Sheila Fitzpatrick's quote above, even in Stalin's Russia, outcomes should not be confused with policy instructions.[1] In cinema policy, the Stalinist party-state failed to achieve its objective of mounting a mass propaganda cinema.

The Soviet party-state had ambitious goals: it wanted to transform an underdeveloped tsarist economy into an industrial powerhouse and a largely backward Soviet population into a new activist society. Cinema too was to become an

---

1. Fitzpatrick, "*Lady Macbeth* Affair," 207.

industrial enterprise that provided controlled cultural and political education to the Soviet population through a massive network of film theaters. Yet the Soviet party-statesmen failed to provide an institutional environment for "cinema for the millions" and took other counterproductive steps. One of their major missteps was to act in an impatient ad hoc manner rather than pursue a long-term strategy in industry development. Stalin and his associates did not realize that to transform Soviet society through cinema the film industry needed a makeover, both structurally and in labor terms.

The Soviet film industry under Stalin continued to function largely as it did under the 1920s New Economic Policy, despite the superficial organizational changes that took place. Although administration of the film industry was partly centralized in the 1930s and film distribution was monopolized in 1938, centralization was not complete. Importation of motion pictures from abroad was largely stopped in the 1930s, limiting the supply of films to Soviet product alone. Yet the exhibition network continued to be decentralized, and how consistent or Soviet the repertoire of each cinema was depended on the agency that controlled it. Soviet studios also continued to operate independently of the center. Annual production plans were coordinated with the central cinema administration but never functioned as orders from above, for the central executives lacked the managerial capacity to develop them and to monitor their implementation. The division of labor was never complete and production continued to be organized around the director, who acted in part as his or her own producer. Studio management changed frequently and was often incompetent in industry matters, and film directors were the only personnel who could control every aspect of production. This gave Soviet directors substantial authority in decision-making, minimizing both studio and central control.

Soviet film directors underwent minimal generational change in the 1930s, and the same talent that matured in the 1920s led the industry through the early 1950s. By and large these directors belonged to the creative intelligentsia, had strong modernist sensibilities, and were not prepared to produce ideologically appropriate mass films. Instead of replacing these directors with an army of new ones, the Soviet government declared them masters and bolstered their elite status both financially and structurally by appointing them to administrative posts. Although the move was dictated by the need to strengthen political self-censorship, its unintended side effect was that artistic incentives dear to filmmakers also received new prominence.

The changes that were introduced in the 1930s to improve censorship produced unexpected consequences. The system of censorship was restructured such that the primary censorship responsibility moved to the industry itself. Industry self-censorship ran into the same problem of weak managers and strong directors that disrupted centralized control. Since industry self-censorship could not successfully preempt problems in preproduction, films had to face a new round of censorship when completed. Many of them turned out not to answer to party-state standards, and the industry was punished by public reprimands. Repeated self-censorship failures left the industry exposed to interventions by Stalin and his associates. However, since such interventions proved both unpredictable and unforgiving, their ultimate effect was to eliminate risk-taking. The presence of Stalin in the system as the test audience and arbiter also made it very difficult for anyone else to make reliable decisions. Plagued by extreme uncertainty, film directors, censors, and executives remained perpetually confused about what the party leaders wanted and thought twice about initiating every production. Systemic confusion and uncertainty resulted in a drastic decline in output.

The problems of Soviet cinema far exceeded those related to political censorship. Censorship was destructive to individual careers and films, as it was before and after Stalin. Under Stalin, however, the problem was not so much censorship as an inability to create content. Soviet studios did not employ screenwriters and the film industry had to rely on outside submissions to initiate productions. As the demand for masterpieces grew, so did the demand for quality screenplays. To externalize responsibility for ideological content and boost quality, the film industry approached legitimate writers for screenplays. The screenplays that the writers submitted were cumbersome from a production perspective and, lacking any other in-house personnel to do the job, the industry had directors rewrite them for filming purposes. Directors could not resist major rewrites, introducing authorship conflicts. Even though, with time, screenplay submissions became better organized through studios' targeted solicitation from select authors, the film industry could never generate enough quality screenplays. In Hollywood there was content control; in Soviet Russia there was content shortage. It is possible that Stalinism was simply not conducive to new ideas. Moreover, the prospect of being arrested and executed for what one wrote was hardly inspiring. Yet, as this book suggests, content vacuum was at least as much a matter of personnel policy and the mode of content development. It was institutional rather than cultural.

In the absence of major reforms in industry structure, production management, planning, screenwriting, and censorship, the Soviet film industry was poorly equipped to satisfy the state. This lack of appropriate institutions compromised both party-state control over the content of Soviet films and the objective of building a diverse and viable mass propaganda cinema. By the end of the Stalin period Soviet film output shrank and genre diversity dwindled, for this dysfunctional system could only handle a very small number of predictable films at a time. After Stalin died in 1953, the extreme censorship uncertainty produced by Stalin's presence was eliminated, new talent entered the industry, and film production picked up. However, the basic institutions of the Soviet film industry that are analyzed in this book—thematic thinking, director-authors, independent screenwriting, and postproduction censorship—persisted.[2]

Was industry dysfunction under Stalin an outcome of neglect or of limited state capacity and therefore avoidable, or were the steps taken to create this system a part of a larger, deliberate logic, which made this situation inevitable? It is possible that cinema was simply never "the most important of the arts," despite Lenin's famous dictum. Indeed, control of print media and literature was a much greater priority under Stalin.[3] As Katerina Clark has shown, the Stalinists seemed to have believed that if they harnessed the textual medium, they could harness everything else.[4] Alternatively, it has been argued that it was never crucial for the Soviet leadership to convince everyone, and the focus was always on the activists and propagandists: those who read the newspapers and wrote for them.[5] As for the limited state capacity, perhaps due to personnel and other shortages, the Stalinist state needed to make choices, and the textual medium rose to the top. After all, print media required less investment and effort technologically. Similarly, one reason why Stalin stopped supporting the Soviet Hollywood project in 1936 was perhaps that cinema was far less important than the news media or the military-and-industrial complex, and these, not cinema, needed investment in the context of a pending pan-European war. That said, shortsightedness and lack of priority do not explain everything about this industry. Stalin did have a cinema policy—albeit not necessarily distinct from his policy in the arts more generally. Although he spent more time on the written media, he wanted a controlled mass cinema and pursued it. His decisions, however ultimately destructive, were not accidental; they had an ideological program behind them.

Soviet Cinema and Ideology

In his fundamental study of socialist economic systems, János Kornai shows that "the main line of causality" in socialist economy flows from the political

---

2. On the most recent discussion of the post-Stalin film industry, see Kristin Roth-Ey, *Moscow Prime Time: How the Soviet Union Built the Media Empire That Lost the Cultural Cold War* (Ithaca, NY: Cornell University Press, 2011), chap. 1.

3. Karel Berkhoff, *Motherland in Danger: Soviet Propaganda during World War II* (Cambridge, MA: Harvard University Press, 2012).

4. Clark, *Moscow, The Fourth Rome*, 78–104.

5. Matthew E. Lenoe, *Closer to the Masses: Stalinist Culture, Social Revolution, and Soviet Newspapers* (Cambridge, MA: Harvard University Press, 2004).

monopoly of a communist party and "the dominant influence of the official ideology." In other words, the socialist economy, including its flaws, inefficiencies, and contradictions, is an outcome of an unchallenged system of ideas. It is ideology, and not accident or mistakes, that determine the features and institutions of the economy—state ownership, bureaucratic coordination, central planning, forced growth, and shortages.[6] The same argument can be made about Soviet cinema. The reason why "quality" prevailed over "quantity" was because the Soviet leadership held that ideological purity of message was more important than mass production. As the Stalin period progressed, instead of a routine consumer product, each Soviet film was treated as a state-sponsored event, and this type of film, an ideological prestige picture, is especially hard to produce in large numbers. Thematic planning was maintained despite its lack of practical necessity because an ideologically important "theme" had to at least nominally lead the thinking behind Soviet film programming. Directors and screenwriters felt entitled to authorship and were given administrative duties because Stalin believed that, when properly motivated, elites would produce the right content. Soviet censors could not function because expectations of ideological purity were unpredictable and unforgiving. Censorship was weak and uninformed because the artists themselves were expected to produce from the position of the party-state, thus eliminating any need for censorship. When the films filmmakers made clashed with the party-state standards, Stalin and his circle reacted strongly with public humiliation and bans, forcing the industry to retreat from trying. In other words, instead of taking practical steps to secure full control and mass production, the Soviet party-state acted in ways that contradicted its own goals—because this made sense ideologically.

The failure of the Stalin regime in mounting a mass cinema was predicated on an ideological position that, when applied to artistic production, led to an irreconcilable contradiction in policy. Stalin expected a large number of predictable films that touted the party-state line, but supported a mode of production where individual contribution and creativity mattered. The Soviet party-state wanted a communist propaganda machine, but it expected Soviet cinema to be of the highest artistic quality, superior to cinemas around the world. In practice, these goals worked at cross-purposes, while they allowed such figures as Eisenstein to become indispensable. The need to mobilize the filmmakers to work for the state conflicted with the impulse to control their product, resulting in an impasse.

---

6. Kornai, *Socialist System*, 360–361.

This book has traced Stalinist ideology in a fundamental domain of Soviet cinema: film-industry institutions. In determining the institutional environment of Soviet cinema, the role of Stalinism was the opposite of what one might expect. The ideological commitment to the artist as the agent of ideology prevented the Stalinist state from producing effective propaganda on a mass scale. At the same time, it allowed Soviet filmmakers to maintain some integrity and continue to express themselves even if within an otherwise limited set of forms. Ideology was conducive of a measure of artistic independence, which worked against the same ideology's propaganda objectives. The institutional arrangement under Stalin, in turn, had consequences for content control. Investment in the director-master weakened the control institutions whose job it was to restrict film content to ideologically Stalinist representations. Instead of precision censoring on the level of the story, scene, or dialogue line, the Soviet film industry was forced to reject whole types of films, rendering cinema inflexible and unproductive. Periodic and unrelenting criticism from the top undermined the initiative and ideological sophistication of Soviet self-censorship, and as a result, the kind of ideological content that made it into Soviet films was circumscribed by already familiar propaganda messages.

Institutional Study of Ideology

By investigating how Stalinist ideology affected filmmaking institutions this book seeks to contribute to the institutional study of ideology. Most existing work on the relationship between ideology and cinema has focused either on individual films or on the broad ideological implications of cinema as a mass phenomenon.[7] In both cases, the causal link between ideology and film texts is abstracted, as the process that embeds ideological content in films is not traced out. Both approaches assume that there is a direct link between ideology and artifacts, that is, for example, that capitalism "produces" Hollywood films or that Hollywood films are products of capitalist ideology.

Textual ideology study, by far the most prolific strain in this area, presupposes that the majority of films "allow the ideology a free, unhampered passage," and

---

7. The classic example of the former is the article by the editors of *Cahiers du cinema*, "John Ford's *Young Mr. Lincoln*," in *Narrative, Apparatus, Ideology: A Film Theory Reader*, ed. Philip Rosen (New York: Columbia University Press, 1986), 444–482. The founding text of the latter is Theodor Adorno and Max Horkheimer's "The Culture Industry: Enlightenment as Mass Deception," in Horkheimer and Adorno, *Dialectic of Enlightenment: Philosophical Fragments*, ed. Gunzelin Schmid Noerr, trans. Edmund Jephcott (Stanford: Stanford University Press, 2002), 94–136.

the task of film study is to expose this ideology.[8] According to this framework, no film can escape the economic system within which it is produced; even the tools of filmmaking are "an expression of the prevailing ideology."[9] If we follow this logic, then Soviet films would be entirely products of communism, promote communism, use communist production tools, and should be exposed as such. Moreover, since the Stalin system differs from Western capitalism, its films must work differently than Western films. The story of the Soviet film industry that I present in this book, however, makes it difficult to subsume Soviet film products under communism or Stalinism. Much of Soviet film technology, storytelling techniques, genres, and stylistic devices developed from or in response to Western influences. Raizman's *Poezd idet na vostok* (*The Train Goes East*, 1947) was inspired by Frank Capra's *It Happened One Night* (1934).[10] Romm's *The Thirteen* was an explicit remake of Ford's *The Lost Patrol*. Dovzhenko held *Citizen Kane* (Orson Welles, 1941) as a model.[11] Even Zhdanov said that Pudovkin's *Admiral Nakhimov* should be "our *Lady Hamilton*" (Alexander Korda, 1941).[12] In many respects Soviet films were international popular entertainment, which puts into question not only their communist belonging but also Western cinema's uncomplicated relationship to capitalism. Given this, we cannot deal with Soviet cinema as the textual study of ideology does.

In their famous critique of mass culture, Max Horkheimer and Theodor Adorno argued that mass art, including mass film, played a homogenizing role in society by naturalizing ideological stereotypes to the point where they became inescapable.[13] The conception of mass entertainment as profoundly ideological has been questioned, most thoroughly by Noël Carroll in *A Philosophy of Mass Art*. Carroll argues that mass art "contributes primarily to the reinforcement of ideology; it is not a major originating source of securing ideological commitment in the first instance."[14] Carroll has also suggested that although films do communicate and produce ideology (as they produce money, stars, prestige, pleasure, etc.), their primary use has been to make art. His position is that "the study of film as art logically precedes the study of film as ideology because art, its

8. Jean-Louis Comolli and Jean Narboni, "Cinema/Ideology/Criticism" in *Movies and Methods: an Anthology*, vol. 1, ed. Bill Nichols (Berkeley: University of California Press, 1976), 23.

9. Comolli and Narboni, "Cinema/Ideology/Criticism," 24–25.

10. Kleiman, "'Drugaia istoriia sovetskogo kino,'" 68.

11. RGALI, f. 2372, op. 8, d. 75, l. 83 ob. In this transcript the film is recorded as *Inzhener Kein* (Engineer Kane), a curious Soviet slippage of the transcriber.

12. Anderson et al., *Kremlevskii kinoteatr*, 724.

13. Horkheimer and Adorno, "Culture Industry," 118.

14. Noël Carroll, *A Philosophy of Mass Art* (Oxford: Clarendon Press, 1998), 408.

forms and its traditions, is the filter through which ideology must pass."[15] This critique of equating mainstream films with one massive formula cannot be more appropriate in the Soviet case, where, as I have argued, artistic incentives contradicted ideological ones. In fact, looking at Soviet cinema as trying to produce art rather than propaganda proves highly revealing.

As powerful as textual and culture-industry approaches can be, they tend to ignore the issue of agency or they situate agency on a level removed from actual film production.[16] Borrowing methodology from film-industry history, but applying it to an industry whose business was ideology, this book offers an alternative that focuses on the domain that ideology affects most directly: filmmakers and filmmaking.[17] If filmmakers and executives, not ideologies, ultimately produce films, this is where the institutional study of ideology must look.

The institutional study of ideology is not entirely new. Edward Buscombe proposed it back in 1975. Buscombe argued that to understand the relationship between film and society we need to study the history of the film industry. Who owns the studios is clearly consequential. That Hollywood studios are part of a capitalist system dictates to studio executives that profits matter more than politics or that, given the nature of American society and state, it might be unwise to make a pro-communist film. But this explains very little about why one film is different from another or why some films—in Buscombe's case those Frank Capra made for Columbia in the 1930s—are more socially conscious. Filmmakers' personal views also influence production. To explain ideological content one has to trace it to the views of each of the film's immediate makers, and specifically of the director, screenwriter, and producer.[18]

Recently the institutional study of entertainment media has been given a major extension in the field of production cultures. Building on industry history, cultural studies, anthropology, and ethnography, John Thornton Caldwell has proposed that to understand screen content one has to investigate all layers

15. Noël Carroll, *Theorizing the Moving Image* (Cambridge, UK: Cambridge University Press, 1996), 378.

16. P. Steven Sangren, "'Power' against Ideology: A Critique of Foucaultian Usage," *Cultural Anthropology* 10, no. 1 (1995): 3–40.

17. Bordwell, Staiger, and Thompson, *Classical Hollywood Cinema*; Balio, *Grand Design*; Crisp, *Classic French Cinema*; Douglas Gomery, *The Hollywood Studio System: A History* (London: British Film Institute, 2005); Kepley, "Federal Cinema." The institutional approach has also been described as historical and archival. See, e.g., Eric Smoodin, "The History of Film History," in *Looking Past the Screen: Case Studies in American Film History and Method*, ed. Jon Lewis and Eric Smoodin (Durham, NC: Duke University Press, 2007), 1–34. The positive concept of institutions is here distinct from Althusser's normative concept of the ideological state apparatus.

18. Edward Buscombe, "Notes on Columbia Pictures Corporation 1926–41," *Screen* 16, no. 3 (1975): 65–82.

of production personnel, both "above-the-line" (producers, writers, and directors) and "below-the-line" (the craftsmen). Textual content, Caldwell argues, is an expression of the "production culture": discourses, debates, ambitions, competition, self-assessment, misconceptions, beliefs, and ideologies of the industry personnel. Similar to Carroll, Caldwell insists that film and television do not just produce culture but are themselves expressions of culture. Apart from showing that a deep layer of agency refracts ideological production, this account makes it no longer possible to speak of ideology in singular terms: for example, as capitalist or communist.[19]

Finally, Jeff Smith has added the institution of criticism to the institutional study of ideology. In his book on American Cold War films of the 1950s, Smith suggests that what in the 1950s was considered communist or anticommunist was a historically contingent interpretation applied by critics as cultural tastemakers. In contrast, the film texts themselves were more invested in the underlying aesthetic and technological tradition of Hollywood filmmaking than in politics. Smith's study emphasizes that we must investigate the historical agents and institutions before we can make any general arguments about the actual ideologies of any group of films. Moreover, what deserves study is not superficial features meant for explicit propaganda but other, more fundamental storytelling and stylistic elements that run through all the films of the period and are more representative of the period's filmmaking culture.[20]

Not unlike these recent works, this book suggests that under Stalin there was no direct pathway between state socialism and the films. Even if an occasional cinema product received full party-state endorsement, the majority missed the mark. Stalin's ideologists had a major difficulty in making Soviet film speak their language. Filmmakers and executives interfered in the direct passage of ideology and toned down and distorted the party-state message, not to mention simply making it impossible to produce more films. Most Stalin-era films glorified labor and personal sacrifice for collective cause, but that was not enough to make this cinema a mighty propaganda weapon. On the other hand, all Soviet films reflected the ideologies of their makers: directors, screenwriters, actors, and censors. The institutional, historical study of ideology proceeds inductively,

---

19. John Thornton Caldwell, *Production Culture: Industrial Reflexivity and Critical Practice in Film and Television* (Durham, NC: Duke University Press, 2008); see also Keith Negus, "The Production of Culture," in *Production of Culture/Cultures of Production*, ed. Paul du Gay (London: Sage, 1997), 67–118.

20. Jeff Smith, *Film Criticism, the Cold War, and the Blacklist: Reading the Hollywood Reds* (Berkeley: University of California Press, 2014).

collecting production histories and histories of industry agents, cultures, and institutions, and determining at each particular nexus what part of industry practice was influenced by state ideology and how.

Like many party-state projects under Stalinism, Soviet cinema was an experiment. It incorporated ideologies, approaches, and operational modes that could not be easily reconciled. This contradictory nature determined its failures and successes. The story of Soviet cinema under Stalin shows that it might be impossible to control cultural production and at the same time demand variety and quality. Similarly, it is impossible to control culture and at the same time maintain an entitled artistic workforce. Under Stalin, the state and the artists needed and influenced each other, and each had to adjust to the other's interests. But when the Stalinist state lost patience, Soviet filmmakers brought Soviet film production to a stalemate.

Acknowledgments

This book originated over ten years ago at a screening room at VGIK, the State Cinema Institute in Moscow, where I saw Abram Room's banned 1936 film *Strogii iunosha* (*A Strict Young Man*). The film clashed with much of what I knew at the time about Stalin-era cinema. I wrote this book to understand how such a remarkable, non-Stalinist film as *A Strict Young Man* could be made under Stalin. I thank my VGIK teachers Nina Dymshits, Klara Isaeva, Vladimir Utilov, Marat Vlasov, Liudmila Kliueva, Vladimir Sharun, Galina Prozhiko, Konstantin Ognev, and Evgenii Gromov for setting me on the path to this book.

The rest I owe to the Wisconsin Project or the people and scholarship associated with the Film program at the University of Wisconsin–Madison Department of Communication Arts: David Bordwell, Kristin Thompson, Vance Kepley, Lea Jacobs, J. J. Murphy, Kelley Conway, Ben Singer, Jeff Smith, Tino Balio, Vincent Bohlinger, Mark Minett, Heather Heckman, Colin Burnett, Pearl Latteier, Katherine Spring, Rebecca Swender, Lisa Jasinsky, Eric Crosby, Bradley Schauer, Charlie Michael, David Resha, Casey Coleman, Billy Vermillion, Kaitlin Fyfe, Tom Yoshikami, Booth Wilson, John Powers, Andrea Comiskey, Jonah Horwitz, Patrick Keating, and Richard Neupert.

This project has benefited in multiple ways from comments from and conversations with Lea Jacobs, Ben Singer, Francine Hirsch, Andrew Reynolds, David Bordwell, Kristin Thompson, Julie D'Acci, David McDonald, Jonathan Gray, Birgit Beumers, Joan Neuberger, Evgenii Dobrenko, Jamie Miller, Vladimir Padunov, Natalie Ryabchikova, James Steffen, Yuri Tsivian, Rashid Yangirov, Val Golovskoy, Ian Christie, Evgenii Margolit, Valerii Fomin, Vladimir Zabrodin, Petr Bagrov, Nikolai Izvolov, Tat'iana Simacheva, Terry Martin, Cathy Frierson, William Todd, Justin Weir, Ana Olenina, Eric Rentschler, Maria Khotimsky, Pey-Yi Chu, Ian Campbell, Justyna Beinek, Rossen Djagalov, Marina Sorokina, Yoshiko Herrera, Sara Guyer, Robert Bird, Lauren McCarthy, Emily Sellars, Colleen Lucey, Molly Thomasy Blasing, Stephanie Richards, Petr Szczepanik, Anna Batistova, Heather Sonntag, members of the Russian History Colloquium led by Francine Hirsch and David McDonald, and participants of the Davis Center seminar series "Informing Eurasia." Vince Bohlinger has been my constant conversation partner and confidant as this project evolved. Before I started my research, Ben Brewster suggested that the director-unit system and the status of the director in the Soviet film industry must have been a problem for the state. All I can say now is yes indeed, it was! My biggest thanks go to my dissertation advisor and mentor, Vance Kepley. Vance has always been there for me with sage advice and deliberate guidance. I learned much from his expertise, care, precision, and ability to keep an eye on the big picture.

Various individuals and institutions assisted me during research. I am thankful to the staff of the Russian State Archive for Literature and Art (RGALI) in Moscow, the Central State Archive for Literature and Art (TsGALI) in St. Petersburg, the Russian State Archive for Social and Political History (RGASPI) in Moscow, and the Moscow Film Museum, where I worked with Elena Dolgopiat and had the good fortune of having once been compelled to share a drink with the museum's director, Naum Kleiman, on his birthday. I am especially grateful to the staff of the Russian State Film Foundation (Gosfilmofond) in Belye Stolby, Moscow Region, and specifically Galina Popova of the Gosfilmofond Archive, without whose hospitality and expertise I would not have had access to some of the rarest documents that informed this book. Thanks also to the hospitality of Mark Zak at the Scientific Research Institute for Cinema (NIIK) in Moscow. I am fortunate to count among my friends the Moscow film experts Larisa Mezenova and Vladimir Zakharov, whose erudition always keeps me on my toes.

My very special thanks go to Boris Lazarevich Shumiatskii, the grandson of one of this book's central characters. I am grateful to Boris Lazarevich for meeting with me and sharing information about his family. Boris Shumiatskii (the grandfather), who was unlawfully executed under Stalin as an "enemy of the people" and whose name was not printed or mentioned in a positive context for decades, is still often considered nothing but Stalin's henchman or a thorn in Sergei Eisenstein's side. I very much hope that this book will revise this perception of Shumiatskii and help us see him as a far more positive, or at least more complicated, figure, which better reflects his role in Soviet filmmaking.

I received funding and support for this project from the Andrew Mellon Foundation and the American Council of Learned Societies in the form of an Early Career Dissertation Completion Fellowship in 2010–2011. I am also grateful to the Davis Center for Russian and Eurasian Studies at Harvard University, and Alexandra Vacroux personally, for hosting me as a postdoctoral fellow in 2011–2012, and to the Department of Communication Arts and the Center for Russia, East Europe, and Central Asia (CREECA) at the University of Wisconsin–Madison for repeated logistical and financial support. Support for this book was also provided by the University of Wisconsin–Madison Office of the Vice Chancellor for Research and Graduate Education with funding from the Wisconsin Alumni Research Foundation.

My enormous gratitude goes also to Cornell University Press and to Mahinder Kingra personally. Without Mahinder's prodding, as well as advice from Roger

Haydon and Cornell's two anonymous readers, this book would have remained a sprawling and unapproachable text. I thank my parents, Evgeniy Belodubrovskiy and Dina Belodubrovskaya, and my sister, Irina Afanas'eva, for their unconditional support. Last but not least, I thank my partner, best friend, and first critic Scott Gehlbach for his immaculate judgment, social-science perspective, and much, much more.

Appendixes

APPENDIX 1   Soviet Feature-Film Production

YEAR	PLANNED	PRODUCED	RELEASED	PRODUCED AS % OF PLANNED	BANNED	BANNED AS % OF PRODUCED	DESIRED
1929	—	**81**	103	—	5	**6**	
1930	138	**108**	90	**78**	11	**10**	
1931	100	**100**	78	**100**	23	**23**	500 in 1932; 620 in 1933; 1073 in 1934[1]
1932	102	**75**	73	**74**	15	**20**	
1933	113	**33**	41	**29**	5	**15**	
1934	72	**57**	46	**79**	4	**7**	
1935	100	**50**	40	**50**	16	**32**	300 soon; 800 to 1000 in the future[2]
1936	95	**50**	34	**53**	7	**14**	800
1937	63	**36**	39	**57**	5	**14**	
1938	48	**37**	38	**77**	1	**3**	
1939	51	**55**	45	**108**	1	**2**	80 by 1942[3]
1940	58	**39**	42	**67**	5	**13**	
1941	45	**40**	40	**89**	6	**15**	
1942	40	**34**	21	**85**	8	**24**	

(Continued)

YEAR	PLANNED	PRODUCED	RELEASED	PRODUCED AS % OF PLANNED	BANNED	BANNED AS % OF PRODUCED	DESIRED
1943	23	**20**	21	**87**	5	**25**	
1944	[30]	**20**	12	**[67]**	0	**0**	
1945	35	**18**	22	**51**	2	**11**	60[4]
1946	30	**23**	18	**77**	1	**4**	100 by 1950[5]
1947	40	**25**	23	**63**	3	**12**	
1948	40	**16**	21	**40**	1	**6**	60 in 1949[6]
1949	21	**17**	12	**81**	1	**6**	
1950	18	**13**	14	**72**	1	**8**	
1951	15	**7**	9	**47**	0	**0**	
1952	13	**11**	11	**85**	0	**0**	
1953	25	**26**	21	**104**	2	**8**	
1954	53	**40**	26	**75**	—	—	
1955	—	**59**	—	—	—	—	
1956	—	**97**	—	—	—	—	

Note: Includes only full-length fiction films (over 1,200 meters or 50 minutes in length) based on original and adapted screenplays, both silent and sound (excluding silent versions of sound films, sound versions of silent films, filmed concerts, filmed theater, and animation). Production and release year sometimes differed, as many films were released months after completion. Primary sources: Macheret, Glagoleva, and Zak, *Sovetskie khudozhestvennye fil'my*; Margolit and Shmyrov, *Iz"iatoe kino*; Anderson et al., *Kremlevskii kinoteatr*; and RGALI. Numbers in square brackets in 1944 indicate that I have not found an exact number or list and this is an estimate.

[1]RGALI, f. 2497, op. 1, d. 37, l. 72. These numbers are given in "full-length units" (or programs), which were made up of not only feature-length films but also short, nonfiction, and agitprop films. The numbers might be deliberately exaggerated.

[2]Shumiatskii, *Sovetskaia kinematografiia segodnia i zavtra*, 9; Aleksei Morov, "Dela i dni kino," *Pravda*, January 28, 1936, 4; O. Afanas'eva, "Uzakonennaia bezdeiatel'nost'," *Kino*, February 6, 1936, 1; Vishnevskii et al., "Boevye zadachi sovetskogo kino."

[3]Kur'ianov, "Chto dast khudozhestvennaia kinematografiia v 1939 godu."

[4]RGASPI, f. 17, op. 125, d. 372, ll. 19, 201, cited by Davies, "Soviet Cinema and the Early Cold War," 53.

[5]Anderson et al., *Kremlevskii kinoteatr*, 741.

[6]Fomin, *Letopis' rossliskogo kino, 1946–1965*, 77.

APPENDIX 2 Soviet Cinema Administrations (1930–1953)

NAME	CHAIRMAN	SUBORDINATE TO	JURISDICTION OVER[1]
Soiuzkino (All-Union Combine for the Cinema and Photo Industry), 1930–1933	Boris Shumiatskii	Supreme Soviet of the National Economy (VSNKh) subordinate to Council of People's Commissars (Sovnarkom), 1930–1932 / People's Commissariat for the Light Industry subordinate to Sovnarkom, 1932–1933	Production, distribution, and exhibition coordination[2] in the USSR. Production, distribution, and exhibition in RSFSR.
GUKF (Main Administration for Cinema and Photo Industry), 1933–1936	Boris Shumiatskii	Sovnarkom	Production coordination in the USSR. Production in RSFSR.
GUK (Main Cinema Administration), 1936–1938	Boris Shumiatskii	All-Union Committee for Arts Affairs subordinate to Sovnarkom	Production coordination in the USSR. Production in the RSFSR. Distribution and exhibition in the USSR coordinated by the Arts Committee.
Committee for Cinema Affairs (or Cinema Committee), 1938–1946	Semen Dukel'skii (1938–June 1939) / Ivan Bol'shakov (June 1939–1946)	Sovnarkom	Production and distribution in the USSR. Exhibition coordination in the USSR.
Ministry of Cinema, 1946–1953	Ivan Bol'shakov	Council of Ministers (successor to Sovnarkom)	Production and exhibition coordination in the USSR. Distribution in the USSR. Production at studios with all-USSR status.

[1] combine prokat (distribution) and prodvizhenie (kartin) (marketing) under "distribution," and kinofikatsiia (cinefication or network expansion) and kinoset' (exhibition network) under "exhibition." All central administrations of the Stalin period also had jurisdictions over film education, film publishing, film export and import, and capital construction (the manufacturing of stock, chemicals, equipment (cameras and projectors), and supplies).

[2] By "coordination" I mean that the cinema administration had nominal supervision obligations in this area but was not engaged in operational management. For instance, both GUKF and GUK signed off on the production plans and films of all the studios, but were directly responsible for managing production only in the Russian Republic (RSFSR).

APPENDIX 3   The Institutions of Soviet Film Censorship

INDUSTRY:

Soiuzkino, 1930–1933

GUKF, 1933–1936

GUK, 1936–1938

Cinema Committee, 1938–1946, with
the Cinema Committee Artistic Council,
1944–1946

Ministry of Cinema, 1946–1953, with
the Ministry of Cinema Artistic Council,
1946–1953

STATE:

Glavrepertkom, 1930–1933 (subordinate
to the RSFSR People's Commissariat of
Education)

GURK (Main Administration for Repertory
Control), 1934–1936 (subordinate to the
RSFSR People's Commissariat of Education)

GURK, 1936–1938 (subordinate to the USSR
Committee for Arts Affairs)

URK (Administration for Cinema Repertory
Control), 1938–1946 (subordinate to the
Cinema Committee)

Department for Repertory Control, 1946–1953
(subordinate to the Ministry of Cinema)

PARTY:

Andrei Bubnov/Aleksei Stetskii Central
Committee Propaganda Department Film
Commissions, 1932–1934

Central Committee Propaganda Department,
1935–1937

Andrei Andreev Central Committee Film
Commission, 1938–1940

Andrei Zhdanov Central Committee Film
Commission, 1940–1941

Central Committee Propaganda Department
(to 1950, then Central Committee
Department of Literature and Art) and
Central Committee Members Zhdanov,
Andreev, and Malenkov, 1941–1953

Primary Sources

Archival Sources

RUSSIAN STATE ARCHIVE FOR LITERATURE
AND ART (RGALI). MOSCOW

f. 631 Soviet Writers' Union

f. 962 Committee for Arts Affairs (1927–1956)

f. 1038 Vsevolod Vishnevskii

f. 2208 Iakov Cherniak

f. 2372 Ministry of Cinema Scenario Studio (1939–1958)

f. 2450 Ministry of Cinema Feature Production Department (1936–1953)

f. 2453 Mosfilm (1938–1966)

f. 2456 Ministry of Cinema/Cinema Committee (1924–1953)

f. 2496 Sovkino (1923–1935)

f. 2497 Soiuzkino (1930–1934)

f. 2498 Sovkino/Soiuzkino (1926–1932)

f. 2753 Vladimir Nil'sen

f. 2769 Tamara Adel'geim

f. 2923 Moscow House of Cinema (1934–1957)

CENTRAL STATE ARCHIVE FOR LITERATURE AND ART
IN ST. PETERSBURG (TsGALI). ST. PETERSBURG

f. 257 Lenfilm

RUSSIAN STATE FILM FOUNDATION (GOSFILMOFOND)
ARCHIVE. BELYE STOLBY, MOSCOW REGION

f. 2 Film files (*fil'movye dela*)

f. 3 Film files (*fil'movye dela*)

RUSSIAN STATE ARCHIVE FOR SOCIAL AND POLITICAL
HISTORY (RGASPI). MOSCOW

f. 17 Communist Party Central Committee

Periodicals

Biulleten' Komiteta po delam kinematografii pri SNK Soiuza SSR
Biulleten' NKP RSFSR
Biulleten' Vsesoiuznogo komiteta po delam iskusstv pri SNK Soiuza SSR
Iskusstvo kino (aka *Proletarskoe kino* (1931–1932); *Sovetskoe kino* (1933–1935))
Izvestiia
Kino
Kino i kul'tura
Kul'tura i zhizn'
Komsomol'skaia pravda
Krokodil
Literaturnaia gazeta
Pravda
Sovetskii ekran (1925–1929)
Vecherniaia Moskva
Za bol'shevistskii fil'm

Secondary Sources

Akhushkov, Sh., ed. *Vstrechnyi: Kak sozdavalsia fil'm*. Moscow: Kinofotoizdat, 1935.
Allilueva, Svetlana. *Dvadtsat' pisem k drugu*. Moscow: Sovetskii pisatel', 1990.
Anderson, Kirill M., Leonid V. Maksimenkov, L. P. Kosheleva, and L. A. Rogovaia, eds. *Kremlevskii kinoteatr, 1928–1953: Dokumenty*. Moscow: ROSSPEN, 2005.
Anninskii, Lev. "Iz zhizni prodiusera." *Kinovedcheskie zapiski* 79 (2006): 41–120; *Kinovedcheskie zapiski* 80 (2006): 6–109.
Artizov, Andrei, and Oleg Naumov, eds. *Vlast' i khudozhestvennaia intelligentsiia: Dokumenty, 1917–1953*. Moscow: Demokratiia, 2002. In English: *Soviet Culture and Power: A History in Documents, 1917–1953*, edited by Katerina Clark and Evgeny Dobrenko, translated by Marian Schwartz. New Haven, CT: Yale University Press, 2007.
Babitsky, Paul, and John Rimberg. *The Soviet Film Industry*. New York: Praeger, 1955.
Bagrov, Peter. "Soviet Melodrama: A Historical Overview." *KinoKultura* 17 (July 2007): http://www.kinokultura.com/2007/17-bagrov.shtml.
——. "Zhitie partiinogo khudozhnika." *Seans* 35/36 (2008). http://seance.ru/n/35-36/jubilee-ermler/zhitie-partiynogo-hudozhnika/.
Balio, Tino. *The American Film Industry*. Madison: University of Wisconsin Press, 1985.
——, ed. *Grand Design: Hollywood as a Modern Business Enterprise, 1930–1939*. Berkeley: University of California Press, 1995.
Belodubrovskaya, Maria. "The Jockey and the Horse: Joseph Stalin and the Biopic Genre in Soviet Cinema." *Studies in Russian and Soviet Cinema* 5, no. 1 (2011): 29–53.
——. "Soviet Hollywood: The Culture Industry That Wasn't." *Cinema Journal* 53, no. 3 (2014): 100–122.
——. "Abram Room, *A Strict Young Man*, and the 1936 Campaign against Formalism in Soviet Cinema." *Slavic Review* 74, no. 2 (2015): 311–333.

———. "The Literary Scenario and the Soviet Screenwriting Tradition." In *A Companion to Russian Cinema*, edited by Birgit Beumers, 251–269. Hoboken, NJ: John Wiley & Sons, 2016.

Belousov, Iu. A. "Dem'ian Bednyi—kritik *Zemli*." *Kinovedcheskie zapiski* 23 (1994): 149–162.

Berkhoff, Karel. *Motherland in Danger: Soviet Propaganda during World War II*. Cambridge, MA: Harvard University Press, 2012.

Berliner, Joseph S. *Factory and Manager in the USSR*. Cambridge, MA: Harvard University Press, 1957.

Bernshtein, A. "Gollivud bez kheppi-enda: Sud'ba i tvorchestvo Vladimira Nil'sena." *Kinovedcheskie zapiski* 60 (2002): 251–257.

Bliakhin, Pavel. "K itogam kino-sezona 1927–1928 goda." *Kino i kultura* 2 (1929): 3–16.

———, ed. *Repertuarnyi ukazatel': Kinorepertuar*. Moscow: OGIZ-GIKhL, 1934.

Blium, Arlen V., ed. *Tsenzura v Sovetskom Soiuze, 1917–1991: Dokumenty*. Moscow: ROSSPEN, 2004.

Bohlinger, Vincent. "Compromising Kino: The Development of Socialist Realist Film Style in the Soviet Union, 1928–1935." PhD diss., University of Wisconsin–Madison, 2007.

———. "The Development of Sound Technology in the Soviet Union during the First Five-Year Plan." *Studies in Russian and Soviet Cinema* 7, no. 2 (2013): 189–205.

Bol'shakov, Ivan. "Nashi blizhaishie zadachi." *Iskusstvo kino* 1 (October 1945): 2–5.

———. *Sovetskoe kinoiskusstvo v gody velikoi otechestvennoi voiny (1941–1945)*. Moscow: Goskinoizdat, 1948.

———. "Za vysokoe ideino-khudozhestvennoe kachestvo fil'mov." *Iskusstvo kino* 5 (September–October 1948): 3–5.

———. *Sovetskoe kinoiskusstvo v poslevoennye gody*. Moscow: Znanie, 1952.

Bordwell, David. *On the History of Film Style*. Cambridge, MA: Harvard University Press, 1997.

Bordwell, David, Kristin Thompson, and Janet Staiger. *The Classical Hollywood Cinema: Film Style and Mode of Production to 1960*. New York: Columbia University Press, 1985.

Boterbloem, Kees. *The Life and Times of Andrei Zhdanov, 1896–1948*. Montréal: McGill-Queen's University Press, 2004.

Brandenberger, David. *National Bolshevism: Stalinist Mass Culture and the Formation of Modern Russian National Identity, 1931–1956*. Cambridge, MA: Harvard University Press, 2002.

———. *Propaganda State in Crisis: Soviet Ideology, Indoctrination, and Terror under Stalin, 1927–1941*. New Haven, CT: Yale University Press, 2012.

Brewster, Ben. "The Soviet State, the Communist Party and the Arts, 1917–1936." *Red Letters* 3 (Autumn 1976): 3–9.

Buscombe, Edward. "Notes on Columbia Pictures Corporation 1926–41." *Screen* 16, no. 3 (1975): 65–82.

Caldwell, John Thornton. *Production Culture: Industrial Reflexivity and Critical Practice in Film and Television*. Durham, NC: Duke University Press, 2008.

Carroll, Noël. *Theorizing the Moving Image*. Cambridge, UK: Cambridge University Press, 1996.

———. *A Philosophy of Mass Art*. Oxford: Clarendon Press, 1998.

Cavendish, Philip. *The Men with the Movie Camera: The Poetics of Visual Style in Soviet Avant-Garde Cinema of the 1920s*. New York: Berghahn Books, 2013.

Chernova, Nina, and Vasilii Tokarev. "*Pervaia konnaia*: Kinematograficheskii reid v zabvenie." *Kinovedcheskie zapiski* 65 (2003): 280–313.

Choldin, Marianna Tax, and Maurice Friedberg, eds. *Red Pencil: Artists, Scholars, and Censors in the USSR*. Boston: Unwin Hyman, 1989.

Christie, Ian. "Canons and Careers: The Director in Soviet Cinema." In Taylor and Spring, *Stalinism and Soviet Cinema*, 142–170.

Clark, Katerina. "Engineers of Human Souls in the Age of Industrialization: Changing Cultural Models, 1929–1941." In *Social Dimensions of Soviet Industrialization*, edited by William G. Rosenberg and Lewis H. Siegelbaum, 248–263. Bloomington: Indiana University Press, 1993.

——. *Petersburg: Crucible of Cultural Revolution*. Cambridge, MA: Harvard University Press, 1998.

——. *The Soviet Novel: History as Ritual*. Bloomington: Indiana University Press, 2000.

——. *Moscow, The Fourth Rome: Stalinism, Cosmopolitanism, and the Evolution of Soviet Culture, 1931–1941*. Cambridge, MA: Harvard University Press, 2011.

Clark, Katerina, and Evgeny Dobrenko, eds. *Soviet Culture and Power: A History in Documents, 1917–1953*, translated by Marian Schwartz. New Haven, CT: Yale University Press, 2007.

Comolli, Jean-Louis, and Jean Narboni. "Cinema/Ideology/Criticism." In *Movies and Methods: an Anthology*, vol. 1, edited by Bill Nichols, 22–30. Berkeley: University of California Press, 1976.

Crisp, Colin. *The Classic French Cinema, 1930–1960*. Bloomington: Indiana University Press, 1993.

David-Fox, Michael. *Showcasing the Great Experiment: Cultural Diplomacy and Western Visitors to the Soviet Union, 1921–1941*. Oxford: Oxford University Press, 2011.

Davies, Sarah. "Soviet Cinema and the Early Cold War: Pudovkin's *Admiral Nakhimov* in Context." *Cold War History* 4 (2003): 49–70.

——. "Stalin as Patron of Cinema: Creating Soviet Mass Culture, 1932–1936." In *Stalin: A New History*, edited by Sarah Davies and James Harris, 202–225. Cambridge, UK: Cambridge University Press, 2005.

Deriabin, Aleksandr. "Vladimir Timin, 'Za bol'shevistskuiu printsipial'nost' v iskusstve.'" *Kinovedcheskie zapiski* 57 (2002): 246–250.

Dickinson, Thorold, and Alan Lawson. "The Film in USSR—1937." *The Cine-Technician* (August–September 1937): 95–111.

Dobrenko, Evgenii. *Muzei revoliutsii: Sovetskoe kino i stalinskii istoricheskii narrativ*. Moscow: NLO, 2008.

Doherty, Thomas. *Hollywood's Censor: Joseph I. Breen and the Production Code Administration*. New York: Columbia University Press, 2007.

Doklad komissii B. Z. Shumiatskogo po izucheniiu tekhniki i organizatsii amerikanskoi i evropeiskoi kinematografii. Moscow: Kinofotoizdat, 1935.

Dolgopiat, Elena. "'V sovetskom gosudarstve—liudi-dvoiniki': Iz istorii sozdaniia fil'ma *Vesna*." *Kinovedcheskie zapiski* 57 (2002): 239–245.

Dubrovskii, A. "O 'predelakh' i vozmozhnostiakh sovetskoi kinematografii." *Iskusstvo kino* 1 (January 1938): 23–27.

Dubrovskii, M. Ia., and L. N. Cherniavskii, eds. *Ezhegodnik sovetskoi kinematografii za 1938 god*. Moscow: Goskinoizdat, 1939.

Efimov, Evgenii. *Sumbur vokrug "Sumbura" i odnogo "malen'kogo zhurnalista": Stat'ia i materialy*. Moscow: Flinta, 2006.

Eisenschitz, Bernard. "A Fickle Man, or Portrait of Boris Barnet as a Soviet Director." In Taylor and Christie, *Inside the Film Factory*, 151–164.

Eisenstein, Sergei. *Izbrannye proizvedeniia v shesti tomakh.* Moscow: Iskusstvo, 1964–1971.

——. "Stalin, Molotov, and Zhdanov on *Ivan the Terrible, Part Two* (1947)." In *The Eisenstein Reader*, edited by Richard Taylor, 160–166. Translated by Richard Taylor and William Powell. London: British Film Institute, 1998.

Erdman, Nikolai. *Kinostsenarii.* St. Petersburg: Masterskaia Seans, 2010.

Ermolaev, Herman. *Censorship in Soviet Literature, 1917–1991.* Lanham, MD: Rowman & Littlefield, 1997.

Filtzer, Donald. *Soviet Workers and Stalinist Industrialization: The Formation of Modern Soviet Production Relations, 1928–1941.* Armonk, NY: M. E. Sharpe, 1986.

Fitzpatrick, Sheila. *Cultural Revolution in Russia, 1928–1931.* Bloomington: Indiana University Press, 1977.

——. "The *Lady Macbeth* Affair: Shostakovich and the Soviet Puritans." In Fitzpatrick, *The Cultural Front: Power and Culture in Revolutionary Russia*, 183–215. Ithaca, NY: Cornell University Press, 1992.

——. "Intelligentsia and Power. Client-Patron Relations in Stalin's Russia." In *Stalinismus vor dem Zweiten Weltkrieg: Neue Wege der Forschung*, edited by Manfred Hildermeier and Elisabeth Muller-Luckner, 35–54. Munich: Oldenbourg, 1998.

——, ed. *Stalinism: New Directions.* London: Routledge, 2000.

Fleishman, Lazar'. *Boris Pasternak i literaturnoe dvizhenie 1930-kh godov.* St. Petersburg: Akademicheskii proekt, 2005.

Fomin, Valerii. *Kino i vlast': Sovetskoe kino, 1965–1985: Dokumenty, svidetel'stva, razmyshleniia.* Moscow: Materik, 1996.

——, ed. *Letopis' rossiiskogo kino, 1863–1929.* Moscow: Materik, 2004.

——. *Kino na voine: Dokumenty i fakty.* Moscow: Materik, 2005.

——. "Sovetskii Gollivud: Razbitye mechty." *Rodina* 5 (2006): 98–105.

——, ed. *Letopis' rossiiskogo kino, 1930–1945.* Moscow: Materik, 2007.

——, ed. *Letopis' rossiiskogo kino, 1946–1965.* Moscow: Kanon+, 2010.

Geller [Heller], Leonid. "Printsip neopredelennosti i struktura gazetnoi informatsii stalinskoi epokhi." In *Slovo mera mira: Stat'i o russkoi literatrue XX veka*, 157–174. Moscow: MIK, 1994.

Gerasimov, Sergei. *Zhizn'. Fil'my. Spory.* Moscow: Iskusstvo, 1971.

Gerasimov, S. "O professii kinorezhissera." In *Voprosy masterstva v sovetskom kinoiskusstve*, edited by B. Kravchenko, 7–42. Moscow: Goskinoizdat, 1952.

Glavnoe upravlenie kinematografii. *Osnovnye polozheniia planovogo zadaniia po iuzhnoi baze sovetskoi kinematografii (Kinogorod).* Moscow: Iskra revoliutsii, 1936.

Glavnoe upravlenie kino-foto-promyshlennosti. *Korennye voprosy sovetskoi kinematografii.* Moscow: GUKF, 1933.

——. *Proizvodstvennyi plan Glavnogo upravleniia sovetskoi kinematografii na 1936 god po proizvodstvu khudozhestvennykh fil'mov.* Moscow: Kinofotoizdat, 1936.

Glavnoe upravlenie po kontroliu za zrelishchami i repertuarom. *O kontrole za zrelishchami i repertuarom.* Moscow: Narkompros RSFSR, 1935.

Gol'din, M. M. *Opyt gosudarstvennogo upravleniia iskusstvom: Deiatel'nost' pervogo otechestvennogo Ministerstva kul'tury.* 2000. http://www.rpri.ru/min-kulture/MinKulture.doc.

Golovskoy, Valery S. "Film Censorship in the USSR." In Choldin and Friedberg, *Red Pencil*, 117–143.

———. "Mikhail Kalatozov—poltora goda v Gollivude." *Kinovedcheskie zapiski* 77 (2006): 271–298.

Gomery, Douglas. *The Hollywood Studio System: A History.* London: British Film Institute, 2005.

Gorlizki, Yoram, and Oleg Khlevniuk. *Cold Peace Stalin and the Soviet Ruling Circle, 1945–1953.* Oxford: Oxford University Press, 2004.

Gornitskaia, N. S. "Dokumenty, materialy." In Gornitskaia, *Iz istorii Lenfil'ma,* 3: 123–135.

———, ed. *Iz istorii Lenfil'ma,* vol. 3. Leningrad: Iskusstvo, 1973.

———, ed. *Iz istorii Lenfil'ma,* vol. 4. Leningrad: Iskusstvo, 1975.

Graffy, Julian. "Writing about the Cinema of the Stalin Years: The State of the Art." *Kritika* 10, no. 4 (2009): 809–823.

———. *Chapaev.* London: I. B. Tauris, 2010.

Gregory, Paul R. *The Political Economy of Stalinism: Evidence from the Soviet Secret Archives.* Cambridge, UK: Cambridge University Press, 2004.

Gromov, Evgenii. *Stalin: Vlast' i iskusstvo.* Moscow: Respublika, 1998.

Gross, Jan T. *Revolution from Abroad: The Soviet Conquest of Poland's Western Ukraine and Western Belorussia.* Princeton, NJ: Princeton University Press, 2002.

Groys, Boris, and Max Hollein, eds. *Dream Factory Communism: The Visual Culture of the Stalin Era.* Frankfurt: Schirn Kunsthalle, 2003.

Halfin, Igal. *Terror in My Soul: Communist Autobiographies on Trial.* Cambridge, MA: Harvard University Press, 2003.

Hellbeck, Jochen. *Revolution on My Mind: Writing a Diary under Stalin.* Cambridge, MA: Harvard University Press, 2006.

Hennig, Anke. "Obobshchenie kinodramaturgii: Ot kinodramaturgii do dramaturgii iskusstv." In *Sovetskaia vlast' i media: Sbornik statei,* edited by Hans Günter and Sabine Hänsgen, 430–449. St. Petersburg: Akademicheskii proekt, 2006.

Hessler, Julie. *A Social History of Soviet Trade: Trade Policy, Retail Practices, and Consumption, 1917–1953.* Princeton, NJ: Princeton University Press, 2004.

Hirsch, Francine. *Empire of Nations: Ethnographic Knowledge and the Making of the Soviet Union.* Ithaca, NY: Cornell University Press, 2005.

Hoffmann, David L. *Stalinist Values: The Cultural Norms of Soviet Modernity, 1917–1941.* Ithaca, NY: Cornell University Press, 2003.

Hoffmann, David L., and Yanni Kotsonis, eds. *Russian Modernity: Politics, Knowledge, Practices.* Houndsmills, UK: Macmillan Press, 2000.

Holquist, Peter. "Information Is the Alpha and Omega of Our Work: Bolshevik Surveillance in Its Pan- European Context." *The Journal of Modern History* 69, no. 3 (1997): 415–50.

Horkheimer, Max, and Theodor W. Adorno. "The Culture Industry: Enlightenment as Mass Deception." In *Dialectic of Enlightenment: Philosophical Fragments,* edited by Gunzelin Schmid Noerr, translated by Edmund Jephcott, 94–136. Stanford: Stanford University Press, 2002.

Il'f, Il'ia, and Evgenii Petrov. *Odnoetazhnaia Amerika.* Moscow: AST–Zebra E, 2009.

Iumasheva, O. G., and I. A. Lepikhov. "Fenomen 'totalitarnogo liberalizma' (opyt reformy sovetskoi kinematografii)." *Kinovedcheskie zapiski* 20 (1993/94): 125–144.

Iurenev, Rostislav. *Sergei Eizenshtein: Zamysly, fil'my, metod.* vol. 2. Moscow: Iskusstvo, 1985.

Iutkevich, Sergei. *Kino—eto pravda 24 kadra v sekundu.* Moscow: Iskusstvo, 1974.

———. "Deklaratsiia pervoi khudozhestvennoi masterskoi pod khudozhestvennym rukovodstvom S. Iutkevicha." In Gornitskaia, *Iz istorii Lenfil'ma,* 4: 128–137.

Ivlieva, N. I., ed. *Repertuarnyi ukazatel' deistvuiushchego fonda kinokartin*. Moscow: Goskinoizdat, 1940.

———. *Repertuarnyi ukazatel' deistvuiushchego fonda kinokartin*. Moscow: Goskinoizdat, 1943.

Jacobs, Lea. *The Wages of Sin: Censorship and the Fallen Woman Film, 1928–1942*. Madison: University of Wisconsin Press, 1991.

Kapterev, Sergei. "Sergei Eisenstein's Letters to Hollywood Film-Makers." *Studies in Russian and Soviet Cinema* 4, no. 2 (2010): 245–253.

Karabel, Jerome. "Towards a Theory of Intellectuals and Politics." *Theory and Society* 25, no. 2 (1996): 205–233.

Katsigras, A. *Repertuarnyi ukazatel': Kinorepertuar*. Moscow: Kinofotoizdat, 1936.

Kenez, Peter. *The Birth of the Propaganda State: Soviet Methods of Mass Mobilization, 1917–1929*. Cambridge, UK: Cambridge University Press, 1985.

———. *Cinema and Soviet Society from the Revolution to the Death of Stalin*. London: I. B. Tauris, 2001.

———. "A History of *Bezhin Meadow*." In *Eisenstein at 100: A Reconsideration*, edited by Al LaValley and Barry P. Scherr, 193–206. New Brunswick, NJ: Rutgers University Press, 2001.

———. "*Bezhin lug (Bezhin Meadow)*." In *Enemies of the People: The Destruction of Soviet Literary, Theater, and Film Arts in the 1930s*, edited by Katherine Bliss Eaton, 113–126. Chicago: Northwestern University Press, 2002.

Kepley, Vance, Jr. "The Workers' International Relief and the Cinema of the Left, 1921–35." *Cinema Journal* 23, no. 1 (1983): 7–23.

———. "The Origins of Soviet Cinema: A Study in Industry Development." *Quarterly Review of Film Studies* 10, no. 1 (1985): 22–38.

———. *In the Service of the State: The Cinema of Alexander Dovzhenko*. Madison: University of Wisconsin Press, 1986.

———. "Federal Cinema: The Soviet Film Industry, 1924–32." *Film History* 8, no. 3 (1996): 344–356.

———. "The First 'Perestroika': Soviet Cinema under the First Five-Year Plan." *Cinema Journal* 35, no. 4 (1996): 31–53.

Kepley, Vance, Jr., and Betty Kepley. "Foreign Films on Soviet Screens, 1921–1931." *Quarterly Review of Film Studies* 4, no. 4 (1979): 429–442.

Khlevniuk, Oleg, ed. *Stalinskoe Politbiuro v 30-e gody: Sbornik dokumentov*. Moscow: AIRO, 1995.

Khokhlova, Ekaterina. "Forbidden Films of the 1930s." In Taylor and Spring, *Stalinism and Soviet Cinema*, 90–96.

———. "Neosushchestvlennye zamysly." In Mamatova, *Kino*, 123–131.

Kleiman, Naum. "'Drugaia istoriia sovetskogo kino,' Lokarno, 2000 g." *Kinovedcheskie zapiski* 50 (2001): 57–72.

Knight, Claire. "Stalin's Trophy Films, 1947–52: A Resource." *KinoKultura* 48 (April 2015): http://www.kinokultura.com/2015/48-knight.shtml.

Komitet po delam kinematografii pri SNK SSSR. *Tematicheskii plan proizvodstva nauchnykh i uchebno-tekhnicheskikh fil'mov na 1939 god*. Moscow: Goskinoizdat, 1939.

Kornai, János. *The Socialist System: The Political Economy of Communism*. Princeton, NJ: Princeton University Press, 1992.

Kossovskii, A. E., ed. *Sovetskaia kinematografiia: Sistematizirovannyi sbornik zakonodatel'nykh postanovlenii*. Moscow: Goskinoizdat, 1940.

Kossovskii, A. E., and V. G. Dorogokupets, eds. *Kinofotopromyshlennost': Sistematicheskii sbornik zakonodatel'nykh postanovlenii i rasporiazhenii*. Moscow: Kinofotoizdat, 1936.

Kotkin, Stephen. *Magnetic Mountain: Stalinism as a Civilization*. Berkeley: University of California Press, 1995.

Kovalova, Anna. "Kinodramaturgiia Nikolaia Erdmana." In Erdman, *Kinostsenarii*, 9–58.

———. *Kinodramaturgiia N. R. Erdmana: Evoliutsiia i poetika*. Candidate diss., St. Petersburg State University, 2012.

Kozintsev, Grigorii M. "Glubokii ekran." In *Sobranie sochinenii v piati tomakh*, vol. 1: 17–356. Leningrad: Iskusstvo, 1982.

Kozintsev, G., et al. "Chto mozhet redaktor: Kollektivnaia povest' ob Adriane Piotrovskom." *Iskusstvo kino* 12 (1962): 40–63.

Kozintseva, V. T., and Ia. L. Butovskii. "*Karl Marks*: Istoriia nepostavlennoi postanovki." *Kinovedcheskie zapiski* 18 (1993): 198–205.

Krementsov, Nikolai. *Stalinist Science*. Princeton, NY: Princeton University Press, 1997.

Kuromiya, Hiroaki. "Edinonchalie and the Soviet Industrial Manager, 1928–1937." *Soviet Studies* 36, no. 2 (1984): 185–204.

Latynina, Alla. "The Stalin Prizes for Literature and the Quintessence of Socialist Realism." In *In the Party Spirit: Socialist Realism and Literary Practice in the Soviet Union, East Germany and China*, edited by Hilary Chung and Michael Falchikov, 106–127. Amsterdam: Rodopi, 1996.

Laurent, Natacha. "L'interdiction du film 'Une Grande Vie': La reprise en main du cinéma soviétique en août 1946." *Communisme* 42–44 (1995): 137–153.

———. *L'œil du Kremlin: Cinéma et censure en URSS sous Staline, 1928–1953*. Toulouse: Privat, 2000.

Lebedev, Nikolai A. *Partiia o kino*. Moscow: Goskinoizdat, 1939.

Lenoe, Matthew E. *Closer to the Masses: Stalinist Culture, Social Revolution, and Soviet Newspapers*. Cambridge, MA: Harvard University Press, 2004.

Lewis, Jon, and Eric Smoodin, eds. *Looking Past the Screen: Case Studies in American Film History and Method*. Durham, NC: Duke University Press, 2007.

Leyda, Jay. *Kino: A History of the Russian and Soviet Film*. New York: Collier Books, 1973.

Liadov, M. *Stsenarii: Osnovy kino-dramaturhiï ta tekhnika stsenariia*. Kiev: Ukrteakinovydav, 1930.

Liber, George O. *Alexander Dovzhenko: A Life in Soviet Film*. London: British Film Institute, 2002.

Listov, Viktor S. "'Nazvanie kazhdoi kartiny utverzhdaetsia Komissiei Orgbiuro.'" *Kinovedcheskie zapiski* 31 (1996): 108–130.

MacAdams, William. *Ben Hecht: The Man Behind the Legend*. New York: Scribner, 1990.

Macheret, A. V., N. A. Glagoleva, and M. Kh. Zak. *Sovetskie khudozhestvennye fil'my: Annotirovannyi katalog*, vols. 1 and 2. Moscow: Iskusstvo, 1961.

Maksimenkov, Leonid. *Sumbur vmesto muzyki: Stalinskaia kul'turnaia revoliutsiia 1936–1938*. Moscow: Iuridicheskaia kniga, 1997.

———. "Vvedenie." In Anderson et al., *Kremlevskii kinoteatr*, 7–78.

———, ed. *Bol'shaia tsenzura: Pisateli i zhurnalisty v strane Sovetov 1917–1956*. Moscow: Materik, 2005.

Mamatova, Liliia, ed. *Kino: Politika i liudi, 30-e gody*. Moscow: Materik, 1995.

———. "Model' kinomifov 30-kh godov." In Mamatova, *Kino*, 52–78.

Maras, Steven. *Screenwriting: History, Theory, and Practice*. London: Wallflower Press, 2009.

Margolit, Evgenii. "Budem schitat', chto takogo fil'ma nikogda ne bylo." In Mamatova, *Kino*, 132–156.

——. "Fenomen agitpropfil'ma i prikhod zvuka v sovetskoe kino." *Kinovedcheskie zapiski* 48 (2007): 255–266.
Margolit, Evgenii, and Viacheslav Shmyrov. *Iz"iatoe kino, 1924–1953.* Moscow: Dubl'-D, 1995.
Mar'iamov, Grigorii. *Kremlevskii tsenzor: Stalin smotrit kino.* Moscow: Kinotsentr, 1992.
Markevich, Andrei. "How Much Control Is Enough? Monitoring and Enforcement under Stalin." *Europe-Asia Studies* 63, no. 8 (2011): 1449–1468.
Marshall, Herbert. *Masters of the Soviet Cinema: Crippled Creative Biographies.* London: Routledge & K. Paul, 1983.
Mayakovsky, Vladimir. "Karaul!" *Novyi LEF* 2 (1927): 23–25.
Messer, R. "A. I. Piotrovskii i stsenarnyi otdel 'Lenfil'ma' (30-e gody)." In Gornitskaia, *Iz istorii Lenfil'ma*, 3: 139–150.
Miller, Jamie. "Soviet Cinema, 1929–41: The Development of Industry and Infrastructure." *Europe-Asia Studies* 58, no. 1 (2006): 103–24.
——. "The Purges of Soviet Cinema, 1929–1938." *Studies in Russian and Soviet Cinema* 1, no. 1 (2007): 5–26.
——. *Soviet Cinema: Politics and Persuasion under Stalin.* London: I. B. Tauris, 2010.
——. "Soviet Politics and the Mezhrabpom Studio in the Soviet Union during the 1920s and 1930s." *Historical Journal of Film, Radio and Television* 32, no. 4 (2012): 521–535.
Monas, Sidney. "Censorship, Film, and Soviet Society: Some Reflections of a Russia-Watcher." *Studies in Comparative Communism* 17, nos. 3–4 (1984–85): 163–172.
Musina, Milena. "'Tut Barnet pereklikaetsia s siurrealizmom!' Stenogramma zasedaniia sektsii teorii i kritiki pri Dome kino, May 28, 1945." *Kinovedcheskie zapiski* 57 (2002): 140–157.
Narkompros RSFSR. *Repertuarnyi ukazatel'*, tom 3, *Kinorepertuar.* Moscow–Leningrad: GIKhL, 1931.
Naumburg, Nancy, ed. *We Make the Movies.* New York: W. W. Norton, 1937.
Negus, Keith. "The Production of Culture." In *Production of Culture/Cultures of Production*, edited by Paul du Gay, 67–118. London: Sage, 1997.
Neuberger, Joan. *Ivan the Terrible.* London: I. B. Tauris, 2003.
Nevezhin, Vladimir. "Fil'm *Zakon zhizni* i otluchenie Avdeenko: Versiia istorika." *Kinovedcheskie zapiski* 20 (1993/94): 94–124.
Nilin, Pavel. *Bol'shaia zhizn': Literaturnyi stsenarii v dvykh chastiakh.* Moscow: Goskinoizdat, 1945.
Ol'khovyi, B. S., ed. *Puti kino: 1-oe vsesoiuznoe partiinoe soveshchanie po kinematografii.* Moscow: Tea-kinopechat', 1929.
Parfenov, Lev, ed. *Zhivye golosa kino.* Moscow: Belyi bereg, 1999.
Perrie, Maureen. *The Cult of Ivan the Terrible in Stalin's Russia.* New York: Palgrave, 2001.
Pisarevskii, D. "Stsenarnye chernoviki *Chapaeva*." In Gornitskaia, *Iz istorii Lenfil'ma*, 3: 230–272.
Pratt, Sarah. *Nikolai Zabolotsky: Enigma and Cultural Paradigm.* Evanston, IL: Northwestern University Press, 2000.
Priestland, David. *Stalinism and the Politics of Mobilization: Ideas, Power, and Terror in Inter-War Russia.* Oxford: Oxford University Press, 2007.
Problems of Soviet Literature: Reports and Speeches at the First Soviet Writers' Congress. New York: International Publishers, 1935.
Pudovkin Vsevolod. *Sobranie sochinenii*, vol. 2. Moscow: Iskusstvo, 1975.
Ryabchikova, Natalie. "ARRK and the Soviet Transition to Sound." In *Sound, Speech, Music in Soviet and Post-Soviet Cinema*, edited by Lilya Kaganovsky and Masha Salazkina, 81–99. Bloomington: Indiana University Press, 2014.

——. "When Was Soviet Cinema Born? The Institutionalization of Soviet Film Studies and the Problems of Periodization." In *The Emergence of Film Culture: Knowledge Production, Institution Building and the Fate of the Avant-Garde in Europe, 1919–1945*, edited by Malte Hagener, 118–139. New York: Berghahn, 2014.

Rimberg, John. *The Motion Picture in the Soviet Union, 1918–1952: A Sociological Analysis*. New York: Arno Press, 1973.

Romm, Mikhail. *Besedy o kino*. Moscow: Iskusstvo, 1964.

——. *Ustnye rasskazy*. Moscow: Kinotsentr, 1989.

Rosen, Philip, ed. *Narrative, Apparatus, Ideology: A Film Theory Reader*. New York: Columbia University Press, 1986.

Roth-Ey, Kristin. *Moscow Prime Time: How the Soviet Union Built the Media Empire That Lost the Cultural Cold War*. Ithaca, NY: Cornell University Press, 2011.

Rubailo, Allentina I. *Partiinoe rukovodstvo razvitiem kinoiskusstva: 1928–1937*. Moscow: MGU, 1976.

Salys, Rimgaila. *The Musical Comedy Films of Grigorii Aleksandrov: Laughing Matters*. Chicago: Intellect, 2009.

Sangren, P. Steven. "'Power' against Ideology: A Critique of Foucaultian Usage." *Cultural Anthropology* 10, no. 1 (1995): 3–40.

Sarnov, Benedikt. *Stalin i pisateli: Kniga chetvertaia*. Moscow: EKSMO, 2011.

Schoeni, Helen. "Production Methods in Soviet Russia." *Cinema Quarterly* 2, no. 4 (1934): 210–214.

Seckler, Dawn. "What Does *Zhanr* Mean in Russian." In *Directory of World Cinema: Russia*, edited by Birgit Beumers, 28–33. Bristol, UK: Intellect, 2010.

Sedgwick, John, and Michael Pokorny, eds. *Economic History of Film*. New York: Routledge, 2005.

Shaw, Tony, and Denise J. Youngblood. *Cinematic Cold War: The American and Soviet Struggle for Hearts and Minds*. Lawrence: University Press of Kansas, 2010.

Shepilov, D. T. "Vospominaniia." *Voprosy istorii* 5 (1998): 3–27.

Shklovsky, Viktor. *Za 60 let: Raboty o kino*. Moscow: Iskusstvo, 1985.

Shumiatskii, Boris. *Kinematografiia millionov: Opyt analiza*. Moscow: Kinofotoizdat, 1935.

——. *Puti masterstva: Stat'i i doklady*. Moscow: Kinofotoizdat, 1936.

——. *Sovetskaia kinematografiia segodnia i zavtra*. Moscow: Kinofotoizdat, 1936.

——. "Zapisi besed B. Z. Shumiatskogo s I. V. Stalinym pri prosmotre kinofil'mov, 7 maia 1934 g.–26 ianvaria 1937 g." In Anderson et al., *Kremlevski kinoteatr*, 919–1053. Originally published as Aleksandr Troshin, "'A driani podobno *Garmon'* bol'she ne stavite?'" *Kinovedcheskie zapiski* 61 (2002): 281–346; and "'Kartina sil'naia, khoroshaia, no ne *Chapaev*,'" *Kinovedcheskie zapiski* 62 (2003): 115–188.

——. "Stalin o kino." In Anderson et al., *Kremlevski kinoteatr*, 81–92.

Shumiatskii, B. L. *Biografiia moei sem'i*. Moscow: Mai print, 2007.

Shumiatskii, B. Z., and Iu. M. Liss. "Vsem trestam, direktoram kinofabrik, direktoram s"emochnykh grupp, rezhisseram, stsenaristam i operatoram." In Soiuzkino, *K templanu Soiuzkino na 1932 god*, 1–4.

Sidorov, Nikolai. "*Veselye rebiata*—komediia kontrrevoliutsionnaia." *Istochnik* 3 (1995): 72–78.

Simacheva, Tat'iana, ed. "Boris Shumiatskii." *Kinograf* 18 (2007): 94–133.

——. "Boris Shumiatskii." *Kinograf* 19 (2008): 55–159.

Smith, Jeff. *Film Criticism, the Cold War, and the Blacklist: Reading the Hollywood Reds*. Berkeley: University of California Press, 2014.

Soiuzkino. *10 fil'm i politprosvetrabota vokrug nikh*. Moscow: Soiuzkino, 1931.

——. *K templanu Soiuzkino na 1932 god*. Moscow: Soiuzkino, 1932.

Sokolov, Ippolit. *Kino-stsenarii: Teoriia i tekhnika*. Moscow: Kinopechat', 1926.

Sopin, Artem. "'. . . Idem na soveshchanie v TsK,' ili 'Sporit' ne o chem': Tri teksta Sergeia Eizenshteina ob odnom predvoennom soveshchanii." *Kinovedcheskie zapiski* 104/105 (2013): 301–313.

Sovkino. *Tematicheskii plan Sovkino na 1928–29 god*. Moscow: Teakinopechat', 1928.

Staiger, Janet. "'Tame' Authors and the Corporate Laboratory: Stories, Writers and Scenarios in Hollywood." *Quarterly Review of Film Studies* 8, no. 4 (1983): 33–45.

——. "Blueprints for Feature Films: Hollywood's Continuity Scripts." In *The American Film Industry*, edited by Tina Balio, 173–192. Madison: University of Wisconsin Press, 1985.

Stalin, I. V. "XV s"ezd VKP(b)." In *Sochineniia*, 10: 269–371. Moscow: Gosudarstvennoe izdatel'stvo politicheskoi literatury, 1949.

Sutyrin, V. "Literatura, teatr, kino." *Na literaturnom postu* 10 (1929): 35–45.

——. "Problemy planirovaniia." *Proletarskoe kino* 8 (August 1931): 4–16.

Taylor, Richard. "A 'Cinema for the Millions': Soviet Socialist Realism and the Problem of Film Comedy." *Journal of Contemporary History* 18, no. 3 (1983): 439–461.

——. "Ideology as Mass Entertainment: Boris Shumyatsky and Soviet Cinema in the 1930s." In Taylor and Christie, *Inside the Film Factory*, 193–216.

——. "Red Stars, Positive Heroes and Personality Cults." In Taylor and Spring, *Stalinism and Soviet Cinema*, 69–89.

——. *Battleship Potemkin: The Film Companion*. London: I. B. Tauris, 2001.

——. "*Veselye Rebiata/The Happy Guys*." In *Cinema of Russia and the Former Soviet Union*, edited by Birgit Beumers, 79–87. London: Wallflower Press, 2007.

——. "On Stalin's Watch: The Late-Night Kremlin Screenings: May to October 1934." *Studies in Russian and Soviet Cinema* 7, no. 2 (2013): 243–258.

——. "On Stalin's Watch: The Late-Night Kremlin Screenings: October 1934 to January 1937." *Studies in Russian and Soviet Cinema* 8, no. 1 (2014): 138–163.

Taylor, Richard, and Ian Christie, eds. *Inside the Film Factory: New Approaches to Russian and Soviet Cinema*. London: Routledge, 1991.

——, eds. *The Film Factory: Russian and Soviet Cinema in Documents, 1896–1939*. London: Routledge, 1994.

Taylor, Richard, and Derek Spring, eds. *Stalinism and Soviet Cinema*. London: Routledge, 1993.

Tematicheskii plan proizvodstva khudozhestvennykh fil'mov na 1954 god. Moscow: Iskusstvo, 1953.

Thompson, Kristin. "Early Alternatives to the Hollywood Mode of Production: Implications for Europe's Avant-Gardes." *Film History* 5 (1993): 396–401.

Timasheff, Nicholas S. *The Great Retreat: The Growth and Decline of Communism in Russia*. New York: E. P. Dutton, 1946.

Tomoff, Kiril. "'Most Respected Comrade . . .': Patrons, Clients, Brokers, and Unofficial Networks in the Stalinist Music World." *Contemporary European History* 11, no. 1 (2002): 33–65.

——. *Creative Union: The Professional Organization of Soviet Composers, 1939–1953*. Ithaca, NY: Cornell University Press, 2006.

Trauberg, Leonid. "O fil'me *Karl Marks*." *Kinovedcheskie zapiski* 18 (1993): 206–209.

Tret'iakov, Sergei. "Stsenarnoe khishchnichestvo." In *Kinematograficheskoe nasledie: Stat'i, ocherki, stenogrammy vystuplenii, doklady, stsenarii*, edited by I.I. Ratiani, 61–62. St. Petersburg: Nestor-Istoriia, 2010.

Trotskii, L. "Vodka, tserkov' i kinematograf." *Kinovedcheskie zapiski* 45 (2002):
    184–188. Originally published in *Pravda* on July 12, 1923.
Tsivian, Yuri. *Ivan the Terrible*. London: British Film Institute, 2002.
——. "New Notes on Russian Film Culture Between 1908 and 1919." In *The Silent
    Film Reader*, edited by Lee Grieveson and Peter Krämer, 339–348. London:
    Routledge, 2004.
Turkin, V. K. "O kinoinstsenirovke literaturnykh proizvedenii." In *Kak my rabotaem
    nad kinostsenariem*, edited by I. F. Popov, 107–147. Moscow: Kinofotoizdat,
    1936.
——. *Dramaturgiia kino*. Moscow: VGIK, 2007. Reprint. Originally published by
    Moscow: Goskinoizdat, 1938.
Turovskaya, Maya. "The 1930s and 1940s: Cinema in Context." In Taylor and Spring,
    Stalinism and Soviet Cinema, 34–53.
——. "Fil'my i liudi." *Kinovedcheskie zapiski* 57 (2002): 251–259.
——. "Gollivud v Moskve, ili sovetskoe i amerikanskoe kino 30-kh–40-kh godov."
    Kinovedcheskie zapiski 97 (2010): 51–63.
Uhlenbruch, Bernd. "The Annexation of History: Eisenstein and the Ivan Grozny
    Cult of the 1940s." In *The Culture of the Stalin Period*, edited by Hans Günther,
    266–286. London: Macmillan, 1990.
Vishnevskii, Vs. *My iz Kronshtadta*. Moscow–Leningrad: Iskusstvo, 1936.
Welch, David. *Propaganda and the German Cinema, 1933–1945*. London: I. B. Tauris,
    2001.
Widdis, Emma. *Alexander Medvedkin*. London: I. B. Tauris, 2005.
Youngblood, Denise. *Soviet Cinema in the Silent Era, 1918–1935*. Austin: University of
    Texas Press, 1991.
——. "Entertainment or Enlightenment? Popular Cinema in Soviet Society,
    1921–1931." In *New Directions in Soviet History*, edited by Stephen White,
    41–61. Cambridge, UK: Cambridge University Press, 1992.
——. *Movies for the Masses: Popular Cinema and Soviet Society in the 1920s*.
    Cambridge, UK: Cambridge University Press, 1992.
——. *Russian War Films: On the Cinema Front, 1914–2005*. Lawrence: University Press
    of Kansas, 2007.
Yekelchyk, Serhy. "Diktat and Dialogue in Stalinist Culture: Staging Patriotic Historical
    Opera in Soviet Ukraine, 1936–1954." *Slavic Review* 59, no. 3 (2000): 597–624.
Zabrodin, V. V. and E. A. Misalandi, "'Sovetskaia komedia—eto svetlyi put' Barneta.'"
    Kinovedcheskie zapiski 45 (2000): 107–119.
Zaks, Boris. "Censorship at the Editorial Desk." In Choldin and Friedberg, *Red Pencil*,
    155–161.
Zelenov, M. V. "'To Prohibit in Accordance with Due Procedure . . .': The Censorship
    Policy of Narkompros RSFSR, 1926," *Solanus* 21 (2007): 49–75.
Zil'ver, E., ed. *Za bol'shoe kinoiskusstvo*. Moscow: Kinofotoizdat, 1935.

Index

Admiral Nakhimov, 146, 206–207, 219
Adorno, Theodor, 219
agitprop film, 17, 20–22, 69
Aktrisa (Actress), 159, 194
Aleinikov, Moisei, 98n28, 152
Aleksandr Nevskii, 106, 193
Aleksandrov, Georgii, 50, 84–86, 88, 141, 159, 194–195
Aleksandrov, Grigorii, 30, 49, 57, 61, 81–82, 95, 102, 106, 126, 142, 146–148, 177, 181, 195, 197, 211
All-Union Combine for the Cinema and Photo Industry: *See* Soiuzkino
All-Union Committee for Arts Affairs: *See* Arts Committee
All-Union Ministry of Cinema: *See* Ministry of Cinema
Alpers, Boris, 208
Andreev, Andrei, 26–27, 42, 191, 193, 230
Angarov, Aleksei, 180, 188–190
Anna Karenina, 162
antiformalism campaign: *See* campaign against formalism and naturalism in the arts
Antipov, Nikolai, 206
Anton Ivanovich serditsia (Anton Ivanovich Is Angry), 84
Antonov, Leonid, 198
Armenfilm, 16
Arnshtam, Leo, 21, 124
ARRK (Association of Workers of Revolutionary Cinema), 109, 120
Artistic Council: ministry level, 59, 101, 104–106, 122, 125–128, 137, 148, 194–195, 197–203, 230; studio level, 58–59, 80–81, 100–103, 109, 122–125, 137, 147
Arts Committee, 31, 179, 186, 188, 191–192
Astakhov, Ivan, 57, 141
avant-garde film, 20–23, 113, 168
Avdeenko, Aleksandr, 157, 192–193
Avenarius, Georgii, 140
Azerfilm, 16

Babel', Isaak, 143, 152, 157n111
Babitskii, Boris, 35, 184, 189
Babitsky, Paul, 99

Babochkin, Boris, 88, 126
Bagrov, Petr, 109–110
Barnet, Boris, 25, 42, 92, 107, 123–124, 143, 163, 195
Bednyi, Dem'ian, 170, 190
Bek-Nazarov, Amo, 102
Belgosfilm, 16
Belinskii, 59
Bezhin lug (Bezhin Meadow), 37–38, 106, 115, 143, 155, 186–189, 191
Bleiman, Mikhail, 60, 94, 101–102
Bliakhin, Pavel, 133, 167, 172
Bliznetsy (Twins), 125
Bogataia nevesta (The Rich Bride), 44, 74
Bogatyri (The Warriors), 190
Bolotnye soldaty (Peat-Bog Soldiers), 193
Bol'shaia zhizn' (A Great Life, part 1), 44, 208
Bol'shaia zhizn' (A Great Life, part 2), 11, 44, 46, 87, 125, 208–211
Bol'shakov, Ivan, 36, 39–42, 44, 49, 57, 64, 77–81, 83–86, 88, 96, 101–104, 107, 122–123, 127, 132, 137, 140, 147, 153–154, 157, 159–161, 194–195, 198–203, 208
Bol'shintsov, Manuel', 60–61, 141
Bordwell, David, 121–122
Bragin, Mikhail, 60
Brandenburgskie vorota (The Brandenburg Gate), 88
Brik, Osip, 55
Briunchugin, Evgenii, 205
Bronenosets Potemkin (Battleship Potemkin), 6, 19–21, 26, 50, 53, 111
Bubnov, Andrei, 206, 230
Budennyi, Semen, 196, 201, 207
Bukharin, Nikolai, 24
Buneev, Boris, 93
Buscombe, Edward, 220

Caldwell, John Thornton, 220–221
campaign against formalism and naturalism in the arts, 31–35, 73, 115–121, 179–180, 190, 208, 210
Cannes Film Festival, 46
Capra, Frank, 30, 107, 219–220
Carroll, Noël, 219, 221

censorship: Boris Shumiatskii, 178–180, 182–190, 204; categories, 14, 19, 32, 35, 40, 42–43, 47, 125, 133, 168–169, 208; censor backgrounds, 137–138, 167, 170–171; Central Committee, 165, 170–171, 174–185, 188–203, 208–209, 212; editors, 34, 47, 75–76, 82, 89, 100, 125, 131, 136–141, 167–172, 180–181, 183, 195, 195n124, 196–203; Glavrepertkom, 21, 133, 166–174, 177, 208; guidelines and criteria, 41, 139–140, 180–181, 197, 203–211; GUK, 36, 179–189, 204; GUKF, 179, 204; GURK, 177, 179–180, 185–189, 192, 203; industry, 34, 165–203; Ivan Bol'shakov, 122–123, 153–154, 194, 208; Joseph Stalin, 166, 172–173, 175–177, 189–193, 204–205, 207–212, 215; multiplicity of authorities, 100, 136–137; opinion divergences, 138–140; party, 170–195; peer criticism, 121–128; prescriptive, 140, 166, 169, 211–212; productive, 6–7, 140, 150, 203, 212; proscriptive, 139–140, 211–212; screenwriting, 128n151, 131, 133, 136–141, 149, 159, 163–164; self-censorship, 10, 42, 103–104, 124, 165–166, 170, 173, 182, 190–194, 214–215, 218; spectatorial, 205; uncertainty, 11, 137, 165–166, 177–178, 191, 201, 203, 208, 212, 215; URK, 192, 200; World War II, 193–194

Central Asia, 16, 43, 67, 87, 125–126, 139

Central Committee (Communist Party): Andreev/Zhdanov Film Commission (1938–1941), 191, 193; Arts Committee, 31; Bubnov/Stetskii Film Commission (1932–1934), 22–24, 42, 66, 174–177, 206, 230; censorship, 165, 170–171, 174–185, 188–203, 208–209, 212; film bans, 44, 46, 83–84, 102, 105, 115, 123–128, 178, 180–182, 186, 190, 192–194; literature, 46, 105, 111, 194; Propaganda Department, 17, 19, 26–27, 29, 31, 38, 47, 73–75, 84, 88, 127, 137, 165, 170, 176, 178–182, 188–195; reactive stance, 178–203; resolutions, 18, 21–22, 46–48, 111, 114, 158, 191, 194; screenplays, 137; Soiuzkino, 16; thematic planning, 53, 57, 66–67, 70, 73–74, 77–78, 83–86, 88; trophy films, 49–50

Chakhir'ian, Grigorii, 137

Chapaev, 6, 21, 26–27, 41, 50–51, 56, 63, 95, 110–113, 148, 175, 177–178

Chapaev, Vasilii, 111

Chaplin, Charlie, 107, 161

Chaplygin, Aleksei, 140

Charge of the Light Brigade, The, 44

Cherniak, Iakov, 136–137

Cherniavskii, Lev, 192

Chernova, Tamara, 199

Cherviakov, Evgenii, 73, 189

Chest' (Honor), 73

Chiaureli, Mikhail, 49, 87, 101–102, 105, 205

Chirkov, Boris, 124, 126

Chlen pravitel'stva (Member of the Government), 80

Christie, Ian, 110

Chudesnitsa (The Miracle Worker), 11, 75, 96, 182–189, 195, 204

Cinema Committee, 38–39, 103, 136, 140, 147, 174, 192, 194

cinematographer (cameraman), 28, 30, 40, 72, 96n22, 101–102, 107, 113, 117

Citizen Kane, 219

Clark, Katerina, 108, 114, 212, 216

Committee for Cinema Affairs: See Cinema Committee

cultural policy: cinema for the millions, 2, 13, 21, 27, 50, 214; content control, 2, 4–5, 9–10, 23, 33, 38, 48, 52, 62, 68–69, 72, 76, 86, 88–89, 94, 105, 120, 129, 136, 160, 164, 208, 215–221; control mechanisms, 7, 190; cultural revolution, 20, 22, 54; engineers of human souls, 94, 105–108, 160; high art, 33–34, 41, 47, 90, 102–115, 121, 128–129; most important of the arts, 1–2, 11, 14, 41, 216; political utility, 7, 33–34, 55, 115, 125; selectivity policies, 13, 22–25, 34. See also antiformalism campaign; censorship; film director; film policy; screenwriting; socialist realism

Daltons Ride Again, The, 201

Dela i liudi (Men and Jobs), 18

DeMille, Cecil B., 107

Deputat Baltiki (Baltic Deputy), 58

Devushka s kharakterom (The Girl with Character), 138

Devushka speshit na svidanie (Late for a Date), 189

director's scenario, 102, 141–159, 183–184, 192, 198–199

direktor kartiny (production administrator), 98–99, 101, 184

Dobin, Efim, 137

Dobrenko, Evgenii, 204–205, 212

documentary film, 20–22, 22n37, 80, 176

Donskoi, Mark, 158–159

Dovzhenko, Aleksandr, 24–25, 56, 67, 92, 96, 102, 106–107, 112, 116, 118, 162–163, 170, 207, 219
Dubrovina, Liudmila, 200
Dubrovskii-Eshke, Boris, 102
Dubson, Mikhail, 81, 100, 104
Dukel'skii, Semen, 36, 38–40, 75–79, 85, 96, 101, 108, 132, 152–154, 158, 191, 204, 208
Dunaevskii, Isaak, 201
Dvadtsat' shest' komissarov (Twenty-Six Commissars), 18, 53
Dzerzhinskii, Feliks, 59, 81
Dzigan, Efim, 57, 62, 81, 97, 102, 161–162, 206, 211

editor *(montazher)*: *See* film editing
editor *(redaktor)*: *See* censorship; screenwriting
Eisenstein, Sergei, 19–20, 24–25, 37, 46–47, 53, 55–56, 67, 81–82, 92, 95, 102–112, 115, 119–120, 142–144, 155, 163, 186, 188–189, 193, 208, 217
Eliseev, Konstantin, 45, 83
Enei, Evgenii, 101
Erdman, Nikolai, 123, 147, 159, 195–198, 202–203
Eremin, Dmitrii, 121, 135, 141, 196–197
Erevan Studio, 16, 102
Ermler, Fridrikh, 21, 49, 58, 62, 92, 95, 101–102, 104, 107, 109–110, 124, 171, 207, 211

Fadeev, Aleksandr, 101
Faintsimmer, Aleksandr, 62, 81, 104
Fairbanks, Douglas, 19
Fatali Khan, 57, 211
Feature Production Department (Main Administration for Feature Film Production), 102, 137, 147, 183, 195, 197, 202
film acting, 4, 21, 25, 28, 72, 96, 103–104, 113, 119, 123–124, 126, 143, 148, 159, 186, 199, 202, 221
film bans, 4–9, 14, 21, 31, 35–37, 41–47, 51, 83–84, 102, 105–106, 115, 120–128, 133, 149, 157, 165–166, 169–175, 178, 180–182, 186–195, 203–212, 217, 227–228
film budgets, 4, 20, 147, 183, 198–199, 201–202
film director: artistic agenda, 90–91, 94, 109–121, 128–129, 214; artistic-production units (KhPO), 98–100; authorship, 5, 94, 96, 108, 141–142, 158, 163, 215, 217; autonomy, 2, 90–91, 109, 128–129; barriers to entry, 93; Boris Shumiatskii, 24–25, 38, 49, 64–65, 67, 69, 75, 79–80, 82, 92, 94–96, 107, 110; categories, 93; compensation,

23, 76–77, 96n22, 108, 142, 201–202, 214; elite status, 5, 25, 90–91, 94, 102, 106–108, 128–129, 166, 214; employment patterns, 4, 7, 24–29, 40, 92–93, 214; group, 5–7, 10, 24, 90–94, 106–110, 121–122, 128–129; Ivan Bol'shakov, 41, 64, 77, 79–82, 107; Joseph Stalin, 49, 94, 105–108; layoffs, 18, 25; leadership role, 6, 9, 92, 96–99, 103; literary scenario, 102, 141–149, 152–155, 158–159; masters, 6, 9–10, 24–26, 48–49, 79–80, 82, 90–97, 106–110, 112, 115, 118–122, 128, 182–183, 214, 218; number of, 4, 24–25, 29, 40, 93; original screenplays, 76, 94, 142; peer competition and criticism, 5, 100, 104, 112, 119–128, 186, 189; political stance, 24–25, 67, 109–115, 124–129, 146, 214; reactions to the antiformalism campaign, 115–121; screenwriters, 62–63, 82, 94, 96, 131, 141–149; self-governance, 40, 94, 100–106, 108, 128; Soviet Hollywood, 28, 107; studio artistic directors, 101–104; thematic planning, 52–53, 56, 61–64, 69, 75–76, 81–82, 88, 94. *See also individual directors*
film distribution, 7–8, 16–17, 20, 26–27, 31, 38–39, 50, 69, 89, 112, 166–174, 179, 193, 214; Europe, 44, 47, 49, 149
film editing, 27–28, 92, 112, 120, 143–144, 146, 148–149, 152–153
film executive: studio head, 55, 94, 96–100, 106, 122, 184
film exhibition, 7, 12, 17, 20–21, 27, 31, 38–39, 89, 214; *cinefication*, 17, 229
film genre, 4, 14, 20–21, 23, 43–44, 48, 64, 70–74, 79–89, 107, 134, 195–203, 211, 215, 219; adventure, 43, 70, 80, 195–203; biopic, 26, 43, 55, 59, 64, 70, 72, 78, 80, 84–85, 87, 104, 107, 112, 207, 211; children's film, 4, 35, 43, 54, 59, 68, 70–72, 77–80, 84; comedy, 54, 61n44, 70–71, 80–82, 85–86, 123–124, 138–140, 150, 177, 181–189, 196–203, 211; defense and antifascist film, 52, 68, 71, 73, 77–80, 86; drama, 23, 43–46, 68, 71, 80, 88, 162, 175, 186, 208–211; fictional documentary, 87; historical and revolutionary film, 4, 43, 52–54, 63, 66, 68–70, 74, 77–81, 84–85, 98, 107, 109, 114, 117, 206, 208; literary adaptation, 53, 68, 71–72, 78, 85–86, 88, 157; melodrama, 71, 126, 168–169; musical, 57, 71, 81, 84–85, 124, 177, 197; prestige picture, 34, 66, 80–81, 95, 104, 205–211; science fiction and fantasy, 70–72, 80; war film, 43–44, 68, 84, 125–128, 195–203. *See also* agitprop film

film industry: dysfunction, 7–8, 27, 213–216; federal principle of organization, 39; lack of vertical integration, 7–8, 17, 39, 214; list of studios, 16; national republics, 16–17, 31, 38–39, 166–167, 229; reform, 6, 9–10, 14, 26–30, 34, 51, 73, 100, 150–152, 159, 215; risk aversion, 3, 10, 24, 35, 40, 42, 51, 102, 104, 121, 194; studio structure, 96–100; studios, 3–6, 15–17, 39–40, 47, 53. *See also* mode of production; Soviet Hollywood

film output, 2–6, 11–14, 17–29, 35–40, 43–44, 47–51, 53, 96, 175, 213, 215, 227–228

film policy: quality (masterpieces), 3–50, 66, 80, 93, 104, 107, 110–121, 131–132, 160, 208, 215–217; quantity (mass production), 4, 13–14, 17–18, 21–23, 26–29, 31–50

film producer, 6, 27–28, 91–92, 96, 98–104, 122, 141, 158n116, 163–164, 166, 178, 220–221; censor-producer, 203; director-producer, 101–103, 122, 214

film production: *See* mode of film production

film stock, 17–19, 96–97, 144, 184, 229

film viewers, 3–4, 15, 22, 55, 78, 111–112, 119, 121, 128, 168, 196, 198

Filtzer, Donald, 39–40

First Five-Year Plan, 15, 20, 22, 32

Fish, Gennadii, 138

Fitzpatrick, Sheila, 212

Fomin, Valerii, 205

Ford, John, 57, 219

foreign films, 3, 8, 12, 15, 20, 38, 112, 174, 213. *See also* trophy films

formalism, 31–35, 55, 66, 110, 115–116, 120–121, 154, 168, 179, 187, 208

Front, 63

Gabrilovich, Evgenii, 62

Galaktionov, Mikhail, 59–60, 105, 126

Gandurin, Konstantin, 167

Gardin, Vladimir, 101

Garin, Erast, 140

Garmon' (Accordion), 145

Gerasimov, Sergei, 58, 93, 102, 124, 147–148

Gerasimova, Valeriia, 59

German, Iurii, 56–57, 59, 63–64

Glavkinoprokat (Main Film Distribution Administration), 39, 200

Glavlit (Main Administration for Literary and Publishing Affairs), 170, 203

Glavrepertkom (Main Repertory Control Committee), 21, 133, 166–174, 177, 208

Goebbels, Joseph, 6

Golovnia, Vladimir, 147

Gorbatov, Boris, 157

Gorskii, Aleksandr, 100

Gosfilmofond, 179, 187

Gosplan, 28

Grazhdanin Sovetskogo Soiuza (Citizen of the Soviet Union), 55–56

Gruziiafilm, 16

GUK (Main Cinema Administration), 31, 36, 39, 97, 179–180, 183–188, 204

GUKF (Main Administration for Cinema and Photo Industry), 17, 179, 204, 206

GURK (Main Administration for Repertory Control), 177, 179–180, 185–189, 192, 203

Hecht, Ben, 162

Hollywood, 1–9, 12–13, 27, 34–35, 39, 47–49, 57, 62, 69, 71, 91–92, 107–108, 130, 132–135, 140–142, 144, 149, 161–162, 164, 201, 213, 215–216, 218, 220–221

Horkheimer, Max, 219

House of Cinema *(Dom kino)*, 109, 116, 186

ideology, 8–11, 15, 20–24, 31–35, 40n105, 44, 50–51, 56, 67, 80, 83–86, 89, 100, 108–110, 114, 118–129, 133, 135, 138, 140, 150, 155–163, 166, 168–173, 178–184, 189, 203–204, 212–222

Il'f, Il'ia, 142, 159

Indenbom, Lev, 184

instructional film, 22, 78n112, 98

intolerance of imperfection, 3, 6–10, 14, 18–19, 31–35, 42–43, 50–51, 91, 133, 150, 203–204, 212

Ioganson, Eduard, 147

Isaev, Konstantin, 63

Iskusstvo kino (journal), 49, 109, 119–120, 158

It Happened One Night, 219

Iudin, Konstantin, 11, 42, 93, 125, 195, 197–202

Iukov, Konstantin, 71, 114

Iutkevich, Sergei, 21, 25, 61–62, 93, 101–102, 107, 111–113, 118, 121, 149, 207

Ivan, 18

Ivan Groznyi (Ivan the Terrible), 46–47, 55–56, 106, 120, 125, 193, 207–208

Ivanov, Aleksandr, 62

Ivanov, Boris, 41, 192

Ivanovskii, Aleksandr, 62, 84, 124

Izvestiia (newspaper), 30, 36, 107, 179, 186, 189, 192

Kachestvo liubvi (The Quality of Love), 55
Kaganovich, Lazar, 18, 177
Kalatozov, Mikhail, 104, 109, 128
Kamenev, Lev, 30
Kapler, Aleksei, 60, 64, 81, 102
Katinov, Vasilii, 47, 82, 137, 197
Katsigras, Aleksandr, 167
Katsnel'son, Leontii, 99
Kavaleridze, Ivan, 117, 168, 179
Kazakhfilm, 16n11
Kepley, Vance, 39, 50
Kerzhentsev, Platon, 19–21, 31, 47, 115, 186, 190
KGB (Committee on State Security), 64, 76
Kheifits, Iosif, 63, 102, 171, 173, 211
Khodataev, Nikolai, 25
Khokhlova, Ekaterina, 173
khudozhestvenno-proizvodstvennoe ob"edinenie (artistic-production unit (KhPO)), 98–100
Kiev Studio, 16, 98–99, 101–102, 138, 152
Kino (newspaper), 25, 69–70, 73, 77, 107, 109, 112, 116, 146, 151–152, 169, 172, 178
Kiva, Nikolai, 81
Kogan, Isaak, 183
Kompozitor Glinka (Composer Glinka), 211
Komsomol (Young Communist League), 41, 59, 66, 192, 200
Korda, Alexander, 219
Kornai, János, 216–217
Korostin, Mikhail, 25
Kotkin, Stephen, 33
Kotovskii, 81, 104
Kovarskii, Nikolai, 125, 137
Kozintsev, Grigorii, 49, 56, 59, 62, 64, 92, 102–103, 112–113, 120, 124–125, 127, 206
Krasnye d'iavoliata (The Red Imps), 200
Kreps, Vladimir, 47
Krinkin (Krynkin), 100
Krokodil (journal), 36–37, 83
Krumin, Karl, 167
Kubanskie kazaki (The Kuban Cossacks), 196
Kudrin, Ivan, 99
Kuibyshev, Valerian, 59
Kuleshov, Lev, 16, 25, 92, 110, 116, 144, 154
Kul'tura i zhizn' (newspaper), 47, 205
Kuzakov, Konstantin, 149, 195
Kuz'mina, Elena, 143, 163
Kuznetsov, Sergei, 200–201

Labirint (Labyrinth), 61
Lady Hamilton, 219
Lebedev, Nikolai, 62

Ledi Makbet Mtsenskogo uezda (Lady Macbeth of the Mtsensk District), 32–33
Lench, Leonid, 43
Lenfilm, 16–17, 26, 39, 43, 55, 57–60, 62–64, 72, 98–104, 122, 124–125, 147, 171, 175
Lenin, Vladimir, 1, 14, 216
Leningrad (journal), 46
Levin, Fedor, 137, 181
Leyda, Jay, 143–144
Literaturnaia gazeta (newspaper), 74, 149, 152
Litovskii, Osaf, 167, 180, 189–190
Lokshina, Khesia, 140
Lomidze, Grigorii, 205
Lost Patrol, The, 57, 219
Lotoshev, Nikolai, 122, 124–125
Lukov, Leonid, 11, 44, 49, 93, 208, 211

Macheret, Aleksandr, 81, 102, 193
Magnitogorsk, 33
Malenkov, Georgii, 42, 50, 88, 193
malokartin'e (film famine), 3, 14
Mal'skaia (Guseva), Fania, 95
Mar'iamov, Grigorii, 87–88, 196–200
Marx, Karl, 64, 125
mass cinema, 8, 10–11, 14, 27, 34, 50–51, 131, 162, 213, 216–217
mass film, 13, 21–28, 34, 38, 66, 214, 219
masterpieces, 3, 6–7, 10, 13–14, 19–24, 26–27, 33–34, 38, 42–43, 50–51, 111, 114, 130, 160, 208, 213–215. *See also* film policy
Mat' (Mother), 111
Mayakovsky, Vladimir, 90
Medvedkin, Aleksandr, 11, 25, 81, 95–96, 182–187
Merkulov, Vsevolod, 121
Messer, Raisa, 58, 100–101, 137
Mezhrabpomfilm, 16, 18, 25, 35, 60, 69–70, 151, 181–182
Michurin, 206–207, 211
Mikhailov, Nikolai, 200
Milestone, Lewis, 107
Miller, Jamie, 8n23, 9n27, 20
Minin i Pozharskii, 80
Ministry of Cinema, 39, 46–49, 105, 148, 194–199, 202
mode of film production, 13–15, 62, 69, 91–92, 135, 163, 217; artisanal mode, 6, 13–14, 50–51, 92, 107, 135; director-centered mode, 10, 14, 25, 90–108, 128–129, 141, 146, 164, 190; lack of division of labor, 9, 27, 92n8, 100, 131, 134, 150–152, 190, 214
Modern Times, 161
Moia rodina (My Motherland), 171–173, 181

Molodoi chelovek (A Young Man), 125
Molotov, Viacheslav, 108, 179
Mordvinov, Nikolai, 199
Mosfilm, 16–17, 39–43, 59, 61, 66–67, 70,
   75, 81, 86, 97–98, 100–104, 122–123, 138,
   147–148, 151–152, 182–189, 192, 198
Moskvin, Andrei, 101, 113
Munblit, Georgii, 124
Muzykal'naia istoriia (The Musical Story), 124
My iz Kronshtadta (We Are from Kronstadt),
   205–206

Na dal'nei zastave (At a Distant Outpost), 205
Na Dal'nem Vostoke (In the Far East), 75
Na otdykhe (On Vacation), 147
*Na poroge budushchego (At the Brink of
   the Future)*, 56
Nabatov, Il'ia, 140
Narkompros (People's Commissariat for
   Education), 54, 166
Nashestvie (The Invasion), 205
Nazarov, Aleksei, 191
Nebo Moskvy (Moscow Skies), 85
Nedobrovo, Vladimir, 55
New Economic Policy, 15, 214
Nikanorov, Mikhail, 181
Nilin, Pavel, 208, 210
Nil'sen, Vladimir, 30, 95, 117–118
1928 Party Conference on Cinema, 19, 54
1935 Cinema Conference (All-Union Creative
   Conference of Soviet Cinema Workers), 41,
   111–116
NKVD (People's Commissariat of Internal
   Affairs), 76, 191, 205

*O strannostiakh liubvi (About the Oddities
   of Love)*, 181–182
Obnorskii, B., 100
Odessa Studio, 16, 39n102, 140, 168–169
Odinnadtsatyi (Eleventh Year), 53
Odna radost' (The Only Joy), 175, 180
ODSK (Society for Friends of Soviet Cinema),
   179
Ogni Baku (The Lights of Baku), 211
OGPU (Joint Chief Political Directorate), 167
Okaiannaia sila (The Accursed Force), 185
Okhlopkov, Nikolai, 126
Oktiabr' (October), 53
Oleinikov, Nikolai, 147
Orlova, Liubov', 95

Pabst, G. W., 124
Padenie Berlina (The Fall of Berlin), 87, 205
Partiinyi bilet (The Party Card), 75, 189

Pasternak, Boris, 160
patronage, 94–95, 100, 105–107, 188
Pavlenko, Petr, 60, 101
Perestiani, Ivan, 200
Pervaia konnaia (First Cavalry Army), 205–207
Pesni (Songs), 171
Petrov, Evgenii, 124, 142, 159
Petrov, Vladimir, 87, 101–102
Petrov-Bytov, Pavel, 101
Piat' nevest (Five Brides), 169
Piotrovskii, Adrian, 58, 72, 100–101
Pirogov, 64
Piscator, Erwin, 16
Poezd idet na vostok (The Train Goes East), 219
Pogodin, Nikolai, 59, 62, 207
Pokolenie pobeditelei (Generation of Victors),
   189
Polikarpov, Dmitrii, 105
politprosvetfilm (agitprop film), 20–22, 69
politredaktor (political editor), 136–137, 167,
   170–171. *See also* censorship
Polotskii, Semen, 125
Popov, Ivan, 161
popular cinema, 50. *See also* film genre; mass
   cinema; Soviet Hollywood
Pravda (newspaper), 14, 26, 30, 32, 41, 47, 50,
   60, 77, 97, 115–120, 149, 160, 172, 179, 186
Pravov, Ivan, 140, 175
Preobrazhenskaia, Ol'ga, 140, 175
Priestland, David, 9
Prizyvniki (Conscripts), 140
production planning, 17, 21–26, 36–39, 55, 63,
   67–76, 227–228; plan fulfillment, 34–50, 75,
   166. *See also* thematic planning
Prometei (Prometheus), 117, 179
propaganda, 1, 4, 6–7, 14, 44, 48, 51, 89, 125,
   129, 198, 202–203, 212–221
propaganda cinema, 1–2, 7–8, 91, 129, 213,
   215
propaganda state, 1, 5
Prostye liudi (Ordinary People), 125–128
Protazanov, Yakov, 16, 25, 107, 124, 181
Prut, Iosif, 57, 100
Pudovkin, Vsevolod, 16, 24–25, 49, 92–93,
   101–102, 107, 123, 146, 207, 211, 219
Pyr'ev, Ivan, 25, 44, 46, 49, 67, 74, 102, 120,
   125, 157, 189, 196, 201–202
Pyshka (Boule de suif), 97

Rafes, Moisei, 135
Raizman, Iulii, 62, 81, 93, 102, 123, 163, 219
Rakhmanov, Leonid, 58
Rappaport, Gerbert, 62–63, 102, 124
Raskin, Aleksandr, 147

Ravich, Nikolai, 167
Razgrom nemetskikh voisk pod Moskvoi (Moscow Strikes Back), 87
Repin, Il'ia, 47
Riskin, Robert, 30
Robin Hood, 19
Rodina zovet (Motherland Calls), 75
Rodionov, N., 197–199
Romm, Mikhail, 25, 40, 49, 57, 62, 81, 93, 97, 101–104, 106–107, 118, 126, 158, 219
Room, Abram, 25, 56, 67, 92, 205
Roshal', Grigorii, 62, 102
Rubinovye zvezdy (Ruby Stars): See *Veselei nas net*
Rzheshevskii, Aleksandr, 139, 155

Saianov, Vissarion, 59
samotek (drift): See screenwriting
San Francisco, 44
Savchenko, Igor', 57, 59, 69, 87, 93, 105, 115, 145, 189
Sazonov, Aleksei, 195
Schast'e (Happiness), 184–185
Schwartz, Harry, 12
scientific film, 48, 53
screenwriting: authored literary scenario, 130, 132, 150, 154–164; Boris Shumiatskii, 132, 150–151; censorship, 131, 133, 136–141, 149, 159, 163–164; Central Committee, 137; compensation, 61, 76–77, 136, 140, 151, 158, 202; directors, 62–63, 82, 94, 96, 102, 131, 141–149, 152–154, 158–159, 192; editors, 58–63, 75–76, 82, 86, 89, 100, 125, 131, 136–141, 151–152, 157, 167–172, 180–181, 195–203; emotional scenario, 154–155, 161; employment patterns, 28, 41, 131, 133–136, 150–152, 156; film quality, 34, 40, 49; film quantity, 21, 38, 131; format, 142, 144–145; iron scenario, 130, 132, 149–150, 153–155, 159, 161, 163; Ivan Bol'shakov, 41, 77, 132, 137, 147, 154, 157, 160, 194; *libretto* (synopsis), 53; literary scenarios, 102, 132, 141–142, 146–149, 152–161, 192; multiple authorship, 130, 134, 151, 153, 155, 159, 162; professionalization, 10, 62, 82, 130–134, 140–143, 151, 155–156; *samotek* (drift) submissions, 69, 74, 86, 133; scenario crisis, 131–135, 137, 141, 149–150, 154–159; Scenario Studio, 47, 57, 60–61, 85, 121, 135, 141, 196–197; screenplay competitions, 61–62; Screenplay Council, 101; screenplay departments, 58, 123, 136–141, 151–153; screenplay vulnerabilities, 131, 139, 156–159; Semen Dukel'skii, 76, 132, 152–153; shooting script: *see* director's scenario;
single-authorship, 130, 137, 151, 153–154, 161–162; specialization, 133–135, 151–152, 155; Standard Screenwriting Agreement, 136, 156; thematic planning, 53–56, 58–63, 69–70, 74, 76, 82, 88, 135; training, 60, 156; uncredited, 134, 142, 159–162; *zaiavka* (screenplay proposal), 53–54, 61, 67–69, 79, 85, 136–138. *See also individual screenwriters*
Second Five-Year Plan, 22–23, 25
Semenov, Nikolai, 59, 81, 123
Serdtsa chetyrekh (Four Hearts), 42
Serebrovskaia, Elena, 59
Shapiro, M. D., 199
Shcherbakov, Aleksandr, 27, 29, 74
Shcherbina, Vladimir, 197
Shchors, 80, 118
Shchors, Nikolai, 56
Shengelaia, Nikolai, 25, 53, 156
Shepilov, Dmitrii, 48–49, 88
Shevchenko, Taras, 57, 87
Shishmareva, Anna, 58–59
Shitkin, Nikolai, 199
Shklovsky, Viktor, 35, 60, 138, 140
Shostakovich, Dmitri, 32–33, 102, 115
Shturmovye nochi (Storm Nights), 168–170
Shub, Esfir', 140
Shumiatskaia, Liia, 95
Shumiatskaia, Nora, 95
Shumiatskii, Boris, 3–4, 13–14, 16–18, 21–31, 34, 36–39, 49, 57, 64–70, 73–76, 79–80, 82, 92, 94–96, 100, 107, 110, 132, 150–150, 172, 174–180, 182–185, 187–190, 204, 212
Shumiatskii, Boris (Lazarevich), 95
Shvarts, Evgenii, 147
Sidelev, Sergei, 189
Simonov, Konstantin, 57–59, 126
Skripitsin, Vladimir, 139
Slavin, Lev, 138
Slepkov, 100
Slobodskoi, Moris, 147
Sluchainaia vstrecha (A Chance Encounter), 189
Smelye liudi (Brave Men), 11, 195–203
Smith, Jeff, 221
socialism, 4, 8–9, 20, 26, 31, 33–34, 40, 43, 100, 114, 123, 160, 182, 184–185, 216–217, 221
socialist realism, 22, 26, 33–34, 110–115, 117, 121, 178, 180n64, 182; simplicity, 113–118
Soiuzdetfilm, 16, 35, 39, 101–102
Soiuzkino, 16–18, 21, 24, 65, 109
Soiuzkinoprokat, 39
Sokolov, Ippolit, 135
Sokolovskaia, Elena, 182, 184, 186, 189
Solov'ev, Aleksandr, 168–169
Sovetskie patrioty (Soviet Patriots), 205

Soviet Hollywood, 6, 8, 14, 27–30, 39, 50–51, 73, 100, 107, 149–155, 216
Soviet Writers' Congress, 23–24
Soviet Writers' Union, 22, 46, 74–75, 104, 110, 155
Sovkino, 16, 19, 53–54, 60, 65
Spadavecchia, Antonio, 201
Staiger, Janet, 134
Stakhanovite movement, 73, 77–78, 80, 84, 181–182
Stalin, Joseph, 1, 3–6, 9, 12–16, 20, 22–23, 25–27, 30–35, 43, 47–50, 55, 64, 86–89, 91, 94, 102, 105–108, 115–116, 150, 166, 172–173, 175–179, 189–190, 192–193, 204–205, 207–208, 210–212, 215, 217; censor, 166, 172–173, 175–177, 189–193, 204–205, 207–212, 215; Kremlin screenings, 27, 176–177, 193; patron, 105–108; producer, 108
Stalin Prize, 43, 56, 158, 193, 196, 202, 204–208
Stalingradskaia bitva (The Battle of Stalingrad), 87
stalinism, 1–2, 5–6, 8, 10, 15, 20, 22, 29–34, 48–49, 89–91, 109, 163, 173, 215, 218–219, 222; aggressive stance, 8–9; control mechanisms, 7, 190–191, 207–208; expert policy, 23–25, 94, 107–108, 160; Great Retreat, 32; Great Terror, 29–31, 40, 97; information vacuum, 173, 190, 212; Soviet superiority, 7–11, 13, 20, 24, 29, 32, 46, 49–51, 160–161, 217. *See also* intolerance of imperfection
Staryi naezdnik (The Old Jockey), 42, 123–124, 195
State Cinema Publishing House, 205
Stepan Razin, 140
Stetskii, Aleksei, 17–18, 171, 174–175, 177, 206, 230
Stolper, Aleksandr, 41, 93, 192
Stroeva, Vera, 189
Stukov, Georgii, 38
Sud chesti (The Court of Honor), 56
Surkov, Aleksei, 200
Sutyrin, Vladimir, 54–55, 95, 154–155, 174
Suvorov, Nikolai, 102
Sverdlovsk Studio, 39
Svet nad Rossiei (Light over Russia), 145, 206–207, 211
Svetlov, Mikhail, 88
Svinarka i pastukh (Swineherd and Shepherd), 44

Tadjikfilm, 16
Takhmasib, Rza, 211
Talenskii, Nikolai, 195

Tamarkin, E. M., 180, 188–190
Taras Shevchenko, 57, 87
Tarzan, 12–13, 50
Tashkent Studio, 16, 122, 139
Tbilisi Studio, 16, 101–102
technical film, 22, 78n112, 98
Tevelev, Matvei, 125
thematic planning: Artistic Council, 80–81; Boris Shumiatskii, 14, 57, 65–76; Central Committee, 53, 57, 66–67, 70, 73–74, 77–78, 83–86, 88; control instrument, 2, 52, 69; creative counterplanning, 52, 65–76, 79–86, 89; directors, 25–26, 40, 52–53, 56, 61–70, 75–76, 81–82, 88, 94; genre, 23, 50, 56, 61n44, 64, 70–74, 79–89; genre diversity, 4, 14, 43–44, 48, 70–71, 80, 88–89, 107; Ivan Bol'shakov, 41, 57, 79–86, 88; Joseph Stalin, 86–89; party theme, 41, 63, 67, 71–72, 127, 180, 197, 209; planning conferences, 24–25, 65, 67–73, 75, 81, 86, 109; post-Stalin, 64; Scenario Studio, 60–61, 85; screenwriting, 53–56, 58–63, 69–70, 74, 76, 82, 88, 135; Semen Dukel'skii, 75–79, 85; Soiuzkino, 65; Sovkino, 53–55, 65; story origins, 56–64, 87–88; *tema* (definitions), 52–56, 74, 79; thematic categories, 4, 7, 52–89, 110, 133; thematic thinking, 53–56, 64, 71–72, 216. *See also* production planning
Third Five-Year Plan, 16
Tolstoi, Aleksei, 158, 172
totalitarianism, 2, 9–10, 105
Trainin, Il'ia, 19, 21
Traktoristy (The Tractor Drivers), 44, 80
Trauberg, Il'ia, 100–101, 138
Trauberg, Leonid, 64, 92, 100–104, 112–113, 124–125, 127, 147, 159, 194, 206
Tret'iakov, Sergei, 151
Tretii udar (The Third Blow), 87
Tri soldata (Three Soldiers), 18
Trinadtsat' (The Thirteen), 57, 219
trophy films, 12, 49–50
Trotsky, Leon, 14–16
Tsekhanovskii, Mikhail, 66
Tsirk (The Circus), 142
Tsivian, Yuri, 109
TsOKS (Central United Film Studio for Feature Films), 43
Turkin, Valentin, 142, 156–157
Turkmenfilm, 16
Turovskaya, Maya, 18, 50
tvorcheskoe ob"edinenie (creative unit), 97

Ukraine, 16–17, 56–57, 70, 74, 87, 169, 187
Ukrainfilm, 99, 179

URK (Administration for Cinema Repertory Control), 192, 200
Usievich, Vladimir, 96, 183, 188
Usol'tsev-Garf, Aleksandr, 122, 139
USSR Revolutionary Military Council, 172–173
Utesov, Leonid, 57, 95
Uzbekfilm, 16

Vainshtok, Vladimir, 95
Vaisfel'd, Il'ia, 86, 137–138
Vasil'ev, Georgii, 21, 26, 93, 101–102, 110, 112
Vasil'ev, Sergei, 21, 26, 62–63, 93, 101–102, 104, 110, 112, 126
Velikaia sila (The Great Force), 211
Velikii grazhdanin (The Great Citizen), 205, 207
Venice Film Festival, 177
Verner, Mikhail, 189
vertical integration, 7–8, 17, 39
Vertov, Dziga, 20, 25, 53, 92
Veselei nas net (We Are the Merriest), 122, 139
Veselye rebiata (Jolly Fellows), 57, 95, 177, 179, 189
Vesna (Spring), 146–148
VGIK (All-Union State Cinema Institute), 93, 109, 154, 156
Vinogradskaia, Katerina, 138–139
Virta, Nikolai, 152
Vishnevskii, Vsevolod, 62, 81, 101, 161–162, 206
VKP(b) (All-Union Communist Party (Bolsheviks)), 140
vodka, 14–16, 28, 50, 199, 213
Volchek, Boris, 102
Volga, Volga, 195, 201
Vol'pin, Mikhail, 123, 147, 159, 195–198, 202–203
Voroshilov, Kliment, 172–173, 177, 206–207

Vostokfilm, 16, 29
Vovsy, Grigorii, 116
Vstrechnyi (Counterplan), 18, 21, 95, 111–112
Vyshinskii, Andrei, 42, 192–193

Welles, Orson, 219
Workers International Relief, 16, 35
World War II, 43–44, 87, 105, 125–128, 195–203, 208–210
writers, 10, 22, 43, 46, 57, 59–60, 67, 72, 74–75, 94, 101, 104–105, 112, 115, 121, 124, 134, 138, 143, 147, 151–164

Yalta Studio, 16
Yunost' Maksima (The Youth of Maksim), 112–113, 124, 175, 178, 205–206

Zabrodin, Vladimir, 124
Zaitsev, Iakov, 35
Zakliuchennye (The Convicts), 75, 189
Zakon zhizni (The Law of Life), 41–42, 83–84, 102, 140, 157, 192–193, 197
Zarkhi, Aleksandr, 63, 102, 124, 171, 211
Zaslavskii, David, 160, 198
Zel'dovich, Grigorii, 34, 130, 183
Zemlia (Earth), 170–171
Zhdanov, Andrei, 4, 41–44, 46–48, 64, 82–84, 86, 88, 94, 105, 121, 124, 137, 139, 177, 192–193, 209, 219
zhdanovshchina (zhdanovism), 46
Zhezhelenko, Leonid, 57, 125
Zhukovskii, 211
Zinoviev, Grigory, 30
Znamia (journal), 46
Zolotoi pesok (Golden Sand), 100
Zoshchenko, Mikhail, 46, 143
Zvezda (journal), 46

CPSIA information can be obtained
at www.ICGtesting.com
Printed in the USA
BVOW03*1401120917
494289BV00003B/4/P